The Salley Gardens

Reimagining Ireland

Volume 106

Edited by Dr Eamon Maher,
Technological University Dublin – Tallaght Campus

PETER LANG

Oxford • Bern • Berlin • Bruxelles • New York • Wien

The Salley Gardens

Women, Sex, and Motherhood in Ireland

Jo Murphy-Lawless and Laury Oaks

PETER LANG

Oxford • Bern • Berlin • Bruxelles • New York • Wien

Bibliographic information published by Die Deutsche Nationalbibliothek. Die Deutsche Nationalbibliothek lists this publication in the Deutsche Nationalbibliografie; detailed bibliographic data is available on the Internet at http://dnb.d-nb.de.

A catalogue record for this book is available from the British Library.

Library of Congress Cataloging-in-Publication Data

Names: Murphy-Lawless, Jo, author. | Oaks, Laury, 1967- author.
Title: The Salley Gardens : women, sex, and motherhood in Ireland / Jo
   Murphy-Lawless, Laury Oaks.
Description: Oxford ; New York : Peter Lang, 2022. | Series: Reimagining
   Ireland, 1662-9094 ; vol. 106 | Includes bibliographical references.
Identifiers: LCCN 2021034403 (print) | LCCN 2021034404 (ebook) | ISBN
   9781800794177 (pbk.) | ISBN 9781800794184 (ebook) | ISBN 9781800794191
   (epub)
Subjects: LCSH: Women--Ireland--Social conditions--21st century. |
   Women--Ireland--Identity. | Women--Sexual behavior--Ireland. |
   Motherhood--Ireland.
Classification: LCC HQ1600.3 .M874 2022 (print) | LCC HQ1600.3 (ebook) |
   DDC 305.42094170905--dc23
LC record available at https://lccn.loc.gov/2021034403
LC ebook record available at https://lccn.loc.gov/2021034404

Cover design by Peter Lang Ltd.

ISSN 1662-9094
ISBN 978-1-80079-417-7 (print)
ISBN 978-1-80079-418-4 (ePDF)
ISBN 978-1-80079-419-1 (ePub)

© Peter Lang Group AG 2022

Published by Peter Lang Ltd, International Academic Publishers, 52 St Giles, Oxford, OX1
3LU, United Kingdom oxford@peterlang.com, www.peterlang.com

Jo Murphy-Lawless and Laury Oaks have asserted their right under the Copyright, Designs
and Patents Act, 1988, to be identified as Authors of this Work.

This publication has been peer reviewed.

For Gabriel, Katie, Marissa, and Orla

Contents

Acknowledgements

We have many people to thank. First and foremost, the young women who generously opened their lives and experiences to us during two research projects for the Crisis Pregnancy Agency between 2003 and 2006 deserve our gratitude. We also want to thank successive cohorts of midwifery students in Trinity College Dublin, between 2006 and 2018 who explored much of this material about the changing contexts for women in Ireland as part of their sociology coursework. Abundant thanks are owed to the following:

Alish Banks, Valerie Blake, Lauren Boon, Clare Brady, Therese Byrne, Liz Cassin, Tasmin Coe, Ellen Cooke, Clare Daly, Sarah Davies, Declan Devane, Lelia Doolan, Margaret Dunlea, Nadine Edwards, Michael Edwards, Doreen Fitzmaurice, Andrea Foley, Sharon Foley, Sinead Fulcher, Anne-Marie Green, Barbara Grimes, Nicole Harper, Kate Harris, Maria Herron, Sian Hodgins, Julie Horgan, Mary Howard, Martina Hynan, Roisin Kavanagh, Cecile Kizenga, Rena Maguire, Leona Mahon, Rosemary Mander, Mary Martin, Ann Maxwell, Sarah McCann, Anne McCarthy, Linda McDyer, Marie McEneff, Claire McNab, Roisin Molloy, Christine Monahan, Rita Monahan, Sophie Moxon, Gerry Mulvenna, Rachel Murphy, Oisín Murphy-Lawless, Brenda O'Brien, Cherisse O'Brien, Sióbán O'Brien-Green, Taylor O'Brien-Pintos, Jim O'Donnell, Emma O'Grady, Stephanie O'Keeffe, Eadaoin O'Sullivan, Karin O'Sullivan, Magdalena Ohaja, Carlos Panero, Ciaran Power, Sean Rowlette, Vic Russell, Kevin Ryan, Bridget Sheeran, Mary Smyth, Olivia Smyth, Malgorzata (Gosia) Stach, Ilona Sulikova, Fleur van Leeuwen, James Webster, Jeannine Webster, Jianwei Wu.

We deeply thank friends, colleagues and students at and beyond the University of California Santa Barbara. The research team provided meticulous copy-editing and skilled assistance to track down and organise needed information. Invaluable have been feminist studies graduate student AP Pierce and undergraduate students Elsie Amador, Dominica Aranaga,

Casey Chen, Tianyi Huang, Ginger Lamb, Teyah Lopez, Olivia Moreno, Katherine Ripley, Aine Roonan, Veronica Varner and Angela Zou. We also want to thank Liz Farsaci for her skilled indexing.

We thank two erudite anonymous reviewers.

Many thanks to Senior Commissioning Editor for Peter Lang, Tony Mason, for his unending patience, commitment and support; thanks also to the skilled staff at Peter Lang for their editorial thoroughness, and to Eamon Maher, the Reimagining Ireland Series Editor for grasping the core of this project with alacrity.

Special thanks to Dominick Jenkins for his consistent mentoring.

Images of Women Present and Past

Yeats' poem, 'Down by the Salley Gardens', is the source for this book's title. The story it presents is of the man who regrets a love lost to him, who has failed to act on his desire for a life with the woman who is confident in hers. With this evocative image in mind, we present the reflections of seventy-three heterosexual women, aged 19–34 years old, on their growing up, forming sexual relationships and, for some, becoming mothers in the last years of 'Celtic Tiger' Ireland, a time of far greater affluence than Irish society has ever before known.[1] The problem of social constraint on the one hand and agency on the other has been at the fore of arguments by feminists about social change in relation to sex and sexuality in Ireland. Women have been freer than any generation before them to shape their sexual lives and to access in ever greater numbers social and sexual freedoms. Yet their efforts to get to grips with what they wanted or needed, the problems they have encountered along the way, have been far from straightforward, and many critical matters remain unresolved. Throughout the book, we share the voices of young women who expressed both hope and despair as they experienced what it means to be an Irish woman – to construct the self – within the inescapable tensions specific to the Celtic Tiger historical moment and simultaneous departures from and pulls to social expectations of the past regarding being a working woman, a sexual woman, a caring woman and a partner, wife or mother. We argue that turning the history of our deep loss towards an exuberant resistance will enable us to effectively

---

1   According to economists and Donovan and Murphy (2004: 16) the term was first used in 1994 by an investment banker working in Morgan Stanley in Dublin.

puncture the limitations of the identities late modern Ireland would have us compliantly assume.

The impact of Celtic Tiger times

The Celtic Tiger term itself was initially used in the overarching spheres of economics and politics but slipped quickly into everyday discourse in the 1990s (Keohane and Kuhling 2004: 139). It provided a self-accepting 'collective identity' (ibid.) as Ireland entered into the boom time of tax-incentivized multinational corporations, export-led industries like the high-tech and pharmaceutical sectors, unrestrained credit expansion in globalized financial markets and feverish property dealing such as Ireland had never seen before. The 'collective moral force' of the Celtic Tiger term was perfectly suited to the global neoliberal economy we welcomed as a society, and it was used to sway people into spending without limit, 'into borrowing and buying' (ibid.: 144), a game promoted by successive governments which did likewise until the economic collapse of 2008 (Allen 2003).

The appendage of 'Celtic' was itself intriguing, suggesting a connection with a transcendent history venerated as 'an heroic age, a timeless time, a Celtic twilight that is also a perpetual dawn' (Keohane and Kuhling 2004: 146), an understanding that conveniently provided us with a one-way ticket out of modern twentieth-century Ireland which had been anything but heroic. Up to 1987, the year domestic unemployment was at its highest recorded level in the last half of the twentieth century, 17 per cent, Ireland with its 'dismal' struggling economy (Geary 1992: 277) had produced a demographic regime completely at odds with Britain and the rest of western Europe. It comprised late marriage, if marrying at all, but high rates of fertility within marriage. Fintan O'Toole (1994: 168–9) has written that when his parents married in the mid-1950s, 64 per cent of the Irish populace was single and he quotes the UCD economist James Meenan that Irish society 'was largely based on the refusal of many of its members of the opportunity to found a home and family. In demographic terms, this was an evil quite as harmful as emigration; in human terms it was more monstrous by far' (ibid: 169). In class terms, social mobility was gained by emigrating from Ireland, not by staying here. In 1987, a mere 6.5 per cent of people from a working-class background had entered the professional and managerial classes (Allen 2000: 1). That was the Ireland swept away by Celtic Tiger times when, from 1994 to 2001, the country's GDP averaged 7.8 per cent, in an 'abrupt leap-frogging from a predominately pre-industrial economy to a post-industrial high-tech economy' (Donovan and Murphy 2004: 19). With 'globalization and Europeanization' coming together (ibid.: 24), the Celtic Tiger exploded into a rapid rise in living standards that introduced us to the gleaming consumer worlds of 'shiny new buildings, business and retail parks … designer stores, gallerias and plazas', along with 'arts centres, theme parks … hotels, golf complexes and housing estates as people with significant disposable income sought easy ways to spend it' (Lucey et al. 2019: 1). Fintan O'Toole (2003a: 49) has rightly observed about this landscape:

> Until we understand the choices made in the course of Ireland's final entry into the global economy in the late 1980s and early 1990s, the nature of contemporary Irish society is incomprehensible. Until we know why some were given a leg up into the roaring 1990s while others were kicked in the face, we won't be able to come to terms with the coexistence of manic affluence and mean despair of boom-time Ireland. (O'Toole 2003a: 49)

This was the Ireland in which our interviewees came to adulthood and then had to live through the crisis-ridden setting which followed on swiftly with the Celtic Tiger's collapse amidst international economic turmoil from 2008 onward. By then Ireland and women's lives in Ireland had changed irrevocably.[2]

The Celtic Tiger era helps explain how contemporary Ireland has come to be far more in tune with the contradictory characteristics of late

---

2   A major review of the boom-time economy in 2010 by Ireland's then largest stockbroking firm concluded that much of the wealth generated during the Celtic Tiger years was wasted because the country failed to invest in important public services, including its schools and healthcare systems, which lagged well behind those of other European countries (see Slattery 2010).

modern societies across the world. Our societies are globalized and fluid, not least in the rapid turnover demanded by consumer capitalism. They are radically unequal societies. They also carry unpredictable risks for individuals in their pursuit of life goals which means there is an ongoing need for self-reflexivity and decision-making, no matter what their social class. Hence core notions for young women in contemporary Ireland are those of agency, identity and choice. Young women expect to exercise their personal agency, to be free to discover unhindered aspects of themselves as sexual beings, to explore what is most important to them about intimacy, to anticipate decisions about their identities and futures, to shape those futures as they choose. As Zygmunt Bauman argues, they embrace willingly the belief that their identity grows and changes as a result of their experiences, that their identity itself is always an 'unfinished task' (2004: 20), and that their sexuality forms a crucial part of their identity. This unfinished task of identity-building in relation to sexuality and the connection to 'choice' as part of the demanding patterns of consumption captures young women's attention daily: globally accessible mass media and internet reinforce what they see in the centre of Irish cities and towns and those innumerable chic shopping pavilions which have been built in recent decades.

Mass media and social media are awash with extensive coverage of the consumer habits, clothes sense, sex lives and often the chic motherhood of international celebrities along with anyone who attracts a following as an internet influencer. One way or another, Irish women must deal with what appears to be a principle of late modern life, an awareness of material consumption which appears to be vital to make sense of their desire to find out who they are and who they might become, how they present themselves and how they learn what to do as sexual beings. They must live with constant change as an imperative of this 'consuming life' which 'cannot stand still' (Bauman 2005: 3). One of the women we interviewed describes how this profusion of messages is received:

> We live in a culture that is a 'McDonald's Culture' which is to say that everything is fast … fast … fast. This has become a country so very different from the one five to seven years ago. Sex and body image are pushed on us all to sell things from toilet roll to ice-cream, and one can't turn on telly or open a magazine without sex being there each and every time. Sex is portrayed as something that is great and casual. It

would seem that everyone is doing it, and if you're not, there is something wrong with you. (Christine, 31, small town, unemployed)

Bauman (2003, 2005) argues that for the individual this seeming fluidity has put paid to older social ties that constrained the body, especially the sexual body, within rigid conventions. This is not done without its own costs. The very fluidity of consumption, of what is new and 'now', contributes to the sense that the individual is always incomplete and is always yearning for what comes next, working to make better 'choices' to achieve that completion. This imperative also recasts the nature of intimate relationships. Bauman asserts that they become 'mixed blessings' in that they can 'vacillate between sweet dream and a nightmare' (2003: viii): ambivalence about relationships becomes a predominant theme in people's lives. Amidst the welter of impressions of how a life can be well lived, we may be doing less than we realize to actively acknowledge and support the validity of women's desires about their lives, most especially in relation to sexuality. Deborah Tolman (2002: 4) has argued that while 'we are supposed to develop a mature sense of ourselves as sexual beings by the time we have reached adulthood', this is a fraught project due to the ongoing social constraints, different to once rigid restrictions, but that are distinctively gendered in their impact. Young women still find it hard to fully articulate sexual desire as a healthy aspiration for themselves in a confident manner, and in ways where they feel they will not come to any emotional or other harm (Durham 2009).

Understanding constraints and agency for women

The problem of social constraint on the one hand and agency on the other has been to the fore of arguments by feminists about social change in relation to sex and sexuality in Ireland. Anne Byrne speaks of a patriarchal society that long sought to confine women to a 'narrow repertoire of permissible identities' (Byrne 2003: 45) and which, in the memorable phrase of Rosita Sweetman (1979) left women 'on our backs'. Similarly,

Pat O'Connor sees the notion of patriarchy as an important starting point for understanding 'the practices and processes' whereby older masculinist and familial ideologies limited the ways in which women 'constructed their lives' (1998: 29).

Contraception is often cited as the technology that gave women in advanced economies a critical edge in ending the most obvious masculinist constraint on the sexual body, namely the burden of unwanted pregnancy that had pushed so many lives into the shadows. Hera Cook argues that the availability of the pill meant that at last women could act on their own desires, insist on sexual autonomy and think of pregnancy as a 'freely chosen outcome of sexual intercourse' (2004: 339). This assertion has special resonance in Ireland. On the fiftieth anniversary of the contraceptive pill being released for use, Medh Ruane (2010) described how 'in living memory', there was a period when no contraception, let alone the pill, could be accessed freely and legally in Ireland and the reality of unwanted pregnancy prevented women from discovering 'the passionate, joyous' aspects of 'women's pleasure'.

Many Irish women born in the 1940s and 1950s will have harsh personal memories related to the legal unavailability of contraception. They will recall their own sense of dread at becoming pregnant, which, if it happened outside marriage, precipitated decisions about marrying sooner than they might have wanted, and possibly marrying someone whom they did not want. Within marriage, they would have dreaded raising a large family. They will recall as well, the haunting stories of young relatives or near neighbours who were forced to go to the infamous mother and baby homes of twentieth-century Ireland and give up their babies for adoption or pretend that the child was born late on to aging grandparents, while the birth mother was conveniently relocated to London or the United States. Some women who might have travelled regularly to and from England or from Dublin to rural areas in Ireland in the 1960s and 1970s will recall discrete and urgent requests that would be made to please bring back 'something' by women who could not face another new baby. In 1971, 41 per cent of women still had a completed family size of four to six children, with 15 per cent of women having a completed family size of seven to nine children (Murphy-Lawless 1987). If married women were lucky, they might convince their GP to prescribe the contraceptive pill which was being legally imported from 1963 as a 'cycle-regulator' for irregular menstruation with the convenient side-effect of limiting their families (Solomons 1992: 23). By 1966, it was reported that 25 per cent of Catholic doctors were prescribing oral contraception (*The Irish Times* 1966: 1).

Several family planning clinics were set up in Dublin in the late 1960s using a loophole in the law (Solomons 1992), and their existence helped to raise the issue more widely of gaining access to effective contraception. Gradually over the next two decades, state and medical opposition to legalising reliable contraception was taken apart. A women's movement which had developed at two levels, locally with grassroots activism and special interest groups, and nationally, with the Irish Commission on the Status of Women in 1970 followed by the Council for the Status of Women in 1972 (L. Connolly 2003), challenged a restrictive legislative and constitutional framework in the courts. This took place alongside the country opening up to the European Economic Community with its insistence on equal status for women and men in relation to employment and welfare issues. The 1972 McGee case, which successfully overturned the 1935 ban on the importation of contraception and contraceptive devices, helped to break the control of a dominant male legislature on this aspect of women's reproductive agency (Speed 1992; Murphy-Lawless and McCarthy 1999; L. Connolly 2003: 142–4).

Strenuous opposition by the hierarchy of the Catholic church also began to be curtailed. Under Article 44 of the 1937 Constitution had enjoyed special legal status 'as the Guardian of the Faith'; that status was removed in 1972 as the force of the official church, at least on this matter of contraception, leached away. By 1980, a majority of married couples was actively ignoring official church teaching on contraception (Lee 1989: 656). The condition-filled 1979 Family Planning Act, leaving GPs and pharmacists in a position to judge if contraception could or could not be issued to a 'bona fide' married couple, was seen by 50 per cent of people in 1984 as being too restrictive, while 60 per cent were in favour of using contraception (Health Education Bureau 1984: 27). The legislation was modified in 1985. By this time, the demographic profile of the country had changed markedly, with over 50 per cent of the population under 30 years of age, and this was to have massive social impact. Betty Hilliard (2006) presents data from her analysis of intimate relationships, taken from the Irish Social and Political Attitudes Survey (ISPAS), that between 1994 and 2002, attitudes about non-marital relationships and non-marital childbearing had shifted to non-traditional emphases, a shift that implicitly underlines women's greater sense of agency over their bodies and their lives.

These changes made it possible for Ruane to observe that 'the prospect of pregnancy after pregnancy is unimaginable now … a past so alien you'd rather forget' (Ruane 2010). O'Connor observes that Irish women in their 20s now had unrecognisably different experiences to their mothers who were possibly more supportive of them, for example, in relation to single parenthood, because of the inescapable harshness they witnessed in their younger lives from their mothers (1998: 29). However, Ruane cautioned as to the incomplete nature of the control women had achieved, 'Ireland 2010 won't face up to reproductive rights and health, through education, better availability of the morning-after pill, making laws to acknowledge the X case … Fifty years on there are battles to be fought' (ibid.).

Ruane was reflecting the reality that restrictive masculinist attitudes, at the level of the individual and of the state, have not been dissolved. In respect of the former, the aftermath of a rape trial in Listowel in 2009 saw some fifty people lining up in the courtroom to shake the hand of the man who had been found guilty and was awaiting a prison sentence, in front of his victim and counsellors from the Kerry Rape Crisis Centre. Rosita Boland reported, 'The fact that so many people in a Tralee courtroom had publicly supported the perpetrator of a sexual assault engaged – you could say transfixed – the country' (Boland 2009).

Their number included the local parish priest, and as one local resistant put it, the supporters 'felt he was an honest kind of a guy', despite the guilty sentence after due process to which there was no legal challenge entered afterwards (ibid.).

The response to the rape trial is one of many indications whereby O'Connor's 1998 conclusion holds, that we have seen both tremendous change and too little change for women. It is a pattern not dissimilar to other European societies. O'Connor observes that the range of cultural and social modalities bound up with patriarchal notions, which defined for so long what a woman was meant to be, were to a considerable extent shared by Irish women with women elsewhere in western Europe, albeit with peculiarly local effects (1998: 5). Cook (2004) has examined the European-wide dimension of this struggle for sexual agency and has pinpointed the period of the 1970s when the northern European marriage system fell apart. No longer were sex and childbearing confined to marriage, when premarital sex, if it took place, was with an intended marital partner only. The technology of the pill was crucial in this revolution, but so was its availability. Women's demands for the contraceptive pill in the far more secularized circumstances of our near neighbour, the UK, were made because they wanted the pill to enable them to have sex when and with whom they chose, marriage notwithstanding. This development reshaped sexual mores (Cook 2004: 326). Even in Ireland, as difficult as it was to obtain contraception legally before 1979, married couples had begun to limit their families so that even while the marriage rate was rising in the 1960s with women marrying at a much younger age than heretofore, by 1970, the numbers of families with four and more children had fallen by 20 per cent (Brown 2004: 247).

Contraception contributed greatly to changing sexual mores in Ireland. We know from the *Irish Contraception and Crisis Pregnancy Study* (Rundle et al. 2004: 66–7) that by the early 2000s, 22 per cent of women between the ages of 18 and 24 had first sexual intercourse before the age of 17, the current age of legal consent in Ireland. The median age for first sexual intercourse for women born between 1981 and 1985 was 18 years of age (ibid.). We accept Ruane and Cook's arguments about the central role the pill has played in enabling women to become sexually active with some sense of self-determination. Women have definitively broken the link between sex and marriage and in so doing have gained new ground for themselves in respect of sexual agency. However, there is a great deal more involved in understanding the position of women in contemporary Ireland on sex, fertility and motherhood than an effective technology. By 1998, Pat, O'Connor argued that 'however powerful the processes and practices of patriarchal control, and however tightly woven the ideological parameters of women's lives, the possibility of social and cultural change or individual resistance cannot be eliminated'; yet, it remained 'difficult' to account for specific phenomena in respect, for example, of the falling marital fertility rate (1998: 23). But fall it did. Finola Kennedy agrees about the specific cultural context, arguing that the important shift towards different family forms and towards far smaller families was concentrated into a single decade, that of the 1980s, and thus Irish women's experiences of 'modernisation', the wide-scale patterns of social change associated with industrialised, technologised societies, was intense and very rapid, albeit with a 'culture-specific context' (2001: 2–3). By 2003, just under 28 per cent of women giving birth had two children, 31 per cent of births were to women with one child, with only 6 per cent of births to women with three or more children. Moreover, the profile of women giving birth outside marriage was shifting. It is 'extremely difficult' to account for how and why women have come to have far fewer children in marriage compared with their mid-twentieth-century mothers and grandmothers, or to become single parents in the numbers which made up our emerging profile (P. O'Connor 1998: 23).[3]

Finola Kennedy (2001: 2) argues that the important shift towards different family forms and towards far smaller families was concentrated into a single decade, that of the 1980s and thus Irish women's experiences of 'modernisation', the wide-scale patterns of social change associated with industrialised, technologised societies, was intense and very rapid, albeit with a 'culture-specific context' (ibid.: 3). Elsewhere in Europe similar changes stretched out over half a century and longer, linked to their longer exposure to 'modernisation'. By the early 1980s, average completed family size in Ireland had dropped to 3.21 children. The total period fertility rate had dropped from 3.23 in 1980 to 2.12 by 1990 (CSO 2004: 59). These

---

3   In 2003, the year that the Crisis Pregnancy Agency initiated a number of key re-
     search projects on women and sex, 40.2 per cent of all births were to first-time
     mothers, with second-time mothers making up 32.2 per cent of the total of 61,517
     live births (CSO 2004: 29). Only 27.6 per cent of mothers had more than two chil-
     dren when giving birth that year (ibid.). Births outside marriage accounted for 31.4
     per cent of all births. The TFR (total fertility rate) stood at 1.98, below replacement
     level (ibid: 25). By 2019, the TFR had fallen to 1.7 (CSO 2020a) with almost 74 per
     cent of the 59,796 births in 2019 to first- and second-time mothers; that year 38.1
     per cent of all births were outside marriage/civil partnerships. Over these first two
     decades, Irish women established familial forms almost unheard of in the 1980s.

statistics convey a sense of greater agency and decision-making about the reproductive body. Yet there remained a powerful distinction between that reproductive, maternal body and the sexual body and, despite the personal decisions implicit in these fertility statistics, the 1980s were perhaps the bleakest period for Irish women in the late twentieth century. The desire for self-determination and having their future in their own hands clashed with very public views of what their roles should be.

Shadows and exemplars

Even though abortion was already illegal under the 1937 Constitution, a bitterly contested pro-life amendment campaign began in 1981 driven by pro-life groups intent on preventing any possible access ever to abortion (O'Reilly 1992). The 'right to life of the unborn' amendment to the Constitution was passed overwhelmingly in a referendum in 1983. Then in 1986, an equally divisive referendum to legalise divorce was defeated. These referenda conveyed a strong sense that women were still being forced to the margins in their decision-making about sex and relationships. This reality was painfully reinforced by three high-profile events in the 1980s. They were followed by the landmark 'X' case in 1992.

The first was that of Eileen Flynn, a secondary school teacher in the Holy Faith Convent school in New Ross Wexford who was forced to resign her post in 1982 when she had a baby with her partner who was separated from his wife. She was seen to have violated the values whereby the school distinguished itself. Flynn appealed first to the state Employment Tribunal for reinstatement. Shamelessly, they ruled against her. She then went to the Circuit Court. This too was unsuccessful. Justice Noel Ryan summed up the Circuit Court case by saying: 'Times are changing and we must change with them, but they have not changed that much ... with regard to some things' (*The Irish Times* 2003a). A final appeal in the High Court was lost in 1985. Justice Declan Costello ruled that the religious order was entitled to interpret Flynn's circumstances as 'capable of damaging their efforts to foster in their pupils norms of behaviour and religious tenets which the school had been established to promote' (Carberry 2008) and thus to deprive her of her livelihood. Flynn never taught again.

In April 1984, the infamous Kerry Babies case began with the discovery of a newborn infant's body on the beach of Cahirciveen, a small town in County Kerry in the southwest of Ireland. The baby had been stabbed to death, and this incident opened up far-older prejudicial beliefs. Similar to the rest of Europe, the child murderess, especially where there was a 'bastard' child involved, played a strong part in Irish folklore, reflected in statutes going back to a formal infanticide act in 1707 which laid the burden of proof on the woman defendant that her baby had been stillborn, condemning her to death if found otherwise (A. O'Connor 1991). This belief about the child murderess, Anne O'Connor argues, took hold especially in the south and southwest of Ireland, persisting into the twentieth century (ibid: 309, 310; see also A. O'Connor 2005). Picking up on this embedded misogyny, and not twelve months removed from the Pro-life Referendum of 1983, the Kerry Garda murder squad quickly focused attention on Joanne Hayes. Hayes lived around fifty miles away in the village of Abbydorney and already had a young daughter whose father was a married man. Hayes had suffered a miscarriage in 1982 before becoming pregnant with her daughter. This was a long-standing relationship and although Hayes continued to live and work on the family farm, there was little attempt to conceal either the relationship or her one daughter. A third pregnancy found her giving birth at home in April 1984, unassisted. The baby was stillborn and after its birth, Hayes concealed the baby's body in a water hole (Inglis 2003; McCafferty 2010), later seeking attention in hospital for heavy bleeding.

The Gardaí conducted private interviews with local doctors eager to cooperate[4] and used the records of Tralee district hospital before subjecting Hayes and her family members to lengthy interrogations. Hayes herself was threatened that if she did not confess there would be dire consequences for her family. She was subsequently accused of not one, but two infant murders. After her arrest, she was transferred to the mental hospital in Limerick for a period, as the authorities were 'concerned' about her mental health

4   Seventy-four of ninety Kerry doctors had signed an anti-abortion declaration during the Referendum campaign (McCafferty 2010: 3).

(McCafferty 2010: 74). The coincidence of the timing of the two births, the fact that Hayes clearly had given birth but had no live baby, that she was viewed as promiscuous,[5] all fruitfully combined to result in her forced confession to 'murders' she never committed on the ground that improbably she had become pregnant by two different men and carried both pregnancies at the same time. This 'theory of superfecundation', postulating that if a woman has sex with two different men within twenty-four hours she can conceive twins (McCafferty 2010: xvii), was the main line of argument in the report prepared by the Gardaí and submitted to the Director of Public Prosecutions, recommending a charge of murder.

The case never came to court. Instead, there were two internal Garda inquiries about the way the investigation had been conducted, followed by a six-month long public Tribunal of Inquiry which, while some Garda procedures, did not reprimand them for forcing the 'confessions' they had obtained and, if anything, further scapegoated Joanne Hayes and her family. The Tribunal extensively canvassed aspects of Hayes' personal life, including her sexual behaviour. As Inglis writes 'a private tragic story ... became part of national history' (2003: 3).

Finally, there is the tragedy of Ann Lovett. For Eileen Flynn and Joanne Hayes, their public tribulations about their sexual lives via formal legal processes took place over an extended period. By contrast, there was no lengthy investigation for Ann Lovett, and her short life ended with dramatic suddenness. The 15-year-old left her home in Granard, County Longford on a bitterly cold, wet January day in 1984, carrying her school bag. She went to the Marian grotto, which was out of sight at the end of the small town, where she gave birth alone to a full-term baby boy. She cut the cord with scissors she had carried with her and lay bleeding and helpless until the late afternoon when three schoolboys hearing her moaning discovered her and her dead baby, the latter placed on a mossy stone. The young girl died several hours later in Mullingar Hospital from haemorrhage and shock. This fact was confirmed at the public inquest three weeks later while the

5   The close surveillance of Joanne Hayes by people in the wider community is a well-established pattern historically, as is infanticide as a response by women to their impossible circumstances. See Rattigan (2008) on similar incidents in early twentieth-century Ireland.

verdict on Ann's baby son was death due to asphyxia during birth (Cowley 1984). Neither family members nor teachers in her school claimed to have any knowledge of Ann's pregnancy (ibid.). These grievous circumstances stunned people across the country. On 23 February, the day after details of Ann's inquest were published in the national press, the broadcaster Gay Byrne gave over his radio programme to reading aloud, one after the other, for fifty minutes, many of the letters that had come in from women moved to tears by Ann's plight which re-ignited brutal memories for those who had become pregnant outside marriage. Through their letters, women conveyed a sense of terrible local retribution against themselves or women they had known. The country heard of women who carried their agony and shame in silence, their pregnant bodies deemed sexually transgressive by citizens of a patriarchal society, men and women alike, bent on denial as to how that had happened. Byrne's programme that day was later termed 'the most dev-astating piece of broadcasting yet heard in Ireland' (F. O'Toole 1998: 154).

The detail of Ann carrying the scissors to cut the umbilical cord remains gripping. If she had been quite unable to prevent pregnancy, somehow she had discovered enough about the process of birth to understand she would need those scissors. Had she been able to give birth in safe, protected cir-cumstances both she and her baby most likely would have been well and healthy if subject to local gossip. Ann's courage in seeing herself through birth unassisted at such a young age continues to invoke strong feelings in women who remember the tragedy, and her circumstances have been the subject of continued reflection. The twentieth anniversary of her death was marked by a number of newspaper articles, while a commissioned piece, entitled *Granard*, was performed by the RTE National Symphony Orchestra. The Irish poet, Nuala Ní Dhomhnaill, placed Ann's death at the centre of her poem, 'Thar Mo Chionn', written soon after we learned the news. Laura O'Connor (2002) commented on how Ní Dhomhnaill's text adroitly took in the abrogation of responsibility on the part of towns-people, the wider community and its institutions, alongside a simultaneous realisation that we were all implicated in how this young girl came to die. 'Lovett's self-marginalising and self-protective journey to the grotto drama-tised the ritual exclusions underpinning the patriarchal social order', argues O'Connor (2002: 1641). For women of a younger generation, it brought home forcibly how the issue of their attaining sexual autonomy continued to conflict with the terrible social rejection of those who became pregnant outside marriage. Diarmaid Ferriter suggests that Ann's death was the 'most poignant' event in a decade when 'delusion and denials' about our hidden sexual past were beginning to be exposed (2004: 8–9). Fintan O'Toole returned to the issue of Ann Lovett's death in 2002, emphasising that

> the version of Ireland that most of us carry in our heads changed for good. It is not that Ann Lovett's awful death stayed at the forefront of our collective consciousness, but it did take up residency in the back of our minds. (O'Toole 2002)

This Ireland of the 1980s was dark terrain, mired in yet another gloomy period of hardship and escalating unemployment that led to large-scale emigration. After a brief respite from this latter aspect of Irish life in the 1970s, the outflow of people, especially those between the ages of 18 and 25, grew rapidly in the 1980s to reach levels similar to those in the 1950s, a decade when Ireland could be said to have been at its nadir.[6] Young women who emigrated in the many thousands in the 1980s might have had great empathy for Eileen Flynn, Joanne Hayes and Ann Lovett, deprived respectively of livelihood, reputation and life, and might have pressed their demands about sexual and personal freedom in sufficient numbers that would have forced a rigid patriarchal social order to shift away from at least some of the constraints it so cruelly imposed. Women activists who remained carried on in what Ailbhe Smyth has described as 'difficult and demoralising years' (quoted in L. Connolly 2003: 58) marked by the expansion of hard-line campaigning on the pro-life and divorce referenda and legal skirmishes around provision of information by student unions on abortion and non-directive pregnancy counselling services. The latter were supported by a host of women volunteers and offered a network of

6   The 1980s crisis was part of the intensifying international economic morass that stemmed from the so-called 'Volcker shock', the abandonment of Keynesian policies and their replacement by strict monetarism tenets whereby a long and serious recession ensued (Harvey 2005: 23–4). The cumulative impacts in Ireland led not only to renewed emigration but also, for example, to severe cuts to the health services and to the redundancy of 20,000 public employees by 1989 (Brown 2004: 353–4).

underground resistance, nonetheless providing invaluable supports for women confronting crises with pregnancy (ibid.: 171–6).

The X case

Activism and resistance have been crucial for feminism with its underpinning by feminist theories about relations of power, especially in relation to reproductive justice, reproductive politics and human rights.[7] The resistance in Ireland to the absence of legal, safe abortion by thousands of individual women was myriad, the numbers charted in relation to the Irish addresses women gave at abortion clinics in Britain: from 1975 when over 1,000 women made that journey, the numbers increased steadily, reaching over 4,000 per annum by the early 1990s (Speed 1992: 96; McGrath et al. 2006: 23). The multiple private, difficult and often lonely actions taken by women, whether to search out facilities for contraception, abortion, foetal anomaly testing, or IVF throughout the 1980s marked a cumulative challenge to state and church, the dual keepers of the patriarchal order. Activists argued that it was that stranglehold of these keepers, their deliberate silence about the many conflicts surrounding the female body, which needed to be resolved if women were ever to realise their personal desires in respect of sex.

The infamous 'X case' in 1992 crystallised public understandings of these private actions in a crisis that overtook both establishments in different ways. The X case ultimately led to a complex series of constitutional referenda and subsequent amendments to the 1937 Constitution. At the outset of the crisis, the state's Attorney General, Harry Whelehan, sought an injunction to prevent a 14-year-old girl, 'Miss X', who had become pregnant as a result of rape, from travelling to the UK for a termination. Miss X had already gone there with her family to Manchester for the scheduled abortion, informing the Gardaí of their action because DNA evidence

7   See Roberts 1998; Solinger 2002, 2013; Luna and Luker 2013; Briggs 2018; Luna 2020; Zavella 2020; Littlejohn 2021.

would be needed in the prosecution of her alleged assailant, when an interim injunction was granted. The abortion was cancelled and the girl's family returned with her to contest the action in the High Court where on the 17 February 1992 the injunction, prohibiting the girl from leaving Ireland for nine months, was granted in full to the Attorney General. The case, he argued, was based on the 1983 pro-life amendment, which made it his constitutional duty on behalf of the state to protect a foetal life despite evidence presented of the young girl's suicidal state. For the next three weeks, Ireland's 'Ceaucescu-style government' (A. Smyth 1992a: 12) aroused intense controversy nationally, with a march of 7,000 people on the Dáil, a record number of letters to the editor of all three major Irish broadsheets (Johnson 1992), while telephone calls to radio programmes were in overdrive.[8] As anger about a carceral state grew, the state came under intense pressure. Internationally, the negative publicity was enormous. Ireland was becoming a competent player on the EU stage, and yet its representatives and workers in Brussels found it hard going: 'In the past two weeks it has become impossible to go to work or to socialize without being confronted with endless questions and often strident and insulting criticism of Ireland and the Irish', one reporter wrote (quoted in Murphy-Lawless 1993: 57). The government became concerned about the impact of this adverse publicity (L. Smyth 2002; Murphy-Lawless 1993) and urged the family to appeal the case to the Supreme Court, offering to pay costs.

The case was heard in February with a complex ruling handed down on 5 March 1992. The ruling, by a 4–1 majority, argued that Article 40.3.3 could only be interpreted as offering equal protection to the life of mother and foetus. In the X case, where there was a 'real and substantial risk to the life, as distinct from the health, of the mother', she must be permitted to seek an abortion. However, the judges were split 3–2 over whether there was a right to travel for a woman in such circumstances. The court called

---

8   Kligman (1998: 5) writing of the Ceausescu regime's policing of unwanted pregnancy and abortion in Romania notes that when reproduction becomes entangled with the 'imagined identity' of the community or state, it actually comes to mean the 'protection and perpetuation of that state in its imagined form', an analysis that precisely describes the actions of the Attorney General in the X case.

on the legislature to clarify issues by passing appropriate laws that could then be tested for their constitutionality.

This illustration of Sylvia Walby's (1990) concept of public patriarchy, at odds within itself as to which of its branches was truly responsible, also saw the judiciary asking some sharp questions about women's agency in ways we had not heard before:

> The failure by the legislature to enact the appropriate legislation, is no longer just unfortunate, it is inexcusable. What are pregnant women to do? What are the parents of a pregnant under age girl to do? What are doctors to do? (quoted in A. Smyth 1992a: 14).

The judgement led to relentless lobbying by the pro-life movement which sought another referendum in an effort to overturn the Supreme Court ruling. If that ruling were implemented in law, it would permit abortion in Ireland if a mother's life were at risk. The legislature avoided the task requested by the Supreme Court, but it did pass the enabling instruments that submitted the electorate to three referenda in November 1992: on the right to abortion for a mother where there was a substantive risk to her life; the right to information and travel; and finally the right to use abortion services in locations outwith the Irish state. The wording of the so-called 'substantive' issue, the right to access an abortion if the mother's life were at risk, specifically excluded suicide.

Pro-life groups took on the November referenda with their predictable outsize energy, but the results were ambiguous from their perspective. The electorate voted 'no' to the substantive amendment, leaving the legal situation uneasily reliant on that historic Supreme Court judgement. At the same time, they voted 'yes' to the right for women to travel and for the provision of information about abortion services. The pro-choice campaigner and feminist, Ailbhe Smyth, urged, 'We should celebrate. It's the first time a pro-choice movement can celebrate anything' (interview in *The Irish Times*, quoted in Murphy-Lawless 1993: 58).

The by now bedraggled 1937 Constitution, with the thirteenth and fourteenth amendments representing these referenda outcomes sitting uneasily alongside the eighth pro-life amendment, left women to get on as best they could.

The upholders of 'traditional' sexual morality

What of the Catholic church in the midst of these controversies? The dominant social and political culture which had so fruitfully tied together the interests of state and church had shown signs of strain for some time (Fuller 2002). The first wave of sexual scandals was to destroy any remaining credibility in the church's hierarchy over the next two decades. In 1992, it was publicly revealed that Eamon Casey, perhaps the only Irish bishop who could reasonably claim a socially radical conscience (Brown 2004: 341; Ferriter 2009: 528–9), had fathered a son in 1974 with Annie Kelly, an American, who kept and reared her son in the United States, ignoring Casey's wishes to have the baby adopted. Casey was forced to resign his bishopric. Over the next seventeen years, continuing up to the 2009 Ryan Commission on the physical and sexual abuse of children in the church's keeping (Commission to Inquire into Child Abuse 2009), the Catholic hierarchy became progressively crippled in its capacity to make meaningful public statements, let alone to intervene directly and forcibly in matters of sexual morality. Permanent damage was done putting distance between them and what had once been an unshakeable constituency, but it went all the way to the 'fourth round' cited by Scally in his book, *The Best Catholics in the World*: the 2021 Mother and Baby Homes Commission (2021: 141).

Lee (1989: 645) argues that the emphasis on sexual morality as the only form of morality worth consideration was convenient for a majority that wanted to remain 'untroubled' about many less savoury elements in Irish society, including public and commercial deceit and violence. It was certainly convenient for a state which displayed 'relative indifference' to social policymaking (Lee 1989: 578), despite terrible inequalities and social ills from the earliest decades of independence. For the most part, neglect and silence appeared to be the preferred position of elite professional and political groups. In 1992, the age limit for the legal sale of condoms was lowered to 17 years, but this was in response to what was seen as a growing crisis in respect of HIV/AIDS. A belated sense of social justice unceremoniously brought down the coalition government in 1994 when the minority Labour party withdrew its support because of the bungled extradition papers in 1991 of the paedophile priest, Brendan Smith, who was to stand trial in Belfast.

Ireland was becoming a more secular society, increasingly grounded in liberal conceptualisations of individual decision-making about sexual and moral issues (Brown 289–90). The state finally began to move: in 1995, the Minister for Health commissioned a research project on crisis pregnancy to help the government understand better the circumstances of women seeking abortions in the UK (Mahon et al. 1998) and also to prepare a Green Paper on the subject. This was the first state-supported initiative that acknowledged the realities of abortion for many Irish women. An *Inter-departmental Working Group on Abortion* was convened in 1998, and the Green Paper was published in 1999 with no fewer than seven possible approaches to resolving the impasse on abortion. The Constitution Review Group, also set up in 1995, considered the issue of abortion and various approaches whereby these might be dealt with, concluding that legislation was the 'only practical possibility at present' (Constitution Review Group 1996: 279). There were two high-profile court actions for young adolescent women needing to travel for an abortion, 'Miss C' in 1997 and 'Miss D' in 2007, both in state care when they became pregnant, one becoming pregnant through rape. Successive activist coalitions, the Irish Women's Support Group, the Irish Abortion Solidarity Campaign, the Safe and Legal Abortion Rights Campaign and others, remained to the fore in helping Irish women make journeys to the UK for abortions, to take legal action against the Irish state and to ensure that the undealt with 1992 Supreme Court decision was not neglected, by publishing accounts of women's experiences of seeking abortion (IFPA 2000; Rossiter 2009).

Three years after the release of the Mahon report on crisis pregnancy, in 2001, the Crisis Pregnancy Agency, a government-funded body, was set up by statutory instrument to help achieve reductions in the numbers of crisis pregnancies through wider provision of education and contraceptive support services and help better understand the numbers of women with crisis pregnancies undertaking abortions (Crisis Pregnancy Agency 2002). Between 2002 and 2009, the Agency commissioned and published a considerable range of original research on aspects of sexual health, sexual practice and sexual well-being in Ireland. The Agency also launched two public health education programmes, Positive Options, to help women with information sources about a crisis pregnancy and Think Contraception, aimed at young adults (see also Chapter 3). These education programmes had extensive public advertising, and in the case of Think Contraception, it was the first time that contraception usage was articulated as an official public health message on television. The state's institutions and health services gradually shifted some practices so that, excepting abortion, issues about sex and sexuality were no longer the massive headline controversies we experienced up to the time of the traumatic case centred on Miss X.

A growing openness of sorts

Irish society at large appeared to be maturing about discourses on sex and sexuality, aided by a younger demographic and a more cosmopolitan population overall, while the voluntary women's sector continued to push vigorously for full reproductive rights and access for all women (Gilmartin and White 2011). The fast-liberalising society of the Celtic Tiger years helped to reinforce the sense that the stories of Eileen Flynn, Joanne Hayes, Ann Lovett and Miss X constituted a threshold between a puritanical and rigid regime that prevailed from the foundation of the state and a much better future. Feminist activists hoped that if only we could move towards a more evolved and responsive politics, we would resolve many of the painful dilemmas about sex and thus change the lives of individual women infinitely for the better. Rosita Sweetman (1979: 50) at the conclusion of her research thirty years ago said that a 'more flexible attitude to sexuality is urgently needed' to move beyond a 'closed' and 'dogmatic' Irish society. Jenny Beale (1986: 18) argued that women born after the 1960s already had 'higher expectations of life, and a more taken for granted degree of equality between the sexes'. Crystel Hug (1999) saw Irish society by the 1990s as beginning to merge with the liberal pluralist values commonplace in the rest of Europe, values that privileged the individual and moved away from the hegemony of the Catholic church in setting down the preferred sexual norms for the country.

Tom Inglis contributed the salient phrase 'moral monopoly' (Inglis 1987) to describe the long-reaching impact of the Catholic church on moral teaching about sex in Ireland and went on to write about how conventional sexual norms were being challenged, with people communicating more openly about their 'pleasures' and 'problems' in respect of sex (1997: 6). In this 'more open, liberal–individualist' climate which saw Ireland move towards 'secular liberal individualism' (Inglis 2008: 7), 'indulgence in private sexual pleasures' was now accepted as the norm and in this sense too we were becoming 'like the rest of the West' (ibid.: 186), moving from deeply negative responses to viewing sex as a positive pleasure (1997: 6). Nell McCafferty concurred: 'If one takes sexual health as the norm against which we are to measure ourselves' then 'Irish people are in a much better state than they were at the time of the Kerry babies trial' (2010: xxvi).

However, the sense of Ireland finally catching up with the sexual mainstream elsewhere in Europe is one that Diarmaid Ferriter (2009) has questioned for its neat symmetry between dark and light. Ferriter has considered the depth and complexity of the transitions about sex and sexuality in Irish society in the twentieth century, citing other debates outwith the Catholic church hierarchy, notably the critical role of the state, the need for public health services and the rise of civil rights, themes common to many western European societies. Linda Connolly criticises the notion of Irish women as 'late developers' compared with women from seemingly less 'traditional' societies. Connolly has been concerned to point out that a notion of Irish women being 'crudely dominated' by objective structures, rendering them 'easily oppressed' and rescued only through influences external to a monolithic Irish society requires more nuance (2003: 8–10). Pat O'Connor (1998: 2–4) argues that while the European Community/ Union project has had very considerable impact on the lives of Irish women, many of these changes, such as the dramatic increases in female employment, were taking place for women elsewhere across Europe at the same time. Recent histories elsewhere do not present us with a straightforward 'modernising' pathway that automatically brings 'progress' for women, in this instance, ending with the contraceptive pill.[9] Connolly, for one, sees the importance of a longer timeframe in which to reflect on dynamic 'processes of mediation, resistance and constraint' (2003: 12) that are woven into women's lives.

This seems important in trying to get closer to the meanings women currently hold about what can be the taken-for-granted good of a liberalising society. The caveats we raise at the outset about an unfinished task are not to suggest that this task is a smoothly progressive move towards liberation; rather they are to draw attention to continuing and painful inequalities for women which are exposed in conflicted gender and class relations. These form major difficulties in relation to sex and sexuality and continue to provoke painful episodes. During the course of our research in 2003–6, there were a number of instances reported in the press of women who had given birth to stillborn babies outside the health care system and to live babies, then leaving them in public spaces (*The Irish Times* 2004c; Reid 2004; Roche 2004; A. Healy 2005). Research carried out in that same period for the Crisis Pregnancy Agency indicated that concealed pregnancy was a complex matter (Conlon 2006), Yet this is not alone an Irish issue, but one relevant in many contemporary settings.[10]

There are sufficient shadows over Irish women's lives for us to understand that making Ireland still more 'modern' and more 'progressive' is neither a straightforward undertaking nor a straightforward solution to

---

9   For example, Collier (1997) documents the gendered shifts of family life in a rural Spanish village from the 1960s to the 1980s, expressing scepticism about accounts 'that portray recent history as a saga of loosening constraints' (1997: 6). She argues that there was a more subtle shift whereby people changed how they defined their sense of self in relation to the changing expectations of others. During a complex period for Spain, individual achievement slowly became a defining source of personal subjectivity over more traditional forms of social status (1997: 209). British society was also perceived as enforcing tight societal norms about sex and sexuality well into the twentieth century, and yet many women sought to work round those actively before oral contraception was available in respect of their sexual desires and practices (Fisher 2006; Szreter and Fisher 2010).

10   Efforts to understand the reasons that lie behind infant abandonment in contemporary western society continue to lag behind legal responses to criminalise women. See Meyer and Oberman (2001), Oaks (2015) and Murphy-Tighe (2017).

embedded social and sexual inequalities. In broad terms, there remain deep tensions between women working to exercise agency in their own right in a state which remains patriarchal. The two women and two young girls in the terrible landmark events from the 1980s and 1990s remain vivid exemplars for us. They let us see how women seek to assert agency and resistance often in the most hopeless of circumstances: that pair of scissors. To reinvoke that unimaginable terrain is not in order to celebrate our good fortune in contrast, but to help us better reflect on our current situation where what Pat O'Connor (1998) terms 'familialism' is still in place as a potent discourse. Lois McNay's (2000) insights are useful, pointing out the contradictory effects on women which the interplay between practical everyday family life and the symbolism about family life produce. These tensions create ambivalent spaces amidst 'variable patterns of autonomy and dependence' (2000: 65). These overlap in the way they provide scope for resistance as much as for the constraints they reveal. We need to hold that awareness of agency as we read through 'women's politics, struggles, theories, knowledges' (Grosz 1994: 163) and perhaps that is best done by employing the longer timeframe of which Linda Connolly (2003) speaks so that we come to understand how, historically, Irish women have struggled to exercise agency, to resist and to experience the quicksilver of desire, even if only partially, on their own terms.

We want to take up Linda Connolly's challenge and intend to explore our contemporary circumstances in light of that longer timeframe which we argue reaches back to post-Famine Irish society in its patriarchal roots. We believe this is a worthwhile undertaking, giving an important backdrop to the actions and inactions of the contemporary Irish state as we attempt to make sense of our current difficulties: for example, the way the state has tried to 'unhear' women whose reproductive health it has directly damaged (Leahy 2018) or the way economic vulnerability stemming from state policies impinges on women as single parents (Holland 2021a). In so doing, we are privileging women's stories of this contemporary Ireland while drawing on the work of scholars including Walter Benjamin (2003, 2005) and Irish cultural theorist David Lloyd (1999, 2008) to help us make sense of both the losses we have sustained and the resistance we require.

In the course of the next five chapters, we explore the implications of this struggle, and throughout the book, we attend to stratified reproduction, a term first introduced by Shellee Colen, which 'describes the power relations by which some categories of people are empowered to nurture and reproduce, while others are disempowered' (Colen 1995; Ginsburg and Rapp 1995a: 3). In Chapter 1, we discuss the extent of modernity in reshaping how Irish people sought to interpret and respond to wide-ranging changes in women's lives and family life into the twentieth century and the legacy of this for women in contemporary Ireland. In Chapter 2, we examine how our interviewees have seen themselves through sexual experiences, images and language. Chapter 3 focuses on negative representations of sexuality, experiences and sexual risk-taking. In Chapter 4, we discuss how women in the early 2000s thought about the risks of pregnancy and what to do when falling pregnant. Chapter 5 explores how young women have considered their life plans and the meaning of motherhood given what many perceive as increased pressures placed on women to 'do it all', balancing children, work, relationships and any other pursuits they may value.

In Conclusion, we examine the lessons from women's stories in light of our current realities. Since 2008, Irish society has tumbled over yet another economic precipice. This complicates the discourse of the progressive, liberalising society based on the story of economic expansion that will enable women to live fuller lives on their own terms. It also complicates our work as feminists in how we make the case for far greater public engagement and acknowledgement of women's complex and impacted experiences of sexuality and motherhood. We know too well how much has imploded for women in the midst of previous such crises. Thus, a core task before us is how to revalue the many ways women are taking up these challenges and, above all, to broaden out the spaces for women's recognition, inclusion and equality.

This research was made possible by the Crisis Pregnancy Agency which commissioned work between 2003 and 2006 on women's understandings of sex, fertility and motherhood (Murphy-Lawless, Oaks and Brady 2004; Murphy-Lawless 2006). The different settings themselves where we interviewed conveyed many of the bewildering juxtapositions of contemporary Ireland during the Celtic Tiger. We were invited into the sitting rooms of expensively rented or mortgaged houses in estates strung across urban areas, often on a Friday evening at the end of a long working week, housemates and partners poised to go out clubbing for the night once our conversations had concluded. We interviewed women in offices, empty lecture rooms, pubs, coffee bars, cramped local authority houses and flats, community centres, training centres and women's centres, some of the latter wonderful, some very down at heel. The reflections of the seventy-three women who were so generous in speaking to us have demanded from us a corresponding sense of commitment to record their perspectives as generously as we can. The entire undertaking has made us rethink what we mean by agency and resistance, revaluing women's actions as they endeavour to value their own lives.

CHAPTER I

'In a field by the river my love and I did stand': Changing Social Forms, Modernity and Resistance

Images of women from the past

How can we take up Linda Connolly's challenge of reflecting on that longer historical timeframe in which women of generations past in Ireland attempted to mediate their lives (Connolly 2003: 12)? What are the more distant social and economic threads that created the historical backdrop to the lived experiences of sex and sexuality for women? A starting point is what Joe Lee (1989: 513) terms Ireland's 'demographic fantasy'. This phrase packs in an extraordinarily dense network of effects on women in respect of sex, marriage, family and work throughout the nineteenth and twentieth centuries. During that long span of aggregate population growth up to the Famine and the collapse of the population thereafter, generations of Irish women had to pick their way as best they could through a welter of conflicting economic and cultural pressures. A singularly Irish form of modernity left its mark on their experiences and lingered to affect current generations. In this chapter, we explore these ramifications.

Population growth and pre-Famine pressures

The voluminous debates and accounts of Ireland's demographic exceptionalism stretch back to at least the 1770s when rapid population growth first became evident (Cullen 1968: 118–9). From that time to the Famine,

1845–51, Ireland was designated a problematic society by observers of the period on the basis of its swelling numbers. It became a staple of the extensive travel literature of the period, English travellers like Arthur Young and James Bicheno, for example, and official inquiries of the pre-Famine period to reflect on the poverty of the growing masses in rural Ireland (Ó Tuathaigh 1972: 108). The fecund Irish peasant woman with her feckless husband, without a care for the future, became the explanation for what was viewed as the major demographic problem in western Europe. Alexis de Tocqueville recorded the view of John Revans, the secretary to the Irish Poor Law Commission: 'The poorer they were the more children they had. They believe they have nothing more to fear' (de Tocqueville 1990: 20). This preoccupation reflected the wider politics of demography in the eighteenth and early nineteenth centuries which was fixated on how to convert the poor into economically productive units, or at least to lessen the perceived burden of the 'unproductive' poor on the rest of society (Foucault 1981: 169). The principal writer on unrestrained fecundity and its consequences for societies, Thomas Malthus, wrote that within the iron laws of food production and population growth, the poor would be punished by starvation and periodic famine if they were so imprudent as to marry and bear children without means to support them (Malthus 2004). The European population as a whole doubled between 1700 and 1835, and Malthusian thinking led some regions in Austria and Germany to impose constraints on marriage, making peasants prove that they could support children (A. Clark 2008: 124).

While population growth continued apace in Europe, the numbers bore no comparison with the rate of growth in Ireland, where the average size of families was far larger, a characteristic that would endure into the twentieth century (Foster 1988: 124). In the last two decades of the eighteenth century, this predominantly rural society was marked by a rapid increase to almost five million people, with the greatest expansion amongst the rural labouring classes. The key economic moment for the nineteenth century, Foster argues, was the ending of the Napoleonic Wars in 1815 (ibid.: 318). As the peak demand for grain to feed a war-time army and navy declined, better-off farmers adjusted to changing market conditions by diversifying to include cattle for export and reduced their need for non-family labourers (Cullen 1968: 119–21). Local wage levels were depressed, while rents for conacre, the strips of fertilised land made available at a price to the rural poor, were subject to proportionately higher increases than commercial agricultural rents, with many agreements to hold the strips even cancelled (Cullen ibid.; Whelan 1995: 26–7).

A growing competition for available land and waged work took shape amongst the cottier class who carried the weight and the consequences of a distorted agricultural economy. The potato became central to their diet, a reality condemned by Malthus who opposed the cultivation of the potato for the poor in England on the grounds that it would bring them down to the level of 'the rags and wretched cabins of Ireland' (Malthus, quoted in McLean 2004: 55). Ó Gráda (1999: 25) estimates that in pre-Famine Ireland, two-thirds of the men worked land which was not their own. The rapid growth in numbers of the cottier class made vital the reclamation of marginal areas to grow the potatoes which were to become their lifeline: 'The cotters are driven to cultivate the inhospitable bogs and mountain lands' (Bicheno 1830: 9). This restructured the landscape, especially in the western part of the country, and the use of 'lazy beds' in areas which could not be ploughed, also created work in abundance for the expanding population, using spades as their main implement.

New communities took shape along previously unsettled uplands, forming what Whelan (1995: 24) terms 'a very modern society' in that it used the potato, a new crop, as its economic base. To accommodate this 'ecological interloper', new understandings of how land was held were required, giving rise to different forms of social relations based on the systems of rundale and clachan (ibid.) which in turn, helped to create a cheap labour force for the better-off farmer. Typically, the farmer rented conacre land to the cottier who then paid the rent with his labour on the farmer's land, sometimes paying as well with part of his potato crop. This 'potato wage' (Whelan 1995: 20), alongside the success of the potato as an abundant crop locked the poorest class into an uneasy dependence on whatever terms were offered to them (ibid.: 26; de Beaumont 2006: 140–1; Ó Gráda 1999: 30). The resulting fragilities for this class of the rural 'untouchable' (Ó Danachair 1985: 103) became apparent in the decades immediately preceding the Famine and contributed to the scale of the Famine.

Women living day to day

What this meant on a day-to-day basis for the majority of women in respect of work, marriage and motherhood is very hard to capture in its
multiple forms, yet certain themes do emerge, especially for women of the
lower classes: poverty, arranged marriages, large families, hard physical
work and emigration. These developments, often associated with post-
Famine Ireland and the very long decline in Irish population into the
mid-twentieth century (Daly 1981; Guinnane 1998), were already evident
in the decades immediately preceding the Famine. As a successful potato
monoculture based on the 'lumpers' grew, supplying the staple food for at
least one-third of the rural population (Crawford 1995: 60), it rendered
unnecessary domestic skills needed to prepare and use grain for bread as a
cooking pot on a hearth sufficed (Ó Gráda 1999: 18). The cottiers

> resorted to the wretched expedient of growing an inferior and coarser potatoe, which
> yields larger crops, and is produced, with less manure, upon a worse soil. That this de-
> teriorated potatoe, called 'lumpers', is extending in cultivation, and becoming more the
> food of the poor … speaks volumes as to their sinking condition. (Bicheno 1830: 142)

In what Foster (ibid.: 295) describes as a 'marginalized rural society'
hit by agrarian unrest and distress, another warning sign for the rural poor
was the number of 'shanty towns' that sprang up on the edge of established
towns (Whelan 1995: 26). The output of commercial agriculture and an
export industry grew alongside this subsistence agriculture (Connolly
2011: 36) and, as long as potato harvests were good, the poor could feed
themselves (Mokyr and Ó Gráda 1988: 229). Nonetheless, periodic potato
crop failures, often weather-related, did lead to acute localised food short-
ages in parts of the country (Connell 1965: 288; Foster 1988: 319–20; de
Tocqueville 1990: 131), and there was a growing inequality of income distribution (Mokyr and Ó Gráda 1988: 211). For the poorest of the cottiers
who had to eke out an existence, it was essential for women and children
to work for any available wages (Cullen 1968: 121; Cullen 1990). Internal
migration for families, with women and children begging and men working
for low wages (Cullen 1990:109), began to extend to seasonal emigration

for men to the fields of Scotland and England. Permanent emigration to the new British industrial towns was well-established before the Famine (Cullen 1968: 122; Ó Tuathaigh 1972; Foster 1988: 322, 324). The rate of population growth appeared to peak before the Famine reflecting problems for the cottier class in obtaining land, the increasing rates of young male emigration and a lower percentage of very early marriages for young women. The overall rate of marriage itself was dropping (Foster 1988: 331–2) as was the birth rate. The population as a whole was set to fall even if the Famine had not taken place (Ó Gráda 1999: 29).

Living conditions for the poorest were stark, yet Ó Gráda (1999: 25), Foster (1988: 220), Kinealy (1997: 5), S. J. Connolly (2011: 37) and others point to the condition of the rural population before the Famine, who in general were noted for their height, strong physique, 'good health and have the clearest skins in the world' (Bicheno 1830: 21). This suggests that if the potato harvest was good, their 'monotonous diet' and ready access to fuel in the form of turf provided reasonable health, even by European standards of the time (Ó Gráda 1999: 25). Literacy rates were growing and education was more available to many, although not for the very poorest who would need to pay a penny per week to a hedge school (Mokyr and Ó Gráda 1988: 223). It was far from a joyless society for many people, however poor. Towards the end of the eighteenth century, Arthur Young wrote of general good cheer and high spirits: 'Vivacity and a great and eloquent volubility of speech … infinitely more cheerful and lively than anything we commonly see in England … Dancing is so universal among them that there are everywhere itinerant dancing-masters, to whom the cottars pay sixpence a quarter for teaching their families' (Young 1897: 104). In the late 1820s, Bicheno spoke of the 'cheerful assistance' rendered to the stranger by the poorer classes and to those even worse off than they were (1830: 38, 232), something also commented on by de Tocqueville (1990: 41, 78, 117), who records perceptions of their being 'gentle, polite, hospitable'.

The cottier classes and smallest farmers who had the least land and landless labourers continued to marry earliest, though not as early as many contemporary observers asserted (Daly 1981: 90–1). This was underlined by testimony to the 1833 Poor Law Commission reported by the Scottish chronicler, Christian Johnstone in her *True Stories of the Irish*

Peasantry, as Related by Themselves, Selected from the Report of the Poor-Law Commissioners:

> It is always the poorest man marries first, because he knows he cannot be worse off by it; it is better for him to marry early, than to seduce the girls, who are so poor and wretched that this would often happen. Besides, we poor people have a strange idea that it is a good thing to have children as soon as possible, in order to help and support us when we begin to grow old. (Johnstone, quoted in Kilfeather 2002: 848)

Bicheno analysed the social meaning of this, where in contrast with the rural poor in England, there were evident bonds of 'affection subsisting between parents and children; and the obligation to support each other is felt to be so imperative, that no excuse can release parties from it' (Bicheno 1830: 253–4). K. H. Connell (1956: 82) argued that marriage in the cottier class followed upon often spontaneous engagements formed 'at will … the first move towards marriage was their own' (1956: 83), rather than following parental direction, not least because 'their customary standard of living' could be secured readily 'on land newly won from mountain or bog' (1956: 82). This was a matter of 'common prudence' for the poorest classes for whom children were the only bulwark in later years. To many contemporary observers, however, those who married when very young lacked prudence and thereby contributed to the problem of over-population: 'The more intolerable their poverty becomes, the more this spirit of improvidence increases' declared a wealthy Catholic merchant to de Tocqueville in 1835 (de Tocqueville 1990: 23). Lee (1973: 4) argues that age at marriage and size of landholdings gave a clue to the highly stratified rural social structure, with those higher up exercising greatest caution to protect their landholdings.

This 'commercial concern' (S. J. Connolly 1985: 85) about what constituted an appropriate marriage, it was argued, led to substantial control over the decisions of sons and daughters of farmers about when and whom to marry, and these marriages were said to be contracted 'without any regard to love, affection or any of the finer feelings' (Poor Inquiry 1836, quoted in S. J. Connolly 1985: 85). Again the contrast was made, whether accurately or not, with the cottier class for whom 'marriages are generally settled between the parties, often at fairs', popular events where the wider family might gather (ibid.: 84).

This does not mean that desire and individual agency were absent from economically more secure families, nor was a purely instrumental and restrictive view of marriage and of women's subservient role absent from men in poorer classes. Family conflict over what was deemed a suitable match within better-off classes could and did occur, sometimes leading to elopement (ibid.). At the other end of the social scale, it was recorded in the Poor Inquiry that landless labourers were searching for a wife 'in order to have a person to attend them, and to wash their clothes etc.' (ibid: 88). Children generally shared the concerns and priorities of their parents who arranged marriages for them and that these priorities were 'not incompatible' with attributes of attractiveness and personality (ibid.: 89). Yet it may have been a 'less restrictive' and 'less oppressive' system than what would come to the fore in post-Famine Ireland (ibid.: 83).

Within marriage itself, conditions for women, especially amongst the poorer classes, were harsh (Cullen 1990). S. J. Connolly (1985: 89) quotes Edward Wakefield, writing in 1812, that the typical husband considered his wife 'his slave'. Bicheno noted that there were 'too many instances of the wretchedness of the women not to be deeply affected by it. If destitution is to be endured, they are the first sufferers' (1830: 37). There is evidence that poor women ate less food in order to feed their families in addition to coping in other ways with their poverty, lack of status and drudgery (Miller, Doyle and Kelleher 1997: 45–4). There appeared to be a restrictive code of sexual behaviour that applied across the class structure, but with uneven effects. While allowing that overt sexual expressiveness and often cruelly sexualised jokes were part of community life, shared by men and women both (S. J. Connolly 1985: 90; Ó Danachair 1985: 100–3), Connolly also argues that the system of arranged marriages would have been jeopardised by widespread non-marital sex.

The social policing of desire and of sex outside marriage highlights the importance of preserving a social system under pressure as best as possible. At the same time, it must have contributed to the hasty marriages with little viable means of support to which the Scotswoman, Elizabeth Grant objected so strongly in her chronicles of Wicklow life in the 1840s. As ever it was the poorest and most vulnerable women who suffered the worst consequences from sexual desire and sexual transgression. Grant gives a vivid picture of a woman she can only call 'the Dumbie', a 36-year-old pro-foundly deaf woman, without family and seemingly without even a proper name, who earned her meagre living by doing heavy work for small tenant farmers. It was one of these men who brought her to 'ruin', the brother of a family called the Pendars for whom the woman had worked for two years:

> She had been bringing in large baskets of potatoes from the field … and was sud-denly missed, looked for and found in the cowhouse with her new born infant. Mrs. Pendar moved her to the hay loft, made her some gruel, but understanding from the poor creature's signs that she accused her, Mrs. Pendar's brother James Butler of her ruin … on the second morning turned this poor creature out on the road, hungry, dirty and naked, for the few rags she had on barely covered her, and her baby was wrapped in a coarse apron. She lay in the gripe of a ditch till dark weeping inces-santly when she made her way to her old master, Dick Gray, about the poorest man in Baltiboys, he took her in, Kitty shared her bed with her, Anne Casey the pedlar who lodges there washed her and cobbled up some old things for the baby. There I found this poor victim of as disgraceful a sin as ever the unbridled passions of man had to answer for. (E. Grant 2004: 147)

The woman's fate was 'to go to Naas to the workhouse, herself and her unhappy baby, whose cries she can't hear and whom she has no means of providing for' (ibid.).

For women in general, the values associated with embourgeoisment in the eighteenth and early nineteenth centuries had already brought about an erosion of women's status, seen in features like a married woman no longer retaining her maiden surname upon marriage as had been done traditionally (Ó Danachair 1985: 109). However, marriage remained a crucial stepping stone to status for a woman within the rural community, giving her independence from her primary family and a sense of respect and authority (Ó Danachair 1985: 100). A line from the *Cottage Dialogues among the Irish Peasantry* by Mary Leadbetter (1811), bears this out. One of the young women domestic servants, Nancy, declares her ambition to marry and take up the habits of the better-off: 'I intend to have tea when I'm in a house of my own, and no thanks to anyone' (quoted in O'Dowd 2002: 514). Whether married or not, women made a necessary contribution to the family economy of poorer households, working at spinning, sewing, bonnet-making, domestic service, childcare, wet-nursing, agricultural work such as weeding and binding, and peddling (Lee 1977: 37–8; O'Dowd 2002: 469, 514; McLean 2004: 26). Here is a description from Michael Corduff from Rossport, County Mayo of women working as peddlers before the Famine, recorded for the Irish Folklore Commission:

> There were no country shops. Women used to peddle some goods through the country from Belmullet which was the nearest town and instead of money received eggs, wool, yarn, stockings etc. for their sales and took these goods back to the town where they received cash for them, or a fresh supply of wares to sell. (quoted in McLean 2004: 26)

Unmarried women enjoyed some level of autonomy as paid workers. Although their wages were small and were often handed over to families directly, especially when they were still adolescents, many single women labourers did have cash to spend on personal goods and did so at country fairs (O'Dowd 2002: 469). Married women did exercise independence over working and the money they could earn, and if much of it went back into the household, the decision to do so lay with the wife (Ó'Danachair 1985: 109). In 1841, women still constituted over half the labour force in non-agricultural work alone (Lee 1977: 37) and, in years when harvests were plentiful, women contributed a sizeable portion of money to the household budget through pig and poultry-rearing, making families more secure and, when the husband had no work, these contributions became even more important (Cullen 1990: 85, 98–9). If families had to rely on begging, it was the women and children who did so. This testimony is from the 1836 Poor Inquiry of a landless labourer in Mayo on why early marriage would not necessarily leave him worse off: 'For when he has no work, if he is ashamed to beg himself, the wife and children will beg and support him' (quoted in Cullen 1990: 110).

The Famine and its empty spaces

Travellers like de Tocqueville (1990: 130–2) recorded that daily life was precarious for many in the lower reaches of Irish society in that final decade before 1845. The Famine visibly changed everything. In the regions most heavily afflicted by death from starvation and fever, by mass evictions and by emigration, the landscape emptied. Prior to the Famine 'the poor were everywhere ... as the remains of whole streets of "bohawn" or mud houses show today even' (quoted in McLean 2004: 28). It was said of Carna in Connemara 'they lived so close to one another that men would chat from house to house without ever coming to the door' (quoted in Ó Gráda 1999: 202).

The ensuing silence, 'this awful, unwonted silence which during the famine and subsequent years, almost everywhere prevailed' (George Petrie, quoted in Lloyd 2003: 206) took on multiple meanings as the catastrophe of the Famine was absorbed. Ó Gráda (1999: 5, 232) argues that the Famine affected all classes across the whole of Ireland, making it proportionately the most murderous of famines in modern times, lasting longer than others and destroying the means of food production for at least one-third of the society. It registered the cruellest of demographic shocks, including the haemorrhage of permanent emigration for generations to come. Many who travelled to the worst-hit districts during the Famine were themselves silenced by the extent of the trauma they witnessed, unable to find words sufficient to capture such 'chaos, death and destitution' (McLean 2004: 78). The Quaker, William Bennett, wrote from County Mayo in 1847, 'language utterly fails me' in trying to describe fever-ridden people 'scarcely human in appearance' who had dug shelters out of bogland in an effort to survive (quoted in McLean 2004: 81). A British government officer who had the task of inspecting the need for public works in County Clare, reported:

> I ventured into the parish this day to ascertain the condition of the inhabitants, and altho' a man not easily moved, I confess myself unmanned by the intensity and the extent of the suffering I witnessed more especially among the women and the little children, crowds of whom were to be seen scattered over the turnip fields like a flock of vanishing crows. (quoted in McLean 2004: 118)

A sense of suffering that was so profound as to be beyond help lay in the silence. Jenny Edkins (2000: 10), in her study of modern famines, notes that 'not only were people killed, they had to endure the total breakdown of social and familial bonds and unimaginable extremities of distress'.

These extremities permeated accounts from the Famine, with many of the visual images centred on women with their children. One of the most famous Famine drawings comes from Moveen, County Clare, and was printed in the *London Illustrated News* in 1849. It portrays Bridget O'Donnell, who was seven months pregnant when her home, from which she had been evicted, was demolished and the cornmeal she had been given impounded, so she could not return. In the drawing, she stands with her arms protectively around her two starving children (McLean 2004: 130). It was said that her baby was born dead, eight days later. Stuart McLean describes how this image was used as a signifier for so much that the Famine destroyed: thousands of tiny villages, an entire class and way of life, 'an historical loss', but it also set up 'a spectral persistence of the vanished past' (ibid.).

Many asserted that the demise of subsistence agriculture was not without advantages.

A number of prominent British thinkers and economists had made the argument prior to the Famine that a complete clearance, albeit without mass starvation, would break up the cottiers and their indigenous patterns and ways of life. The profligate Irish, lacking 'modern' virtues of hard work, would thus have created for them, whether they willed it or not, the space for a more orderly, progressive, rational and modern society, and new forms of land ownership (Lloyd 2003: 213–5; Nally 2008: 731). Relying on a Malthusian ideology, they argued that the Irish had brought it on themselves through their lack of discipline.

Some Irish observers responded differently, mourning the loss of a cultural order. The disappearance of the largest single class of the population appeared to create an irrevocable dividing line between past and present, the point at which there was no return to what were deemed pre-modern ways of life. William Wilde, writing in 1849 at the Famine's height, lamented the 'great convulsion which society of all grades has lately experienced' and how it had 'broken up the very foundations of social intercourse' leaving 'the remnant of the hardiest and most stalwart of the people [to] crawl about, listless spectres, unable or unwilling to rise out of their despair' (Wilde 1850: 1–2). He was stricken at the sweeping away of the very people who had carried an oral culture within the fabric of their daily lives: 'All the domestic usages of life have been outraged' (ibid.: 2), bewailing this terrible loss 'on the one hand and the spread of education, and the introduction of railroads, colleges, industrial and other educational schools on the other' (ibid.).

Before the Famine, the Irish administration under direction from the British government had already begun to transform major aspects of Irish life in efforts to 'modernise' this unwieldy society. The schools to which Wilde refers were part of a national school system to educate the poor that began to take shape between 1831 and 1832, a move that would replace the indigenous hedge schools. The Irish Railway Commission was established in 1836, the same year that reforms to the police force created a sophisticated Irish constabulary, vital from the state's perspective to deal with the wide range of violent agrarian protests that emerged following the agricultural collapse of 1815 onward (Lloyd 1999: 44). Oliver MacDonagh has argued that these new functions of government were characterised by specific moves on the part of central government to undercut and diminish local power and local custom, in effect to impose a streamlined uniformity and professionalism before 1850 (2003: 37). During the Famine, the government reformed the medical dispensary system, also setting up a system of national inspection (Nally 2008: 720). These developments, building on the work of two centuries to remake Irish institutions in order to deal with the 'Irish question', were well in advance of moves in Britain and its other colonies, and made Ireland a laboratory for modern government (Ohlmeyer 2003: 58). Crucially, they opened up possibilities of a biopolitical regime, that key undertaking of nineteenth-century liberal governmentality, in which all aspects of a population became subject to regulation (Dean 2002; Legg 2005; Nally 2008). In Foucauldian terms, this new state machinery was positioned to help set in motion new social norms about and connections between the individual and the social body, in order to solve 'the political problem of population' (Foucault 1997: 70). Thus while Wilde sees the Famine as eradicating the old social order, it had already been encroached upon by these measures, let alone the other pressures that were building cumulatively in the 1830s, including emigration.

The state intervention with arguably the greatest impact was the Poor Law of 1838 that brought with it the division of the country into 130 unions, each with its own workhouse. This legislation had as much to do with set-tling the perceived problem of what the English Poor Law Commissioner, George Nicholls, termed Ireland's 'superabundant population' as with alle-viating poverty (Nally 2008: 723). It is notable that the centralising work of the state in Ireland ensured the rapid establishment of workhouses com-pared with a far slower and 'patchy' development in England (McDonagh 2003: 34). The two outstanding conditions of the Poor Law were designed to break the communitarian, agricultural way of life of the cottier class and to deprive them of possession of land. In line with the economic thinking of a rapidly industrialising England, the emphasis was now put on 'freeing' a man's labour which was his 'only protection from actual want', on which he should rely (ibid.). The government's strategies to bring relief were in-dissolubly bound up with the task of reforming agricultural production and land ownership to bring about an absolute expansion of the market economy (ibid.: 728–9). Thus while the potato blight itself could not have been anticipated, the catastrophe the Famine became was built into how the state promoted a new economics and its 'concern for the regulation and control of the population' (Edkins 2000: 2). The intent of this modern project was to 'radically restructure Irish society' (Nally 2008: 730).

Implications of the Famine: Post-Famine accommodations

As Bauman has argued, modernity and the modern state set out to 'free' people from a past where they were presumed hopelessly entangled by archaic traditions and customs, and to replace that with a rational order, refurbishing the 'social space' (Bauman 1993: 83). Of course, that dividing line between pre-modern past and present is never as clear as its propon-ents might wish. The past is 'fluid ... constantly shifting'; it is not a linear unproblematic progression through to a 'better' present with its 'radically individualized subject' (McLean 2004: 128, 44), free to pursue life on un-fettered terms. Moreover, the ambitions of powers that promote modern-ising, commonly the nation state, underscore the aspirations of powerful groups that may be radically different to what other groups in the population can discern as needful. McLean (ibid.) argues that maintaining a sharp division between past and present is a way of authorising only one account and one set of concerns about a past, excluding multiple concerns and stories: those who vanished during the Famine, seen one way by the authorities at the time, were ultimately seen by a newly independent Ireland as a kind of repository of 'a timeless national essence' (ibid.: 20) to be mined whenever discussions or assertions about 'Irishness' arose.

This also became a useful tool to dismiss any ongoing resistance to the social forms that came to dominate post-Famine Ireland and this had implications for women. A small but significant example can be found in how the Irish Folklore Commission, established in 1935, went about its work of collecting and classifying memories and stories from the mid- to late nineteenth century. There simply were no women collectors or recorders sent out (McLean 2004: 22) which fact ultimately will have changed the nature of what was recorded, however rich that material was.

Overlooking women as agents in this retrospective gathering of folk memories, eliminating their active presence, parallels the representations of women as silent during the Famine. Given the nature of the conservative patriarchal society that was to develop from the 1850s onward, both are telling in their consideration of women's voices, and their status. Women figured prominently in visual depictions of the Famine, most commonly as mothers, as with Bridget O'Donnell, and portrayed as passive, voiceless victims. Margaret Kelleher (1997) has argued in her work, that either as mother heroines, trying to find food for their children or trying to bury them, or mother anti-heroines, killing their children and worse, women came to represent the breakdown of society. They were also made to represent a society that was vanishing, in which maternal affection had become a symbol of nourishing the wider domain, albeit with no political power (Kelleher 1995: 245). This same sense of women as mothers driven to break crucial social boundaries, but without genuine power to alter their circumstances, is also found in Folklore Commission accounts (McLean 2004: 135). The elision between women as suffering motherhood and the country as a whole appears central in the many attempts to make sense of the extent of the loss (Kelleher 1995). They became a signifier for the cottier class that was being wiped out. McLean (2004: 139–40) suggests that the need to preserve women as silent symbols helped a (male-dominant) society to step between an imagined past and a bleak present during and just after the Famine.

Yet women were far from voiceless, passive or agentless on the eve of the Famine when, for example, their industrious begging kept their families alive (Cullen 1990). At the point of death even during the Famine, women retained subversive spaces in oral culture at least, so that the traditional keening, the *caoineadh*, not only was undertaken solely by women, it enabled women to express their anger at male violence towards individual and community life and their resistance (Bourke 1993; Whelan 2005: 141–2). When committed to the workhouse during the Famine, women were often able to turn the rules of these institutions to fit their needs (McLoughlin 1990). Literate women from the middle class produced an extensive range of fiction about the Famine in which women's voices were heard (Kelleher 1997: 113–4). The wholly admirable Asenath Nicholson, an American, kept a journal of her years during the Famine providing relief for women who had fled to Dublin in which she relates their 'cool calculation' on their chances for survival as they scraped to keep their families alive (Nicholson 1998: 44). As it happens, men fared worse than women during the Famine. The analysis of mortality (Boyle and Ó Gráda 1986: 554–5; Fitzpatrick 1997: 52–3; Kelleher 1997: 9–10) indicates that age-specific death rates were higher for men than for women.

Boyle and Ó Gráda (1986) calculate that there were one million Famine deaths while 1.3 million people left Ireland in the Famine years. As for births, 'lessened to an extent scarcely credible' (Wilde 1850: 68), Boyle and Ó Gráda estimate that there were over 300,000 births in the Famine years that did not take place owing to the ravages of death and emigration (1986: 555). These losses contributed to shaping that rather more recognisably 'modern' society that slowly emerged in the decades after the Famine. Between 1851 and 1871, almost two million people emigrated and, over the next six decades, nearly six million people left Ireland. It meant that for many decades to come, people could leave more easily because there was a widespread community of settled emigrants with whom to connect immediately. Ongoing emigration was undeniably an outcome of the 'disaster

paradigm of social improvement and population regulation' which comprised the Famine (Nally 2008: 733). As a society, Ireland continued to
rely on emigration as a mechanism 'a distinctive form of disciplining' for
those men and women with no personal future within its restructured
economy (Lloyd 1999: 12).

Those who remained built an account of the Famine as a catastrophe
for the classes who were most culturally backward, the marginal classes
closest to that line between culture and nature (Lloyd 2003: 215). The
Famine as a 'natural disaster', courted by people who refused to become
'modern', deflected any political or economic analysis of causes and consequences for all the major power groups in post-Famine Ireland. Ireland's
modernity thus became a 'skewed culture' built on complex layers of an
unworked-through loss, where the (British) state project of rationalising
post-Famine land ownership meant that the empty spaces were of benefit
to many who stayed behind: 'There were … others who rejoiced that all
around them were evicted so that they fell in nicely for their places. We
have them around here since, people whose ancestors did that – but we
must leave it so and press it underfoot' (Donegal chronicles, quoted in
McHugh 1956: 430).

Wholesale emigration was the most prominent effect: the continued
outflow into the middle of the twentieth century of the most disenfran-
chised meant that population projections made in 1922 of fourteen million
by 1990, would never be achieved (Lloyd 1999: 102), nor with it the secure
economic success of the conventional modernising European model. If the
'non-modern' Irish were punished first by death and then by ongoing emigration, their 'unwelcome spectres', occluded within the official accounts
of the Famine, haunted the conservative order of post-Famine Ireland and
yet were denied representation by that order.

This was perhaps nowhere more so than in women's lives where their
daily realities went unrepresented by official Ireland. The cultural (male-
led) constructions of women as passive and suffering and identified with
motherhood, objectified women and their everyday experiences and left
little space for them to represent themselves as dynamic and powerful in
their daily lives (Moane 1999: 50–1). The regulatory mechanisms introduced
by the British and seen at their most developed in pre-Famine Ireland in

the Poor Law, became 'powerful tools of association' (Nally 2008: 723) with the potential to expand their reach for a number of groups in rural Ireland who grew in influence in the immediate post-Famine years. Most important of these groups were farmers, both the tenant farmers and larger landowners. Small tenant farmers were able to expand their holdings in one generation and added their numbers to the weight of a conservative rural ideology. For median holdings over one acre, their size grew from 10.8 acres in 1844 to 18.5 acres in 1876 (Clark 1979: 107). Larger Catholic landholders, as well as middlemen and professionals, all had an abiding interest in re-inforcing socially conservative norms. Mac Laughlin (2001: 150–1) defines this broad grouping as akin to the 'reactionary bloc' (Gramsci 1971: 74) in late nineteenth-century Italy that came about through 'binding together of the various rural groups' sharing the same 'material and ideological' interests. This reactionary bloc went on to push for governmental and social forms that would be to their advantage. Mac Laughlin characterises the ensuing nationalist vision as one of 'rural fundamentalism, patriarchal property rights, and all the moral and cultural capital that accompanied these' (2001: 337).

The Catholic church was well-positioned to benefit from this height-ened identification with norms and individual discipline and the general climate of conservatism. In 1835, de Tocqueville, on the whole praiseworthy of the enormous efforts by individual priests who sought to alleviate the suffering of their parishioners, had made this prescient observation, when speaking of the then Bishop of Kilkenny:

> There prevails in his language a certain note of triumph, which indicates the head of a party who arrives in power after having been oppressed for a long time. I believe that he is very sincere in wishing that the church should not be part of the state, but I wonder if he does not think, at bottom, that the state would do well enough as part of the church. (1990: 62)

The reforms imposed by Archbishop Cullen on his return from Rome in 1849 and the subsequent imposition of ultramontanism (a highly cen-tralised church on the Roman model) from 1850 onwards beginning with the Synod of Thurles were all too successful in expanding clerical power at a time when the country was at its lowest ebb. The Catholic church worked to achieve a sophisticated education system, encompassing a Catholic university, while also suppressing popular religious beliefs and customs (Doherty and O'Riordan 2011). A streamlined clerical organisation added to their religious duties, appointments as patron, manager, guardian and chaplain in the temporal settings of school, workhouse, infirmary and so on (Clarke 1979: 193–4; Whelan 2005: 138–9). The interests of churchmen at local level, reflecting the Catholic hierarchy, merged with the prevailing social conservatism that came out of the wreckage of the Famine, simultaneously providing a useful 'symbolic identity' (Whelan 2005: 138–9) for the wider community, as well as a power base.

The continuing exchange of prevailing beliefs among male-dominant conservative farmers, the professional classes and churchmen at all levels, and their collective capacity to foster a dense network of social and legal regulations were to wreak havoc with women's lives in post-independence Ireland. While this was not necessarily a peculiarly Irish development as Mac Laughlin (2001) and others indicate, it had particular force and expression in a depleted society. Thus, by the twentieth century, the Catholic church extended its symbolic identity to become the major cultural force speaking out against 'secularism', at a stroke reinforcing a version of Irishness that was grounded in patriarchy (Kilfeather 2005: 106).

Marriage based on the wider family needs of a rural society, the use of dowries and arranged marriages, and emigration were set to dominate lives in the late nineteenth and early twentieth centuries. Continuous population decline from the time of the Famine, 1845–51, to 1956 (including only the twenty-six counties of the Republic from 1922 onward), of massive emigration, of deferred marriage for many and permanent celibacy for a significant minority, of high marital fertility once women did marry, defined the country as a demographic oddity for over a century.

Of the generation born between 1896 and 1900, 30 per cent of men and 25 per cent of women were still single at the age of 50 (Daly 2006: 13). The impact of the Famine on women's lives in rural Ireland was considerable. Lee (1977: 38–9) points out that women's loss of economic independence and status as a result of a rapidly contracting work force and the shift to pasturage away from tillage, made unmarried women far more dependent for their value on a dowry system and therefore on their fathers who paid that dowry. In general, women had three fates: to gain a match through a matchmaker, to remain unmarried, or to emigrate, while men with little or no land had least chance of attracting a wife (Fitzpatrick 1985: 120). Dowries changed to a purely cash payment and rose in cost, so that a passage to America was actually cheaper than a dowry (Fitzpatrick 1985: 121). At the same time, impartible inheritance and a more rigid system of property began to influence the decision to marry much later (ibid.: 118; MacCurtain 1993: 17–8). Parents were pleased to place their adolescent daughters in domestic service in middle-class households, where they learned the domesticity that might increase their value on the marriage market, or to hire them out as farm workers. The reliance on male power and the consequent problematic status of young women can be read through K. H. Connell's bleak picture of relationships and marriage, in post-Famine Ireland:

> By the time they did marry, they were likely not only to have outlived the years when sexual attraction is most adventurous, but to have lived them in an environment ill-attuned, admittedly by the subtleties of human nature, but equipped by a harsh persistence to lop and stretch the emotions. The Famine was remembered and described too starkly and too vividly for men [sic] to disregard the folly of impetuous marriage. (1958: 5)

That phrase 'equipped by a harsh persistence to lop and stretch emotions' points to a daunting task for women if they were to try to explore a sense of agency and desire. The bleakness of severed emotions for men and women reverberates in the fictionalised biography by John Throne of his maternal grandmother in early twentieth-century Donegal (Throne 2006). In 1910, this young Protestant girl of 13 was hired out as a farm labourer by her impoverished tenant farmer father to a man who beat her, systematically raped her and got her pregnant, after which the local Protestant landowners and local bishop found another poor farmer to marry her before the baby was born. Through five more pregnancies, she worked to feed and protect her children, shielding them from her husband's physical violence, placating him, knowing she needed him to keep her and her children from the workhouse. She died in her 21st year. Her mother is portrayed as helpless to speak out against the authority of her own husband, or the local hierarchy of male power (the young girl's family was considered too poor to attend the local church, yet the Protestant clergy ruled on her fate). Her own daughter, Throne's mother, who was unable to work free of the prevailing ideologies, conveyed to her son, Throne, when she was an elderly woman and anxious for him to know the 'truth' about their family, that her mother, Throne's grandmother was a woman who had committed a terrible sin in becoming pregnant outside marriage.

After 1851, the low rate of marriage overall and high rates of marital fertility suggest that the decisions attached to sex and marriage either lay outwith the scope of many women, or possibly represented too poor a return for them to pursue. Emigration or internal migration to the larger cities was an exit strategy that became central to the life plans of many hundreds of thousands of single women, albeit dependent on the passage they could afford and the work they could hope to find, either domestic service or unskilled factory jobs (Guinnane 1997: 105; Hearn 1990; Miller, Doyle and Kelleher 1997). By the twentieth century, the argument which sprang up around emigration concentrated on the death of Ireland as a nation, resorting to that elision between the loss of women as mothers of the future, and Ireland as Woman: 'Potential mothers of families lost forever to Ireland ... emigration has been like a huge open sore on the bosom of Ireland, robbing her of her lifeblood' (O'Brien 1954: 26).

Through extensive scholarship, much of it by feminist historians, we have come to understand the broad outcomes of the Famine on the lives of women. They were not evenly distributed and contain many anomalies. In respect of marriage, for example, Caitriona Clear (2007: 74–7) points to regional and local variations of age at marriage. Late marriage was not a firm rule of thumb across the country as a whole, nor even necessarily tied to the issue of farm holdings to be passed on to the next generation. A rising middle class across Europe sought later marriage in any case (ibid.), while in Ireland, the wealthiest farmers were least likely to marry (Guinnane 1997: 206). There were difficulties in meeting and courting due to changing employment patterns in both urban and rural areas (Clear 2007: 82–4). In general, 'uneasy relationships' prevailed between unmarried men and women whether they lived in town or country (MacCurtain 1993: 18). Clear also observes that women themselves may have been reluctant to marry into the hard work of a farming background, preferring spinsterhood. For women in the upper-middle and upper classes, 'husband-hunting' was a serious undertaking but not all would be fortunate to marry at the same or higher level of social status and so some might choose not to marry at all (Clear 2007: 85–6).

Like pre-Famine Ireland, post-Famine Irish society was patriarchal, but with quite different meanings for women in its 'cultural singularities' (Lloyd 2003: 215). Women's location and class were crucial to how they experienced these singularities. However, resistance in the sense of women seeking to rework their situations and to create other possibilities amidst these 'radically different forms of social change' (ibid.: 218) was never absent in this period.

'She bid me take love easy': The quicksilver of desire

The woman portrayed in the folksong which Yeats refashioned into the poem, 'Down by the Salley Gardens', gives us a fleeting glimpse of someone who appears to have a deep sensibility about loving and living.[1] The anonymous male narrator of the poem tells us first

> 'She bid me take love easy, as the leaves grow on the trees'
> and in the second verse, he relates
> 'She bid me take life easy, as the grass grows on the weirs'
> He tells us that each time he understood too little what she meant
> 'But I, being young and foolish, with her would not agree'
> and in the final line, he declares
> 'But I was young and foolish, and now am full of tears'

Yeats, whose intention was to fuse folk music and literature, wrote the poem in 1888 and later said that 'This is an attempt to reconstruct an old

---

1   We are indebted to Gerald Dawe for directing us to the 1992 edition of Yeats' poems edited by Daniel Albright which explains how Yeats came to learn the original folksong. See Yeats and Albright (1992).

song from three lines imperfectly remembered by an old peasant woman'
(Yeats 1992: 424). Yeats was to explain further in a 1937 radio broadcast:

> I went from cottage to cottage, listening to stories, to old songs ... Some of my best
> known poems were made in that way. 'Down by the Salley Gardens', for instance, is
> an elaboration of two lines in English somebody sang to me in Ballysadare, County
> Sligo (ibid.).

We can only surmise how the imagined young woman of that old
woman peasant's song might have fared without her erstwhile lover, whether
she might have found another, or no one she wanted. The song poem implies that she, the young woman, knew what one as a woman most needed
to understand about love and desire. Perhaps the old woman knew that
as well. Yet the long trajectory of post-Famine Ireland into the twentieth
century is not noted by historians as a generous space within which Irish
women might develop gentle and profound perceptions about sex and
sexuality, quite the reverse as we have seen.

Siobhán Kilfeather, in her introduction to the section on sexuality in
the *Field Day Anthology*, quotes Terry Eagleton, the cultural theorist on
nineteenth-century Ireland: 'The sexual culture of the nation belonged to
a complex economy of land and inheritance, property and procreation. As
far as sexuality goes, we are speaking less of the erotic and psychological
than of dowries and matchmakers' (Kilfeather 2002: 826). This version of
late nineteenth-century Ireland became a kind of official version, backed
as it was by the oppressive tactics of those with power at local levels as with
John Throne's family. K. H. Connell wrote of the impact in rural Ireland
of the impartible family farm and the role marriage came to play in protecting the farm:

> The peasant-father exploited his power of giving in marriage ... in his daughter-in-
> law the father hoped to find, not simply the appropriate dowry, but strength and
> submission, the promise of fertility and skill in a woman's duties in the house and on
> the land. 'Not very purty!' a father is said to have exclaimed about his own daughter,
> 'Faix, I'll make her purty with cows.' (1956: 88–9)

Kilfeather (2002: 826) takes issue with this thesis about a solely material expression of sexuality and argues that despite its prominence as an

explanatory model, it is 'inadequate to the lived experiences of women'. She suggests an alternative exploration of 'yearning' and 'desire'. Women did hold and keep those responses and they formed a resistance to a conservative and deeply hierarchical stranglehold, based on class and gender in late nineteenth- and twentieth-century Ireland. It is undeniable that this was a power base shot through with 'violent authority' (Clark 2005: 391). Even so, women worked to redefine their lives. So, even if girls were seen as 'largely redundant', it was in fact girls who profited most from increasing rates of literacy (Fitzpatrick 1987: 164). Over half the female population, who were adolescents at the time of the Famine, summoned the means to emigrate, and if they lacked status when they left, the very act of going gave them a chance to improve the scope of their lives, compared with their mothers before them (Fitzpatrick 1990: 173–5). In the 1860 painting of Molly Macree by Thomas Alfred Jones, an adolescent country girl is portrayed wearing a frieze skirt, a soiled work apron and a highly patterned blue and red shawl. She is also portrayed as socially competent. Margaret MacCurtain (1993) perceives a kind of calm, intelligent confidence in her gaze, something which is 'unrepresentable, disturbing – truths that lurk below the surface … in the years following the Famine' (ibid.:14). We might name that unrepresentable something desire and we might say it is bolstered by resistance.

That same resistance is there even in accounts of women who enter the workhouses. Dympna McLoughlin (2002) writes of the independence and spiritedness that pauper women displayed. Many of them appeared capable of handling non-orthodox relationships with men, whether the women were married or not (McLoughlin 1990: 128). Although women and children were meant to be separated from men, not least to monitor sexual relationships, there was constant movement in and out of the workhouse. It depended on the availability of work outside and women knew whether that was changing in their favour so that they could leave even on a temporary basis. Day discharges with women going off to sort out family affairs or going to nearby fairs and festivals were also common. In 1852, a group of women from the South Dublin Union went out for the day and came back drunk (McLoughlin 2002: 724). In 1850, the Minute Books of the Lismore Workhouse record the following:

9th January, 1850.

An inmate, Mary Tobin, is reported to be pregnant. Her husband is dead since
March 1849. On being questioned by the Board of Guardians, it was discovered
that she was the mother of nine children and that she did not know the name
of the father of the present child. She claimed that when she was on an errand
for the Master she met the man on the road between Lismore and Tallow. The
Officers expressed indignation at her conduct and ordered that her ration of milk
be stopped every other day until her lying-in, providing the Medical Officer approved. (Nolan 1995: 114–5)

With no further detail, we know nothing about the nature of Mary
Tobin's encounter on the Tallow Road, whether it was a liaison that she
sought, a serendipitous meeting, or a forced encounter, but whatever the
context, it was not an uncommon occurrence (McLoughlin 2002: 724),
nor was it uncommon for women who were caught in such circumstances
to be 'quickly and severely punished' (ibid.: 725). McLoughlin (2001: 83–
4) has presented evidence on a wide range of sexual relationships in the
nineteenth century, including the 'irregular unions' that the poorest had,
without recourse to church or state. Instead they gave a very small fee to
a 'couple beggar' to witness their union. The range of relationships gives
a glimpse of how women continued to remake social boundaries in their
own favour.

Anna Clarke's (2005) work on young women inmates in the South
Dublin Workhouse in 1860 also indicates how agency could be exercised.
The official expectation that these young women would be 'passive and
dependent' (ibid.: 391) because of their non-existent social status and because of the mechanisms to punish them and hold them in check, was
continually frustrated. The authorities were unable to prevent them from
subverting their workhouse uniforms by wearing caps at rakish angles,
from finding ways to knit and sell fancy stockings to buy luxuries for themselves like tea, from making their hair more stylish, shiny with castor oil
and scraps from the kitchen. A fracas in April, 1860, where fifteen young
women were searched forcibly by workhouse officials looking for stolen
goods and leading to 'indecent' exposure, ended in a parliamentary inquiry about their treatment. One of their group, Eliza Bergin, was said
to have stated: 'Although we were mendicants and in the South Dublin

workhouse, we were not to be treated in so barbarous a manner' (quoted in Clark 2005: 394).

Women were marginalised in a multitude of ways economically. By the end of the nineteenth century, they had been steadily moved on from heavy physical work and were confined to jobs in the farmyard and more genteel housekeeping skills. This clearly more gendered division of work had mixed consequences. Fitzpatrick (1987: 167) observes that the growth of machinery in connection with dairy-farming hastened women's redundancy in milking and churning butter and that their increasing restrictions spoke volumes about their diminished status. Nonetheless, they inched back to take space as best they could. If women lost ground in contracting labour markets (teaching was one of the few areas where numbers went up by 1911, see Bourke 1993: 33), if through changing patterns of agricultural production and the need to 'modernise' agriculture, they lost control of processes like butter-making, they remade their roles. They took back at least a modicum of autonomy through egg money from the hens they kept, or through new jobs in shops in towns and the big cities, or sewing factories, or domestic service away from home, or through accepting an intensifying embourgeoisement and becoming more involved in household management and childcare as their exclusive domain (Bourke 1993). Kilfeather describes this as negotiating 'a subtle and complex place for sexual expression within their families and communities' (2005: 100). Some who left claimed their independence in a different way and, having worked 'to slave and scrape till they have a little treasure collected', returned as women of means to reject their fathers' matchmaking and choose their own husbands (Lynd 1909: 45). In respect of life as a farming wife, the picture was mixed across the country by the twentieth century. Many women were effectively farm managers (O'Hara 1998) and also took on the more skilled work of accounts and book-keeping (Duggan 1987: 57–60). O'Hara argues that despite the constraints of patriarchal structures, women did bring a 'unique influence' to bear on the shape of farming coming into and through the twentieth century and were 'powerful actors in their own right' (1998: 38–9).

At one level at least, this everyday influence could help some women jostle against that strange early twentieth-century modernity in Ireland which arguably became far more implacably opposed to any threat of women's sexual

transgression as the decades wore on. A socially conservative order implicitly supported the 'stem family', for example, a consequence of having the
farm pass to one child only who married fairly late on and whose wife then
moved in with her parents-in-law. However, rural communities where these
patterns remained strong saw shifts from the 1930s and 1940s onward (Clear
2000: 171–3; Hannan and Katsiaouni 1977), along with changes to strict sexual
divisions of labour. Rising levels of wealth and consumption were germane to
these changes, as well as a change, albeit very gradually, to a wider social life for
women outside the home (Clear 2000: 208–12). Beyond farming life, Clear
(2007: 27–8) points to the rise in apprentices and skilled women workers in
the small and larger towns, including an increase in dressmakers and milliners
by the 1880s. The need to appear smart, no matter what one's work, opened
up the market for ready-bought clothing for women by the beginning of the
twentieth century and with it, work in clothing factories for young female
apprentices. Shop work too expanded creating openings for young women
and if, they had the funds for training and education, teaching and nursing
also became possible (ibid.: 30–3).

    David Fitzpatrick (1985: 119) argues that children continued to be
seen as assets in post-Famine Irish society and that women, if and when
they married, had powerful motivations to bear children. Kennedy (1973)
concurs, seeing this pattern carrying into the twentieth century. He argues
that the childless marriage would have meant a life filled with boredom for
women already constrained by the social mores of the period not to work
outside the home (ibid.:18, 186–7). Clear argues that pragmatic considerations of what might comprise a 'good' marriage could and did co-exist
'with sexual attraction, friendship and joy' (2007: 85). Towards the middle
of the twentieth century, Hannan and Katsiaouni (1977: 183) document
a move towards more 'strong emotionally supportive relationships' and it
was in that period that the nuclear family became the dominant family
form.[2] Yet this did not create a more comfortable social sphere for many
women. Between 1946 and 1951, there was a massive outflow of people from
farming, four times greater than the number in the previous twenty years
put together (Quinn 1969: 120–1). The number of women emigrating from

2   The interviews with elderly women in the 2010 documentary by Ken Wardrop, *His
      and Hers*, gives some flavour of the growth of companionate marriages in rural and

Ireland in this period doubled to over 14,000 per year (ibid.: 122), leaving behind them an aging population, even as many who did stay moved from rural areas to Dublin (ibid.: 126–7).

Terence Brown's description of a 'dishevelled present struggling to achieve modernity' (2004: 352) might well describe the social context in which women worked to build their lives. For many married women, their investment in their relationships with their children perhaps was a way to re-channel desire within often difficult and disappointing marriages. We can read John McGahern's *Memoir* in this light, and his portrayal of his mother as a woman who continued to work as a school teacher and who reared her seven children living semi-independently from her unpredictably violent husband, a Garda sergeant, until she became terminally ill with breast cancer.

In her semi-autobiographical novel, *Never No More*, Maura Laverty paints a different account of a woman breaking free, her mother acutely frustrated by the narrow parameters of motherhood and domesticity flourishing only when she can move away to become a successful businesswoman as a dressmaker and shop-owner. Laverty's 1942 novel is a finely drawn picture about a girl coming of age and learning about sex and sexuality in the post-Independence years. Laverty includes details of irregular sexual relationships, including a woman who worked in the town of 'Ballyderrig' as a prostitute, but who was not completely shunned socially, this at a time when the policing of women and men was thought to be at its height through such machinery. The 1935 Dance Halls Act for one saw the state and local clergy acting together, the priests opening up parish halls for a fee, while the state collected the license income from the priests (Ó hAllmhuráin 2005). The sense of desire, of taking that chance, and then of reconciling it with local social realities is beautifully observed in William Trevor's *Love and Summer*, set in 1950s Ireland. After her institutionalised childhood with the nuns, and her fortunate elevation from domestic hand to a farmer's obedient young wife, Ellie Dillahan discovers sexual desire with the transient photographer, Florian. The brief relationship is watched from afar

---

small-town settings in the Irish midlands in the mid-twentieth century and also a sense of women's modest success in placing boundaries around some aspects of their married lives to retain some sense of autonomy.

and with care by the town's respectable spinster, Miss Connulty, who herself had been forced by her father into a backstreet abortion up in Dublin when she was a young woman. At the end of the novel, Ellie will go back to her quiet older husband, and will possibly have a baby for him, but not his baby, and there is a sense that she will be whole albeit in a complex way.

In the 1950s, Sean O'Faolain laid out the scathing responses from young men to his newspaper column asking why men did not want to marry (O'Faolain 1954). The fearful contempt in which women were held by many young men if women acted on their own wishes, in the clothing they bought or the drink they requested in a lounge bar, comprised a kind of social horror story. Yet O'Faolain, wily critical voice that he was, pointed out the extent to which the state had failed to support its people in the most basic of social needs, health services and housing. A political meanness met the extant meanness of spirit sustained by state and church in the 'lies and half-truths about Ireland' which O'Faolain himself vigorously contested (McCaffrey 2005: 144). Young people lived with that meanness and many learned to distrust marriage. The sense of danger in associating with the opposite sex, that relationships were problematic for the unmarried and that supervision and surveillance for adolescents especially was vital, comes through the writing of the 'agony aunt', Angela MacNamara in the 1960s (Ryan 2011). It was all about keeping a lid on things and, for the poorer classes just scraping by. Beleaguered working-class women carried the burden of poverty and ill-health, accompanied by grievous rates of infant mortality, 100 per 1,000 live births in 1932, compared with a national rate of 72 per 1,000 (Earner-Byrne 2006: 262). For young women, especially from socially marginalised backgrounds, who were sexually active and became pregnant with no chance of marriage, the Magdalen laundries became their fate, and with that incarceration, yet another form of silencing and forgetting closed in on women, with the state's active engagement (Smith 2007).

A 'curtain of silence' (Sweetman 1979: 15) needed to be torn asunder in many different directions. In 1966, RTE screened a programme produced by the social commentator Michael Viney, about large families and the need for contraception, 'Too Many Children'. Dublin Corporation had a ruling at that time that no couple could be accepted on to the local authority housing list before they had three children, upping the pressure to have those children very close together. Several women on the programme recounted how they had considered contraception and as a result, had been refused absolution by priests in confession leaving them to abandon the church. The psychiatrist, Ivor Browne, interviewed for the programme, related that the majority of women coming to his public clinics in Dublin were married, in poverty and burdened by too many pregnancies. They had 'never had their heads above water since the day they married' (*The Irish Times* 1966). The programme provided a telling example of how the ideology of rural, conservative Ireland was reinforced by the concrete practices of state machinery, in this instance refusing entry to housing lists, as much as by cultural practices and rulings of the church.

Even so, there were exuberant images of desire and pleasure to be found. Edna O'Brien's Caithleen and Baba in *The Country Girls*, O'Brien's 1950s semi-autobiographical account, has this delightful curiosity and edge about it as they set off for their first dance in Dublin: 'Fellows; we'll have them swarming round us. Christ, if you take any fellow of mine I'll give you something to cry about' (O'Brien 2007 [1960]: 168). When the pair go on to meet the middle-aged Harry and Reginald in a hotel and get taken to the latter's house, frustrated non-sex on Harry's part with Caithleen does not prevent their being driven back to their digs by him at their request, although he does so with a 'venomous' shake of his car keys.[3]

The encrustations of a society that had been obsessed with the economics of poor land, too little work, mass emigration, respectability and a rigid interpretation of Catholic morality, all to the detriment of young women for at least 120 years did begin to dissolve in the 1970s. This was

---

3   Similar sexual energy and curiosity are found in Patricia Craig's memoir of growing up in Belfast in the 1950s, feeling let free when going to the Rannafast Gaeltacht:

It's only the *muintir na háite*, the people of the place, as far as we are concerned, who are endowed with adequate allure. Why is this? They are rough wild country boys for the most part, turf-cutters in summer, migrant workers at other times of the year; not student material, not our type at all. Yet we latch on to them instantly. I suppose it is partly that the sudden freedom, the escape from family pressures, has gone to our heads a little; we're experimenting in waywardness, trying out certain posters, estimating how far we can go. The *muintir na háite*, with their boldness and rumpus, suggest anarchic possibilities to which we respond with an equal measure of attraction and alarm. I am perfectly well aware that I will try to

when emigration was finally reversed and young people began to return to
Ireland. They did so in a period where it was beginning to be possible to
admit to what the accommodations about sexuality and about familialism
were based on, and how they had to be negotiated against a network of
contradictions and deep inequalities. On the far side of that divide of
the 1970s, the work of Laverty, McGahern, Trevor and O'Brien gather
up many of the conflicting strands of women's lives as they attempted
to reconcile themselves to the society which contained these unstable
contradictions. These are vital stories about yearning and desire co-ex-
isting amongst the peculiar distortions that formed modern Ireland and
contributed to forming our subjectivities as Irish women. We are cautious
about any one-way account that suggests that being modern is always an
improvement (Williams 1983: 208–9). We suggest that individual women
exercised agency where they could in that long period as Irish modernity
took shape and that the actions of many indicated the strength of their resistance. However, in very real senses, resistance went underground where
we could not see it.

Agency as resistance often goes underground. It becomes more fluid
to bend round seemingly intractable social roles and the rigidity of loss,
leaking into motherhood, amongst other spaces. However, the quicksilver of desire is ever-present, its forms of expression ever-changing, and
resistance is still a necessary part of how women build agency for themselves. If not as stark as the period of Ireland's high modernity, there are
continuing conflicts that are threaded through the late modern accounts
of women that they are constructing, even as they work to resolve the

get out of any sticky situations in which I find myself – that a point will be reached
at which timidity, prudence, social conformity or whatever will come on strong.
Yet my entire being is geared towards inducing just such a sticky situation. (Craig
2007: 92)

The sexual regulation of women in Northern Irish society, sanctioned by the
Protestant mini-state of Stormont paralleled the Irish Republic in many key areas,
despite the differences in religious affiliation (McCormick 2009). The emphasis on
the 'moral purity' of northern Irish women and their 'traditional' roles which stood
out against 'modernity' are also similar discourses (ibid.: 182–3, 207).

conflicts. Women continue to speak about their needs and desires about sex, motherhood and all they wish to be from within a cultural and political setting where equality and its implications are ill-understood or even deliberately misunderstood. The always present, if always shifting, nature of constraints does not undermine our emphasis on the importance of women's agency.

CHAPTER 2

'Young women saying "I love having lots of one-night stands" is still not quite acceptable': Making Sense of Sexual Experiences

'We talk a lot about this stuff'

In this chapter, we explore how young Irish women in the first decade of the 2000s came to view themselves as sexual beings. Using their images, language and experiences, we explore how they came to understand and interpret their changing needs and responses to evolving sexual relationships. What are the symbolic and practical meanings associated with a young woman experiencing sexual intimacy for the first time, or carrying condoms, or using the contraceptive pill? How do young women negotiate feelings of confidence and responsibility when they access sexual health services? The sociologist Tom Inglis writes that 'in the present era, in which sexuality has become differentiated from religion, being sexual revolves around being fit, healthy, attractive, engaging, enticing and flirtatious' (1998: 103). Fulfilling this sets huge challenges for young women. Medb Ruane, reporting in the *Irish Independent* on the rural follow-up study to our 2004 Crisis Pregnancy Agency report, wrote that the studies brought home a complex and often negative contemporary reality: 'Once it was social suicide to have sex outside marriage. Now it's social suicide not to' (Ruane 2007). Although this level of urgency does not characterise all young women's views, some do feel caught up by such expectations.

As young women reflected on their sexual lives and understandings, good and bad, words like these recurred in our interviews: exciting, exhilarating, lovely, frightening, difficult, lonely. Young women articulated what had become commonplace, having sex outside marriage, short and long-term relationships and casual relationships, and through all these how they were attempting to define expressions of sexuality and sexual intimacy on their own terms. For this generation of women, unlike their mothers' and grandmothers' generations, their conversations about needs and desires had ceased to be ones that were limited to largely internal dialogues and otherwise referred to only obliquely. As one woman said, 'We talk a lot about this stuff.' This held true amongst close friends, let alone the broader changing contexts. This far greater openness about sex and desire marked a significant change in Irish society. Social norms have adapted in Ireland to the extent that no young Irish woman now will be expected to marry and have large numbers of children or indeed any children if she does not wish to do so.

Still, a pervasive theme holds across generations, as captured by Máire Leane's interviews with women born between 1914 and 1955 about their sexual knowledge and experiences 1920–70, that 'keenly emphasise how difficult it was for women to assert a sexual persona that did not comply with prevailing norms and practices' (2014: 53). In other words, women's understandings of their sexual selves are characterised by complex negotiations of self with cultural ideals around sexual activity and sexual identity.

In our interview participants' mothers' generations of the 1960s and 1970s, sexual activity as a source of personal identity was still overdetermined while not altogether silenced by the location of the traditional Irish Catholic church as the chosen moral arbiter in Irish society (Inglis 1998; Hug 1999; Hilliard 2004; Ferriter 2009). Talk about sex was confined to the confessional with an audience of one and in language approved by the church (Inglis 1998: 36). A woman interviewed by sociologist Betty Hilliard in 2000 who was 'against contraception' in 1975 though 'still very religious' reflected, 'We were very scrupulous Catholics, we were all damned but I think the people are changing their views about the Church now. I would say the family … should be limited, have the amount of children you think yourself that you can keep comfortably and educate' (quoted in Hilliard 2004: 157). This developing perspective is remarkable compared with the dominant social and Church views of the past. A woman who became a mother in the 1950s–60s recalls of that period, 'It was a worrying time to be honest with you. We were reared in a time when you had to obey your husband, we couldn't refuse them' (Hilliard 2004: 140). Fear of pregnancy completely overshadowed enjoyment of sex for many women: 'Anytime you did have sex you were afraid of your life next day, you have this dread … the dread! … ah, no it was like a disaster trying to cope again and you're not able when you were trying to look after all the small babies as well' (Hilliard 2004: 145). These women were not free to view sex as having a 'recreational dimension' not least because of the extreme difficulty of obtaining contraception or contraceptive knowledge (Hilliard 2004: 143). But women in this time period did have strategies for rejecting sex. Said one, implying some level of her husband's cooperation, 'We used to work by that – the rhythm thing … that and saying you've a headache. I had to do it, otherwise I could have twenty children now' (Hilliard 2004: 144).

This self-appointed task of the churches, one reinforced by state institutions and state machinery, had much to do with the perceived need to hold back the tide of secularism and its ally materialism. It was a task shouldered across the island of Ireland by Protestant churches as well as Catholic: the theme of the purity of Irish women, with their free exercise of sexual expression curtailed and corralled, was used symbolically north and south to distinguish Irish women from their too secular English counterparts (McCormick 2009). Tom Inglis has argued: 'The deployment of sexuality through the regulations and principles of the Catholic Church and state-sanctioned inheritance and legal systems established "a sexual self which denied sex to itself"' (Inglis 1997: 13; quoted in B. Gray 2004). While we are not positing that individuals in past generations did not have 'sexual selves' or view themselves as sexual beings, of course, we can agree that forms of expression, moral beliefs and social supports were radically constrained compared with contemporary perspectives, where in any case different constraints have emerged. For example, historian Cara Delay argues in her study of women's life writings 1880–50, 'while communities, the Catholic Church, and the Irish state did indeed attempt to contain young women's sexuality, those attempts were not always successful. Girls actively sought out knowledge about their bodies and sex, and some found pathways around the restrictions of the day' (Delay 2015: 167).[1]

---

1   Delay maintains that 'Irish sexual prudery came of age in the post-famine era' (Delay 2015: 165), but that 'pervasive regulation of the female body' started decades

A specific component of change in the 1960s was with what Ryan (2012) describes as the 'informalisation of emotional life'. A strict demarcation between private and public lives was breaking down. Almost imperceptibly the very notion of sex became an easier thing to speak about in all sorts of ways. Inglis (2003: 236–7) argues that the shift from the post-Famine Catholic culture of 'self-denial and self-sacrifice' to this newer culture of 'self-expression and self-indulgence' dug in quite quickly in under two decades from the 1980s, though others mark the late 1960s as the starting point of intensified social change (see Ferriter 2004: 571). Inglis notes that as young people began to act out what they saw in films and imported television programmes like *Dallas*, Ireland did not become a sexually promiscuous society, rather that love and romance were becoming sexualised. The western sexual revolution which was late in reaching into Ireland had to do with 'a decreased sense of guilt and shame about sex' (2003: 237). Inglis describes changes in rural Kerry in the 1980s regarding sexuality in an optimistic light, yet its exercise was still filled with negative consequences:

> But young people were increasingly distancing themselves from the Church's moral teachings, particularly in relation to sexuality. They were beginning to make up their own minds about what was right and wrong. This was not an easy journey; it was full of contradictions, personal turmoil and family conflict. More young people might have begun to have sex before and outside marriage, but they were playing a high-risk game of pregnancy – a form of Irish roulette. Even if they wanted to use contraceptives, many chemists did not stock them and, even if they did, they were available only to married couples (Inglis 2003: 11).

Relatively speaking, a far more liberal and officially countenanced regime in relation to sex and its meanings permitted widespread discussion over the semi-state airwaves and in the press (Inglis 1998: 123). The *Late Late* Show, first put out by RTE the state television broadcaster in 1962 soon after it was established, exemplified this change with the 'the bishop

---

before the Great Famine. Yet 'Alongside tragic stories of sexual control, abuse, and exploitation … other narratives tell a different story, one of curiosity, experimentation, and even resistance' (Delay 2015: 164).

and the nightie' incident in 1966 one of the best remembered (Ferriter 2004: 539).[2] In his analysis of RTE's contribution to prising open frank exchanges on sex, Diarmaid Ferriter quotes from the memoir by the novelist Colm Tóibin on how the many discussions which the *Late Late* hosted over the years were 'mesmerising' for a national audience which included many people 'who had never heard about sex' (2009: 376). Domestically produced Irish women's magazines and newspaper self-help columns began to publish advice columns on a spectrum of sexual dilemmas that hitherto had not reached Irish print. The Irish Censorship Board (still in existence) did not oppose the launch in 1996 of the sale at newsagents of *Playboy Magazine* which had been banned up to that point, and within a year 40 per cent of all the magazine's sales in the British Isles were in the Republic of Ireland (Myers 1997).

The growing freedom to have sex outside marriage was related at least in part to the commodification of sex as exemplified by the availability of films, television programs and other media forms that exposed all younger Irish people to sexualised versions of love and romance. In the 1990s, an explosion of public talk about sex within hearing-range of young people erupted in a number of other forms: reports and legal trials of Irish priests

---

2   During the *Late Late's* 'Bishop and the nightie' incident, husbands and wives in the audience were asked as part of a quiz what they knew about each other. One woman in response to the question about what colour nightie she wore on her wedding night, responded that she could not recall, and perhaps had not worn any, drawing laughter and applause from the audience. Bishop Tom Ryan of Clonfert was infuriated and rang the *Sunday Press* to say he would be denouncing the programme in his Sunday sermon; all the newspapers covered the controversy the next day. Eileen Fox, the woman who made the comment in innocence, died in 2015 and Gay Byrne, the *Late Late's* host, paid tribute to her soon after her death on another famous RTE programme, *Liveline*, which has also aired its fair share of controversial issues on sex and sexuality. Inglis (1998: 38–9) argues that the media changed all the older views about sex as the problematic side of love, a threat not just to the moral values of chastity and purity and health of the individual, but to the social order as a whole. Ferriter's analysis of correspondence between the Director General of RTE and Archbishop John Charles McQuaid shows that by 1966, the writing was already on the wall for any substantive church control over the media (Ferriter 2009: 376–9).

for consensual sexual affairs, homosexual practices and sexual exploitation of children (see Ferriter 2004: 734–9); the Department of Education's 1997 institution of a national, school-based Relationships and Sexuality Programme and controversy around it (see Inglis 1998) and legal contests over contraception, abortion, homosexuality and divorce (Hug 1999), all acting as crucial lightning rods for a rapidly evolving social space. Sex shops, advertisements for sex talk lines in phone books and newspapers and internet sex sites all became part of Ireland at the turn of the twenty-first century.[3] Strange overlaps remained: on the night of Pope John Paul II's death in April 2005, the national semi-state broadcasting agency, RTE, ran coverage of the event on their main channel throughout the evening with solemn-faced anchormen, commentators and reporters dressed in black while on their second channel an American film with explicit sexual scenes was being screened.[4]

3   In 1999, a UK chain store, Ann Summers, which billed itself as selling 'lingerie with attitude' but 'absolutely not a sex-shop' and which was described by the managing director Jackie Gold as offering an atmosphere that 'is feminine ... sexy [and] fun', opened a branch on Dublin's main thoroughfare, O'Connell Street. Despite *The Irish Times* reporting on 1 October that the shop 'opened without so much as a raised eyebrow' the previous day (O'Brien 1999), the same paper noted that within hours Dublin Corporation filed legal charges that the shop was in breach of the Integrated Area Plan (Haughey 1999). It was soon followed by 'Fantasia's Adult Boutique', on South William Street, and numerous adult video shops which became part of the urban wallpaper. The UK chain store opened a second shop in Cork in 2004, adding this commercial outlet to its so-called Party Plan business in Ireland, with women as party organisers hosting women in their homes and taking in several hundred euro per session for sex and lingerie merchandise (O'Connor 2004).

4   Up to the beginning of the last third of the twentieth century, it was possible to argue that regular church attendance could be a measure of active Catholicity that would probably reject a loosening of the moral code on sexual mores. The data on church attendance has indicated an absolute decline since the 1970s when the figure stood at just over 90 per cent. By the early 2000s, the average figure stood at 65 per cent, still high in comparison with European averages (see Ferriter 2004: 733). In 2015, 30 per cent attended a Catholic church weekly, fewer than in the U.S. (Kennedy 2015; see also D. Scally 2021: 254–5). The sexual abuse scandals which progressively destroyed the credibility of the Catholic church are a massive factor in this decline (ibid.: 187–8). Throughout this period, it has also been argued that Irish people became more confident about developing their own moral

By the early 2000s, there was a general expectation that young women should be reasonably adept at handling the complex gendered scripts that ensued in this new climate. The plurality of developments which had overtaken Irish society included the strong sense, linked to second-wave feminism, that sex and sexual pleasure should remain in the grasp of each individual as she determines. However, we discovered that while some women perceived the increased access to sexual information, discussion and images as enabling a broader expression of self, many women also voiced ambivalence, anxiety and tension around a perceived demand to see themselves primarily as sexual beings and to view others only in sexual terms. All these experiences were screened through the ongoing framework of heterosexuality which, as Lynne Segal (2015) observed two decades ago, has posed an impossible conundrum for women. This remains so despite the work feminism has undertaken as a social movement to make heterosexuality less binary-driven, less phallocentric, and far more about pleasure, desire and vulnerability, both women's and men's, on an equal plane.

These challenges to male-dominant heterosexuality initially arose alongside the notion that sexual desire is a core part of the late modern self (A. Clarke 2008: 11) and the expectation of gaining sexual fulfilment and pleasure has been facilitated throughout western countries by accessible and reliable methods of contraception. Deborah Tolman has defined sexual subjectivity as 'a person's experience of herself as a sexual being, who feels entitled to sexual pleasure and sexual safety, who makes active sexual choices, and who has an identity as a sexual being. Sexual desire is at the heart of sexual subjectivity' and this can and should be at the heart of

---

standards about sexual issues independent of church teachings (see Tovey and Share, 2003: 404–7; Hilliard 2004), and that this was evident even in rural areas beginning in the 1980s (Inglis 1998: 11). Joan, an Irish woman living in London, talks about a 'Catholic culture' when she says, 'being Irish is being Catholic, from a very young age … the whole environment is Catholic … I wouldn't be particularly dogmatically anything, but I feel very *culturally Catholic* … it's my culture … I am Catholic till the day I die … and the chances are that when I'm dying, I'll scream for a priest … "I'm sorry I'm a lesbian, anoint me with your oils'!"' (quoted in B. Gray 2004: 47, emphasis original).

responsibility in sexual decision-making (Tolman 2002: 5–6).[5] Extending this argument, Hera Cook (2004) asserts that becoming competent at sexual activity can be fairly described as 'work' because of how important sex has become to the self-identity of younger generations of women.[6] Pat O'Connor notes that the mothers of young Irish women, who were adults when the women's movement began to influence Irish society and policies, have a pattern of inspiring resistance among their daughters that encourages self-reflection and a need for self-knowledge (2006: 115) and part of this self-knowledge is sexual self-knowledge.

Yet the work of 'dismantling the old gender regimes of marriage and male privilege' (Segal 2015: xvi) has been cut across by the instabilities and practices generated within late modern society, so that the situation of the 'working woman', for example, without equal wages and guaranteed access to childcare, leads to a continued dependence on men and male-dominant thinking (ibid.), so often enmeshed with the failure of a still male-dominant state to follow through on equality policies. Young women have a further series of constraints to negotiate in settings where, Linda Grant (1994) argues, the promises for women of the 'sexual revolution' so that they could pursue their desires have been reconstituted as part of mass marketing and commodification. More complicated still, the lack of success for feminism and other social movements of the 1970s and 1980s to gain more radically open social spaces, a general political drift to the right which appreciably worsened issues of economic and social inequality, a specific inability to shift the understandings of heterosexual norms away from a male-dominant hegemony and finally the advent of AIDS leading to moral panics about sex, led to a backing away of political engagement by many feminists with sexual equality and with arguments for heterosexual practice as a prime locus for expressions of female desire. Grant identifies the contraceptive pill as problematic in these shifts and the complex trajectory that emerged alongside them: women had to move from saying no to sex in the early 1960s because of fear of pregnancy to having to say yes all

5   Many others elaborate theories of the 'sexual self'; see, for example, Foucault (1981), Gray (2004), O'Connor (2004), Hirsh and Khan (2020).
6   On the concept of 'sex work' within long-term heterosexual relationships, see Duncombe and Marsden in Weeks and Holland, ed. (1996).

the time to saying no because of feminists' questioning of male intractable standards to finally 'learning a constructive yes' (1994: 15) that communicates clear and enthusiastic consent; quite a journey.

Many Irish women distilled what they could from the grand narratives of feminism in trying to make sense of their everyday sexual experiences. Any success in doing so was cut across by class and status and by the historical weight of an 'isolated, protected conservative Ireland' and the 'immense prestige' Irish people attached to that belief system (F. O'Toole 1999: 288). It was a loading from under which young women had to extricate themselves and this was not without difficulty. Ann Marie Hourihane writes of how the 1983 Pro-life Amendment Campaign 'was really the death of the Irish Left, but for a while we didn't know, so we just kept walking. You didn't have to be a socialist to be a member of the Irish Left; you just had to want contraception' (2000: 37).[7] Slowly a modernising project, in Irish terms aided by EU membership in 1973 with all the gloss that leant to the major expansion of consumerism (F. O'Toole 1999), supplanted older beliefs and became the backdrop to a relatively safer space in which to have sex, as long as an unwanted or 'crisis' pregnancy was not a result.

Sex under this new regime has not been without emotional, social and financial cost, a factor which is related to that same consumerist expansion which at cultural levels has become a compulsory activity and is seen in Ireland through the cappuccino and shopping centre phenomena that Hourihane (2000) charts so effectively.[8] Feminist cultural theorist

7   The pill was imported in Ireland as a cycle regulator, not a contraceptive, in 1963 (Solomons 1992: 23). The first Irish family planning clinic was opened in Holles Street, Dublin, in 1967, then closed following the Vatican's 1968 release of *Humanae Vitae* (Ferriter 2004: 573) which reiterated the Catholic Church's ban on use of 'unnatural' methods of contraception. In 1969, the Irish Fertility Guidance Company opened in 10 Merrion Square in Dublin, carefully working around laws against the sale of contraceptives by providing them free (see Solomons 1992: 28–9). Co-founder Michael Solomons wrote of this time, 'Even in 1969 the majority of Irish people would have been unwilling to visit a family planning clinic, believing the use of "unnatural" methods of family planning to be a sin' (1992: 30).

8   Shopping centres became entrenched within commercial property development by the early 2000s as the Irish economy expanded. An estimated thirty new shopping centres were planned to open between 2005 and 2010 with many of the newer

Angela McRobbie (2008) questions the validity of 'a post-feminist language of personal choice and freedom' that has much less to do with the older dream of freeing up sexual desire and much more to do with 'new technologies of the self' which have come to the surface through 'commodity feminism'. McRobbie sees commodity feminism as reinstating an 'insurgent patriarchalism hidden beneath the celebrations of female freedom' (ibid.: 539) which has actually narrowed and limited possibilities for young women. It is quite a distance from Segal's hopes for how women might enjoy sex with men, 'confident in the knowledge … that this is what we want and how we want it', that women can 'do sex' (Segal 2015: 266). For example, the American television series, *Sex and the City* made exactly these claims about its four main characters, but Angela McRobbie reads the influential series in a far more normative framework. She identifies how in all their adventures with the potential for transgression, the women choose to return to a 'familiar and knowable heterosexuality' alongside a 'straightforward endorsement of the joys of consumption' (2008: 542) restabilising gender roles to the advantage of insurgent patriarchalism which has dismissed feminist concerns as irrelevant. The stream of opulent images like those furnished in *Sex and the City* are part of the 'saturation marketing techniques' of late capitalism (Walkerdine et al. 2001: 8) which have contributed to an increasing number of concerns for young women, who with perhaps fewer analytical tools than an optimistic feminism once furnished, must plunge into the persistently gendered problems surrounding sexual desire.

The sexual double standard has retained considerable power and is used to label young women negatively even as they work to portray themselves as agentic, knowledgeable and desiring subjects and to avoid being constructed as objects of desire only. Jackson and Cram (2003) note this in their work with young New Zealand women, and it holds true in Ireland as well. Young Irish women practice strategies of social policing of each other's sexual behaviour through language, rumours and knowledge of individual sexual practices, many of which are rooted in the sexual double

---

developments aiming for a luxury market trade (Beesley 2005). This was fuelled by the growth of the EU as a single market with no border controls which contributed to a vastly increased importation of goods.

standard that honours men and stigmatises women as sexual beings (Lees 1986; Tanenbaum 2000, 2015; Tolman 2005; Orenstein 2016, 2020). There is resistance to being constructed as passive objects of heterosexual desire but this is neither collective nor collectively voiced (Jackson and Cram 2003) and it is the collectivity of voice that is vital if these scripts are to change for the better.

Despite the continuing court cases and social turmoil over abortion law and the Eighth Amendment, things moved on quickly in the late 1990s and early 2000s so that being open about sexual desire felt publicly endorsed. It was an Irish television network, TV3, which carried the *Sex and the City* series, for example, while focus groups with 15–19-year-old Irish men and women about their perceptions of media representations of sex revealed no objection to the fact that these were pervasive (MacKeogh 2004). They enabled discussion about sex and a way of learning although for young women, this was helpful in gaining knowledge of their sexual identities, whereas young men voiced their experiencing a kind of pressure not to think about emotions but to follow a narrow script that valorised just having sex, not relationships (MacKeogh 2004: 84).

At the time of our research, younger women were discovering that sex itself can be articulated as a site for pleasure, bearing out Deborah Tolman's argument that sexual desire for adolescent girls is 'important and life-sustaining' and that their minds and hearts should help them make sense of strong sexual feelings as part of their embodied selves (Tolman 2002: 19; see also Garcia 2012; Orenstein 2016, 2020). Yet this is significantly challenging, as Orenstein in *Girls & Sex: Navigating the Complicated New Landscape* argues with her observation that 'Girls shifted between subject and object day by day, moment by moment, sometimes without intending to, sometimes unsure themselves of which they were' (2016: 15). Identifying one's own desire is complicated by this interplay.

Tolman makes the distinction between exploring desire and actually having sex and argues convincingly that if we are to be truly supportive of our young women and of their exercising agency in their lives, we need to be enabling young women to talk about desire in very different ways. This is one way to build strengths that enable young women to challenge patriarchal norms. Such work has to lead to greater safety in being sexually active and must carry across class lines in order to challenge the class basis whereby public moral codes continue to regulate teenage sexuality (Walkerdine et al. 2001; Garcia 2012; Orenstein 2016, 2020). In these mixed messages, teenage pregnancy for young middle-class women needs to be avoided as a disruption along the pathway of academic and career success while working-class teenage pregnancy is viewed differently, as leading to long-term welfare dependency (Walkerdine et al. 2001: 188–9) and carrying more opprobrium for that reason, with the lack of social and educational equality neatly hidden from view (ibid.; Redfern and Aune 2010: 53).

The expansion of consumer culture to include an intensified focus on young women's body images and body management, masquerading under a 'rhetoric of choice' (Walter 2010: 14) has also brought new pressures, increasing anxieties at the same time that young women are being encouraged to become more sexualised in ways which objectify them (Redfern and Aune 2010: 52–3) and turn them into 'living dolls' (Walter 2010). Young women in more socially precarious circumstances can find the continuing reinvention of self and body that is now taken as a norm for all is double-edged, a way 'to keep at bay loss of status and poverty' (Walkerdine et al. 2001: 8) while they simultaneously lose out on qualifications and greater job security (ibid.: 67). Regardless of class many young women struggle when 'it becomes difficult to discern your desires among the clamour of voices telling you what you should be feeling and doing, even what you should find a turn-on' (Redfern and Aune 2010: 52). This is what Ann Marie Hourihane found visiting the nightclub scene in Dublin in the late 1990s where young women were being paid to dance provocatively: one 19-year-old explained that 'they said if I get a good reaction, if people are looking … that's fair enough' (2000: 64). Similar scenes of objectification are described in Laura Stepp's exploration of hookup culture, where young people accept and actively seek having sex with no emotion and no connection, because that is what is now expected, and are averse to the notion of emotional intimacy as part of a physical relationship (Stepp 2004; see also Bogle 2008, Wade 2017, Orenstein 2020). Peggy Orenstein's in-depth interviews with over 100 young men ages 16–22 from across the U.S. found that hookup culture 'aligns with the values of conventional masculinity: conquest over connection, sex as status-seeking, partners as disposable' (2020: 79).

Redfern and Aune (2010: 50) argue that the sexual double standards which shape the lives of young women are maintained in a number of specific ways: objectification, so-called 'raunch' male culture, pressure to have sex before they feel they want to, irrelevant sex education, heterosexism and constraints on leaving relationships all create constraints on women being able to explore sex and sexual desire confidently in order to identify what they want and need at their own pace.

Many of these issues and struggles came up in our interview discussions, indicating if nothing else an absolute end to that dream world of an isolated, conservative Ireland anchored by unvarying female identities of daughter, wife and mother. At the same time, the very liveliness of the women who talked with us indicates the ongoing potential for Irish women to upend their understandings of sexuality. Luke Gibbons argues in his essay, 'Unapproved Roads: Ireland and Post-colonial Identity', that people in Ireland have a strong sense of being able to do this by creating 'lateral journeys along the margins' (Gibbons 1996: 180) and hybridising what appear to be rigid social categories. At the broadest level, young women are endeavouring to take on the responsibility of defining their life choices in ways that must now become seen as 'Irish' despite the departure from Irish life options of the past. This difficult work is accomplished in settings where there remains great uncertainty about how women can exercise their rights to develop their own rationales and approaches to being sexually active, as we turn to next.

Thinking about sex, thinking about self

Irish novelist Anne Enright describes vividly what it felt like in the 1980s to have one's sexual self gradually emerging, all the jumble of feelings and emotions at once amidst utter public uproar about sex:

Ireland broke apart in the eighties, and I sometimes think that the crack opened in
my own head. The constitutional row about abortion was a moral civil war that was
fought out in people's homes – including my own – with unfathomable bitterness.
The country was screaming at itself about contraception, abortion, and divorce. It
was a hideously misogynistic time. Not the best environment for a young woman
establishing a sexual identity. (Enright 2005: 186–7)

That uproar has lessened considerably since that time, in part due to
legalisation of contraception, abortion and divorce. However, the noise
surrounding sex and sexuality remains pervasive if different to how women
in Anne Enright's generation experienced it. We recognise, along with feminist scholars including Jessica Fields, Deborah Tolman and Lorena Garcia,
that young people are 'engaged in sexual lives, regardless of whether they
are formally sexually active' (2006: 73). In other words, young women
and young men come to see themselves and their peers as sexual beings
not alone through sexual experience, but through all the media images,
conversations, prohibitions and fantasies that constitute understandings
of sexuality (Inglis 1998; Orenstein 2016, 2020). The unconscious side of
the development of a sexual self is expressed well by this young woman
living on the outskirts of a small town:

In my neighbourhood there was a lot of older boys, and they just like talked about
stuff like that constantly, so you just picked it up. I don't think you're actually even
aware when you're actually picking it up of what it all is. Just one day, someone starts
talking about it and you realise you know. (Joanne, 23, unemployed, outskirts of a
small town)

The paradox that young women now confront is that while Irish society is more open to sex and women's rights to separate sex from motherhood, becoming sexually active remains hard work. Sarah, a teacher in a
metropolitan area, characterised the opportunities and limits placed on
women's sexual selves:

I think there's a kind of a contradiction. I think there is more openness, you are able
to discuss the very fact that you are sexual being, and things like, you know, the ability
to enjoy sex. But there's also sort of a level of insecurity and discomfort about that.
So I think it only goes so far. There are set lines that you can't break, rules that you
can't break as a woman. (Sarah, 30, teacher, metropolitan area)

It is much harder work if young women are living in more marginal circumstances, be they social, economic or geographical. There are differences in supportive frames of reference and access to resources for women from lower social class backgrounds and differences as well between urban and rural and small-town areas. Caoimhe, a project manager in a rural area, noted that for rural women it is more difficult than their urban counterparts, 'to even talk about it [sex], to find out how to be ... have a healthy attitude to it [sex]', while Joanne relates how a young woman's having sex could feel like a transgression:

> It was like you'd done something so bad that you couldn't tell anybody about it. But it wasn't so, it wasn't like you committed a murder or something, do you know? But nobody could talk about it. (Joanne, 23, unemployed, outskirts of a small town)

We see that some women are more comfortable in *speaking the word sex*, while others use the word 'it' to communicate, knowing that the listener understands the coded meaning of 'it'. The uneven and contradictory messages young Irish women receive influence the creation of their 'sexual selves'. Sarah pinpoints part of the new pressures placed on young women:

> There's more 'Shoulds'. You *should* enjoy sex. You *should* want to have it a lot, or more than you did. There's also the kind of *Cosmopolitan* culture that I think is going round, where young girls are under pressure to be a certain type of woman. (Sarah, 30, teacher, metropolitan area)

Women of every generation have felt the pressures of gendered norms. Today, the commercialised centring and indeed celebration of sex as a positive aspect of a woman's self-definition, yet the pervasive nature of this sexualised consumer culture gives little substantive comfort or real support to women as they begin to explore sexual feelings and relationships. We see this impact in the exchange below where women are speaking of how their younger adolescent selves were drawn into having sex without really having the scope to think of precisely what they wanted. Their desire to have sex was influenced by a flood of competing images and imperatives to 'feel right' that worked at quite different levels which they felt were continuing strong determinants for young teenagers:

You know like American TV drama where, like 'American Pie' where they have to all lose their virginity on prom night. And now they're all thinking, and I know this stuff at that age, it doesn't matter who it is, but it's romantic if you do it on prom night. Because you'll feel all lovely, and your hair will be done and you'll be wearing a nice dress. (Elizabeth, 27, occupational therapist, small city)

One of your friends slept with a boy, and they tell you, and how great it was, and you're going to sit there and think 'Oh, that sounds good, I might have a go.' (Ciara, 27, nurse, small city)

And you've no idea how you're going to feel after it! Like you actually have no idea. You might think that you're going to feel great, but you're not. It's not a bed of roses, as such, by any means. And they're just rush rush into everything like. (Niamh, 26, nurse, small city)

Niamh's comments about the pressure to rush along and especially her judgement that first sex may not be 'a bed of roses' alert us to why at a minimum, very young women need a sympathetic individual or group to help anchor them as they try to develop self-belief and not to focus on self-doubt for not measuring up to the welter of sexualised images that confront them daily. Mona had a close group of teenaged friends to help manage the pressures while Marcella had her sister:

Going back to before I had sex, when I started going out with boys, we were pretty innocent about them, but it wasn't wide eyed naiveté. (Mona, 26, health worker, small town)

I think for our generation we're much luckier in terms of the openness and the acceptance. Me and my sister were of a similar age, and we were both in kind of long-term relationships when we were about sixteen, so there was acceptance really. (Marcella, 28, civil servant, small town)

Put another way, some women have been more fortunate in being able to deal successfully and more dynamically with the split between knowing about sex in an abstract way and sorting through their feelings about sex, about when they decide to have sex, and what they do or do not want:

I think that I thought that sex was just a part of life and it was just something that you did do. And if I chose to do it earlier in life than some women did, that was just me choosing to grow up as fast as I chose to grow up. (Maureen, 33, self-employed, small town)

I think it's a very progressive thing ... the ages between fifteen and eighteen were my most complicated. During that stage you're a changing personality, continuously growing and discovering yourself. And now I'm nineteen and I just go with the flow. Whatever feels comfortable for me, I go towards it. (Lisa, 19, student, suburban area)

At its best, it is just as Lisa expresses it, accepting oneself and one's needs and desires as they evolve and having 'the confidence to say "No I actually don't want to do that" and the boys will still like me, you know?'

Memories and meanings of earliest sexual experiences

Young women, collectively and as individuals, need to resolve for themselves that they have a right to social spaces where they are enabled to be sexually active on their own terms. However, despite the fact that talk of sex plays a prominent part in conversations and perhaps even the expectations of many adolescents, few of our respondents articulated their first sexual experiences in terms of a right.

Echoing Maureen's decision, above, about actively choosing to grow up earlier and have sex earlier rather than later, Karen, 23, who lives in a very small rural townland, began to have sex with her boyfriend just before her 14th birthday. She relates that there was peer pressure from both boys and girls, with girls continually asking one another about 'doing it'. However, Karen is clear on the matter of her personal desire: 'I did want it to happen.' She continued to have sex with her boyfriend through her final year at school, leaving at 15 without a Junior Certificate, and then took up hotel work. She was already pregnant. Despite becoming a mother at such a young age, and looking back eight years later, Karen says explicitly, 'I don't feel strongly that I should not have been having sex.'

Karen's experience, her decision at the time and her retrospective judgement open up the issue of how prepared we are as a society to help support very young women in a safe exploration of their sexual selves. As Tolman argues about young women, 'to leave pleasure out or to deny its importance is, quite simply, to misrepresent sexuality' (2002: 80). Karen's decision cannot just be written off as unsafe and unwelcome because it exposed her to the dangers of sexual desire, in her instance, unprotected sex leading to a crisis pregnancy with no recourse to abortion. However reluctantly we do so, once we concede as a society the positive force of sexual desire, it shifts the responsibility back on to us as to how we intend to create safer spaces for women, especially early teenagers. This cannot and should not happen in a vacuum, and thus be dependent on individual pure luck. As matters stand now, finding safe spaces is a personal task for each young woman and contingent on personal circumstances and resources.

Mona had luck on her side in deciding what she wanted to do. She describes her progression through a reasonably confident adolescence where she felt she could explore sexual feelings physically with adolescent boys, but without undue pressure to have sex fully. The latter decision she postponed until she became a college student with the scope to decide what she wanted:

> [At] student discos, people would disappear out the front of the disco, in the field, and they'd be gone for two hours and … in a way it was kind of a safe thing because you knew that at two o'clock, you'd come back to the others and get the coats and go home. And that was really good. And then when I got to college, then the whole thing started that you could go over to other people's places, so you had opportunity as well as motive and that's when I started really kind of thinking 'Well what do I want to do here? Do I want to have sex?' and I thought no, I just don't feel comfortable with the idea of having sex. And when I do I will, and until then there's plenty of other things to do. I had certain lines [to say no] and I just wasn't going to go there. And then I got into second year, and started thinking more about it. And the way I thought about it was I've got two options. I can wait for the romantic perfection, but then he's going to turn out to be human like everyone else, and if that's what I'm pinning it on, then, how much of a let-down is that going to be? So I figured my other alternative is, you know, you find someone who you get on with, and you trust and it's nice and you see if you like it. And that's pretty much what I did. And that was fine, you know, grand. It was someone who was older and very laid back about the whole thing, and it was really nice … and that was grand. (Mona, 26, health worker, small town)

Both Karen and Mona thought through the issue of sexual desire, but a number of factors worked in Mona's favour so that she could more successfully act on it, setting her own terms and focusing on the 'plenty of other things to do' beyond intercourse that are sexually pleasurable. The circumstances of a particular secondary school helped: it was one where everyone came from the same surrounding small community of middle-class parents and where there was a strong sense that young people would go on to college. This created a useful backdrop to the expectation that a young woman should be learning to make life decisions. For Mona, it meant that she had a wider repertoire of decisions available and to make in relative safety. The school discos allowed peers to keep an eye on one another:

> The girls and myself have said it since, that the experience of going out, the four of us, kind of consolidated that, we always went out as a four and we came home as a four, and that was the pattern of things. So we were pretty confident and just not being taken in by bullshit. (Mona, 26, health worker, small town)

These were protected opportunities in that they provided the chance to explore and to access information and understandings about sex and sexuality. That standby of young college women, the student health service where people could expect to be treated as adults with the benefit of being anonymous, was mentioned by Mona and other college-going women as 'very straightforward, they were completely non-judgmental'. At the same time, Mona's experience of proceeding at her own pace is not a common one:

> I think I was pretty assertive about it, I was prepared to go as far as I was prepared to go and no further, and no one was going to intimidate me or *plámás* [Irish, meaning flattery to persuade] me into anything otherwise. (Mona, 26, health worker, small town)

The commodified 'openness' about sex and sexuality does not necessarily translate to an openness about one's experience of first sex despite the boasts of 'doing it' that appear to circulate especially amongst younger teenaged women. For many of our other respondents, there was a considerable gap between their first experiences of sex and any sense of sexual intimacy and pleasure. Having first sex was something which you could speak about retrospectively most often in those narrow terms of having 'done it'.

> I was rather a late developer I guess, in the sexual field. I was nineteen the first time I had full blown sex. And it was, it was alright. It wasn't, you know, it was just 'Oh

OK'. There's always this kind of anti-climax, I think especially for women, you know, what the fuss was all about, I really don't know. (Joan, 34, civil servant, small town)

It's like a big secret, weren't it? You couldn't tell anyone like. (Marie-Therese, 24, re-training scheme, village near a small town)

This naming of first sex as 'a big secret' illustrates that the symbolism of virginity loss can be heavily weighted and again suggests the need for a protected space (Thompson 1996; Carpenter 2005; Valenti 2009; Garcia 2012; Orenstein 2016, 2020; Hirsh and Khan 2020). That space may or may not be within the family. Stating that she cannot recall how she learned about the pill, Jane shared her experience of embarking on a sexual relationship and searching out the pill to protect herself well in advance of her mother's well-meaning but hopelessly idealised timeline for her daughter to experience the sexual dimensions of a relationship:

I remember my mum sitting me down once when I was about seventeen, and telling me that soon, myself and my boyfriend might kiss. We might kiss, but it wasn't to go any further, and in about five years' time, if we were still together, she'd sit me down and give me a talk about contraception. Which I thought was hilarious, because at the time, I was on the pill. (Jane, 28, scientist, small city)

These accounts of early sex demonstrate above all how contingent women's circumstances are in pursuing their sexual desire. Whether they can identify it or not, they are relying on sheer luck and on factors such as a fortuitously well-grounded sense of self, the ability to state what they want and access to contraception, within what remains a guarded and primarily unreceptive wider social setting.

Emotions and uncertainties about desire

In interview discussions, we consciously sought to address the complexities of sexual expectations and experiences respecting completely each individual's account of her decisions. What we found was that women were often uncertain about the path on which they had embarked, and their discussion of their own and others' first sexual encounters reflected this and other concerns. Emotions are far from straightforward in the wake of having first sex, in particular whether sex then equates to a relationship. Eve reiterates the strong sense that very young women may well need this complexity explored before they have sex, although how and by whom is unclear:

> Yeah. I think so. And, you know, the whole how will you feel afterwards, in terms of if he's going to be still there if that's what you want, just making sure that what you think you're going into is what you want. (Eve, 29, marketing administrator, metropolitan area)

What are the terms of engagement for young women who may feel they should give in to having full sex if they are to be able to have a boyfriend in the more traditional sense, if they really long to have that status? Can having sex be once-off, or part of a very short relationship centred only on exploring sexual desire? Clare and Lisa both struggle with these dimensions as they described all the questions they had:

> Like if it's someone that you fancy, like that you've really fancied for a long time as well, and it's kind of come to the crunch and you're kind of wondering like, should I or shouldn't I? And if I don't, I'm never going to see him again. And somewhere in your own head you should be saying, 'Well you know if he really likes you he's not going to mind waiting for a while.' But you don't think like that, you're just like 'Right if I have to keep him, I have to do this.' And like you don't want to come across like some … like if you actually said 'do you have condoms?' and he said 'no', you'd just kind of be like 'alright'. Like you just wouldn't do anything about it because you just so be too afraid that he'd, because of the way boys are, just up and leave, and you'd be left there. (Claire, 20, unemployed, outskirts of small town)

> Like I said earlier, sex isn't something that I found you can just stop, start, stop, start. Like, I started with one person, and when that relationship finished with that one person, it went on with other people. So it wasn't something that 'Oh yeah, blah blah blah. I'm going to wait until I'm in a stable relationship.' How can you be in a stable relationship at seventeen? How? In this culture; I'm not talking about any other culture. (Lisa, 19, student, suburban area)

The progressive learning curve about sex demands that young women deal explicitly with their anxiety around whether and when to have sex. It also demands that they become quite skilled at reading their own desires through often conflicting demands from others yet we encountered no clear understanding from young women as to how that might be accomplished. How can young women reach the point where they can do this work of interpretation of their often multiple emotions and handle male desire in a way which is not to their own disadvantage? The sense that you might be falling behind with a developmental milestone if you do not have sex earlier kept emerging in the interviews and it has become part of the adolescent mindset for many young women:

> Yeah, when friends are all going, 'Why haven't you done it already, just get rid of your virginity, I've done it and it's great and like you read in [magazines], fifteen and sixteen,' like, 'I still haven't lost my virginity, and all my mates have.' (Kathryn, 34, animal groomer, small city)

> It's become the norm. And everyone else is talking … you know that type of thing. And in a way it was, it became that kind of way. So yeah, that wasn't the way it happened in the end for me, but I think that could happen for a lot of people. (Eve, 29, marketing administrator, metropolitan area)

> Because it's all peer pressure, yeah. You're constantly, 'What's the norm, what are we supposed to be, what's the coolest thing to do?' And it's the most important area. And people need confidence and need to be told, yeah, they're probably under pressure. Because you think it's the thing you should be doing. Rather than having the confidence to just go and say 'No I don't want to.' (Nora, 27, local authority worker, small city)

The issue of the norm and of being cool is picked up in Hyde and Howlette's (2004) study of Irish teenagers' perceptions of sex and sexuality. In their group of very young women interviewees who had not yet had sex, virginity loss was anticipated as an accomplishment and a stage in one's life-course (see also Thompson 1996; Carpenter 2005; Valenti 2009; Garcia 2012; Orenstein 2016, 2020). This view worried our older respondents as they reflected on their own experiences and they expressed concern about how teenaged women might find that a too early engagement with sex lent itself to negative feelings or unrealistic expectations about sex (see also Hyde and Howlett 2004: 67–8). Ciara, Roisin and Elizabeth try to analyse this in terms of privileging enjoyment and the 'right' person over 'doing it' at a younger age to get it out of the way:

Very much that part that you should enjoy it. Because you don't want young ones to think that it's this terrible thing out there. If you're comfortable enough to say to them like, that it is wonderful and that they are going to enjoy it, but they need to wait for the right person. Rather than saying 'don't have sex with anybody because it's wrong' and they might be able to start thinking about it in a different way. (Ciara, 27, nurse, small city)

I think they're having sex too young, and they don't realise really what it is. Like I was seventeen, and I felt even at the time, or maybe later, that maybe that was too young, that maybe I should have waited longer. Because then you really understand what you're doing, and you know, you enjoy it, it's not just this quick thing behind the bike sheds or something. And I was with a guy for two years, and I felt it was how it should have been, and I didn't regret it. And I've talked to my younger sister, and she was fourteen, and she says she does regret it, and would have preferred to have waited longer. So I think helping people to understand that, and to maybe delay sex a bit longer is needed. (Roisin, 25, mature student, small city)

Yeah, wait, wait till you're actually with somebody. (Elizabeth, 27, occupational therapist, small city)

Waiting for the 'right person' seems to suggest waiting for someone who might be safe or kind, but it is then bound up with the problem of whether one is in a relationship to have sex or not which, as we have already seen, is deeply confusing. In Hyde and Howlett's group of young teenaged women, they stated that their ideal of losing their virginity was within a relationship and with a 'special person' (2004: 68). Tolman (2002: 80–1) is helpful in reminding us that because sexual pleasure for young women is either condemned or cast aside for consideration by mainstream social discourses where the emphasis is on 'risk and avoidance', young women must inevitably split their consciousness about their sexual development into what they want and what gender relations will permit. This 'dual consciousness' (Tolman elaborates on this term, quoting Michelle Fine) came up consistently in our conversations with our respondents. Several women commented on the need to develop skills in handling sex with men, especially if sex takes place before a relationship is well-established or an ongoing relationship is not desired by the man. The dual consciousness enforces an additional layer of responsibility in dealing with gender relations and women may or may not be successful in how they deal with this:

I didn't actually become sexually active till I was 19. I was going out with somebody from 16, but I wanted to wait till I was over 18 and I wanted to wait until I had finished school. That was a conscious decision. My sister, now, she had sex younger and he wasn't quite as patient, her boyfriend was constantly pressuring her. Whereas with me that wasn't an issue at all, it was when I was ready and that was it – there was no pressure at all. It was a very different situation I think. I suppose I was lucky really. (Marcella, 28, civil servant, small town)

Women reflected about these aspects in relation to the settings where they became aware of sex, and to varying degrees, safer sex. They also point out their aspirations for young women for the future, knowing that matters must change from what too often feels an exploitative social context. Comments about young women's discomfort with exploring sex and a lack of putting forward women's own sexual desires emerge strongly, as do efforts to recasting their own experiences, the missing link being how to encourage assertiveness and thus to shift gender relations away from the male dominance of which Garcia (2012), Segal (2014), Orenstein (2016, 2020), Hirsch and Khan (2020) and others write, and which is what women see:

I mean, if we were seventeen and we were at a party, and we've had a few drinks. And suddenly you find yourself in some situation. Because you don't really know what the boundaries are. Like, you have a fair idea, but as a teenage girl, you're really going to be talked in by a teenage boy to a lot of stuff. I think. And there's a lot of peer pressure as well, and a lot of talk. (Michelle, 26, administrator, metropolitan)

I think a girl, even if she's confident, when she gets into a situation like that, and a boy is, someone's more confident than you, you automatically kind of assume they're right or something? If someone's in your ear, I think teenage girls need to be more assertive. Definitely. (Bridget, 30, computer programmer, metropolitan area)

One woman, studying as a mature student, related how taken aback she was when working in an Irish bar in Munich to discover a sense of having sex as a perfectly acceptable undertaking without the drama of matters here:

And the difference in girls, German girls our age, and the Irish girls that arrived over that had never left Ireland before, you mention the word sex, they go red and die, and the German girls are sitting there going, 'What's the problem like?' (Lucy, 24, mature student, small city)

This feels an audacious position to several other women because it opens up the problem of the 'slut discourse':

> The only difference I would say that I think is really obvious is that, I would always have thought that it's fair enough for women to be sexually active, but for women to openly say that they want sex, and that they want this and that and the other, then it's like 'Oh my god, slapper!' you know? There's this whole thing. (Aisling, 24, mature student, small city)

> You have a name then … oh you're a slut, like. (Emer, 20, student, small city)

> If it's a man it's fine, if it's a woman, it's not. (Sorcha, 24, mature student, small city)

In all of these exchanges, women point out implicitly and explicitly that *even if a woman is confident about what she wants*, she may bend to what she perceives others think about sex. Hyde and Howlett argue that young women did not feel active peer *pressure* to act certain ways sexually, but did feel peer *influence*, characterised by the desire to keep up with what their friends were experiencing (2004: 67) and of course that is framed by what current gender norms demand. What we see is a constant process of consideration and revision of one's actions in relation to those norms. It means that we cannot assume that recent changes in openness about sex observed by Irish scholars and journalists translate easily to greater access to positive sexuality and experiences for young women. Women are coding their own sexual pleasure as need where pleasure as a notion for women is absent (see Tolman 2002; Holland et al. 1998; Hyde and Howlett 2004: 75; Garcia 2012; Orenstein 2016, 2020; Hirsh and Khan 2020). These women resist characterising Ireland as having changed for the better, and note enduring double standards about how women and men see sex:

> I think it's probably gone from, yeah. No. I wouldn't see a huge change, or kids as opened or teenagers as more open. They would have a lot of drink and then be more open about it, but that's, like, you know what I mean? They would use some substance and then they're OK. But ask them and they still would be a bit giddy, with their sexuality and that whole thing. You know the way you were when you were twelve years of age? There's still women like that. (Deirdre, 30, community worker)

> And that goes back to women don't see they have a need. They're engaging in sexual activities, they don't see that they have a need as well, do you know what I mean,

that it's still a man's, he gets his needs met and that's it. And then the woman ends up in the situation of no condoms. (Sharon, 28, drugs support worker, working-class metropolitan area)

How sexual desire and sexual needs are defined is in flux. Television and as we have noted above, the now ubiquitous debs ball ('prom night') were mentioned as key influences in the belief that first sex should be accomplished by the time one reaches a certain age, before the end of one's teenaged years. The gendered dimension to this was brought out by one woman who suggests that the traditional pressure placed on boys to have sex before a certain age now falls on women as well.[9] Note that there are different standards placed on young men and women in Marie's view, as she cites 16 as the outer limit for men and 18 for women to have first sex, both of which timeframes peers consider 'normal':

> I mean, if a fella's, sixteen or whatever, and he hasn't as such 'done it', it's this whole thing. And even it's got to the stage with girls, they're coming up to eighteen, and they're like 'Oh my God, I can't be eighteen and haven't done it!' (Marie, 24, unemployed, outskirts of a small town)

The pressures that many women express and the lack of positive talk about sexual pleasure and desire alert us to home much more work needs to be accomplished in changing mainstream discourses.[10] This is the case in multiple contexts for young women. For example, Lorena Garcia interviewed working-class Latinx students in Chicago and found that young women could easily discuss sexual pleasure in the context of what they had read or others had told them, but also then hesitated, and, 'searching

9   The big dance held at the end of secondary school, the 'debs', has been a magnet for over-consumption: see 'How much does the average Irish girl spend on her Debs?' (Reilly 2012).

10   Hyde and Howlette's research indicates that young men also express anxiety about sexual knowledge and performance and there are decided pressures on them to conform to gender and social norms about 'doing it' which hinders their and their partners' sexual pleasure (2004: 72–4). Orenstein found that young men 'struggled not only with unexpected feelings of connection and vulnerability, but with other emotions: inadequacy, anxiety, insecurity, confusion, disappointment, embarrassment–none of which, as guys, they felt permission to express' (2020: 81).

for words to articulate why they enjoyed engaging in sexual activities, they pointed not to bodily sensations or to their sexual desire, but rather to their relationships with their boyfriends' (2012: 137). This type of evidence, alongside our interviews, leads us to underwrite Deborah Tolman's argument:

> *Not* feeling sexual desire may put girls in danger and 'at risk'. When a girl does not know what her own feelings are, when she disconnects the apprehending psychic part of herself from what is happening in her own body, she then becomes especially vulnerable to the power of others' feelings as well as to what others say she does and does not want or feel (2002: 21, original emphasis).

Irish women's reiterated concerns about young women succumbing to 'peer influence' and their comments urging more 'confidence' on the part of young women reflect this underlying message.

Changing cultural norms about sex and being feminine

The availability and proliferation of sexual content across most public areas of Irish life, centred on the media, advertising and social media suggests widespread social acceptance of sex as a commonplace activity. However, we discovered ambivalence amongst the women we interviewed about how open Irish society actually is about sex, whether it should be more open, and if so, what might that openness needs to look like.

> I think we are more open. Not to the extent of the US obviously, I can safely say, but I still think there is a bit of a taboo, I suppose it's just the history of the Catholic religion. (Jacqueline, 30, financial services, suburban metropolitan area)

> Yeah I think we are. Yeah definitely. Like people are definitely more comfortable talking about it in the last ten years [since the mid 1990s]. It was very taboo years ago, you know what I mean? We talk between our friends about it. A few years ago our friends weren't so open about it, but in recent years you do. (Heather, 26, local authority worker, small city)

> I think there's a kind of a contradiction. I think there is more openness, you are able to discuss the very fact that you are sexual being, and things like, you know, the ability

to enjoy sex. But there's also sort of a level of insecurity and discomfort about that. So I think it only goes so far. You still should be in a long term and stable relationship and enjoying sex. But saying 'I love having lots of one-night stands' is still not quite acceptable. (Sarah, 30, teacher, metropolitan area)

You're not going to get a group of young women on the 'Six One' news or on 'Nationwide' at seven o' clock in the evening talking about their enjoyment of sexuality. What you often get is hygiene related kind of conversations. Nobody is actually going out and saying 'It's wrong to have sex' but the focus would be on the health risks of sex. (Sadbh, 31, computer operative, metropolitan area)

The role played by the media is seen as useful in discussing sex as part of everyday life, but also in exposing some of the bleak aspects of sex, including sexual violence:

It's on the television and it's just making it that you see it, and that it's part of our life like. It's just part of society. And people, you know, if what happens is bad … they had another story last week around a rape of a young girl on *Fair City* as well like, so they're constantly kind of covering those issues in it. I suppose it's a lot of positive exposure around it. (Caoimhe, 25, project manager, rural area)

At the same time, the media also reinforces strong gender stereotypes which can dig deep into the consciousness of young women:

First of all from media, movies, TV, I got two lessons. One was the man wanted to have sex and the woman basically laid there until it was over. Lots of images of the woman staring up, like 'Is it almost over?' And the second one was that boys masturbated and girls didn't. So like, boys enjoyed sex, and girls didn't. And it was only really in my mid-twenties that I dispelled both of those strange ideas. (Maureen, 33, self-employed, small town)

The *Sex and the City* phenomenon may have dispelled some of these ideas to a certain extent and seems to be helpful in at least enabling people to talk more freely about sex as pleasure:

I think it's a great programme and I would watch it religiously every Thursday night. Maybe, it is very blunt, it is very kind of out there. It may not be that our lives are like that, but it's something that's enjoyable to watch that you think there are … that these women do exist, you know. They aren't completely fictional, there are women like them, they do represent women like that somewhere in the world. I think it's a very light hearted kind of programme and I think it is liberating for women, the kinds of issues that they do bring up and it makes it kind of … It makes it easy to talk about sex and sexuality, and it's comfortable to talk about it and you shouldn't have any hang-ups around it. (Kate, 30, health services administrator, rural area)

I've watched it [*Sex and the City*] a couple of times and they are at brunch … and every sexually practice and technique comes out, and [Samantha] has a great booming voice and she comes out with some sexual technique that no-one has ever heard of before and the others are stunned … as you say there is that openness about it. And it's very different to the *Fair City*, *Coronation Street*, where sex is always crisis. Whereas with them sex is play I suppose. (Molly, 29, restaurant worker, small city)

How helpful this might be, however, turns on the matter of the com-modification of sex and the vulnerability of women to that message that as McRobbie (2008: 531) argues concocts a 'specific modality of feminism' which turns on a 'ideal subject category of "girl" ' that fits perfectly within a neoliberal culture. Sarah picks up on some of these issues:

I find that it's [media] causing pressure on young women too, it's still not allowing them to find out what it is they would like as individuals. Things like *Sex and the City* and the advertising and the teenage magazines are all promoting a particular model of sexuality, and there's very little room for people to actually find what their own sexual identity is. (Sarah, 30, teacher, metropolitan area)

Christine lived through the far bleaker dimensions of sex, having experi-enced childhood sexual abuse and then became pregnant at 17, and she is concerned at the trivialisation of sex in programmes like *Sex and the City*:

Sex is portrayed as something that is great and casual and something that we do and when we are finished we just get dressed and go have a coffee with our friends and sit in our designer clothes and mull over the size of his penis or the colour of his socks. The problem is there are no warnings or guidelines to help us make an informed decision about what is a very important area of our lives one that will affect us both emotionally and physically. It would seem that everyone is doing it, and if you're not there is something wrong with you. My feelings are to conclude that young women don't have any part in the decision-making process with regards to sex. The media has made the decision for them, sex has become an almost subliminal programming by people in suits to sell products and the humanity has been stripped away. (Christine, 31, unemployed, small town)

Women reflected on the additional pressures which come from the media they all face, especially younger adolescent women. One's appearance

as a sexual person, the need to dress in a fashionable but sexualised way in
order to command attention from young men, all these dimensions need
to be dealt with at the same time young women are trying to learn about
themselves. Lisa gives a graphic account of what this feels like:

> I think sometimes you don't even understand what's happened to you, by dressing
> that way. But I think, when you dress like that for a long time, you become an object,
> you're dressing to become an object. And you don't realise it, at the time, it's like, you're
> buying the clothes because they look good. And they do look good, they're pretty,
> you look at yourself in the mirror you think 'Wow, I look good!' and 'Woo-hoo!'
> and it's a lot of power for a young lady to have. And especially to be able to control
> young men by getting them to look at her, it's very exciting. And for someone of fif-
> teen or sixteen, it's an awful lot of power that you can have by wearing something,
> or by putting your hair a certain way. And so you learn to work it. You know what
> I mean? (Lisa, 19, student, suburban area)

An accompanying lack of strong female role models in the media was
cited, where women could be celebrated for skill and self-worth that extended beyond a commercialised sexy appearance:

> I was watching Heidi Klum [German-American Victoria's Secret model, business
> person and TV host] yesterday on the telly and I was like 'oh my God, I'm never
> eating a bite again … till next week!' and I'm twenty-six years of age! So I mean,
> where is a fourteen your old, you know what I mean? Like, whether they're going
> to get to know themselves, they're still going to go out and have sex. Or experiment
> in some shape or form, with either alcohol or drugs, cos at that age, everyone has
> very low self-esteem. They don't know themselves. You can have all the talking in
> the world about it, but they're still going to go and try it out. A lot of it again is the
> peer pressure. (Niamh, 26, nurse, small city)

> Maybe I'm being, I dunno, far too old here but, I wonder that girls' role models, it
> is all very sexually pointed. There's like, Christina Aguilera, there's Britney Spears
> [American singers], and you do look at them and go 'Jesus, I'd love to look like
> that.' Whereas men have a lot more sports role models, and there's a lot more posi-
> tive image I think. It's easier to see something different, the rugby players, let's face
> it, are hideous, as are GAA [Gaelic Athletic Association] players, and yet they're
> a very positive role model, because they feel good about themselves, and they're
> not this kind of, I dunno, actor-type looks. Whereas I don't think girls have that.
> And I think they, girls, tend to have very bad feelings about themselves because
> they don't live up to these absolutely ridiculous role models. I mean, that's very

naïve to think that but I did, that's what happens. (Elizabeth, 27, occupational therapist, small city) [11]

Being more assertive: Sex and sexual practices

If sex is now openly part of everyday background noise in Ireland, women being able to set terms for themselves is not. Understanding better what woman want from sexual relations and how to assert themselves remains a very uneven and unsupported undertaking. Luck, a fortunate discovery, happenstance all continue to be underlying determinants into how one might meet a partner with whom one can be open about sex, be it short-term or otherwise. There were plenty of examples of continuing negative attitudes, and here Denise argues that women have to absorb those attitudes and try to negotiate around what remain strongly male-dominant mores to achieve their own sexual desires, even though they do not have the scope to fully control male behaviour:

> Still goes that same way, that lads that go out and do what they want to do and have sex with as many women as they like, they're still the studs at the end of the day. Whereas if a girl goes out and does it, they're still classed as a slut or a slapper. Whichever way you want to put it. But I think if you want it bad enough, you can get most of it. Men, and sex is something that's going to be out of your control most of the time, you know, but I think it depends on the way you see yourself as well, as to how much value you're going to have in relationships. If that what you want to do, if you just want to have sex, then it's got to be between two people who know that's all they want or, as many people call them now, shag buddies. (Denise, 25, office worker, suburban area)

11 There have been improvements in the visibility of younger Irish women as potential role models. For example, in 2015, the Irish women's rugby team won the women's Six Nations receiving at last this kind of press attention: 'Winning is the lifeblood of Ireland's women rugby champions: The strength of our women rugby players should be cherished' (Commiskey 2015).

We encountered one quite positive example of a young woman who had learned how she wanted to have sex outside the parameters of a long-term relationship, how to assert herself and to protect herself without putting off her male partner:

> I actually developed this habit really early on, because I found that um obviously the problem was because you know, there's all the politeness and mind games involved in it which used to make me sort of giggle because you're in this very unconventionally unpolite situation, but what would always happen is you get somebody to put on a condom, and of course that would dampen their fervour a little bit. Which of course then if you went on to have sex immediately afterwards would be crap. And so what I used to do is go 'Okay, look, will you just put on the condom now, and forget about it, but you're not going near me for another while', so that, you know, that made a huge difference. You know, those kinds of things. (Mona, health worker, 26, small town)

Bernadette's suggestion of an alternative 'peer power' that empowers friends to stay within their comfort zones is also a creative one:

> So it's not even so much educating people, but making people realise that it's OK to want to protect yourself. That that's a valid way to be. I mean, I'm thinking of groups of girls in the areas that suffer the most [from teenage pregnancy]. And it's not just a question of getting the leaflets out there or getting the information out there. They still go, 'My friends aren't doing it, I couldn't do that, my boyfriend wouldn't have that'. You know. So we need something else, something more than that, to make these people stronger. And turn peer pressure on its head. Peer power. (Bernadette, 30, catering manager, small city)

Yet we have no clear way of getting there, no series of appropriate efforts to encourage agency and self-knowledge on which Irish society can agree at family and community levels, never mind at the level of the state and its policy machinery. Our respondents have been open, honest and deeply reflective, and through their accounts we can see that matters have definitely moved on from where their mothers were, that they do not have to be 'in the dark' now, but they see too, the fissures in Irish society that have left this work of openness and support stalled and which can leave young women stranded still:

> Well I certainly couldn't say that it's as bad as it used to be. I'll put it this way. I'd much rather be a young woman today than a young woman growing up in the 1970s,

or the 80s ... So I think that women, and before that time, were really in the dark and they, they couldn't even identify what they wanted, and they certainly couldn't mention anything they wanted in terms of sex, sexuality and choice. Whereas women today can. And although it's poor, they can access information, they can even approach a GP with less of a fear that the GP's going to report them. So I think they're working less in the dark than they were. But I also think things have got stuck and become stagnant. And there are other conflicts coming in that maybe aren't recognised, maybe because we're so focussed on the repressive, um, Catholic thing, that we missed out some of the pressures that are coming from an oversexualised idea of women, where your whole identity is sex, which comes from another influence. So I still think there are huge conflicts. And that if girls are going to progress any further, and resolve those conflicts, they need older women to start things moving again. (Kathleen, 25, social worker, small town)

Women are stating these issues, some gains and more unexpected conflicts within a now familiar globalised sexual culture. Young people need to be confident in order to make the right choices for themselves. How are we to get there?

Sexualised contexts and demands to develop and inhabit sexual selves

There have been significant social changes that influence how we perceive the sexuality of young women and young men, and how they perceive themselves, as Tom Inglis hoped in the late 1990s:

> The shy, demure Irish boy and girl, uncertain of themselves and their sexuality, are gradually being replaced by bright, confident, outward-going people, able to proclaim their desires, demonstrate emotion, and anxious and willing not just to display their bodies and sexuality, but to engage in sex. (Inglis 1998: 167)

Women are under pressure to appear more knowledgeable and more sophisticated about sex than they may be feeling. They need to know so much more, for example, about sexual techniques and how much of a repertoire they wish to acquire. They urgently require an expanded repertoire of responses to help them deal with their emotions. To use Cook's phrase again, it needs 'work' to become competent at being sexually active (Cook 2004; see also Duncombe and Marsden 1996). However, knowledge is being gained in a piecemeal way while women deal as best as they can. Their outward visage has to appear as quite urbane to the point where they can participate in jokes about sex without appearing to be compromised. The message that sex is an integral part of one being a sophisticated young woman, that sex is 'good', is built in to current daily life.[12]

There have been some gains. We can see that some young women are more confident than their counterparts have been in the quite recent past to identify female desire and remove themselves as best they can from speaking about sex having only the language traditionally associated with young men (Inglis 1998: 141–2). Interestingly, Irish women do not appear to be in quite the same space as either their British or American counterparts. For example, Hyde and Howlett's group of young teenaged women who stated their desire to lose their virginity with a 'special person' (2004: 68) stands in contradiction to recent American-based literature on young women and sexuality which elaborate two poles of young women's experiences: exercising their sexuality openly through the hookup culture, often without wishing any emotional connection, or protection of self through abstinence pledges, foreswearing sex for the immediate future as a form of identity-building (Kamen 2000; Carpenter 2005; Mullaney 2006; Stepp 2007; Rupp et al. 2014; Wade 2017). Activists and policy groups in Britain note that experimentation is important for young people and they need to be able to learn for themselves, but the higher rate of teenaged pregnancy in Britain has cut across the development of a more multi-stranded dialogue and been complicated by formal sex education in the schools which has positioned sex as dangerous and risk-laden (Lee and Jenkins 2002).

The young women we talked with have helped us to see that many emotions and feelings, including the crucial need for trust, are part of sex for women, even in the context of short-term relationships:

12   Weeks (1997) has argued that the market exploitation of sex to increase the commercial viability of an expanded consumer market has changed our relationship with sexuality, a relationship which must have particular impact on younger women and men.

There's all kinds of identities tied up with sex. And most of the issues around how women field sex. I think sex is still used as a tool in some sort of way. Whether that's a woman who won't have sex with a man the first time she goes out with him because she might be perceived as easy. Or 'I won't have sex with him because then he's more likely to ring me again, because he won't have got what he wanted the first time'. (Deirdre, 29, community worker, metropolitan area working-class)

I think that women do want something with some more feeling attached. Something a bit more emotional. And it doesn't have to be committed for the next however many years, but it's with somebody that you feel that you trust. You feel that you're comfortable with, that you feel they're not going to do anything after you've opened yourself up like this. Because sex is something like this I think. Where you open yourself up to, to be quite vulnerable. And I think that's what women want. And that's where it comes into short- or long-term relationships. (Bernadette, catering manager, 30, small city)

We cannot paint a portrait of a 'generation of women' believing and acting a certain way around sex or of an entire society shifting in sexual attitudes and practices. Change is uneven, and diversity will always be present. As Peggy Orenstein (2001) employs in her analysis of women, work, relationships and motherhood in the United States, the concept of flux may best capture how social patterns ebb and flow, and how diversity is maintained within any society. Despite the notable differences from past decades, Irish society still has a distance to travel in being more open about emerging patterns of sex and relationships. Women voice a need to change what remains of the older, more repressive culture:

It's like everything. We all know what goes on, but we'd rather it didn't. We'd rather it went on within wedlock. My mum always called it 'wedlock' and I hate that term so much. (Jane, 28, scientist, small city)

You know, it needs to change at a much more basic level. Because the condoms or the pill or whatever are just the tiny piece in a much bigger picture that's still very much muddled in Ireland. (Elizabeth, 27, occupational therapist, small city)

For women like, you were in the house, you done what you done, you made your bed and you lie in it. And that's whether the man had the right over what he done. Do you know what I mean? And even my Ma today would not have a clue about sex. And yet she had twelve kids. And that still continues, that the man has the upper hand in society. Yeah, it's changing when people and women are beginning to get stronger. Because they're going to women's groups and they have more

confidence in their personal development. And it has to start in the family. At a
very young, very very, young age. (Deirdre, 30, community worker, metropolitan
working-class area)

So-called 'traditional Irish values' about the primary place of sex, marriage and motherhood in women's lives remain present, aspects of which
are perhaps felt more powerfully by women living in rural areas than urban
settings, mostly to do with the reticence of how to speak and practice sex
actively without public ridicule. What comes through clearly in the discussions we had and indeed also through media representations of Irish
women is the great diversity, and a remarkable self-reflection with which
young Irish women are voicing their understandings about their sexual expectations and experiences. The near-blinding rapidity of change toward
a global, consumer economy in a very compressed Celtic Tiger timeframe
calls attention to the Irish case. Young women are challenging expectations by seeking to expand the types of socially acceptable sexual selves
in Ireland today. Yet, at the same time, they must contend with the way
that both enduring expectations of young women's roles and emerging
expectations challenge their ability to create and inhabit positive sexual
spaces and identities.

Young Irish women's perspectives on sex, sexuality and sexual health
services must be seen as an important component of social change. Young
women are challenged with determining sexual and social roles for themselves in a society that has been perilously slow to recognise a broadened
variety of such roles. As Deborah Tolman (2002) puts it, positive narratives
of girls' understandings of their own sexual desires reject the agentless statement of 'it just happened'. For many young Irish women, 'it just happened'
is a vestige of the conservative, traditional past, whereas now, women and
men have the responsibility (and burden) to design sexual selves and experiences in a society only recently flooded with sexualised marketing, increased contraceptive availability, greater acceptance of single motherhood
and consumer-driven expectations about how teenagers ought to present
themselves sexually. Determined not to be seen to abandon Irish young
people again in this epoch, others have voiced increasing concern, as with
this recent commentary:

> The old [Ireland] denies them sex and relationships education as well as access to contraceptives and basic privacy. Meanwhile the new [Ireland] commands them to have sex with the promise it will bring love and everlasting happiness. (Ruane 2007)

Young women becoming sexually active are exercising their agency and are being responsible. But the message that often comes over is that they are not seen like that. Is it responsible and empowered to begin to be sexually active or am I being under-handed, doing something my mother has always warned me against doing? We stress how critically important it is that the basic building blocks are put in place with which to enable young women to establish their sexual selves as safely as the adventure of sexual experience can be made. They have their eyes on their elders in this:

> It's the whole deal really. Certainly government, and policy making needs to be put forward. But policy makers can only make policy if the government is supportive of the policy that you're trying to make. So you can produce loads of really fantastic ideas, and they can just be left there. But it's a cultural shift that has kind of started off, and stopped to a certain extent. (Marcella, 28, civil servant, small town)

The next chapter explores particularly difficult challenges in doing so as a result of persistent double standards about acceptable social and sexual behaviour that stigmatises some women for their sexualised self-presentation or behaviour, shakes their confidence, and works as a potent form of social control.

CHAPTER 3

'And she didn't know what to do': The Many Obstacles to Sexual Freedom

The burdens of negative representations

By the beginning of the twenty-first century, young people were increasingly distancing themselves from the Catholic church's moral teachings, particularly in relation to sexuality (Inglis 1987; McAuliffe and Kennedy 2017; D. Scally 2021). This was not an easy journey; it was full of contradictions, personal turmoil and the potential for family and relationship conflict. More young people might have begun to have sex outside marriage, even when they did go on to marry, but they had the concern of often playing a high-risk game of pregnancy – a form of Irish roulette. If they wanted to use condoms, many chemists did not stock them (Inglis 2003: 11) and access to other forms of contraception remained out of reach for many. So while enjoying all the seeming benefits of a sleek consumer culture, Irish society was predictably slow to give young people vital support to have sex safely, a crucial prerequisite for women. Deborah Tolman (2002: 80) points to the inescapable contradiction that 'under current gender arrangements', sex for women holds 'both pleasure and danger'. The principal Irish institutions which might have otherwise contributed to supporting young people, the education and health services especially, have continued to send a confused and condemnatory message to them and their parents: active sex is risky and in the course of your everyday lives, there is little help for you to mitigate those risks. There was – and remains – a more acute problem still in relation to 'stratified reproduction', the concept we laid out in the book's introduction that trains our focus to see that within any given setting, power relations are such that some groups of women are ceded relatively more power over their reproductive lives 'while others are disempowered' (Ginsburg and Rapp 1995a: 3). If gender already forms a problem of conditionality for women, class, ethnicity, sexual identity and other forms of marginalisation contribute still more to a loss of personal agency, and the notion of 'stratified reproduction helps us see the arrangements by which some reproductive futures are valued while others are despised' (ibid.). In this chapter, we extend the concept of stratified reproduction to help us see how women's experiences of having sex can be read through social, economic and, to an extent, geographical contexts which can be more or less supportive of a woman's personal agency.

If we consider some of the accounts of first sexual experiences in Chapter 2, we find Joanne who related how you could not talk to anyone about having had sex, its clandestine nature marked out for her as a young, working-class adolescent with no access in a very small town to any person or organisation to counsel her about contraception. Mona, living in a larger more urbanised setting and with middle-class credentials to help her, did have access and support and an adroit sense of how to use contraception. Their situations are indicative of the mid-2000s, when a series of obstacles confronted young women which they had to try to resolve for the most part individually.

Condoms had been deregulated in 1992 in the wake of the Virgin Stores controversy in Dublin (see Enright and Cloatre 2018). In 1988, a peer group project developed by the Irish Family Planning Association as part of its education programme was supported by the IFPA to open a stall selling condoms in Virgin Stores. This was in direct contravention of the 1979 Health (Family Planning) Act. Virgin Stores were convicted of selling condoms without a license and fined in 1990, gaining international media coverage. An appeal was rejected in 1991, and the size of the fine increased. Starting on Valentine's Day in 1992, an AIDS activist campaign called 'Condom Sense' illegally installed 140 condom vending machines in clubs and pubs (Enright and Cloatre 2018: 274). Finally, in July 1992 and framed as the government's response to AIDS, in the Health (Family Planning) (Amendment) Act, the age at which a person could buy condoms was lowered to 17 years while the restriction of needing a medical prescription for condoms was abolished. Thereafter condoms were available from a number of sources including, in theory, any chemist's shop; vending machine sales and free condom distribution was prohibited (Enright and Cloatre 2018: 276). Ferriter notes that neither of these moves prevented a steep rise in the numbers of sexually transmitted illnesses (STIs) – an apparent marker for far greater sexual activity although family sizes were coming down equally dramatically (Ferriter 2009: 426–7). One outcome was that the 1993 legislative step to regulate condoms as prophylactics and not as contraceptives kept in place the reality that 'Women's reproductive freedoms had reached an impasse; they could obtain contraceptives from their doctor at home, or an abortion abroad' (Enright and Cloatre 2018: 277–8).

A breakthrough in the public visibility of the contraceptive need to use condoms occurred in 2004 when the dynamic Crisis Pregnancy Agency launched its 'Think Contraception' advertising campaign on Irish television, a major first. The campaign targeted young people, aged 18–25 years of age. The Agency had commissioned the research which gave concrete meaning to the need to speak out about contraception. Published at the same time the television advertising campaign was first viewed, research at that time indicated this was the cohort most likely to have had early sex, that is, sex before the age of 18, while 25 per cent of the 18–25 cohort did not use contraception consistently (Rundle et al. 2004: 65, 68). The younger end of that cohort not only had sex earlier in their teenaged years, but they also were less likely to use contraception. Social stratification also came into play, with differences in the levels of education a disturbing proxy about contraceptive use. Those people who had least educational attainment were least likely to use contraception consistently (ibid.) whether from diminished opportunities to access any or diminished exposure to the very limited and patchy sex education available in schools.

These overview figures, helpful though they are, lend no insight into the impact on young women's selves of having to live with the negatives of having sex, including unwanted pregnancy and the risks and stigma attached to sexually transmitted infections (STIs). Adina Nack (2008: 5, 16) has observed in relation to STIs that there are 'social and psychological costs' to living with these and that although we 'teach' in a broad way about the 'risks' of having sex, the negative impacts of sex are felt by individuals in a complex process. She argues that this process inevitably begins before even contracting, say, a sexually transmitted illness, and implicates the 'social dynamics of gender, race, class and sexuality' in ways that our impoverished approaches to sex education do not capture (2008: 16).

Putting this in a broader perspective, bell hooks writes that before the feminist movement began to pull apart how patriarchal culture works, 'most women found it difficult, if not downright impossible, to assert healthy sexual agency' because of the way that culture taught them that 'the domain of sexual desire and sexual pleasure was always and only male' and that women must not 'lay claim to sexual need or sexual hunger' (2000: 85). Many women still do find it difficult, and younger women engaging in sexual experiences for the first time can find it especially daunting. Patriarchal norms continue to determine how the female body 'is experienced, and relations of power maintained. Bodies are given or denied meaning, regulated and regularly demeaned, within institutions and discourses which give value to what is seen as efficiently "masculine", and actively "heterosexual"' (Segal 2015: 253).

The overarching influence of the Catholic church for the first eight decades of the twentieth century on what Tom Inglis terms the field of sexuality (Inglis 1998), but with a reduced impact thereafter as a once monolithic regime reminds us of the harsh realities for a great swathe of the population and its project of social control fitted well with the interests of the post-1922 state in securing stability and conformity. The state relied heavily on the church as a cultural agent of great force which helped to maintain the continuing commitment to rigidly patriarchal norms which both entities shared. Although this punitive Catholic discourse was radically decentred by the 1990s (see Ferriter 2004: 665–6; Hilliard 2004: 152–4; Leane and Kiely 2014; Kiely 2015; McAuliffe and Kennedy 2017), it led on to no less difficult realisations of how state-enforced patriarchal relations have been sustained and imposed on women's lives within this more recent period.

Numbers of feminist critics have pointed out how the Irish state has held tightly to the ideology of famialism in pursuing its social and economic policies very much at the expense of women's equal status, so that women's self-identity, apart from being a wife, partner or mother, has been troublingly hard won (Byrne 2003; Mahon 1994; O'Connor 1998; Yeates

1999; Brophy and Delay 2015). Nicola Yeates comments that the biopolitics of Irish social policy is consistent in its 'normative prescriptions of women's role as homemakers': 'Women's social and reproductive rights have been the explicit focus of family law and social policy' (Yeates 1999: 608). It is the continuing impact of this multi-layered reality that Evelyn Mahon (1994) terms state-supported private patriarchy. If in the past the Catholic church has supplied the zealous frontline cavalry of a deeply conservative patriarchal society inflicting so much damage on women, it has done this alongside state ideologies which have had no less focused an intent, if a broader field in which to preserve patriarchal relations.

This is clear within Irish education and its particular management structures which favour a hierarchy of control (Devine et al. 2011; Lynch and Lodge 2002; Lodge and Lynch 2004; Lynch 2004). There has been an ongoing problem of church patronage, by definition patriarchal, of the majority of Irish primary schools and approximately half of its secondary schools (B. O'Toole 2015), but this control has been underwritten by a frequently quiescent and conformist civil service which has failed to challenge substantially masculinist values. First observed by sociologist Patrick Clancy (1986) the role taken up by successive ministers of education and the civil service itself from independence in 1922, effectively committed the state to that of a subsidiary force, paying for almost the totality of Irish education, whether private or public, but permitting educational values to be set and dictated elsewhere. Barbara O'Toole (2015) observes that the long historical timeline of the Catholic church as 'an instrument' of Ireland's social and cultural modalities, fully controlled primary school education in particular, from the mid-nineteenth century down to the 1960s, so that what was originally meant to be a non-denominational system was de facto denominational (2015: 90). That started to shift, but in no substantive way, with the beginning of the Dalkey School Project and beyond that, the Educate Together movement from the 1980s, helping parents to organise non-denominational schools within the Department of Education's ambit, but this is a tiny movement. The 1998 Education Act, endeavouring to establish the principles of pluralist values in education in an increasingly diverse society, nonetheless had to work alongside the 1998 Employment Equality Act which itself contained a loophole exempting

organisations with a specific 'ethos' from fully conforming with the legislation (O'Toole 2015: 91).

The Department of Education, always cautious about challenging the
dominance of Catholic social values even as Ireland has grown steadily more
diverse in its population make-up was finally forced to tackle the basis for
admissions to Catholic-run schools with the 2018 Education (Admission to
Schools) Act, preventing Catholic-run primary schools from giving priority
of enrolment to schools to parents with evidence of baptism (C. O'Brien
2018). In a curious pairing with its cautious approach about perceived
social values, it has been in latter decades firmly committed to neoliberal
doctrines, pursuing 'education' as a mechanism for participating in a neoliberal labour market (Lynch 2001, 2006). This leaves un-interrogated and
undisturbed the continuing economic and social inequalities (O'Sullivan
2019) within Irish society, and this includes sexual inequalities. Kathleen
Lynch (2001: 402) describes this as a problem of 'non-recognition, mis-
recognition and misrepresentation' so that these damaging inequalities are
cemented into how schools work. While contemporary critical educational
theory emphasises how to help reinforce 'solidarity, intimacy, trust and care'
in our societies (Lynch 2001: 397), anchored in the 'affective domain ...
concerned with relationships of love, care and solidarity' (Lodge and Lynch
2004: 2), these are objectives with little status or meaning in current Irish
educational priorities and structures (O'Sullivan 2019). The current pre-
occupations with training and labour market outcomes (the Department
is currently known as the Department of Education and Skills) and its
long history of unreformed hierarchical relations, makes schools far from
the best settings for serious work with pupils about the affective domain
that takes in sexuality.

There is an underlying 'compulsive masculinity' in Irish schools,
maintaining in turn a 'heterosexual hegemony' which too readily feeds
sexism and homophobia (O'Higgins-Norman 2009: 4).[1] Schools are 'not
neutral actors' (Lynch 2001: 399) with the result that even when teachers do
address education about sex and sexuality, they must do so within those strict
hierarchical arrangements and with the agreement of school management

---

1   For how this plays out in the U.S. context, see Fields (2008) and Garcia (2012).

committees, teachers and parents. The Department of Education has not
entirely ignored sex and sexuality. Work on the Relationships and Sexuality
Education programme goes back to 1995 and 1996 when the Department
of Education first issued circulars requesting policies to be developed on
RSE in all post-primary schools, and from 1999, as a specific part of the
national curriculum, material was to be introduced across the school years
for all students no later than 2003.

It has been at best a dismal performance. Inglis (1998: 177) noted that
the RSE programme would require 'a new relationship between teacher
and pupil', a dialogic one to replace the old rigidities of Irish education.
This was not forthcoming. In a research report on the Department's RSE
curriculum, published in 2007, the authors (Mayock et al. 2007) carefully
treads a line between the joint publishers of the research, the deeply cautious Department itself and the Crisis Pregnancy Agency. In the foreword
to the report, the then Minister for Education, Mary Hanafin, spoke of
'significant progress' being made with the implementation of the RSE programme, though much remained to be done (ibid.: 2).

Research which had already been conducted by the Crisis Pregnancy
Agency pointed out all too clearly how unprepared psychologically and in
practical physical terms many young people were when they first engaged
sexually, reflecting not least the failure of 'sex education', often described as
'the talk', to be in any way helpful. By the mid-2000s, the Agency's research
programme had established that possibly up to a third of young people
were sexually active by the time they were 17 (Layte et al. 2006: 26; Mayock
et al. 2007) and that the steady decline in age at first sexual experience was
accompanied by a critical appraisal on the part of students themselves on
how inept they found school initiatives (Hyde and Howlett 2004: 40–1),
especially so for early school-leavers (Mayock and Byrne 2004). If schools
were asked to respond where parents appeared to find it hard to talk with
their children about sex (Mayock et al. 2007: 2), they fell disastrously
short. Far from being dialogic, the RSE programme gave the appearance
of something to be got through by teachers, who tended to rely on narrow,
text-based material rather than active discussion. There was a focus on the
biological and technical aspects of sex, and with significant gaps in knowledge, an overall approach to speaking about sex and sexuality that from

the perspective of pupils was 'too little, too late' (ibid.). The 2007 research report established that the numbers of schools delivering some aspect of an RSE programme had increased considerably to over four-fifths of the school-going population.

Yet students overall reported having little confidence in what was being delivered. More than the Catholic orientation of many schools was problematic; teachers themselves were judged by students as being embarrassed and not 'able to handle' the class (Mayock et al. 2007: 241) and while in-service teacher training to help them to teach the programme was praised by teachers, there was a sense that this entire subject was best left to 'outside' facilitation. This itself is disturbing, given that many teachers in the early 2000s would have ranged in age from their mid-20s to their mid-40s and thus would already have moved to create considerable latitude in their personal lives in how they dealt with sex and sexuality. Seemingly, however, they could not extrapolate from their own journeys what a younger generation might require.

Kristin Luker (2006) and others writing about sexuality education in the United States, including Janice Irvine (2002), Jessica Fields (2008), Lorena Garcia (2012) and Peggy Orenstein (2016, 2020), describe many of the same fault lines and issues that we have seen here in Ireland between 'conservative' and 'liberal' adult worlds reacting to and interpreting how young people should deal with having sex. Determined as both lobbies are to advance what is a 'curious mix of values and pragmatism' (Luker 2006: 253) about sex education, targeting crisis pregnancy in particular, they too often end by delivering a 'motley grab bag of experiences' (2006: 250) which ignores the primary issue of gender and the situation of young women. Luker warns us that 'the debate about sex education gets its passion from deeply felt ideas about gender and women's roles in particular' (2006: 258) and that we need to deal with this complexity. In the Irish context, we must meet this challenge by enabling young people to understand the depth of meaning that lies behind that composite phrase and patriarchal relations of control. Sexuality education should really pull apart how such control continues, the extent of its damage for young women and for young men, and how it is supported implicitly and explicitly by a rake of contemporary institutions and organisations and cultural bodies.

Identifying the meanings of sexual desire and the limitations for women of accepted heterosexual frames of reference would be a good start, but if the goal of RSE work has been to enable young women to exercise sexual agency, it has been hopelessly unsuccessful on these grounds. From a Foucauldian interpretation of the state regulating sexuality, Elizabeth Kiely notes the 'narrow subjectivities' on offer and in her analysis of the politics surrounding the introduction of the RSE programme in the late 1990s, also contends that the teaching material for both primary and secondary schools sought as one of its principle aims to develop 'a healthy attitude to sexuality and relationships' entailed in its early phases (2015: 111). But this faded to the background especially due to 'trade-offs and resource commitments to keep religious bodies and the key educational stakeholders on board with the programme implementation' (ibid.). These trade-offs included opt-out clauses for both parents and teachers who might have objections in conscience to teaching any of the material.

As cautious as the programme material was, it did lead to public debate in the media between perceived liberal and conservative factions of Irish society about teaching what were in fact very narrow interpretations of what knowledge young people might need. For example, proponents of RSE wanted to see an RSE programme which would reduce sexually transmitted illnesses and pregnancies amongst young people reduced (ibid.: 121). It is highly unlikely that these would have been the key matters in knowledge-building for young people themselves: those 'narrow subjectivities' (Kiely 2005) were no route to help them recognise themselves as sexual beings. Its conservative reading with a 'preoccupation' about penetrative heterosexual sex and the potentially disastrous outcome of a crisis pregnancy steers students towards a binary choice between only abstaining from sex or having penis-in-vagina sex: 'Limiting notions of sex to one act means that other pleasurable and, in some instances, safer conceptions of sex are unlikely to be given due consideration in lessons' (Kiely 2005: 257). It also puts in place the sense that one person – male – wants penetrative sex and the other person – female – must say yes or no, rather than encouraging young people to think of a mutually responsive and responsible stance towards one another as sexual beings. At the same time there is a strong public health tone to much of the programme, the 'liberal' approach to sex education, implying that postponing sex because of pregnancy risks is the sensible middle-class choice in terms of schooling and onward career trajectories (ibid.: 262; see also Kiely 2015).

The notion of desire as a positive force shaping how we might relate to one another is absent, its place filled by silences about the potential of the sexual body. Instead, the programme underwrites the strongest building block to preserve patriarchal relations, copulation, while largely neglecting STIs and furthermore reinforcing negative stereotypes of the female body. In a severely distorted body-conscious age, the teaching material refers to how an adolescent woman's hips get wider to 'prepare' her for 'childbearing' (Kiely 2005: 258); so much for a woman's personal agency there. Kiely quotes the feminist ethnographer, Michelle Fine, who noted these problems with sex education in 1980s America and the extent to which the avoidance of teaching about desire as a positive thing for women severely handicapped young women, most especially poorer women, 'as actual and potential victims of male desire (Fine 1988: 32)' (ibid.).

The impact of no relevant sex education for more marginalised women

This brings us firmly back to the huge problems of stratified reproduction and how individual problem-solving to achieve good sexual health at the levels of both physical and mental well-being is simply insufficient for young women in a society as unequal as Ireland.

These grievous failures may well contribute to how young women perceive themselves as having no latitude about 'giving in' to men in demands for penetrative sex. There is no question but that this is a problem made worse when other inequalities run alongside this basic one. One young woman we talked with, now a single mother with two children and who had left school at 14, vividly explains what this non-negotiable demand feels like:

> I think it's very dirty here. Definitely. I think it's very, they're very mean here. They're very … When I lived in England and I didn't want to sleep with a fella, not all fellas in England, now don't get me wrong, but the majority were fine, they were brilliant about it. Here … I think they're very nasty if you don't sleep with them. (Marie, 24, unemployed, outskirts of a small town)

Marie grew up with her grandparents in the southeast and when she left her convent-run school, she ran away to England, having her two daughters there before returning to Ireland, to that same small town. Her experiences have left her well able to judge male pressure about having sex and she simply finds it harder to deal with this pressure in an Irish context, possibly and not least because she is a single mother, with no immediate family and no father to her girls living nearby. She feels her status as a single mother coping alone does not gain her any respect, quite the opposite. It leaves her wary and very cautious.

Marie was at least fortunate in having gone to England, she was able to avail of NHS reproductive health services free at the point of use and she gradually learned about appropriate contraceptive care.

> There's a lot more help and support in England. Because they have all drop-in centres and stuff you can go to, and there's people you can talk to about … obviously, there's a place you can go and get condoms. And if I was in trouble or I was scared, I could go into them and talk to them. (Marie, 24, unemployed, outskirts of a small town)

By contrast Ireland's health policies and health services have remained stubbornly less accessible to younger unmarried women with factors of both class and geography worsening matters considerably for individuals. Condoms, for example, which should have been zero-rated when they were deregulated in 1992 have always been subject to VAT (Value Added Tax), with the 21 per cent rate only reduced in 2008 to 13.5 with continued calls to lower the VAT to zero, consistent with contraceptive pills, implants and injections (Finn 2019). This is a burden falling especially hard on those who are poorer and those who have come from smaller towns and rural areas where even getting hold of condoms can be difficult to do discreetly. Young women, and especially younger adolescent women, can easily be sexually active but will not have a medical card of their own to cover the costs of other forms of contraception.

In 1995, the Department of Health issued guidelines to all of the then
eight health boards administering primary care that 'family planning' services and related modes of service delivery needed to be evaluated so that
a comprehensive programme could be made available. The Department
repeated the same mistake made by the NHS in the UK several decades
earlier where clinics carried the name 'family planning' so as not to be seen
to be actively encouraging young women to have sex (Cook 2004: 272) In
the Eastern Health Board planning document from that time, reference
was made to 'persons with special needs such as teenagers, travellers and
drug misusers' and the need to have 'flexible methods of delivery' for such
groups (Eastern Health Board 1995: 17) without specifying how these flexible outreach services were to be developed. Otherwise, access to any forms
of contraception other than condoms could be gained only through GPs
and private charities such as the Irish Family Planning Association and
Well Woman clinics which were not widespread throughout the country
and which had to charge for their services.

From the early 2000s, the Crisis Pregnancy Agency developed and
promoted its Think Contraception programme through media advertising,
online sites, teaching DVDs and through active distribution of condom
packets at large-scale music venues and once-off events, all emphasising
the need for sexually active young people to get into the habit of consistently using contraception. While the Agency carefully pointed out in its
materials that the age of consent for sexual activity in Ireland is 17 years,[2]
it also pointed out that there is no minimum age in relation to providing
contraceptive advice and prescriptions. The IFPA, for its part, reached in to
completely new territory with a community action programme that piloted
comprehensive sexuality education for women from five disadvantaged
communities in the eastern counties, with the objective of women as parents
becoming peer educators on sex and sexuality within their communities

2   There was a change in the age of consent in the 2006 legislation, with no set min-
     imum age in Ireland at which contraceptive advice and prescriptions may be pro-
     vided. The age of consent to sexual activity is 17 and it may be a criminal offence to
     have sex with a person under the age of 17. This means that providers of contracep-
     tive services are entitled to refuse to provide those services to people under 17. In
     general, the age of consent for health services purposes is 16.

(Murphy-Lawless et al. 2008). The course was wide-ranging and was a distinctive policy response to overturn the barriers and problems of school-based sex education by building confidence and capacity directly within communities in need through the sixty-three women who participated from the five settings. The aim of giving the participants formal accreditation in sexual education training fell before the complexities of the inflexible processes laid down through the Department of Education,[3] but the programme itself was a significant undertaking by the IFPA with the participants arguably receiving a better grounding in sexual health and sexuality than that afforded to teachers within the official RSE programmes.

Rurality, poverty and the reinforcement of masculinist norms

At the other end of the country, in 2002, another critical community intervention began to take shape in Letterkenny Women's Centre, now Donegal Women's Centre. As a voluntary organisation, the centre had been providing contraception and sexual health services for women across the county since 1989. GPs in Donegal were ill-equipped to deliver a full range of contraceptive services with less than half of the GP cohort having any training in contraception (Mason 2003). The centre was acutely aware that class, status and stigma combined with older Catholic attitudes on the part of many GPs also played a role in excluding women, and that its services could step in when conservative GPs were reluctant or refused outright to respond to women's stated needs. It received health board funding to provide its services in quiet recognition of these bald facts. Donegal, a very poor county with high levels of unemployment (Combat Poverty 2005), was also a county with a young demographic profile, and those factors interacted to impinge on young women's well-being and life chances. Local community and youth workers and the centre's volunteers were very aware that although the services they were

---

3   And we note the importance of accreditation for adult women who were also early
     school-leavers.

providing were of huge assistance to women, they were less able to reach very young women who were left largely unprotected. One youth worker framed the broad issues this way:

> In rural areas, you see they haven't moved on, how stuck they are. Young women are thinking they have to get a man. For those who leave who can get out, things move on. But if you go back, you find that the difficulties in rural areas are the same while only some of it has moved on. Getting the boy is nearly the most important in their lives for girls and having sex to keep him is part of that. The traditional aim of getting a man and pleasing him is now crossed up with demands to have sex. (Emma, 31, community worker, rural area)

Knowing about the pressure to have sex, but with young women lacking clear structural support, the centre set out to document their needs and then respond to this younger group. An initial wide-ranging research report, with 153 respondents aged 17–25, documented a sorry catalogue of inadequate sex education, along with the high cost of contraception, poor communication with GPs who often stigmatised sexually active young women and poor to non-existent access to any alternatives (Kavanagh 2005). The overall recommendation, to establish a standalone sexual health clinic for young women aged 17–26 finally led to the establishment of the Ilash clinic in 2011 which was advertised through mobile apps and other social media. The clinic was delayed in starting up because of funding issues in the wake of the economic collapse of 2008 onward. In the meanwhile, the centre went ahead and developed a holistic education course on sexuality and sexual health for young women who had left school early (Higgins and Murphy-Lawless 2009), a programme which continues to run still.

What is important about the IFPA work on sexuality peer educators and the work of Donegal Women's Centre is that both initiatives proceeded from the bedrock feminist principle of beginning with women's experiences, voices and agency in determining vital practical change. This must be the starting point in identifying how and why the mainstream institutions of the Irish state continue to leave in place essentially misogynistic practices in health service provision, which we discuss in Chapter 6. These practices are visible to many women in their daily lives when they consider how the state continues to regulate their bodies by omission in failing to support them as they need on issues of sexuality education and sexual health services. However, trying to achieve any level of empowerment in the Irish health services is notoriously difficult (Burke 2009; M. O'Connor 2007) and it has consistently required a sense of political imagination and commitment to move out with the conventional modes of thought of a conservative state. From this perspective, the IFPA, Donegal Women's Centre and the Crisis Pregnancy Agency, which was a statutory agency at that time and which initiated crucial research and outreach work and helped to fund the Donegal initiatives, showed singular determination not to represent the state as usual.

With too little of such work around the country, the burden of negative experiences for women has been a heavy one and it has borne down heaviest of all on those most subject to social and economic marginalisation. We now turn to how women expressed the realities of negative experiences.

Sexuality and the remains of the Catholic church

The philosopher Michel de Certeau (1988) writes of the 'inertia' of belief in everyday living and how there is at the same time a process of '*ebbing-away*' of what people once believed that runs alongside an '*absence* of a stronger credibility' (1988: 178). We can see this at work for some of our older interviewees who found themselves in an interregnum of sorts, no longer strictly Catholic in their practices, but not yet in a completely different space. Inglis argues that in twentieth-century Ireland the confessional was the place where people admitted to their desires and passions and to the 'pleasures of the flesh': 'Priests became the experts with sole jurisdiction in this area' (Inglis 1998: 36). Betty Hilliard has also written on this, noting that in her research, it was the women who had children in the 1950s and 1960s who remembered the fear of going to confession when they were trying to avoid pregnancy because they would not be given absolution. Some came to recognise that some priests were more sympathetic than others (Hilliard 2004: 147–8) while other women refused to confess aspects of their sex lives (2004: 150). In the 1990s, the

cumulative toll first of priests' paternity cases and then the successive
scandals of sexual abuse perpetrated by clergy fatally diminished the
confessional as a site for sexual talk (see Ferriter 2004: 665–6; Hilliard
2004: 152–4). One of Hilliard's interviewees, in her 60s, articulated the
unmasking of this hypocrisy: 'That time you felt guilty, then as you got
older and hear what the priests were at – the cheek of them!' (Hilliard
2004: 152). By the late 1990s, very much younger women were picking up
on this contradiction and challenging the very idea that priests could have
any authority about sexual matters or that the confessional was in any way
a private encounter where any trust could be found in speaking out about
sex (Inglis 1998). Thus one teen talking in the late 1990s recounted her
friend's woes with her parents, she having gone to confession in the then
still customary manner:

> A girl I know, she had sex with her boyfriend and she got worried about it. And she
> went to the priest, and the priest said, 'Everything is confidential here', but he went
> back and told her parents, and told her boyfriend's parents, and she was grounded
> and they had to break up. So they're not allowed see each other anymore. That's not
> on. I mean priests just haven't really got a clue. (quoted in Inglis 1998: 139)[4]

That last statement, not having a clue, effectively became the way younger
women thought about the once powerful clergy. Amongst our interviewees, Siobhan, a 30-year-old trainee solicitor from rural Ireland, identified the Catholic church's highly publicised sex scandals as the reason
for its failure to be a force any longer in respect of sexual morality:

---

4   Hilliard (2004) documents the confusion, hurt and anger felt by women who
     recalled a lack of Church support for their poor families and desires to limit the
     number of children they had. Looking back on her distress yet acceptance of
     Church teachings, one exclaimed, 'And then I'd say, was I a simpleton? … we're
     all very cross about it. I think all the ones around my age (she was 66) are angry'
     (2004: 151). One woman in her 60s recounted the day she learned about the Bishop
     Casey affair on the radio while ironing, concluding, 'I can say it damaged my whole
     life.' She also was left vulnerable to her daughter's challenge, 'well Mam, what have
     you to say for yourself now?' and recalled, 'I sat there and I hadn't the answers for
     her but I said, "to be honest it is a bigger shock to me than it will ever by to you'"
     (Hilliard 2004: 152–3).

> The Catholic Church aren't as vocal on it [sex] because I think they're more wrapped
> up with defending their whole sexual abuse cases … I don't think they have time to
> be preaching from the pulpit about sex, because they'd have to take an about turn.
> (Siobhan, 29, solicitor, rural area)

Siobhan had been living with her partner for several years and was married just before we talked to her. Though she planned a church wedding, she refused to do the premarital course once she had spoken with her local priest about its content. Siobhan shared her reaction to what she saw as inappropriate teaching and 'a really frightening lack of insight into a sexual relationship and communication'. She was also struck by an inappropriate exercise of authority for the local parish priest to insist on a premarital course as a prerequisite for a church wedding. She argued this diktat was out of touch with where women and men are now in making their own decisions. Siobhan recounted the priest's stance:

> He said 'Right. OK then. It's part of my job, I have to recommend it, and you don't
> want to do it and I'm not going to stand in your way. I will let you be married anyway.'
> And that kind of shocked me that there was this whole permission aspect to it, as in
> 'I think you're a suitable person to be allowed to get married.' And I kind of wonder
> about people manage who maybe aren't as vocal or aren't as questioning or aren't
> as forthright in their views about sex with the whole Church and marriage thing.
> (Siobhan, 29, solicitor, rural area)

Siobhan encountered head on the tense relationship between individual rights and a decision to marry and the preferred norms about marriage which the church and its clergy were no longer able to enforce. At the same time, Siobhan is representative of the process de Certeau describes, that belief ebbs away and practices are attenuated, yet this does not happen all at once. Inglis (1998: 53) describes a shift at the end of the 1990s which at best transformed remaining practicing Catholics, who are generally older, into 'loyal critics' as people came to reflect on the importance of individual autonomy in developing a personal morality. Younger people, far more secularised now, are further away still from this position but appear to 'make room' for Catholicism as part of their cultural and historical identity of being Irish (Andersen 2010: 36). Thus Siobhan is typical of younger Irish women in that the church remains an important symbolic place for a wedding because it is space for a community to share but on terms to be negotiated with the clergy, no longer holders of significant power.

The other setting where our interviewees have directly encountered Catholic mores on sex and sexuality is within convent schools. Hyde and Howlett's research with Junior and Leaving Certificate year students found that nearly every student commented on the 'lack of influence the Church has over their lives' (2004: 33; see also D. Scally 2021). That applies to all schools, if more so for convent schools. This is not to say that nuns have not tried to exercise some control. However, it would appear from our interviewees that this ranged from the hapless to the somewhat more connected in about the realities of increasing shifts in sexual morality. Trying to avoid the topic merely made young women want to gain greater accountability from the nuns:

> Like they have health education in the convent, and like, they'll just do anything but. You'll have the workbook, and you'll see the sex education part coming up. And you can't wait, because it's actually something interesting. And they'll stay off it for as long as they can. And when they finally touch on it, it's for half a class, and that's it, it's gone. It's done as far as they're concerned. And they'll spend four weeks doing like personal hygiene, or something stupid like that. And it's just ridiculous. For schools and convents like, you'd have to go to the nuns and say 'If you're so against teenage pregnancy, why won't you let people in to talk to us?' and I know they're against contraception as well, but even to make them aware. (Una, 22, retraining, village near a small town)

Sarah describes how her class in a convent school took advantage of a much older nun who had been given the task of attending to sex education:

> I remember a specific event with an old nun, she must have been sixty-five, seventy, in our social studies class, gave us our sex education thing. And our class asked a lot of questions. We asked, and I think a lot of the questions, we wanted to ask, but a lot of them were asked probably to put the nun in an uncomfortable position. She answered all of our questions, but we got into trouble later over it. That ... we should not have done that. (Sarah, 30, teacher, metropolitan area)

Any discussion on sex and sexuality appeared to work at least partially if the nuns endeavoured to connect personal development with a wider education on social issues and to bring in outside facilitators:

It was, it was Catholic. It was the Holy Faith, but yeah, it was nice, it was just part of the religious programme. I mean some weeks we'd have [Irish] Travellers come in, we'd have people from Amnesty come in, various religious groups … we had refugees come in, it was great. (Jennifer, 24, shop assistant, city)

Actually our school wasn't bad, we went to a convent school, and we were all fully expecting the talk to be sort of 'Keep your knees together young ladies!' But we had, I'm not quite sure where she was from, possibly the Catholic Marriage Advisory Council, a sort of speaker in. And she was excellent. She went through all the different options in a very, very matter of fact way. (Sadhbh, 31, computer operative, metropolitan area)

One young woman represented something of an exception for a number of reasons. She adhered to her parents' Catholic tenets about sex and sexuality, was engaged to be married but had no intention of having sex until she was married although she would, she said use the contraceptive pill so as not to have children straightaway:

For me it would have been my parents. I would have been brought up I suppose in quite a religious kind of background, I'm RC northern. I think in the north you're brought up with a very strong sense of Catholic identity so to speak. For me it would have been primarily at home yeah. I suppose my mother more so than my father probably but, definitely it was at home. And to be honest I haven't used any contraception, the main reason being I'm a virgin. So I'm actually getting married next year, and I would think to use the pill, yeah. (Caoimhe, 25, project manager, rural area)

This young Northern Irish woman, living and working in the Republic, and her explanation about the importance of Catholic identity may be linked to how a more conservative Catholicism continues to play a role in Northern Ireland, less as a marker of national identity and more to do with community-building post the peace process (Mitchell 2005).

Sex education from other directions

The absence of reliable, open and informative sex education in all schools, convent or otherwise, came over strongly from almost all our interviewees.

In pace of solid education was neglect, negativity, mis-information and also an attempt to shock:

> Nothing except in first year we had a lady who came in two Fridays in a row, who explained the basic facts to us. And it was not discussed in the rest of school, except for within friends. (Agnes, 29, financial advisor, metropolitan area)

> We had it in fifth year, the teacher, she was the one who actually would sit there and tell us that French kissing was a mortal sin because the boy was entering your body. I mean, we were just sitting looking at her going 'Riiiight … whatever.' And I remember my sixth class teacher talking about 'You know, you see those girls, hanging around the town centre … the girls with prams'. (Mona, 26, health worker, small town)

> I mean, ours was drawings, cross sections, and a sample of a tampon, that was it like. That's what we had. But certainly nothing about relationships and emotions. (Bernadette, 30, catering manager, small city)

> I think more education in school and more open discussion in small groups of young people, rather than someone coming in. When I was at school a woman came in and taught us about sex with matchstick men. Like it was so ludicrous and it was just a lecture for us and we all went home. Whereas small group discussion, open frank discussion about the reality of STDs and pregnancy and just being able to say no. The reality of becoming a sexually active being. That's the most important thing. (Marcella, 28, civil servant, small town)

This woman, looking back at her teenaged years, commented on how schools end up concentrating on exactly the wrong thing which they do not wish to explore in depth in any case:

> There's a piece of all that missing in our education system, around people getting to know who they are and what they are. Sex is just a small piece of it. You don't know how to say no or how to say yes or what you want unless you've explored some of that. (Ciara, 27, midwife, small city)

One retrospective view of sex education in school awarded brickbats to the Department of Education:

> Nah, it's a bit faffy about, really, it's very vague. It's a typical department document, characteristic of loads of policy documents, and training documents that come from the government, which is aspirational in some ways, and then translates into non-specific stuff. And I also don't think that a document on its own, or a training package on its own is enough. You've got to have the backing of the schools and the teachers

behind it. And then you have to have family support. It has to be a whole deal. And I think it has kind of been pushed to one side, and I think there's a tendency for schools who don't want to deal with it, they don't have to. So it's not a holistic thing at all. (Joan, 34, civil servant, small town)

In this societal vacuum, parents did what they could. Many did not try to talk with their daughters beyond the absolute basics of menstruation. Others who attempted to discuss sex with their children appeared hobbled by naivete and embarrassment, repeating the mistakes and omissions of the schools:

I daren't go to my parents about anything to do with sex. And I was terrified about my mother asking me did I know about it, because I'd have to say no, and then she might tell me, and I was 'Oh my God!'. But myself and my brother would have tried to discover information together. I remember getting the instructions from the Tampax box, and the two of us looking at it, and looking at the inside of a woman! We must have been really young at that point. (Roisin, 24, student nurse, small city)

In regards of like sex and stuff like that, it was never spoken about, that stuff because she never knew, and that's the way she learned from her parents. She learned from her parents, and I, like, I was young. I even thought by kissing a fella that you could become pregnant. You know? Or even touching. Everything runs through your head and you think 'Oh my God, could I be pregnant?' And you kind of, that stays there with you until the end of the month when your period comes. Because we didn't know enough. And we didn't, schools never taught us enough in regards to that end of things. And regards of STDs. They never said a word, never. And they still don't, to this day. (Danielle, 27, unemployed, working-class city area)

First birds and bees, it was my mother and I was ten. And believe it or not, I had absolutely no suspicion before she told me so I was like 'No way! You're kidding me!' And the way she did it was so sweet. She produces this book which was one of these rather holy catholic books, but it was nice, it was meant to be sort of accessible for children. The first thing they talk about is all about how mummies and daddies fall in love, and God is a big blue triangle, but he's a nice big blue triangle. (Mona, 26, health worker, small town)

Aoife, remembered her mother broaching sex and contraception, seemingly with the knowledge that her daughter was sexually active:

There was one sit-down session, that was really broad and general, and pretty much went through everything. And she was really embarrassed, and I was kind of sitting there just being embarrassed for her , then throughout my life, she'd just kind of say 'Now you are being careful?' … and she'd do it in the most delicate ways, like 'Take care of yourself.' (Aoife, 22, shop manager, city)

A few women had supportive mothers who apparently drew on their own experiences in enabling them to grasp the issue. Sarah's mother did so from the outset:

My mother would have been very much a pro-choice and out there, a bit of a campaigner. So, certainly found out about sex and how it works at a very early age, three or four really, and there was no issue about not being able to discuss that. When I was eighteen, I got contraceptives for my birthday even though I had no intention of doing anything with them, so it was like a symbolic 'Go out there and have fun!' (Sarah, 30, teacher, metropolitan area)

My mum's a pharmacist and I mean because she sees so many young people coming into her in the chemist looking for the morning after pill because they can't afford to pay the doctor. That's why I think she's so, open. It's the same with my two older sisters, once they had boyfriends that was it. And I mean it was a completely open thing, and if she knew like, if you went into her in the shop you'd get the talk in front of no matter who was there! Like if you had come in for an antibiotic, she'd be 'Now you know this doesn't work, your pill doesn't work with this.' And she'd always, it wasn't a case of being subtle, that's probably the best way. She'd be the same to any of our cousins. (Marie-Therese, 24, retraining scheme, village near small town)

Friends, peers and older sisters also became an inevitable mainstay:

Mainly friends in school. Like, not my Mum, she gave me the basic sex education talk, which was nothing. It was always my friends at school. (Maureen, 33, self-employed, small town)

My peer group, pretty much totally. And then as I grew older and got less embarrassed talking about it, it would have been my sisters. But certainly in school, yeah, you go by what you hear from your friends. And that's pretty much all. It wasn't discussed in any kind of a class or anything like that. (Agnes, 29, financial advisor, metropolitan area)

And I suppose stuff came from older sisters as well. I'd say something and they'd say, 'No, that's crap, listen here.' (Louise, 24, customer services, city)

I think if you're from a bigger family you learn from your older brothers and sisters. Because I had five before me, so you do learn. My younger sister was a lot sharper and quicker than all of us, at that age of eighteen. (Brenda, 28, farmer, rural area)

The other source of support became the British teenaged magazines aiming at a young female teenaged-market:

> Probably where I learned most practical stuff was English teenage magazines. We'd have these, *Just Seventeen* and *Nineteen*. There were kids of thirteen, fourteen writing in going 'Oh I want to have sex with my boyfriend' and they would always say, well, if you think you're ready for it, be really sensible, bla bla bla. And it was all really sensible advice. It was absolutely the only place that gave you any sensible copped on advice about sex. To the extent of explaining words that you'd hear, and of course couldn't possibly let on that you didn't know the meaning of at fourteen years of age, and I'd say they were probably the lifesaver. (Jane, 28, scientist, small city)

> We used to get, what was it, the one with the position of the fortnight, *More*. And I remember we used to get it every two weeks, and most of the magazines, we all got them. And they were then banned in the school, and my mum was saying just don't bring them in, she didn't have a problem with it, she'd rather us know. She had the book out, I think at about thirteen or fourteen, and we'd sit around and all talk about it and discuss, and it was the worst, to sit with your sisters, but you did it like, and then it was out of the way. But yeah the magazines were all banned, and we weren't allowed have them. (Lucy, 24, student nurse, small city)

In the face of parental embarrassment and the almost complete dereliction of duty on the part of the Irish education establishment, young women nevertheless seized on what material they could to inform themselves and to help them think about their emotions and feelings.

Problems of contraceptive access and expense

What the official silences, educational lacunae and parental discomfiture create unwittingly is a negative weighting for women about what is viewed as the worst consequence of having sex, namely unwanted pregnancy. This makes it harder for women to be clear about the necessity of having access to and using contraception:

> If you educated beforehand, if you make contraception available to people, if you make them understand what the consequences are, like disease or pregnancy, then

maybe people would take more care. But it's not in your face, it really isn't. (Hazel, 29, sales manager, city)

In and of itself, this creates a sort of nervous response of, 'it won't happen to me', either having sex or becoming pregnant. Having sex and not thinking about consequences can be recast as individuals being 'stupid' rather than a failure on the part of the Irish state and society to address women's sexual protection:

> When I was young, I didn't do anything that was stupid, but there again, I didn't think about it. And if I had been in a position where I didn't know any better, and I didn't really think about it, and no one was blowing it in my ear the whole time, like 'use a condom, use protection, use contraception', I probably would have gone off and did what I wanted to do, like. You were like 'Ah sure, it'll be grand.' (Louise, 24, customer services, city)

Yet people are 'stupid' in the course of their ordinary social lives precisely insofar as they are not enabled or encouraged to think about their needs in being sexually active:

> You know, where somebody picks you up, or you pick them up or you get together in the pub, and one thing leads to another, that's the way these things happen. (Aisling, 24, nurse, small city)

> Women don't see they have a need for contraception. They're engaging in sexual activities, they don't see that they have a need for that as well, do you know what I mean, that it's still a man's thing, he gets his needs met and that's it. And then the woman ends up in the situation of no condoms. And if it was open from the start, the woman would have known what to do. (Clodagh, 25, IT worker, suburban area)

> Like, you get a young girl that has gone into a nightclub, pissed out of her head, and she ends up sleeping with this fella. I mean, I had to learn this myself, I had to learn myself, and I was the one who that carried condoms with me because my first partner was HIV+ and I found out I needed to protect myself. So you need more information, and you need it more around the nightclubs and stuff. (Deirdre, 30, community worker, working-class city area)

As we have already alluded to in Chapter 2, gaining access to contraception is easier for older teenaged women or young adults from a middle-class background or, for example, where there is access to college health services. Women's access to safer sex information, knowledge, and methods varies widely, as does their experiences of social support for 'taking care of themselves'. This reflects not only individual confidence and whether or not women have the skills to seek resources, but also takes in geographic location and social support. The primary gatekeepers include parents, particularly mothers, doctors or pharmacists, sisters and friends. Having to deal with gatekeepers raises concerns about privacy and how one would be seen if seeking contraception and we found these were paramount in many women's minds.

This woman expresses exasperation as she attempts to act sexually responsible, yet is reprimanded by her mother:

> I went to the doctor to get the pill, and I was seventeen, and eh ... I went in and he was grand, and I just said I wanted to go on the pill, and he didn't ask me. I was thinking he's going to ask me my age and he's going to ask this and that. But it was 'grand, right, there you go, if you've any problems, come back' and that was it. And he was grand like. And I was worried cos he was my family doctor and I was going, 'I know he's not supposed to tell, but what if he does?' And then at the end, cos my mother kept going on about 'make sure you don't get pregnant' and all this, and I left it out on my dresser in my bedroom. And then she comes in 'Don't be leaving your pill out for me to see!' I was like 'What do you want?' You know? 'Try to reassure you that I'm being careful like, and then you're giving out to me for it!' (Aisling, 24, student, small city)

It seems that this mother's message, 'don't get pregnant,' was interpreted by her daughter to mean 'use safer sex' and not 'don't have sex' (see Garcia 2012). Communication between them about their expectations of one another was anything but direct. Negotiating parental expectations is a complex area, especially when parental concerns focus on not getting pregnant and parents are slow to offer positive and practical support to ensure that young women are protected from pregnancy. Claire describes a good 'talking to' that she received from her mother when it was discovered that she was sexually active. She was told of the bad consequences of having sex and possibly becoming pregnant:

> More like, 'You have your whole life to look forward to and what's the point?' Because at the time two of my cousins were pregnant and the father didn't bother sticking

about. And it was a case of [my boyfriend] 'will do the same to you if you got pregnant, and the fella'll not bother to stick by you' and all of that. (Claire, 20, unemployed, outskirts of a small town)

Joanne described how her mother was not willing to discuss sexual topics with her. This silence had to do with her mother's discomfort and perception about her daughter's sexual knowledge:

My mum wouldn't be open at all. When we were growing up I think she just decided to herself one day that we already knew everything so she wouldn't bother telling us. Like she never, you know the way some mothers will sit down and be like 'So ...' and you know they're about to start having that topic, and you're like 'Ah no mam, it's OK, we learned it at school' and they're like 'OK!', she didn't even do that! She just assumed that we knew. (Joanne, 23, unemployed, outskirts of small town)

Many young women also struggle with how to find contraception and with what form of contraception might be appropriate:

And access to contraception, personally I wouldn't have had any problems accessing contraception, mainly that's because I've been in a position where I could access it. But I'm sure there's plenty of women who find it very difficult to access contraception, and don't have any options possible when it comes to, you know, even around types of contraception, knowing the pros and cons of which methods. (Laura, 26, accounts manager)

Positive first sexual experiences are far less likely if young women must face alone the responsibility of contraception. Despite all the talk of sex, being sexually active remains hidden in many women's younger years. This is complicated further by their lack of knowledge about forms of contraception and where to obtain any without calling unwelcome attention to one's self. In other words, a young woman cannot *with confidence* announce that they are active sexually, whether or not they are 'responsibly' seeking contraception. This poses a considerable risk for much younger women, as with Karen, who began to have sex while still 13 years old:

I was still so young. I knew nothing about contraception. It was nothing really discussed by anybody. I knew of it, the name, but nothing really about it. (Karen, 23, back to work trainee, village)

If women are fortunate, disclosure to friends can be a real help:

> When I was around seventeen and I was still at the convent, one of my friends, she
> was in the relationship for a few months, and she'd never had sex. She came to me
> and she knew I had been on it [the pill] for a couple of years like, and she knew at
> that stage I knew all about it. And she was like 'I think I'm ready, and I really want to
> do it like.' And I says right, 'You're not doing anything unless you go on the pill.' And
> she was like 'Right what do I do like?' and I was like 'Right we'll go to the doctor and
> get you on the pill, and you can do it afterwards like.' So I made the appointment,
> and I went with her. (Marie-Therese, 24, retraining scheme, village near a small town)

> There's a girl that we would know locally, she was like sleeping with different people
> a lot. So I said 'Maybe you should just go on the pill.' I had just got the thing in my
> arm (contraceptive implant) at the time, and she was mesmerized by this thing. 'That
> stops you getting pregnant! Imagine!' And I said 'Why don't you just go on the pill
> like.' She was what, twenty-one at the time? She first of all thought that she couldn't
> get pregnant because she couldn't have an orgasm. And then she says 'Well, how does
> the pill work?' (Pauline, 23, unemployed, village near a small town)

Women continue to have to negotiate feelings of confidence, stigma,
blame and responsibility when they do find their way to sexual health services and providers. Yet women have a right to an understanding about the
messiness of this most intensely social activity of having sex and of being
secured from any adverse consequences. Our interview participants could
see the former as an abstract principle but struggled with the latter and with
the consequent labelling of their decisions, often by the women themselves:

> But there's a certain stigma, attached to going in, a young girl going in and saying 'I
> want to go on the pill.' That's the problem. If you could go in without people looking
> at you and saying 'Look at her!' That is the problem. That's why young girls aren't
> going in and that's why young girls are getting pregnant. But I don't think you're
> going to solve that, I think that … that's the way people's attitudes are. (Liz, 20,
> bank clerk, small city)

The search for contraception is complicated by a lack of anonymity and
consequent stigma which is an especially difficult issue in small towns and
more rural areas:

> Yeah, there's huge issues around confidentiality and embarrassment around going
> into a local chemist for contraception. I grew up in a rural area but I don't live there

anymore. But I can't imagine if I was living there, how I would access that contraception. I probably wouldn't know as much as I do now anyhow, and I wouldn't have that access if I was still there. I'm sure it'd be the talk of the town as well like. Local chemist, everybody knows each other, it's just there's huge barriers there like, and the person that works in the doctor's is your neighbour or whatever. (Kate, 30, health services administrator, rural area)

The increasing number of chemists' outlets in nearby small towns and, of course, latterly the internet helped to widen access to condoms as contraception if nothing else, but the issue overall continues to be complicated by the strong feelings of lack of privacy and the fear of being exposed or condemned for being sexually active:

I mean, unless maybe you're living in a massive city somewhere, where there's a chance you're going to go in somewhere and not know anybody like. But nearly every chemist in the town, you know somebody, or someone'll see you, someone who doesn't work there will be there and you know, you always seem to get caught in the act of walking to the counter with something. (Una, 22, retraining, village near a small town)

There has been an intense concern about being identified as a sexually active young woman within a smaller community and the fear of being judged, either by health care personnel or by people within the wider community, and this can weigh heavily:

It's really, really daunting … because people are driving past and they can see you going in, and they're like 'well'. You're being judged yeah. (Claire, 20, unemployed, outskirts of a small town)

There has also been a strong sense of needing to defend one's status as a sexually active young woman often by having to deny that status. In this instance below, Emer's boyfriend actually took on this task but avoided stating directly that they were in a sexual relationship:

I remember about two years ago being in the doctor's surgery, just because I had like a stomach ulcer. And my boyfriend of the time was with me, and like about two weeks later we were out, and one of his kind of mutual friends, he wouldn't know him really well, and he was like 'Oh, I hear she's pregnant' and he was like 'No, she's not like.' And it was like 'Oh such-and-such seen the two of you up at the doctor's surgery', and he was like 'And is that all you can go to the doctor's surgery for?' So

> I mean, if they're thinking that about a doctor's surgery, do you know what I mean? (Emer, 20, student, small city)

Managing one's contraceptive needs in relation to emergency contraception (EC) was problematic up to 2011 when it was made available over the counter:

> Well I actually know as well from one of my friends last year, she needed the morning after pill, and it was on like a Tuesday. She didn't know where to get it. She just didn't know, and it was in the evening, and by the time he had gotten out of her bed and left and gone home it was like evening time and the doctor's surgery was closed. And she didn't know what to do. (Joanne, 23, unemployed, outskirts of a small town)

Trying to access EC also means managing potential disapproval and judgmental attitudes from health care providers. Here is Sonia's account of being referred to a health centre GP for EC:

> So literally, when you open the door you say 'We were referred over here' and he was like 'Oh right, the morning after pill?' But I had to get it. And then about a month later I had to get it again. And I didn't want to go back to him and say 'Right I need it again.' So I went back with this rigmarole about how the girl that I live with needed it, and she had been home for the weekend, and she couldn't get it in her home town because her mother knew the doctor, and she was really badly stuck and all the rest. And he was like 'Right, well only this one time, I really shouldn't give it to you, she really should be here and I need to talk to her.' I just felt like, it's not even that he'd tell anybody, I was kind of gone past that. Like it doesn't matter who he tells. Like he actually did say he knew some of my family from up around here, he knew the name. It wasn't that, it was more that he would actually judge me. You know, that he would be like 'What is she doing?' (Sonia, 19, student, suburban area)

There is a hint of defiance in Sonia's voice as she speaks about not caring who might or might not be told locally about her seeking EC. But there is no particular trust in any professional undertaking of confidentiality, especially when a doctor in that context, even perhaps in a friendly conversational way, comments that he knows a woman's family. She feels vulnerable about being judged by him as irresponsible.

Ellen, seeking out EC when she was away from home, traveling round the country for her work, rang up the nearest GP she could find in the local telephone directory prepared to hold her ground. While the encounter worked out for her, even she felt obliged to say to the GP that she was not drunk, and she wondered how a much younger woman with far less confidence might cope:

> I said 'Listen, I'm going to be very straight with you. I'm looking for a prescription of the morning after pill' and he said 'That's no problem, do you know where we are? Can you come in now and I'll see you now, in between appointments.' So that was a very positive experience. And I walked in, and he was a fairly young guy, probably about my age. And I kind of said 'I wasn't drunk or anything!' and he said 'Oh that's not my problem anyway!', he was very easy going about it and it was a very positive experience. But what we thought about after was, what if it had been a sixteen-year-old local, looking for the morning after pill, and the only place I can get it is freaking Limerick, and how do I get to Limerick? I have to go to school, do you not understand? So that was a very, very strong eye opener for me, in that OK, here I was thirty something, with a car, with my partner, with money, you know, we could manage this, it wasn't any hassle. But what if it had been a different situation? (Ellen, 33, self-employed small business, rural area)

As Ellen implies, it is a far greater burden for younger women and dependent on whom they encounter:

> I remember going for the morning after pill. I was dating someone, I'd say for about a year or two, and it [period] was late and the fear set in. And I went into one of the family planning clinics. I would have been in my Leaving Cert. year when I went in, and petrified wasn't the word like. And you're trying to be responsible, but you don't feel that responsible, you feel like you've actually done something wrong. I didn't know much about it, I didn't know how the morning after pill worked, but I was at the door the first thing in the morning. The nurse was lovely, the doctor was horrible. Horrible. Did I think I was silly enough not to use a condom? Like, with me it was a burst condom and I was trying to explain that I hadn't been stupid enough to have it without a condom and in the end I just shut up. Out the door, out past the nurse, last time I was ever going to enter into anything like that. Oh, they just make you feel like dirt. It really is an awful experience, especially when you're young like. (Lucy, 24, nursing student, small city)

Reflecting on the meaning of 'responsibility' and her own experience of having taken EC pills three times, Sadhbh stated:

> One occasion, just due to my own stupidity. I blame half a bottle of wine. And the other two times just due to an accident with the condom. And obviously it's preferable

to the alternative [seeking a termination], but still not the most fun experience. (Sadhbh, 31, computer operative, metropolitan area)

Judging oneself harshly for not dealing well with contraception was commonplace could be made worse depending on the responses of service providers:

> I've been to the _____ on _____ Street a couple of times, and I have to say I don't like them. Or possibly I don't like a particular doctor that I saw there. I saw her for the morning after pill once, whereupon she managed to get the impression that I was being horrendously irresponsible for not being on the pill … I was already feeling reasonably bad because, 'Oh my God, this mightn't work!' Angry, actually. Really, like, 'Stop, don't lecture me, I'm in here trying to do the best I can for myself.' But as I said, in sharp contrast to the _____ people who have been very much like, 'Oh well, better safe than sorry', and very helpful and very informative. (Heather, 26, local authority worker)

Sadhbh's and Heather's comments reveal distinct negativity about how they and others deal with sex. Sadhbh labels herself as 'stupid' for not using contraception all the time, while Heather relates that a clinic doctor made her feel 'irresponsible' because she'd opted against the contraceptive pill. She also suggests that lecturing and disapproval are not appropriate health care responses, and that she had internalised 'feeling bad'. Sadhbh points out that young Irish women could usefully demand as best practice in sexual health service provision the lighter message, 'better safe than sorry' and that service providers ought to respect women's feelings that by seeking EC, they are trying to do 'the best they can' for themselves.

Not surprisingly, in addition to consideration of the meaning of accessing contraception, the expense – in all its forms – was certainly an issue for young women:

> First I used condoms, and still do cos I can't take the pill, as I discovered. So yeah, the first thing I realized I was going to be resigning myself to considerable expense. Condoms are very expensive. Extraordinarily expensive. And obviously they aren't as foolproof as other methods, which means you open yourself to the possibility of unwanted pregnancy or having to take the morning after pill, which is also phenomenally expensive. (Jacqueline, 30, financial services, suburban area)

I find with the health checks in the clinics, you go in for your six-month prescription, and you pay for the doctor's appointment, which is basically just taking your blood pressure and your weight. And no one has ever checked my body, or told me how to examine my breasts or whatever. Just weight and blood pressure and you're out the door. And you're given six month's supply, and that'll be seventy Euro for that. (Eilish, 24, IT programmer, suburban area)

And if you're so broke, you have to say to yourself, I can't afford to go back to the doctor's and then you come off the pill. That's what happened me, I came off it because I can't actually afford to go to the doctor. (Molly, 29, restaurant worker, small city)

Several respondents spoke of how their fear of pregnancy had induced almost an obsession about using contraception:

For me, I know that I got through my teens with, almost like a mantra of 'Don't get pregnant, don't get pregnant, whatever you do, don't get pregnant.' It's only in the last couple of years I realized that's still going on in my head and I have had unprotected sex once in my life. Unprotected from a pregnancy perspective. I have almost always been on the pill or using a diaphragm or something like that. (Maureen, 33, self-employed, small town)

At the same time, this fear of getting pregnant did not translate for all women into consistent contraceptive usage, underscoring firmly the fact that fear alone is not an adequate prophylactic or basis for the practice of safer sex. With the exception of one respondent, all had experiences of unprotected sex. Thinking back to what she would have wanted in place at the time she started having sex, Aine, who fell pregnant as a teenager, shared wistfully:

I suppose, when I got into the relationship with [my son's] dad, to be able to go to somebody. But I was very shy. Very, very shy. Just to have had the confidence, like my Mam had never said to me, 'If you want to go on the pill, or whatever, come to me and I'll go to the doctor's with you.' I would have liked her to be able to have said that to me. Or to have the confidence myself to go to the doctor and ask for it myself. But I just didn't have it. (Aine, 24, invoicing clerk, city)

The reiteration of the need for young women to have greater confidence in coming to terms with their sexual desires and safer sex is remarkable in that the burden of sexual responsibility continues to be on a woman. The emphasis is on an individual's safer sex goals, as distinct from a couple's shared safer sex cooperation. Protection from pregnancy, rather than sexually transmitted infections, was the highest expressed concern we heard from women, and the contraceptive pill stood out as the perceived 'best' method. Use of the pill is inevitably dictated by the need to feel secure about not becoming pregnant once a woman is sexually active, and is a method that is invisible to others and controlled by her alone. Yet it is difficult to consistently use the pill, and a woman is reminded daily of her sexual responsibility, or transgression of it, if she fails to take the pill for any reason (Littlejohn 2021). There is no correlate for men yet, despite scientists' efforts to develop a so-called 'Male Pill,' or male hormonal contraceptive methods (see Oudshoorn 2003; Oaks 2015; see also Almeling 2020). This should not mean, however, that women ought to shoulder solely the burden of safer sex. Few women pointed this out, demonstrating how engrained the individualised message about 'protecting yourself' has become.

Making sense of contraceptive responsibility

If women judge themselves harshly about not using contraception, reflecting the often-poor attitudes of sexual health services, it can and is often fraught when making a decision about whether or not they alone are responsible for each sexual encounter and much depends on relationship status.

> Dealing with relationships and the being sexually active, it's complicated. To what extent are you with a fella, for just a night, or are you with him longer? I think it's probably more acceptable to be with someone for a one-night stand than it was like. But whether that's throwing up issues about contraception too. (Aine, 24, invoicing clerk, city)

As Aine states, what counts as 'responsible' sexual and contraceptive behaviour for a woman when with from her sexual partner can be deeply complicated. While women have varied emotional and physical preferences for different types of safer sex methods, they also implied that while they understood safer sex messages, younger women in particular were far less likely to heed them, directly related to that lack of wider social support from education and health services.

This sense of not being able to see their actions as responsible colours women's experiences of when they do not practice safe sex and the reasons that lie behind that non-practice. There can be major difficulties in negotiating with a male partner about whether he or the woman is responsible for contraception. A woman may through a series of often precarious encounters, where to raise the issue of safe sex or to refuse sex is to risk being left on one's own, unless a woman has the confidence to insist:

> Yeah. And a couple of times I've slept with fellas, and I've spoken to them about protection, and as soon as I've said protection, they kind of walk away. Some fellas they don't want to use it. So if you really like this fella and you want to sleep with him, then you'll sleep with him. (Pauline, 23, unemployed, village near small town)

> Last year this guy, and I think he's nearly forty, and he wasn't going to use a condom, and I was like, I was really shocked, really, really shocked. It was like 'Are you mad?' And he was going 'Oh, I never thought of it.' I was kind of going 'You don't know where I've been either like!' I could have been around anywhere, you know what I mean? Not saying that I've been anywhere, but really that's how he should treat it. Like he doesn't know where I've been, he doesn't know who I've slept with, and who they've slept with. I was really shocked. (Shauna, 26, nursing student, small city)

Not expecting contraceptive responsibility from a man with whom one is having occasional, once-off or unexpected sex may simply be easier within a heavily male-dominant paradigm within which women still have limited possibilities to exert their own autonomy. Even then, women may not construe their actions as responsible, because the issue of safety from pregnancy may be defined as more important, despite the other issue of STIs:

> Well for me, I'd stay on the pill. I'm not in a relationship now, and I'm still on it, because, you know if that does happen, at least you are covered for yourself, more than anyone else. You know, that's the main priority. (Linda, 29 unemployed, rural area)

> They just don't care. As long as they're getting some, they don't care what the circumstances are, who you've been with or who you are or where you've been, or anything,

they just don't care. They really don't. I have never ever met anybody that does. (Orla, 22, Ban garda, small town)

Kathryn actually eschews that her use of the pill is a responsible action despite her indicating the failure on the part of men she has encountered to be pro-active about contraceptive use. It simply could not enter the conversation:

> Responsible would be a bad word. I take the pill because I'm happier knowing I'm in control. So it wouldn't be I feel responsible for it. Partner wise, I've never been in … like it's never really come up. Like, yes, there is the fellas there that I wouldn't, they'd be gone, you know they'd be gone. And they'd be the ones that would be gone. But they'd never turn 'round and say 'No, I'll do something about it [contraception].' So it's, no, I'm taking the pill and that's it. (Kathryn, 34, animal groomer, small city)

Even within the relative stability of a relationship, there is only a bit more freedom to assert your contraceptive needs:

> I think there's more freedom to kind of, once you're in a relationship, to be who you want to be and do what you want to do. But I think, especially on one-night stands or on those sort of times, if there's someone you like and you're starting to have sex with that person, or making a decision whether to have sex with them or not, I think there's a lot of issues around that still. I think there's still a hell of a lot of people, even with sexually transmitted diseases and HIV, I think a lot of people aren't using contraception. I mean it's quite common for peers of mine, you know, when I spoke to them, to say, 'Oh no, we didn't use anything.' (Emily, 29, community worker, small town)

This ambivalence about being sexually active seems to create a pattern of variable contraceptive usage moving across a mix of no use and EC to condoms to using the pill in a steady relationship:

> If I wasn't in a relationship, I probably wouldn't be on the pill. (Sinead, 27, nurse)

> Well most of the time I'm mostly in a relationship, so it's kind of that I would use a condom for the first while, and then after, I dunno, maybe after like, two months or something. (Caoimhe, 25, project manager, rural area)

> But then I think you're reluctant to go on the pill when you're not in a relationship. There's a real feeling of declaration about that, do you know what I mean? And I'm conscious I'm still feeling it now. That going on the pill if you're not in

a long-term relationship says 'I'm a big fucking slag!' And even though all of your
lovely Contemporary Woman, post-modern maturity goes 'No! You're taking responsibility bla bla' but you just have the hangover from whatever it is … whatever
baggage it is. (Mona, 26, health worker, small town)

Emer, whose experiences of summer work in a German bar we have encountered above and which led her to see sharply contrasting attitudes,
was amazed at how a young German woman responded to being sexually
active:

I know one German girl in particular. I mean, she was a lot younger than, she was
only like seventeen. And there was girls there who had just arrived over, about four
or five Irish girls, and they were going out on the night out. And your one says 'Right,
has everyone got their condoms and everything?' and if you saw the four new Irish
girls' faces hit the floor and come back up. And your one took out her bag, handed
a condom out to everyone, and like lipstick or something! Everything had to be
there for a good night out, just in case, phone, fags, lipstick, *condoms!* (Emer, 20,
student nurse, small city)

Such a matter-of-fact insistence on contraceptive preparedness was rare
amongst the young women we spoke with.

Carrying the weight of 'slut', 'slapper' and 'town bicycle'

The suggestion of carrying condoms opened up the issue of whether
women have the 'right' to have sex when and how they want which brings
us to what is accurately termed the 'slut' discourse. As Leora Tanenbaum
(2000, 2015) has written at length, this is a punishing labelling of women
which has its historical roots in the absolute denial that young women
should have any sexual desire whatsoever. It shadows the lives of many
women still:

And I think women still feel, well in my experience anyway, obviously I'm
generalising here, but women still feel carrying condoms at times will make them
to be perceived as kind of easy, or expecting to have sex. (Emily, 29, community
worker, small town)

While many of our interviewees acknowledged without difficulty that they have had numbers of sexual partners, the notion still prevails that they must be careful in how they are seen to do so. The double standard of sexual morality continues to have real and concrete effects for them and carrying condoms in their handbags, as the young German woman was doing, sends out a potentially risky message.

> I would always have thought that it's fair enough for women to be sexually active, but for women to openly say that they want sex, and that they want this and that and the other, then it's like 'Oh my God, slapper!' you know? (Louise, 24, customer services, city)

> It still is like if I had condoms in my bag, I would be like hiding them in my bag. Like even older friends would think things if I had condoms in my bag, because it looks like you're going out looking for it. You know that kind of way? (Maeve, 26, financial services, small city)

> I think it is quite ironic, because if you talk to men, and you said to a man, well if you went out tonight and met a girl and she went home with you and slept with you, what would you think of her? 'Oh slapper'. And I'm saying 'But what if she wanted it, she wanted you, she went out and got you, and she got it and that was it?' 'Ah no, no.' They'd be saying 'It's not the same for men as women.' (Molly, 29, restaurant worker, small city)

The effects of this double standard remain very deep-rooted, particularly in small towns or rural settings, where they linger in young women's lives especially:

> If it's a man it's fine, it's perfectly acceptable for a fella, a guy to go on, and boast about it, but if it's a woman, totally opposite, there's this whole thing. (Aine, 24, invoicing clerk, city)

> You have a name then. 'Oh you're a slut', like. (Jennifer, 24, shop assistant, city)

In a small town, the potential for licentious stories to spread can be felt as truly damaging:

> And then there's this thing where men, I've heard this a few times, where they'll say 'Oh that wan's a right wan, and it's all well and good to go out with them or whatever, but you wouldn't marry her, bad reputation, she's not the type.' Because she's had a few partners. (Pauline, 23, unemployed, village near a small town)

Younger women can fall into the trap of describing one another this
way, presumably in order to disassociate themselves from their own
vulnerabilities about having a potentially vulnerable reputation. This
exchange between three interviewees shows this disturbing dynamic
at work:

> Here's a girl in the town and she's just like (Marie-Therese, 24, retraining scheme,
> village near a small town)
>
> A slapper! (Claire, 20, unemployed, outskirts near a small town)
>
> The town bicycle, you know what I mean. And everybody in the town knows that
> they would catch something off her. But at the end of the day, every single one of
> them'll go and have a go at her. And then the next day it's like 'Oh you're mad, you
> could catch something off her!' and he was like 'Oh, a shag's a shag' like, and all that
> kind of craic. He doesn't care, and he probably wouldn't have used anything like. But
> they just don't care like. (Una, 22, retraining, village near a small town)

We argue that partly what is at work here is the impact of stratified reproductive chances and stratified life chances. These are young women either
unemployed or on short-term job creation schemes, perhaps quite possibly in the same social class, and vulnerable in many ways as the young
woman whom they describe. That young woman may well be in need
of good sexual health services. They may all be in need of approaches to
sexuality which would strengthen their sense of personal agency. What
these women did not come to terms with was how this double standard
continues to be replicated. Instead, they were broadly accepting that this
is how matters stand and that they must fall in with it. However, stratified
life chances do not account for all the instances we encountered of this
deep ambivalence.

Two other exchanges will illustrate how difficult it is to manage this
ambivalence. One group of women ranging from 19 to 24 years of age, three
of them with good careers conferring status and financial independence
on them and the fourth an IT student with bright employment opportunities awaiting her, had been discussing how women are growing more
confident about being sexually active and that as one put it, 'We all have
our own minds and we know what we want to do.' Yet immediately after
this statement, they all agreed they had not carried condoms when they

became sexually active. This next extract indicates how the fear of becoming labelled as a 'slut' becomes internalised to the point of being an unquestioned, albeit deeply conflicted part of one's behaviour:

> The reason I wouldn't have carried one [a condom] is not, it wouldn't be because I'd wonder what the guy would think about me, I never even thought about that to be honest. It was more just 'No I don't feel comfortable carrying them.' I think it's the guy's job, now that might be very naïve, but that is the way I do think about it. I would never dream of going into the pub and buying a condom. But then it depends on your situation, it depends on if you're going out and you do think you're going [to have sex] yeah and then well, better safe than sorry. But I've never been in that situation, I've never deliberately gone out to buy a condom, no, never. But that's just my own, it wasn't because I thought the guy would think I'm … because I'd rather be safe. (Eilish, 24, IT programmer, suburban area)

We did not press Eilish on these contradictions and hesitancies. But her discomfiture, her belief that it is a man's 'job' to have condoms, and her sense that she is 'safe' from being labelled by not seeking sex out and not carrying condoms potentially leaves her being unsafe in respect of crisis pregnancy and STIs. A younger interviewee in another group corroborated this level of acceptance, apprehensiveness and confusion. She too speaks early on in the interview about young women being more confident and assertive about sex:

> It's just that we're learning now that we can do it too, without feeling ashamed about it. There's no shame about a man doing that [having sex when he wants], and nobody talks about it. Nobody cares. But now among your friends like, they kind of get the gist of it now. But the fellas still won't, they just don't understand that if they can do it, we can do it too. But that's what's come about, we've realized that we can do it too. (Jean, 19, student, city)

Later, when taking about sex education in her family, she tells us that her mother was the first person to call her a 'slut':

> My mother is a typical Donegal woman. And you can imagine, ten years behind the rest of the world like. And I never got any information at all about sex. She was relying on the school to teach me. But once I hit about fourteen, she said I was a slut. I don't know why. Now I would hang round an awful lot of boys. But they were friends. (Jean, 19, student, city)

To compound Jean's confused position, as she argues that sex education in the school ought to be made available at an early age, she unselfconsciously uses the word 'slut' to label another very young woman:

> The way I see it, why don't you just give them the information, if they wanted to have sex. Like when I was in first year [of second level school], I hung around with a few sluts. That's the only way to put it. In a bush, happy days. (Jean, 19, student, city)

The damage from this double standard is evident: just because you can cope with it, does not mean that it does not leave an impact. To begin with, it affects women's sense of how open we are in Ireland about sex:

> No, we're not necessarily more open. It still goes that same way, that lads that go out and do what they want to do and have sex with as many women as they like, they're still the studs at the end of the day. Whereas if a girl goes out and does it, they're still classed as a slut or a slapper. (Denise, 25, office worker, suburban area)

We are saturated daily with sexual allusions and sexually charged material, yet this does not lead to greater self-awareness and confidence about sex and sexuality, for young women and for young men, quite the opposite. The double standard, the absence of consistent structural support for teenaged women to explore in safety what they need and want, the incapacity of many adults, parents and teachers, to focus and listen more responsively to the teenaged women and men for whom they have responsibility, contributes more than we are prepared to admit to how younger women come to have sex and then regret doing so. In an important working paper published in 2007, Richard Layte and Hannah McGee reported data from their Celtic Tiger period 2005–6 national survey on sexual knowledge that fifty-two per cent of women who had first sex before the age of 17 later regretted it (Layte and Magee 2007: 10). Crucially, age was not the important predictor of this outcome, rather it was a lack of knowledge and a lack of the personal skills needed to articulate what they felt comfortable in doing which led to a lack of preparedness for sex and on occasion to feeling 'coerced' into having sex (ibid.). The number of women reporting that they experienced regret is ultimately attributable to the failures of major Irish institutions to put in place the requisite space and knowledge that young people – and their parents – need.

While we did not ask specifically about instances of abusive behaviour nor did we ask about sexual assault or childhood sexual abuse, nonetheless several women did bring personal experiences of these into our conversations. They served as a cruel reminder of how in a conservative society where a male voice and male power simply matter more, a spectrum that can run from disregard about men's responsibilities to attend to contraception, to disrespect about women's sexual needs and sexual desire, can and does end in forms of sexual violence.

If there is too often an expectation held by men that women cannot really state for themselves what they need and want, women may well experience the kind of abuse described here by Marie, who lived in a very small town and wanted to disclose a deeply humiliating incident. She began to weep as she did so:

> I'll be honest with you. It kind of happened to me not so long ago, that I kind of slept with a fella, I didn't, and this is why I'm telling you this, I didn't want to sleep with him, and I ended up sleeping with him, and I ended up stopping it halfway because I didn't feel comfortable. And there's a rumour going around that I pissed all over him. And I think, why can't you just say something else? But people goin around ... yesterday I was in town, there was a few fellas and they were laughing at me in the car. I knew exactly what they were on about because they're friends with this fella. Like, make up a different thing, a silly thing, but not something so low, that you could say a woman pissed all over you ... do you know what I mean? I can't talk to anybody about it. I'd like to be able to tell my family what's, you know, things like that going round the town about me. It's hard really, you've nobody you can talk to, there's no groups here that you can talk to, about stuff like that. And that's just the way it is. (Marie, 24, unemployed, outskirts of a small town)

What is especially disturbing is that Marie did exercise agency in bringing to a close a sexual encounter she decided she did not want, but that she then paid a price of vicious public ridicule for having done so. Her story is one of many that prompts us to recognise how deep-rooted patriarchal attitudes remain in Ireland and how easily these can be reflected in the behaviours of young Irish men who, like young women, lack secure spaces in which to develop healthier attitudes towards sex.

Structured silences and deep contradictions around sexual subjectivity

With deep insight, a youth worker based in a small town whose brief was to provide a limited but nonetheless concrete intervention in providing much-needed stopgap education on sexuality commented to us that whereas, say the 1950s version of sex in Ireland – do not have premarital sex – led to huge damage and ostracism for so many young women, it did comprise a set of rules, however rigid. For young people now, their parents are frequently ambivalent while schools and teachers are largely ineffective and sexual health services limited in appropriate access. On the other hand, young people are bombarded with images of sex from the media, from teen magazines, from all over. They have very little owner-ship over the issue and their views of it are very clouded. They are given neither space nor guidelines where they can take their time to sort out their own position and their own needs, space that is supportive of their development, space to support an analysis of what having sex might mean for them. They are left in a vacuum.

At a more analytical level, Michelle Fine wrote almost thirty years ago of 'structured silences' (1988: 34) and how these silences blanket 'female sexual subjectivity' and how the 'expressions of female voice, body, and sexuality are essentially inaudible when the dominant language and ways of viewing are male'.

At the time of our research, the mid-2000s, Ireland remained a male-dominant society in the ways that Fine suggests, for all the reports an-nouncing relevant policymaking in key education and social arenas. This Ireland, on such a different scale to the 1950s, nonetheless let its young people down again with difficult and negative consequences for its young women. Elizabeth Kiely (2005) in her analysis of sex education argues that official adult domains in Irish society work instead to eliminate those structured silences which so badly disadvantage young women, to drop its fixation with what might be termed a public health anxiety about sexuality and sex amongst younger people, and to work instead with the positives of sexual desire, seeing sexuality in a much expanded way with a 'set of ethical practices and relations' to match this (2005: 263; see also Kiely 2015).

Where now for more positive messages for young Irish women?

Where will we find such energy, commitment and understanding as Kiely calls for at this juncture to break the structured silences? That public health discourse is so convenient for the conservative set of institutions which constitute official Irish society, including the medical profession. These institutions are not prepared to shift the masculinist discourse at its base. This can be upended, young women can make sense of women's agency in seeking out sexual relationships on their terms, as perfectly exemplified by the 2019 ITV *Love Island* edition with Maura Higgins in a starring role. Cultural critic Tanya Sweeney was quick to observe the obvious outcome of that edition:

> Love Island is saying more about gender relations, toxic masculinity, consent and sexuality than several other TV shows put together … Until a fortnight ago the gender roles on Love Island were pretty cleanly delineated, just as they often are in dating in general. The men were the pursuers, women the pursued. Women were the coquettish givers of sex, men the takers. And, by that reckoning, women don't enjoy sex quite as much as men do. And then a Longford lass arrived and, with a few choice moments, blew it all out of the water … Amid the sun-drenched horseplay and the banter, and the copious footage of women using their GHDs [good hair days], Love Island should be hailed for offering its young audience as potent and pertinent as message as that (Sweeney 2019).

Padraig O'Morain rightly commented that 'when Maura struts her stuff it's as though she is dancing on the grave of an Official Ireland that denied the reality of real women, ruthlessly, for too long' (O'Morain 2019). The women from whom we have heard in this chapter would roundly applaud. But, in glaring contradiction, the current generation of young women continue to cope with the dilemmas of sexual engagement that confronted Maria, who spoke of how 'dirty' a manner in which young men play the heterosexual power game. The difficulty for them, for all of us, is that the message so provocatively delivered by Maura Higgins, is that the Love Island package is wrapped up within the commodification of sex, which carries its own freight of problems for young women. In reality, young women's sense of the possibilities of their sexual selves remains limited by torpor on the part of official Ireland. The most egregious example, Irish abortion policy, is what we turn to in the next chapter.

CHAPTER 4

'It's not the right time for me, I can't go through with this pregnancy. And it should be free choice': Abortion as the Loneliest Decision

Public dissonance and the obliteration of personal agency

Young women who have sex as a result of willing consent, eager antici-
pation or pressure, and who do not have access to contraception have
to confront the possible negative consequence of a crisis pregnancy.
Historically, societies have been remorseless towards women who faced
unwanted pregnancy and they have been left to struggle on their own
within extraordinarily limited circumstances. Ireland's laws and social attitudes have been especially cruel, and in Chapter 1, we discussed some of
these cruelties and the outcomes for women. Cliona Rattigan (2012: 1), in
her book on infanticide in early twentieth-century Ireland, provides historical evidence about individual women's lives. There is the story of Ena
P, who was 20 years old when she came up from the country to Dublin
searching for employment. This was a pattern for many young unskilled
women that lasted up to the last few decades of the twentieth century.
They got jobs as servants, childminders and in hotel kitchens, as with Ena
P, doing basic labour, and despite the accepted strictures in place in that
period, they had sex. Ena P worked in a hotel on Eden Quay and was
arrested in March, 1932, when the body of the baby boy to whom she
had given birth and at once killed and buried beneath the floorboards in
her room, was discovered. The haunting statement from Ena P, recorded
by the Garda, was 'What else could I do?' and Rattigan comments that
the 'sense of passivity and helplessness is quite striking' in Ena P's official
statement (ibid.). Ena P's lack of defence underscores the almost total absence of options for young women like her.

Infanticide was a logical outcome of a repressive social regime in which women, especially those in poverty who had no positive status whatsoever and who became pregnant outwith marriage tried to survive in the newly independent Irish state (Rattigan 2012). The 1949 Infanticide Act replaced the 1707 Infanticide Act which had carried the possible sentence of hanging although when women were charged with murder, even pre-1922, the sentence was commuted to life imprisonment (Rattigan 2012: 7). In practice, from 1922 to 1949, women generally faced a charge of 'concealment of birth,' usually heard in the Circuit Courts, and only sometimes as manslaughter in the Central Criminal Court. Sentences for both crimes were prison, incarceration in a Magdalen home or sometimes both (Ferriter 2009: 246–7; Rattigan 2012: 2). Under the 1949 Infanticide Act, it also became possible to sentence women found guilty of murder to the Central Mental Hospital by reason of insanity. This treatment of infanticide exposes directly how the logic of the independent Irish state was aligned in its actions with the entrenched authoritarian culture of post-Famine Catholic Ireland. That culture, which Diarmaid Ferriter (2018) has characterised as 'a mix of charity and snobbery [that] gave rise to cruelty', recast the ostensible duty of the good Catholic to respond to the poor and most vulnerable by instead obliterating their personhood through the unquestioning recourse to institutionalisation.

Less visible, less spoken, and only recently receiving significant scholarly attention is evidence of illegal abortion procured at home, mainly in urban working class and low-income rural regions (Kavanagh 2005; Delay 2018). Cara Delay argues that her research on the period 1922–49, 'provides evidence for the ordinariness of abortion, which, for many, was woven into the fabric of everyday life' (2018: 11). Both single and married women carried out clandestine abortions with domestic tools, including tea kettles, spoons, basins, cloths and tablets, as a way to privately manage reproduction. Criminal trial court documents indicate that some pregnant women fell ill or died, however, safe home abortions were practiced in a supportive community of mothers, grandmothers and neighbours (Delay 2018).

In Chapters 2 and 3, we have discussed the often-fraught experiences that Irish women have gone through in very recent times to gain more grounded understandings of their sexual beings and identities. Tom Inglis

(2003: 11) posed this as an uneasy journey for women in mental and emotional terms, and what Inglis refers to as a journey applies all too literally in respect of abortion. In this chapter, we explore the complexities around abortion decisions, contextualising celebration of the recent liberalisation of Irish abortion policies within the disparate and often wrenching family, relationship and medical care challenges that women face before, during and after the Celtic Tiger period. Listening to women, we gain a dynamic understanding of how legal abortion represents but one component of support for women's sexual and reproductive agency.

Women in Ireland simply had no legal access or choices, save the limited option since the 1967 legislation on abortion in England, Scotland and Wales to travel to end a pregnancy and, following the passing of the 2013 Protection of Life During Pregnancy Act access to a legal abortion in Irish hospital settings when a woman's life was at risk. Hard-fought for as that 2013 Act was, it was hardly a woman's 'choice', given the critical clinical conditions she would have to be facing for a hospital to initiate the abortion at all.[1] Positing that Irish women's sexual agency has been aided by the possibility of migration, Breda Gray comments that 'Migration would appear to have operated both as a resource in concealing pregnancy and as a means of expanding sexual possibilities for many women' (2004: 27; see also Delay 2019a). In the mid-2000s, at the time of our research interviews, women with their own means or the capacity to discretely borrow funds could travel for an abortion. They also might still avail of that common enough course of action in the mid- to late twentieth century of living outside of Ireland for a time to conceal their pregnancy and thus 'keep up appearances' at home (see Gray 2004: 27). In one of our interviews, this recollection was shared:

1   The Protection of Life During Pregnancy Act was passed by the Oireachtas on 30 July 2013, and was commenced on 1 January 2014. From that date until 1 January 2019 (when it was repealed under Section 5 of the Health [Regulation of Termination of Pregnancy] Act 2018), ninety-eight abortions in total were carried out under its terms of reference. The annual numbers were listed in five brief reports submitted by the HSE to the Department of Health in accordance with Section 20 of the Act between 2014 and 2019, and then made public through a departmental press release, the last one appearing on 27 June 2019 on the Department's website.

For instance, there was a girl on my road, we all knew she was pregnant, her family wouldn't admit she was pregnant, we all knew it. They went off to Spain for their family holiday as they did very year, and she came back, now this girl used to come back the most amazing colour from Spain, and she came back as white as snow you might as well say. And we all found out later that she had been shipped off to a home in Scotland, she had had the baby over there, the baby was still over there, and she was home here trying to figure out what she wanted to do. (Denise, 25, office worker, suburban area)

Marella Buckley contends that England has been central to Irish women's 'inner picture of the reproductive life-choices for some considerable period', and that most women 'know that if they needed an abortion or a non-accusatory climate for childbirth or a relationship, one available option is to try to get to England to find it' (cited in Gray 2004: 27). Joanna Mishtal notes: 'The ordeal involves anxiety, fear, indignity, secretiveness, and unknown places' (2017: 201), and Delay observes, 'For Irish women, the main narrative of abortion is often one of continuity, marked by secrecy, stress, and an encounter with unknown places and spaces' (2019a: 218). Some women in Ireland, including asylum seekers, are barred from traveling and subject to Ireland's restrictive policies (Luibhéid 2004, 2006; Conlon, O'Connor and Ni Chathain 2012; Yogalingam et al. 2013; Bakhru 2014; Side 2016) underscoring all of the inequalities that women must confront in relation to their individual reproductive needs.[2]

Young women have dealt with access to abortion care against what has been the most bitterly contested fault line in Irish society, and continues to be contentious since the 2018 referendum that affirmed the legalisation of abortion care in Ireland under specific circumstances. At every level, women have struggled with heavily freighted negatives about abortion even as society gradually pulled away from previous generations' experiences of a repressive social and political regime controlling sex and sexual

---

2   Non-citizen women living in Ireland have resorted to backstreet abortions (see L. Smyth 2005: 144). Kavanagh (2005) provides insight into the underground abortion business in Ireland from the 1930s through the 1950s. Delay and Liger (2019) analyze how historical courts and the press framed abortionists as 'others' and the practice of abortion as against Irish society and 'national values'.

expression. Asserting that the abortion issue has held a particular power in Ireland past and present, the late Dr Anthony Clare, then a psychiatrist and Medical Director of St Patrick's Hospital in Dublin, stated in oral evidence to a government committee on abortion in 2000:

> 'With due respect to the Celtic Tiger and great changes of an astonishing kind in people's moral and intellectual positions, I still feel this one [issue] touches something very, very basic in the heart of every Irish person. I think that is why the debate here in Ireland is sometimes the most thoughtful, the most serious as well as the most appalling and disagreeable. It is because it matters' (quoted in L. Smyth 2005: 123).

In Ireland and elsewhere, abortion 'matters' in different ways to different people, and most immediately and seriously to women facing what in Ireland is called a crisis pregnancy.[3] The decision to terminate a pregnancy is at once a concrete one for a pregnant woman and an abstract one for legislators, policymakers and advocates on either side of the debate over the legal status of abortion the world over.[4]

Contests over legal abortion are certainly culturally and historically specific, however, key components are shared: opposing views on the roles of women, sex and motherhood, competing ideologies about what constitutes life, and disagreements about who should have the power to determine whether and how pregnant women can make their own reproductive decisions.[5] Rickie Solinger (2001) observes that motherhood is a class privilege in America, and she and other scholar-advocates' emphasis on how race and class inequalities constrain reproductive decision-making is

---

3 The term crisis pregnancy was first used in the 1998 government-sponsored study by Mahon, Conlon and Dillon. Following the definition used by the Crisis Pregnancy Agency, we define 'crisis pregnancy' as an unplanned or undesired pregnancy that represents a personal crisis for a woman, and/or a pregnancy that becomes felt as a crisis due to a change of circumstances despite it being planned or desired (Crisis Pregnancy Agency 2003: 6, cited in Rundle et al. 2004: 7).

4 Ginsburg and Rapp 1995; Georges 2008; Munson 2009; Halkias 2004; Haugeberg 2017; Stettner et al. 2017; Barmpouti 2019; Mason 2019.

5 Roberts 1998; Luker 1991 [1975], 1984; Ginsburg 1998 [1984]; Ginsburg and Rapp 1995; Ludlow 2008a,b; Goldberg 2010; Barry 2016, 2018; Briggs 2018; Cullen and Korolczk 2019.

relevant beyond the United States context and is core to the concept of reproductive justice.[6]

It follows that even in conditions of legal rights, *access* to sexual and reproductive health as well as abortion care in many places is tightly restricted, uneven and stratified.[7] Advocates for reproductive and abortion access and their allies are practiced at working around restrictive laws in Ireland particularly[8] and in other places and times (Kaplan 1997; Nelson 2003, 2015; Reagan 1997; Singer 2019; Delay 2018, 2019a, 2019b), which creatively has included international waters (Gomperts 2002; Best 2005). At the same time, activists seek strategies for safe, accessible, supported and legal abortion care.

The vexing politics of abortion in Ireland

In Ireland, the movement to revise abortion laws has involved multiple public referenda, a series of court cases that over time have made more visible the circumstances of women's lives and decision-making (see IFPA's 'History of Abortion in Ireland'),[9] underground support networks and ongoing concerted public activism since the 1980s (A. Smyth 1992a, 1992b). Legislated in 1861 under the Offenses against the Person

6   See also Petchesky 1990; Fernández Kelly 1992; Kligman 1998; Bhattacharjee and Silliman 2002; L. Smyth 2002; Gutierrez 2008; Lopez 2008; Bourke et al. 2015; Orr 2017; Lowe and Page 2020; Luna 2020; Zavella 2020.

7   For example, in studies of Northern Ireland up to 2019 when the law changed (Side 2006; L. Smyth 2006, Thompson 2018), Catalunya (Ostrach 2018), the U.S. (Joffe 2010; Cohen and Joffe 2020), Mexico (Singer 2017), Poland (Fuszara 1991; Mishtal 2015), the UK (Lee 2003; Lowe and Page 2019), and Spain, Portugal, Uruguay, Argentina, Chile and Italy (Blofield 2008).

8   See Rynne 1982; A. Smyth 1992a, 1992b; Murphy-Lawless 1993; Porter 1996; Luibhéid 2006; Rossiter 2009; IFPA 2012; García-del Moral and Korteweg 2012; Side 2016; Mishtal 2017; Earner-Byrne and Urquhart 2019; de Londras 2020.

9   Northern Ireland's abortion laws and history of legal struggle are distinct from the Republic of Ireland's and the UK's (see Fegan and Rebouche 2003; Fletcher 2005;

Act, abortion was already illegal when the 1983 Eighth (also known as the Right to Life) Amendment resulted in a reassertion in the 1937 Irish Constitution of the coupling between Irish Catholic ideologies and a ban on abortion with the strictest laws in Europe. The Amendment, which stipulated that abortion was criminal except to save the life of the pregnant woman, was approved by 67 per cent of voters (see Rynne 1982; Hesketh 1990; Solomons 1992; T. O'Brien 1998). The 1983 referendum chimed with deeply conservative far-right movements in other countries, specifically the U.S., and represented one aspect of political backlash against the gains of the women's movement and social changes around women's roles.[10] In 1992, following the contentious 'X Case' that began when the 14-year-old teenager we encountered in the Introduction became pregnant as the result of rape and whose family then reported the assault to the Gardaí, with the circumstances that led to the March 1992 Supreme Court decision (A. Smyth 1992a; Murphy-Lawless 1993), but legislation in line with this decision was never prepared and brought to a vote in the Oireachtas, leading the European Court of Human Rights to rule in 2010 that Ireland had violated the European Convention on Human Rights (see J. Taylor 1999). Within that timeframe, as this book's introduction explains, other women's cases propelled slow, but forward, changes in Irish law with turbulent public discourses.

One woman we interviewed shared a critical view of anti-abortion tactics in Dublin when women were coping with travelling for abortions abroad:

> The way the anti-abortion lobbyists parade pictures on O'Connell Street, and they are very, very gruesome pictures, people that are thinking of going through with [an abortion] that don't want to see that. They're thinking of, 'It's not the right time for me, I can't go through with this pregnancy.' And it should be free choice. (Denise, 25, office worker, suburban area)

Side 2006; L. Smyth 2006; Delay 2018; Thompson 2018; Meredith 2018; Earner-Byrne and Urquhart 2019).

10   See Hesketh 1990; O'Reilly 1992; Solomons 1992; Murphy-Lawless 1993; Oaks 2002; Mullaly 2005; Muldowney 2015; Delay 2019a, 2019c.

In the mid-2000s, this view simply was not widely discussed. Arguments for legal abortion accelerated following the 2010 European Court of Human Rights ruling in the *A, B, and C v Ireland* case that the three women who had lodged the case (in 2005) had no effective way of determining whether they had any legal remedy open to them under the X case Supreme Court ruling of 1992 ruling, because the Irish government had failed to pass legislation (see Side 2011). In 2011, the government, obliged to respond to the European Court ruling, set up an expert advisory group. In April 2012, the Independent 4 Change TD, Clare Daly, introduced a bill into the Dáil to implement the X case ruling of 1992. Although the bill was defeated with only 20 TDs voting in favour, it was the first time that abortion was debated not in terms of a tragedy but as a 'health and human rights issue' (Daly 2015: 264).

Later that year, tragedy was made visible. In October 2012, Savita Halappanavar, a 31-year-old Indian dentist living in Ireland with her husband, died in Galway University Hospital. Savita was denied an abortion having been admitted as an in-patient while experiencing a septic miscarriage at seventeen weeks of a desired pregnancy. News of her death, which would have been entirely preventable, broke a month later, causing a widespread national and international outcry against the spirit and consequences of the Irish abortion ban (K. Holland 2012).

Savita's death occurred at the very time when the expert advisory group reported its conclusions on the need for legislation to implement the 1992 X case ruling and to bring Ireland into line with the European Court on Human Rights ruling. Despite the efforts of a number of TDs, including Clare Daly, to include grounds of rape, incest and fatal foetal anomaly in the bill, the ensuing 2013 Protection of Life During Pregnancy Act provided only the narrowest of circumstances for legal abortion in Irish hospitals: emergency cases, risk of loss of life from physical illness and risk of loss of life from suicide, with the proviso that there had to be a formal assessment and review procedure as to whether a specific abortion being sought under any of these three categories case was legally permissible. The Act also continued to criminalise any effort at securing an abortion outside these narrow grounds of a risk to life. In respect of the risk of loss of life by suicide, psychiatrists quickly came to see the Act as unworkable and as putting them 'in the firing line' to make a judgement about an individual woman's circumstances when the very nature of their work was to respond to mental ill-health, not to take decisions about abortion on behalf of Irish society (K. Holland 2017a). This followed on from such difficult cases as that of a young woman who had come to Ireland seeking asylum, found herself pregnant and became suicidal; she was denied an aborting ad the baby was subsequently delivered by caesarean section (Holland and Mac Cormaic 2014). So although it was true that the 2013 Act was 'the first time that abortion in any form has ever been legislated for in Ireland' (Bacik 2013: 105) and meant that at least some women's lives might be saved under its provisions, it was not going to hold.

From 2015 to 2017, a series of United Nations bodies, including the Convention on the Elimination of All Forms of Discrimination Against Women (CEDAW), cited the restrictive nature of Irish legislation and the necessity for reform. These international reviews helped to intensify calls to revise the strict policy, and above all to rid the country of the constitutional burden of the Eighth Amendment. In March 2017, the distinguished British obstetrician, Professor Sir Sabaratnam Arulkumaran, who had carried out the critical review of Savita's death at the request of the HSE, returned to Dublin to address a session of the Irish Family Planning Association on the need for relevant woman-centred abortion legislation. In an interview afterwards, he stated that under the 2013 Protection of Life During Pregnancy Act, it was impossible for doctors to quantify life-threatening risk clinically and not to face the risk of going to prison themselves for an incorrect decision (Shannon 2017). He addressed specifically the 2014 case in which a pregnant woman suffered a catastrophic incident and was pronounced brain dead but was kept on a ventilator for twenty-four days by hospital staff because the foetus was still alive and the hospitals involved feared the legal consequences of withdrawing life support.[11] Arulkumaran contended that the woman had been treated like a 'container' and that

---

11 The case of Natasha Perie arose in December 2014 when fifteen weeks pregnant with her third child, Ms Perie experienced a catastrophic ruptured brain cyst, but despite being pronounced clinically dead was kept on life support by hospital staff who feared they would be violating the right to life of the foetus under the Eighth

appropriate legislation had to be developed and that medical professionals required a legal framework in which to respond adequately to women's needs: otherwise, 'if you really look at the woman's perspective she is not getting her sexual and reproductive health and rights' (ibid.).

The momentum to repeal the Eighth Amendment through activist, political and medical coalitions was consolidated in the historic recommendation of the Citizens Assembly in April 2017 that the Eighth Amendment should not be retained, but should be replaced. That recommendation forced the hand of the government to establish a 25 May 2018 referendum on the Eighth Amendment.

The dynamic referendum campaign emphasised women's reproductive autonomy on one side and support for foetal rights on par with women's rights on the other; 'Yes campaigns advocated compassion and care for women who were forced to travel from Ireland. No campaigns advocated compassion for foetuses as "unborn"' (Side 2020: 111).[12] The Yes vote to Repeal the Eighth Amendment won by a two-thirds majority, illustrating the scope and depth of social change, Savita Halappanavar's father approved of the Yes campaign using her image on posters and materials, saying, 'I am surprised change has not been implemented, I request that all Irish people vote Yes for this law to change' (quoted in K. Holland 2018). Further, the Taoiseach, Leo Varadkar, head of the Fine Gael, the old behemoth Civil War party campaigned for repeal, as did Micheal Martin, the leader of Fianna Fáil, the other old Civil War behemoth party. Only one constituency in Ireland voted to defeat the referendum, and by a 51.9 per cent narrow margin (Bardon 2018).

On 1 January 2019, abortion in Ireland was instituted under the Health (Regulation of Termination of Pregnancy) Act 2018, legalising free, legal

---

Amendment. Ms Perie's family had to take a case to the High Court where a panel of three judges delivered their judgement on St Stephen's Day, 26 December, stating that Ms Petrie's life support should be turned off at once as the only future facing the foetus was 'distress and death'. Ms Perie's family subsequently sued the HSE and were awarded damages (Carolan 2019).

12 See also de Londras and Enright 2018; de Londras and Markicevic 2018; Field 2018; O'Riordan 2018; Griffin, O'Connor and Smyth 2019; Boylan 2019; Browne and Calkin 2020; Browne and Nash 2019, 2020; Side 2020.

abortion up to twelve weeks of pregnancy, requiring a three-day mandatory waiting period from time of medical consultation and having surgical or medical abortion (pills). The law allows for abortion later in pregnancy in circumstances of a threat to the woman's life or serious harm to her health and in fatal foetal anomaly cases. It retains criminalisation for anyone assisting a pregnant woman beyond the stipulations in the Act, and conscientious objector provisions can result in some regions having few or no abortion providers. Fewer than 50 per cent of all maternity hospitals had services available on 1 January 2019, and some general practices were prepared to offer medical abortion care (Bray 2019a). The MyOptions confidential helpline launched by the government received an average of forty-five to fifty calls per day, seeking access to support services for all options and also post-abortion counselling (Bray 2019b). Following the referendum – marking a symbolic if not real shift of service provision from church to state – Cura, the Catholic crisis pregnancy counselling agency established in 1977, closed, ending the employment of two full-time and fourteen part-time staff, citing 'decreasing service demands' (McGarry 2018).[13]

Scholars and activists argue, following other global examples, that while establishing sexual and reproductive health education as well as legislation and policy is important, decriminalisation, access and destigmatisation of abortion in Ireland remains crucial to meeting women's and girls' needs (see Cullen and Korolczuk 2019; Hogan 2019a; Browne and Calkin 2020). Laws do not address all needs, and access to abortion services and social acceptance of abortion even in legal circumstances is certainly not guaranteed. And laws and their enforcement may change. The Irish law that went into effect in 2019 has a three-year review component, so any legal changes next become possible in 2022.

The embodied and emotional abortion journeys that Irish women have had to undertake outside of Ireland, which some will be forced to continue to do, reverberate with the long historical Irish experience of emigration and of institutionalisation which has borne so heavily on women. Women's knowledge, means and access to life experiences either to conceal pregnancy

13 Cura received Crisis Pregnancy Agency funding in the mid-2000s, and was embroiled in controversy when the Catholic bishops banned the organisation from distributing HSE PositiveOptions pamphlets (ibid.).

temporarily or to live abroad permanently as a direct consequence of a crisis pregnancy have always reflected the realities of stratified reproduction. Perhaps the starkest reality, stemming from the worst constraints faced by unmarried, marginalised and pregnant women, was the short journey to the Magdalen laundries run by Irish Catholic nuns and lay organisations. It is estimated that up to 30,000 'fallen women' entered these institutions, some for life, forced to surrender their newborn infants and do hard labour for their moral 'crimes' (Smith 2007); the last such institution was closed in Sean MacDermott Street in Dublin's inner city in 1996 (Culliton 1996; see also P. Kennedy 2002; Brogan 2004; Luddy 1991).[14] These Magdalen institutions symbolise pervasive disrespect for the contexts of stigmatised young women's lives:

> While they raised serious questions about the Church's approach to vulnerable women, they [the laundries] could not have been operated without co-operation from society at large, particularly the many parents who consented to their daughters being sent there, and co-operated with the Church to force them to give up their babies. (Ferriter 2004: 538)

Those women who died in Magdalen homes, even after years of working in them, were buried in unmarked graves (P. Kennedy 2002: 62; Smith 2007); a gravestone in Glasnevin Cemetery had the word 'Penitents' etched into the stone. It took many decades for that regime to begin to fail, but fail it did, as we discuss in the book's final chapter.

Tom Hesketh (1990) in his authoritative account of what he termed the 'second partitioning of Ireland', the 1983 abortion referendum, quotes a prescient Dáil speech by John Kelly, a Fine Gael TD in 1983:

---

14   Luddy (1991) notes that it is difficult to tell from historic documents the 'moral cries' that led to these women being placed in 'reform' institutions, but prostitution seems the dominant one until the twentieth century. In the twentieth century, the subjects of the asylums were not prostitutes, but unmarried mothers and 'wayward daughters' (1991: 737). Luddy's phrasing seems more accurate than Ferriter's because she recognizes lay and Church-based Magdalen homes: 'Both the Catholic public and the religious communities colluded in removing these "shameful objects" from public view' (1991: 737).

The groups promoting this legislation [the bill leading to the referendum itself] have created unwittingly what has never existed before, that is, a large secular platform from which in the future repeated attacks will be launched. (quoted in Hesketh 1990: 378)

Slowly changing attitudes about single motherhood and the impact of the 1967 UK Abortion Act in a far more secular society led to different parameters over time. For those women who had some means to travel to the UK mainland, safe abortion became a reality.

A significant advance in the Irish government finally openly acknowledging the circumstances of women's reproductive lives was a study it commissioned in 1995. The resulting government-sponsored book, *Women and Crisis Pregnancy* (Mahon, Conlon and Dillon 1998) was an historic and ground-breaking report on the complexities of abortion. It gave us in-depth data on women who were able to exercise this decision. Just over 2,000 women formed the sample for the study and although some women self-reported as being in their 40s and in a stable relationship when they faced a crisis pregnancy, the majority of the sample were similar to our interviewees, mostly younger, not in a stable relationship and dealing with a crisis pregnancy which was also their first pregnancy.

The subsequent consultations on the 172-page government *Green Paper* on abortion in 1999 (Hardiman 1999), and the All-Party Oireachtas Committee on the Constitution recommending the establishment of the Crisis Pregnancy Agency, which was set in train in 2001, continued an emphasis on the greater visibility of women's pregnancy decision-making experiences. Journalist Mary Holland, among the first Irish women to publicly reveal in 1980 that she had an abortion, critically noted that not a single woman who had had an abortion brought forward her experience to the All-Party Oireachtas Committee on the Constitution; only eight of the 700-page report are devoted to 'The Experience of Abortion' (M. Holland 2000; see also *The Irish Times* 2004a,b; Ferriter 2014). In response to Holland's drawing attention to the 'deafening silence of women who have faced an unwanted pregnancy', the Irish Family Planning Association published *The Irish Journey: Women's Stories of Abortion*, which documents women's crisis pregnancy experiences and includes a chronology of Irish abortion law and list of counselling, support and educational resources (Ruane 2000). The book's preface, written by then-director of Pregnancy

Counselling Sherie de Burgh, grounds the issues around abortion as pervasive, noting 'Not every woman will have an abortion, but any woman could' (2000: 5). Adding to the outpouring of evidence through abortion narratives, the first ever large-scale survey on Irish adults' attitudes toward sex and pregnancy, published in 2004, indicated that crisis pregnancy was a known experience for the majority of adults between 18 and 45 years of age (Rundle et al. 2004). Sixty-eight per cent of participants stated that they knew someone personally who had experienced a crisis pregnancy.[15] Despite these efforts, legislation remained stalled while social practices around sex, relationships and motherhood continued to change and women endured the reality of needing to seek abortion care outside of Ireland.

While this new data was being gathered, including ours, scholars were analysing changes in social perceptions and practices around abortion and motherhood, although we recognise that given the secrecy of many women's abortion journeys, studies likely do not reflect the full reality of Irish abortion experiences. The growing percentage of births taking place outside marriage in the mid-2000s was especially striking in a society which even in the recent past had treated women in such circumstances so harshly (Inglis 2003). In a national Irish survey on sex and pregnancy, 84 per cent of respondents agreed that it was 'acceptable' for a woman on her own to raise a child without a stable relationship with the baby's father, and 89 per cent stated that there should be no pressure on a woman to have her child adopted (Rundle et al. 2004: 18). With nearly a third of all babies being born into non-traditional family forms by the beginning of the twenty-first century (CSO 2004), it appeared that there was little or no social stigma remaining for a woman if she became pregnant outside marriage, especially if she were in what was perceived as a stable relationship.[16]

15   When describing why the pregnancy was a crisis, women (41 per cent) and men (39 per cent) explained that it was not planned. Other common themes were being too young, being unmarried, having relationship difficulties or being in a relationship that was new or not steady (Rundle et al. 2004: 20).

16   At that time, Irish figures were comparable to figures for seven other EU countries, with Sweden and Denmark having the highest percentages of births outside marriage at 55 per cent and 44 per cent respectively (Eurostat 2003).

Alongside such shifts in attitudes about single motherhood in Ireland, there have remained ambivalent and often deeply painful reactions to an unexpected or unwanted pregnancy in Ireland, whether in or outside marriage, and whether abortion is sought or not. A number of factors were converging in the mid-2000s period to enable a majority of women to have more decision-making over unwanted pregnancy, including greatly improved access to contraception, despite the low base from which those policies began to have substantial impact (see Crisis Pregnancy Agency 2003). Gathering and providing information has been particularly important. Launched in 2003 the Positive Options programme – the umbrella effort that promoted state-funded, agency-based crisis pregnancy counselling services in Ireland – widely publicised its services and ran an in-demand text information service (*The Irish Times* 2003c). In 2010, the second broad-ranging Irish Contraception and Crisis Pregnancy study on contraception practices and crisis pregnancies recorded that 62 per cent of all crisis pregnancies (the study defined a crisis pregnancy as one which entailed a crisis or trauma at the outset or which developed into a crisis as it progressed) ended in the baby's birth and with the birth mother parenting that baby, while 21 per cent ended in abortion, 16 per cent in miscarriage and 1 per cent in adoption (McBride et al. 2010: 24). The reported number of Irish women travelling to Britain for abortions and giving Irish addresses peaked in 2001 at 6,673, but fell each year up to 2009 by then totalling 4,422. In the era of much cheaper air travel, a much smaller number of women had also begun to access abortions in Netherlands (HSE Crisis Pregnancy Programme 2010).

Still, women can be left painfully exposed and the issues around stratified reproduction are never far away from these vulnerabilities. The lack of complete scope for a woman to make safe decisions about pregnancy is highlighted by the abandonment of babies, often in prominent places where it must have been hoped that the babies would soon be discovered: the three-day old, healthy baby girl in the car park of the South Infirmary Hospital in Cork in October 2003, a baby left in a bus shelter near the Coombe University Women and Infants Hospital on a bitter February morning in 2004, and a third baby in the porch of a church in Leixlip in April 2004 (Reid 2004). In the spring of 2007, a rural 21-year-old Irish woman moved to Australia five months pregnant keeping it secret and then abandoned the newborn (K. Healy 2007). Dozens of abandoned, dead newborn babies have been accounted for across fifty years, making starkly visible the lack of compassion, care and support that some girls and women experience in Ireland (see A. Healy 2005; Boland 2020). It is impossible to guess at the resilience women needed to come through these experiences (see Oaks 2015).

These tragedies perhaps reflect the fact that public opinion about the acceptability of women's pregnancy decisions depends for many people on the 'cause' of the crisis pregnancy. One in a series of highly public and contested cases of Irish women's legal challenge to seek abortion in Britain was the 2007 Miss D case, involving a 17-year-old pregnant woman whose foetus was diagnosed with anencephaly. Miss D intended to travel to Britain for an abortion, but was prohibited from doing so by the Health Service Executive (HSE), then was granted the right by the High Court (*The Irish Times* 2007). A June 2007 poll found that 43 per cent supported legal abortion if a woman believed it was in her best interest while 51 per cent remained opposed. Eighty-two per cent favoured legalisation for cases when the woman's life is in danger, 75 per cent when the foetus cannot survive outside the womb, and 73 per cent when the pregnancy has resulted from sexual abuse (O'Sullivan 2007). Here, we see in 2007 that a woman's legal right to abortion on her own terms was respected by less than half of the public, whereas public support was behind legal abortion in specific situations. This history provides a basis for understanding the 2019 restrictions on legal abortion following the repeal of the Eighth Amendment's abortion ban.

Despite a lack of public visibility or broad social support, in the early 2000s, women who wanted an abortion continued to have to travel outside of the Republic of Ireland, and the key legal cases and the string of national referenda discussed above certainly attracted international media attention to the plight of Irish women.[17] Reflecting on the constraints on

17 For the analysis of competing public discourses, see Murphy-Lawless 1993; A. Smyth 1992a, 1992b; Oaks 1998, 1999, 2002, 2003; L. Smyth 2005; Conroy 2004; de Londras and Enright 2018; Griffin, O'Connor and Smyth 2019; Boylan 2019; Browne and Calkin 2020.

Irish women's pregnancy choices, sociologist Lisa Smyth noted before the repeal of the Eighth Amendment, 'More than two decades of debate and five referendums on abortion have not reduced the abortion rate, enhanced women's rights, or promoted women's capacity for self-realisation. It remains to be seen whether this will change in the future' (2005: 146). Despite the current legalisation of abortion in some circumstances in Ireland, alongside other scholars and activists, we remain extremely concerned about women's crisis pregnancy options and what changes Irish society and government agencies can continue to make to assist women.

What *really* matters for young women experiencing crisis pregnancy: Support and resources

Turning from the historical and present aspects of abortion policy, we explore how women we interviewed in the mid-2000s and who experienced unintended pregnancy felt a dearth of social and personal support at a time of rapid social and economic change in Ireland. This lack was the result of the lack of any substantive policy response and a continuing ambivalence at the seat of government and historical cultural and religious opposition to even open discussions of sex and pregnancy, even though as we stated above, more young women were opting to raise children outside of marriage. The stories of the women we interviewed reveal how state and social support provides for or constrains their abortion decisions and single motherhood. Women's experiences and views on the 'problem' of unintended pregnancy and its 'solutions' point to the complexities involved in framing individuals' options within social, cultural, economic and historic constraints on sexuality, marriage and motherhood. Personal experiences are shaped by public understandings of what are acceptable responses to crisis pregnancy.

The women we talked with offer insight into the complicated issues involved with young Irish women's pregnancy decisions. Speaking about the topic of abortion decision-making and the isolation of Irish women who experience abortion, one stated,

> I think that abortion is the great undiscussed subject, you know, I have three friends
> who had abortions, and it wasn't talked about … But you had to go and get it done,
> and not talk about it, and not tell anybody, and then accept it within yourself, and
> you got no counselling or whatever. (Agnes, 29, financial advisor, metropolitan area)[18]

Liz, a young mother, spoke about her immediate reactions to a crisis
pregnancy and what it meant for her life path, which she had to handle
on her own:

> I think anybody who says they don't think about abortion is … they're fooling
> themselves, because you do. You do. What it is is because of all the emotions you're
> going through, it's because of the worry of what other people are going to say and it's
> because … well I mean the major worry is what way is your life going to go? I mean
> still today, my baby is thirteen months old and still today I have worries of where
> my life is going to go. So you have to, you have to think about it. It's not something
> that you want to think about or you don't want to think about. You *have* to think
> about it. (Liz, 20, bank clerk, small city)

The 1992 X case altered at least some of the not knowing in the public
media about women's reproductive needs:

> Like I remember saying this, even when we were growing up, even the ads for tam-
> pons and stuff, there was none of those on telly when I was growing up, and all of
> a sudden they're there … I think the X case was the first one about the abortion.
> (Kathryn, 30, animal groomer, small city)

When we talked with Marie, she explained that she had lived in
England where she became pregnant three times, raising her daughter
and then having two pregnancies ending in termination. Upon returning
home to Ireland, she found herself unable to mention the abortions at all
because she feared that she would be ostracised by her family. Yet she also
found it very difficult not to feel guilty about having had her terminations:

> I haven't been able to talk to a lot of my family about it, because obviously my family
> are all Catholics, and they don't agree with terminations, which is fair enough. But

18   Mahon and Conlon (1996) found that only ten per cent of Irish women re-
     ceived counselling before travel to England for an abortion (cited in Mahon et al.
     1998: 183).

at the time, I had to have them. It wasn't … I didn't have to, no one put me down and made me have it done, but I thought at the time it was the best thing to do. Now looking back, I'm feeling guilty and I'm feeling wrong, and I can't go up to my family and say 'this is what's after happening, this is how I feel'. There's no little place you can go to and talk to someone. (Marie, 24, unemployed, outskirts of a small town)

She explained her own experience and the difficulty with what Agnes, quoted above, called 'accepting it within yourself:'

I know there's probably them that would say that you got rid of your baby, and get on with your life now. Because I didn't do it, I didn't fall pregnant just to go in and have a termination and come out and feel alright like. It happened, it shouldn't have happened, I shouldn't have fallen pregnant, I didn't want to be on my own, with a child at that time. You know, it's hard to do. I'm still not the same after my terminations like. No way. Not even just my mind like, my body. (Marie, 24, unemployed, outskirts of a small town)

Marie's experiences point to a continuing painful split that women can and do experience in negotiating the consequences of unprotected sex in a society that describes itself as liberal in so many ways, but that remains conservative and grounded in forms of institutional and cultural patriarchy that often leave women isolated. Her feeling that some people might urge to her 'get on with your life now' despite her feelings of profound and unavoidable self-change also suggests the imperative to provide appropriate post-abortion counselling and support services to women who may worry about their reactions being judged.

The late Director of Pregnancy Counselling at the Irish Family Planning Association recognised so well the complexity and the burden shared by so many: 'Irish women's abortions often become dark secrets because of the fear of judgement, and the journey to England almost always involves cover stories and lies. For many women it is the first major life event that is kept secret from family and friends. The lies are often told to protect those same loved ones from having to cope with this awful crisis' (Sherie de Burgh, quoted in Ruane 2000, 4; see *The Irish Times* 2017). So, we see how abortion matters to women, who find they must contend with pressures to act in socially acceptable ways, concealing their difficult experiences, struggling internally over their sense of what abortion means to their sense of self, their families and their friends. Women have been vulnerable due to the uniqueness of pregnancy in that particular woman's life along-side the historical lack of abortion services in Ireland. Women contend with ambivalent and often deeply painful reactions to an unexpected or unwanted pregnancy in Ireland, whether in or outside marriage, whether because of violence, timing, the need to preserve or restore physical and emotional well-being, myriad reasons. As Lucy Watmough described it in 2015, 'I try to act normal around friends and family, attempting to hide my morning sickness so as not to arouse suspicion. At home, surrounded by people I have never felt more scared or alone' (quoted in Mullally 2018: 21). Underscoring this, one of our interviewees shares her struggles similarly a decade before Lucy's experiences:

> I think everyone should have the choice whether they would like a termination or not. You're the one that's going to have to either live with the fact of you saying 'What I did, then was right' or 'What I did then was wrong.' I think most people would say what I did then, for me, was right. Even though I mightn't like it now, what I did then was right. I think the reason that there is so many unwanted preg-nancies now, and why so many young girls are taking the choice of keeping the baby, is because they can't afford to go to England (200–300 pounds sterling). For sixteen-year-old girls, that is a lot of money. How are they going to get to England without their parents knowing or finding out? It's all this is what they're afraid of, and it all builds up at the end of the day to 'I can't do this'. Where at least if it as an option open to them here, they would be able to go to a counsellor to talk about it, 'Do I want to go through with this? Is this what I want to do?' it wouldn't be 'Oh my God, how am I going to get to England? Oh my God, how am I going to get the money together? I'm going to have to fly over and come back and no-one's to know about it.' Where at least here, there could be some kind of system built in, to help people deal with what's going on. Because it is a traumatic thing. (Denise, 25, office worker, suburban area)

Her suggestion is a logical one: that to avoid seeing single motherhood as the only choice, young girls need access to counselling and services that would allow them to process the range of options and be able to secure funds should travel for an abortion be their ultimate choice. Denise was one of the women who expressed how commonly there was a socially en-dorsed pervasive emphasis on the fear of sex outside marriage because it might result in pregnancy. She continued:

Well, I think abortion is still a very taboo subject. And still in some families, and if you're raised in a very strict family, contraception would be a very taboo subject: 'Oh no I don't believe in it.' But everyone has their own choice to make. If you're not, what is it my mother said, 'If you're not willing to take care of your own business, then refrain from having sex.' If you're not willing to be careful, even if you're with a fulfilling partner, and you could be with him for years, there's still risks at the end of the day. If you're not willing to be careful, to be responsible, just say no. That would be me looking at it though. (Denise, 25, office worker, suburban area)

But 'being responsible' is not the only factor shaping how young women view what their options are. For example, Sharon, a teenager when she became pregnant, did consider abortion, although her family wanted her to have and keep the baby. Her isolation arose from not being able to discuss abortion as an option in addition to a resource issue. Sharon simply could not find the money:

And then I was trying to get the money up then to go [for the abortion], and I couldn't get it anywhere anyway. Like, he's thirteen now, thank God I didn't do it. But like even the family then wouldn't let me go. They said no. I really had nobody to talk to about it. (Sharon, 28, voluntary drugs worker, city)

One interviewee vividly recalled being socialised in schools against teen motherhood:

The whole thing was you didn't do it outside marriage. I remember my sixth class teacher talking about 'you see those girls, hanging around the town centre … the girls with prams' … and it was very firmly in my mind that there were 'girls with prams'. And they were something that we didn't become because 'we're not that kind of people'. (Mona, 26, health worker, small town)

In contrast to this teacher's imperative to postpone sex until after marriage, almost all of the women we spoke with have had unsafe sex at some point, finding themselves at risk of becoming pregnant. In the unsupported circumstances women experienced in Ireland and with unsafe sex a commonplace in women's lives, it has been an inevitability that crisis pregnancies are occurring. It has the feel of a lottery for many young women. Unsafe sex takes place in many different contexts: it may be casual sex; it may be sex in a short-term relationship where the woman is unsure whether she wants to commit herself to using the pill; it may be inexperience of younger women; a sudden letting go of any sense of caution. It may be forgetting to take precautions. It may be as a result of coerced sex. Some women may be lucky, some women can effectively use emergency contraception and some women end up experiencing a crisis pregnancy.

Many have experiences of either family members or close friends who have had a crisis pregnancy, outside the context of an established co-habiting or married relationship. In some ways, a change in the general social climate is seen to have made things easier, because marriage in such circumstances is no longer forced upon women who become pregnant. Reflecting on a friend's experience coming from a rural background and changing social attitudes about marriage as a solution to crisis pregnancy, Kate confided:

> I had a very good friend that fell pregnant unexpectedly when we were at college. Now, I don't think there would have been anybody looking twice at it, but at that time, it was a huge issue, and again a rural background and completely unexpected ... I think it's a good thing, the attitude now, because I think a lot in the past people were rushing into marriage, and really, and they weren't ready for it to be quite honest with you, and it was always seen as the answer, and it was wrong because nine times out of ten you were dealing with two very young people that would change a lot in ten years. So I think the attitude now is a lot more positive. (Kate, 30, health services administrator, rural area)

And even where the pregnancy is a shock to traditionally minded parents, some parents work at being supportive:

> But like say, my mam and dad would be big into religion or whatever or Catholic or whatever. But they'd be still not liberal now, but understanding. Like my sister had her baby when she was 23 but she wasn't married. And when she came over to tell Mam and Dad she was pregnant, we were like all going 'Shit, this is going to be terrible' but Dad just shook his head and said, 'Sure what can we do about it?' And Mam cried of course, but apart from that, Mam was the ultimate support. The way she saw it, it wasn't that, you know, she was Catholic and this was wrong, you know. Mam saw it as like 'I'm a Catholic and I'm a Christian and it's up to me to do my best to help and make the best of the situation.' (Orla, 22, Ban garda, small town)

Ellen had an abortion after unsafe sex at 20 years of age, and remembered the high anxieties of that time in her life, and also her mother's support:

I was really afraid, really afraid. So my mother went with me to the abortion clinic. (Ellen, 33, self-employed, rural area)

Subsequently, Ellen had a 'one-night stand', became pregnant and decided to have the baby and has 'absolutely no regrets' about her decision, even though the father of the child has never been involved, at her request.

But for many women this remains an extremely difficult time for family relationships, because of the family trauma and because the individual involved may feel obliged to conceal the pregnancy as long as possible. If she decides on a termination, the secrecy may be extended over a very long period of time:

My friend got pregnant. She hid it from her family till she was six months pregnant. And I don't know how she managed it. Nearly the whole pregnancy behind their back. And she was terrified to go to the doctor, she was terrified to go to the clinic, she was five months pregnant before she went to see a doctor. (Jean, 19, student, city)

My sister had an abortion about two or three years ago, but she waited nearly a year until she could tell me. And she's still, I mean, she was destroyed at the time, she even contemplated killing herself when she came back from ____ and it was just awful. And she couldn't tell any of us because she felt she'd done such a wrong thing. And she still hasn't got over it, I mean she never will I don't think. It's a huge loss. (Marcella, 29, civil servant, small town)

The secrecy of the decisions, we heard, impact all family members differently. Particularly important for forming their views on sex and relationships, younger female family members may feel the burden of a crisis pregnancy:

Like we got an awful lot of hassle, I think as well because my older sister had gotten pregnant when she was young. We were like, you know, every time you were going anywhere, it was 'Don't you get yourself in trouble! Don't drink because you never know what'll happen.' (Shauna, 26, student, small city)

You know, I think the older generation as well, if their daughter gets pregnant at a young age, the mother thinks, 'If that had've been me years ago, I would have been forced to give up the baby or I would have been forced to go into a home, so why should my daughter be forced to have to go through that?' so then grandmothers say 'Oh no, you'll be fine, we'll look after things. It'll all be OK.' (Denise, 25, office worker, suburban area)

These two views point to dual messages in the context of Ireland: individual pregnancy risk-taking results in crisis pregnancies ('don't drink') *and* changes in the social acceptance of single motherhood shape that option as a better one than abortion within some families and communities.

But family members do not have all of the social power, and friendships also strongly influence women's perspectives. Elizabeth reflected both on learning from a friend's experience and on how being from a rural community had additional negative weight that a crisis pregnancy brought to her when she accompanied her friend to a clinic in Britain:

> I remember sitting in an abortion clinic with my friend in _____, and I think for me that was a big realisation of what that experience is like, and of what becoming pregnant is like. And I think especially, if you're from a more rural background as well, it's just such an 'Oh my God she's pregnant!' (Elizabeth, 27, occupational therapist, small city)

Working through these accounts brings home vividly the need for women to have had a safe, non-judgemental space to return to in the wake of an abortion decision to help them resolve all the ways in which a socially burdensome issue became their personal burden.

The multiple, competing pressures on young women

Clearly, the vast majority of young women we spoke with were making decisions about sex and reproduction within a context that offered them few, if any, 'good' ways of meeting their needs. The pressures were rooted in dissatisfaction with relationships and family, inadequate sexuality education, the reality of the costs of contraception and abortion, and feelings about one's own health and well-being. The foundation of women's reflections on these areas was that it is unfair that women must endure these burdens. One complained legitimately with an 'insult to injury' argument:

> And also having to shell out [for emergency contraception], the last time I had to take it was last year, and it was something like seventy Euro! It was astronomically

expensive! All for something that made me feel sick and cranky. It was something in the region of that figure. I just remember staggering out of the surgery going 'I feel bad enough about my situation without having to spend my earnings' and obviously if I had to go to England [for an abortion], it would be considerably more expensive and more traumatic. But I was really appalled at how much it cost. (Sadhbh, 31, computer operative, city)

Christine told us that she experienced crisis pregnancies several times, and each carried its own trauma and pressures. Christine decided to keep her baby – she was a teenager when she became pregnant – but in the mid-2000s had an abortion after she was raped. She described the journey to Britain and the experience of abortion as 'harrowing', in part because she was going against her outspoken values and in part because she was on her own and angry. The unsupported context of her decisions is epitomised in the way Christine found out where to go for the abortion, from the back pages of *Cosmopolitan* magazine:

It was like travelling down the longest darkest tunnel. I found out where to go for the abortion from an ad on the back page of *Cosmo*. I remember all that stuff about it being illegal for women to travel [the X case]. I really argued against abortion. It was going against all my principles before when I went for the abortion. I ended up with one set of beliefs and being pulled the other way. I flew to _____ and I'll never forget the taxi ride from the airport to the clinic. The taxi driver knew why I was going there, he said 'So many come over from Ireland. Everything will be alright.' What did he know? You had no privacy and they were cold there in the clinic. I told very few people when I came back. The whole taboo, you just can't talk. (Christine, 31, unemployed, small town)

Aine, Liz and Sharon talked about crisis pregnancies and their decision to keep the baby. For two of these women, denial and isolation were features when they first discovered they were pregnant:

I was four months pregnant before I went to anyone. (Aine, 24, office worker, city)

I would say for about six months I was in denial. (Liz, 20, bank clerk, small city)

This silence seems understandable in the context of the lives of both of these young women; their disclosures were met with an initial complete lack of parental support:

It was very, very hard. I mean my mother wouldn't talk to me for about two months. (Liz)

My mother went absolutely ballistic. Because I was always told not to come home pregnant and that was that. And I was very innocent till I was seventeen years of age. I didn't even have a proper boyfriend till I was seventeen. And it was just one of those things. Literally just one of those things. It was like the second time or something that I wasn't careful, I got pregnant. And just like that. And she just said 'Don't come home. Don't come home pregnant. Don't come home and tell me you're pregnant.' (Aine)

Aine recounted further both the assistance of a friend and how they had an entirely unsupportive response when she went to a Dublin maternity hospital to have the pregnancy confirmed:

My friend persuaded me to go into _____ hospital. So not knowing where to go I went in, and my friend went up to the desk and she said, 'My friend would like to take a pregnancy test.' And the girl behind the counter said 'OK take a seat.' And the next thing this woman comes out, a nurse or a midwife or whatever, and ate the head off me. 'Who did I think I was, walking in off the street, asking for a pregnancy test. Did I not know what chemists and doctors were for?' And 'they weren't here to provide that kind of facility'. So I've never been back in there since. So I just cried all the way home. And then my friend went to the chemist and got me a pregnancy test. So that was it like. You don't, there wasn't support there at all. (Aine, 24, office worker, city)

Speaking to another aspect of support, some young women shared with us that a lack of such education and never learning about sexual consent raised the risks of pregnancy. Claire, who became pregnant at 17 years of age grew up near a small town and completed her Leaving Cert, had become sexually active in her middle teens without incorporating contraception into her life. She had no option whatsoever of obtaining an abortion. She had not been given any grounding by her mother or school in sex education; it simply was not discussed. She experienced family rejection as a result of the pregnancy and now wonders how she did not understand that she could have refused to be sexually active if she had wanted, ultimately blaming herself and not a lack of information:

It was totally unplanned. My family didn't react to it well at all. Because I was left on my own for months on end. I had to tell my mam straightaway, because I was in a relationship at the time and he had told his Mam. And I thought I'd better tell mine before they found out from somebody else, which would more than likely happen. My Mam was angry. Like how could I be so stupid and that? But at the end of the day I didn't hear anything from them about sex education or anything. I learned all I knew from friends or magazines or TV. To be honest I'm not blaming it on this or anything, but to me, I was never taught to say no, or you that you could say no like. And that's a couple of years, like she's three now. And whenever I started becoming sexually active or whatever, that I didn't realise, it was probably stupid of me, but I didn't think 'I can say no here'. (Claire, 20, unemployed, outskirts of a small town)

Women have faced overlapping pressures, being worried about negative reactions to having sex, seeking pregnancy testing, telling family and friends, and feeling settled in making decisions for themselves. Distress was compounded by the absence of responsible, responsive sex, sexuality and relationships education, including, as Claire emphasises, communication about desire and consent within gendered sexual scripts and constrained agency.

The contentious place of men and heterosexual relationships

Although we did not interview men, the presence of relationships, sex and family ties with men are woven throughout young women's experiences and important in discussions of abortion care. A report published soon after our research concluded, *Men, Sexuality and Crisis Pregnancy: A Study of Men's Experiences*, provides some context for these issues during the Celtic Tiger period (Ferguson and Hogan 2007). All but six of the forty-five heterosexual men between ages 18–67 reported having been involved with a pregnancy scare (ibid.: 30), and there were twenty-two crisis pregnancy experiences reported. Only eight men went through an abortion experience, and all but two (who learned of the pregnancy after an abortion) actively participated in the decision. A number of the men provided money and offered to travel to England, but only one relationship lasted after the abortion (ibid.: 95). The experience had a range of financial and emotional significance, and 'All eight men expressed some emotion about the abortion experience, be it sadness, despair, anger, relief or a sense that it gave them the opportunity to plan their own life-courses', and one man reported it had 'ruined his life' (ibid.: 94) and others had mixed feelings.[19] The report recommendations include sex and relation-ships education, widely available condoms, framing condom use as a re-sponsible sexual practice for men, recognising grandparents (particularly grandmothers) who provide support, and arguing that 'services that re-spond to crisis pregnancies need to be promoted as open to and inclusive of men unless this is inappropriate' (ibid.: 15).

We agree that recognising the diverse forms of power that women and men bring to heterosexual relationships and working to adequately sup-port all sexual partners – through social change and healthcare access – is a crucial goal. So do women we interviewed. Commenting on the disjunc-ture between clinic staff attitudes and their desire for men to take shared responsibility and be treated with mutual respect, one woman talked to us with great energy about the position of women and their male partners going to non-governmental organisation clinic providers for contraceptive care and for counselling on abortion. She shared that several of her friends had reported clinic staff as being judgmental and unpleasant. She queried a possible conflict between the overall philosophy of providers and indi-vidual practitioners on the rota which led to less than optimum support of male partners in such circumstances:

> If they went with their partners, their male partners would be treated like shit. I've had one person I know who went for termination counselling with her partner, they had made the joint decision, they had been together a good few years, and her partner was also treated disastrously. Which is surprising, but it's there. And it seems to me that there's a conflict there. There's a very pro-choice thing, but then the individual

---

19   Some men espoused anti-abortion views, but the practicalities of finances, rela-tionships and the fatherhood role played more of a role in their decision-making (Ferguson and Hogan 2007: 94). Others discussed how they coped emotionally, including a 27-year-old professional: 'I was fucking freaked out: I didn't know what to do, because I'd nowhere to go to. I could have told some of my friends but she asked me not to tell them so I wouldn't, for her. I couldn't go to my family because it's not the type of thing you talk about in the house' (quoted in Ferguson and Hogan 2007: 106).

doctors, you know, the organisation may have a certain philosophy, but that doesn't necessarily apply to the individual practitioners that come in on a rota system. This would have been happening to them in their late twenties, and they kind of feel, 'look, I'm a mature person, I don't need to have this lecture at twenty-seven. I don't need to sit here in front of you and have you giving out to me'. And if I bring my partner, it means that I have a very good relationship with a very good man, who should be respected as well, and that we're making a joint decision, and he didn't impregnate me, he's not some irresponsible boy of nineteen. (Sarah, 30, teacher, city)

Showing the difficulty of suspending judgement in the area of reproductive health decisions and relationships, Sarah, while arguing for respect for couple's decision-making, does mobilise a stereotype of the irresponsible teenager. This runs counter to the responsibility and caring narratives of some men in Ferguson and Hogan's study, including Patrick, a 20-year-old skilled labourer, who said, 'And I tried to stay as impassive to my own emotions as possible. I tried not to give, I knew she had enough on her plate as it was with the whole, dealing with the pregnancy thing, wanting the abortion thing, I knew it was hard enough on her as it was, I didn't want to land my stuff in on top of her so I just thought, "Look, I'll deal with this myself"' (quoted in Ferguson and Hogan 2007: 106). Taking this all into account, we underscore that the most equitable position is to argue for access to support to assist unique challenges when facing a partner's crisis pregnancy, at any age, and including teenagers.

We heard some positive stories about men's support and participation in pregnancy decisions. Una had a termination with her first pregnancy, became pregnant a second time at 21 years of age and decided to keep the baby. She had become sexually active in her mid-teens and had not used contraception. Una believed she was infertile and continued not to use contraception when she moved away from home, and was attending a course when she became pregnant. This first pregnancy came as a shock:

At a young age when I seen other people, I always said if I ever got pregnant, I would definitely have an abortion. And I did get pregnant and I did go and have an abortion. Because it was, you know it was an accident as well, but it was totally like the timing, I was in my first year in college and the timing was just all wrong ... For about five months in college, [I had] just constant unprotected sex and then suddenly, bang, I was, my period didn't come, and I was like ... 'OK what?' (Una, 23, unemployed, outskirts of a small town)

Una did 'feel panicked', but her boyfriend supported her financially and emotionally, and she arranged to go to the UK for an abortion. When she became pregnant the second time, she was completing her college course. She ultimately decided to keep the baby, recalling,

> It wasn't actually planned. But I didn't panic the way I did the first time at all. I wanted to put my studies first before I had a child. But then I fell pregnant then like, so I had to stop like then. I wanted to stay at home here near the fella and my family. (Una, 23, unemployed, outskirts of a small town)

However, the issue arises as to why she was not able to explore approaches to contraception that would be more protective, especially given that she had the same boyfriend throughout that time and pregnancy changed her life-course, leading her to prioritise motherhood over college studies. Joanne told us that she did have family support and the support of the father of her baby, even though the relationship did not endure.

The need for support for young men and for recognition of their unique roles stands out when we review these experiences. Opening more discussions in Irish society about both the pleasures of sex and sexual relationships and the possible difficulties would be beneficial in many ways for all young people and would help take burdens of the shoulders of young women.

Legal abortion cannot change everything

Just as with finding out about contraception (Chapter 2) and establishing a sexual self (Chapter 3), what these young women's stories tell us is that even in rush of consumer capitalism in Celtic Tiger Ireland in the mid 2000s, you had to pick up what you needed to know as you went along, without clear resources, support or information structures. Hearing from young women in urban and rural areas across education levels and age reveals the unevenness of reproductive health services, stigma, family approval and financial safety nets. The more impoverished women were, the fewer resources they had, the more rural their locations, the more difficult a crisis pregnancy proved for them. It is crucial that we recognise these differences and how they may persist, and not subscribe to progress narratives that suggest that a more just present – symbolised by pointing to the legalisation of same-sex marriage, divorce and abortion – provides equity for all.

We see, for example, the recent changes legalising abortion in limited circumstances and public discourses recognising women's need for abortion care certainly as positive steps, as Irish feminist Ailbhe Smyth notes:

> We are freer about sexuality and sex in Ireland than we were twenty-five or thirty years ago. There's no doubt about that. Two generations out there now grew up in a very different world, where being able to be at least more open about your sexuality and about your own sexual behaviour, your sex life, your partners, and so on, is much more taken for granted than it used to be. That makes it easier to talk about personal experiences to do with abortion. (2018: 138)

The professional legal and healthcare structures which have been built out since January 2019 have begun vital work for women. However, these structural changes require that long arc of social change which can be sensitive to the work of resolving the residue of all that women, their sexual partners and their families have carried in memory. Kitty Holland poignantly communicates this, writing about the significance of post-abortion counselling she received:

> I spent those months, and since, thinking about how we women, from girlhood, are taught to think about others' needs, to care and share and never be selfish. These are good lessons, of course, but I believe, as we grow into women, we are taught to care too much about how other are, how others think of us – to worry deeply about how we look, how we are seen, how kind and caring and giving and selfless we are ...
> I thought about how women of all classes are taught to accept that our ambitions just might not be fully realised because others' – men's? – ambitions are possibly more important than ours; how perhaps we are better than men at fulfilling a caring role – running a family – and that is really what we want. Or should want. (2018: 51–2)

It is not just that young women need wider access to reproductive health and abortion services where they feel safe and respected. We agree with reproductive justice advocates that it is crucial to 'look beyond resistance and survival to create conditions of thriving' (Luna 2020: 15). In a country where young women's sexuality and crisis pregnancies have been publicly debated for so long while being privately kept secret, meeting young women's needs has do with establishing a wide public respect for women's agency and sense of self-confidence and above all, a sense of entitlement about how they engage with and enjoy sex and sexual relationships. Crucially, it also has to do with a reproductive justice movement that is also grounded in the wider social and economic realities which have led contemporary Ireland to being so unequal. As Kitty Holland stated in 2017 about the Repeal the Eighth campaign:

> Accessible abortion services is fundamentally not about being able to choose abortion. It is about a woman who becomes unexpectedly pregnant being empowered to regain control of her body, to be able to take choices about her life – her education, her career, how many children she can afford, how many children she wants, if any. Accessible abortion is essential if women are to achieve economic and political equality with men, and it is absolutely essential if the poorest, most marginalised women are to achieve economic and political equality with their middle-class sisters. (Holland 2017b)

As we explore in our next chapter, the issues that Holland outlines are intimately connected to the subject of what it means to be an Irish woman, which for generations has been constrained with images of ideal motherhood, while the very idea of motherhood has entailed new pressures within and beyond the Celtic Tiger period.

CHAPTER 5

'It's not just about having children – how can you build a life?': Motherhood Becomes Another Country

A site of dissonance and desire

In this chapter, we present what women said about motherhood and their decision to become a mother, or to say no to that possibility. We were especially interested in how they perceived the complexities that surround motherhood and parenthood in Celtic Tiger Ireland, a time of rapid social and economic shifts. The desire for children is complex, as the psychologist Daphne de Marneffe (2006) has written, one in which for some women at least, motherhood feels like a freeing of self, free to care and nurture. Eija Sevón argues that the desire 'can be a strong, overwhelming power that is only partly tellable or explicable' (2005: 472). De Marneffe quotes the Black American writer, Toni Morrison, who described motherhood as something 'liberating', leaving that space to nurture her baby and small child in total acceptance of who she was:

> Somehow all of the baggage that I had accumulated as a person about what was valuable just fell away. I could not only be me – whatever that was – but somebody actually needed me to be just that. (quoted in de Marneffe 2006: 48)

In 2010, Victoria White (2010: 14–5), an author and journalist who has four children with her husband, spoke simply of her need for 'wholeness', leading her to reassess what she wanted in becoming a mother. Ultimately it led her to give up her job as a full-time journalist with *The Irish Times*.

A decade on, Eliane Glaser is much less certain about assertions of 'wholeness', about the sheer cost of motherhood. Willing to write that she is 'well resourced and well supported … a very happy mother', she nonetheless argues: 'Here we are with more than 100 years of feminism under our belts … Yet mothers are still underpaid, overworked, exploited, overlooked, frazzled, isolated, and perpetually guilty' (Glaser 2021). Clare O'Hagan (2015: xii) in her study of working mothers in neoliberal Ireland has written that Irish society continues to use 'maternity to divide women in the public and private spheres', copper-fastening the problems at the centre of gender inequality. Her interviewees have struggled to deal with what they are told is their choice to be both a mother and to work outside the home. This seeming choice is belied by the realities of mothering in a patriarchal society unprepared to underwrite their decision-making with concrete social and economic policies to make their lives more viable.

This is just one of the currents leading women to reach conclusions at odds with the conventional image Irish society wants to portray about women as mothers. Bernadette Fallon (2019) has written that however women come to it amidst the confluence of life's circumstances, the decision to be 'childless' or an acceptance of childlessness means that one can face crude judgements, for example, of being a cold-hearted career woman. Fallon points out the many contradictions in contemporary Irish attitudes about having a child and how a woman can be more easily discounted if she has not had a child 'as if she mattered less', yet Ireland which now has only the third highest total fertility rate in the EU is a society where just short of 18 per cent of women in their mid-40s are remaining childless, many by deliberate choice (ibid.). An increasing number of Irish women live this way, with a clear emphasis on 'lifestyle' issues (Ní Chonchuir 2014; Carey 2015).[1] One woman quoted in Fallon's piece observes, 'Being

---

1   The word itself has a history bound up with the consumer economy taking shape in the twentieth century. In his autobiography *Timebends*, Arthur Miller recounts how in 1955, during a rent strike for better public housing in New York City in which he was involved with the sociologist and social activist, Richard Cloward, Cloward explained to him that collective action was already being whittled away by issues of 'lifestyle', a term Miller had never heard before. Cloward explained to him that it meant 'competing styles of life … essentially meaningless differences in clothing, speech patterns, taste in food, cars and so forth … Identification will be more and more in terms of style – the self-image will be politically neutralised that way. It's going to be style-conscious, not class-conscious' (A. Miller 1987: 362–4).

childless makes life easier – so many of my friends say they love their children through gritted teeth' (Fallon 2019). Perhaps that last comment is explained by a 2018 Everymum survey of 3,708 mothers of children from babies up to the teenage years which captured a number of contradictions and ambivalences: 86 per cent of the women who participated reported they were 'happier' since becoming a mother, while 73 per cent felt 'overwhelmed' and 62 per cent reported being 'lonely' (*Irish Examiner* 2018). Women who experience infertility find difficulty to negotiating that issue at a social level, in addition to their sense of personal grief and loss. Jill Allison (2013) in her analysis of infertility and involuntary childlessness concludes that absence becomes an ongoing present that women who are infertile must carry given what she terms the Irish heteronormative progression from marriage/partnership to motherhood.

Taking on that expected pathway and becoming a mother falls hardest on the shoulders of women who are economically least secure. In their study of poorer women dealing with the economic pressures of motherhood in Northern Ireland and Scotland, Lisa Glass et al. (2013) point to the increased burden of expectations on them: 'On the one hand she is to seek employment and work hard to lift herself and her family out of poverty and on the other hand, intensive mothering is positioned as necessary to secure children's well-being' (2013: 200). However, childcare costs make paid employment difficult for poorer women: the ESRI 2018 study on maternal employment and the cost of childcare in Ireland (Russell et al. 2018) concludes that Ireland, with one of the highest rates of childcare costs in the EU, allows those costs to fall disproportionately on lone parent families and families in the lowest income decile and that government policies need to better support these costs in order to lift households from poverty. That argument about employment being a key route out of poverty for less skilled women is itself less tenable in the face of the demands of a neoliberal labour market. In 2015, by which time Irish society was being asked to 'pay' for the collapse of the Celtic Tiger, with the EU/ECB/IMF troika of imposed austerity measures, Alice-Mary Higgins, then a policy officer in the National Women's Council of Ireland noted:

> Recent figures from the CSO tell us that 50% of all women workers are now earning €20,000 or less. Women are being faced not just with the loss of jobs but with a

dangerous erosion in the quality and security of jobs. Aggressive casualisation and the lack of affordable, accessible childcare are pushing more women workers into low pay and precarious part-time work. (NWCI 2015)

In many ways, that precarity goes unseen at the everyday levels of family living. For example, mothers who are already marginalised economically find it hard to make their voices heard about their children's needs in school settings (O'Sullivan 2019). When the precarity is exposed, through escalating housing costs, pushing women and their families into homelessness and emergency accommodation (Hearne 2020), when women have their children taken into care because they cannot cope with poverty and related personal difficulties (Deegan 2019), when there are disturbing increases in mothers committing suicide in poorer areas (Holland 2018c), the complexity of mothering is laid bare in acutely uncomfortable ways.

Given how these widely differing circumstances sketched out above are contingent on a range of factors well beyond the scope of the individual woman to 'solve', what are we saying to ourselves as a society about what we think a woman as mother can be, the quality of her life?

Feminist thinking on motherhood

In late modern societies, women face continuing tensions between the desire to mother and the constraints on how we mother while attempting to remain in any way faithful to what we consider as our own person and identity. Sevón (2005) suggests that while motherhood has become a choice for many, with the availability of contraception and safe abortion, it is a complex decision for all women because of the growing self-reflexivity that is part of late modernity. A decision to become pregnant, as distinct from the pregnancy that happens without being 'planned', is 'multilayered', full of contradictions and far from 'clearcut', dependent as it is on social norms, individual circumstances and relationships, and the vexing issue of when is the best moment, if that latter can even be defined

(Sevón 2005). Lowe (2016) argues that what appears as choice – because of the potential to control fertility, and thus our choice as women to move out of the domestic sphere in the name of greater gender equality – consistently runs across the normative discourses about 'good motherhood' which inevitably centre on notions of 'maternal sacrifice': 'At its heart, maternal sacrifice is the notion that "proper" women put the welfare of their children, whether born, *in utero*, or not yet conceived, over and above any choices and or desires of their own' (2016: 3). Not alone will women be judged by external critics as to how well they do so, if they fail to reach certain standards in the eyes of public authorities, they will risk their children being removed from them, as in the Irish case of the carceral system of Magdalene homes to contain women pregnant outside socially accepted norms prevented from keeping their babies (Smith 2008). In recent decades, in the United States, public discourses on the 'proper' or 'good mother' ignored the contingent circumstances of growing rates of poverty and racism affecting women and the nature of stratified reproduction, instead passing laws in every to designate 'safe havens' allowing women the option of giving up their newborns at a legal site and anonymously, and with the promise of 'no questions asked' (Oaks 2015). Advocates of these laws, motivated by cases of the death of babies who had been unsafely abandoned or 'dumped', focused on outreach to teenagers, women of colour and poor women, encouraging them to relinquish motherhood, deflecting attention to the root causes of 'unplanned' pregnancies and avoiding pregnant women's need for medical care and social support (ibid.).

The 'unplanned' pregnancy can indeed carry its own range of ambivalent responses for women in more secure circumstances, for as both Victoria White (2010: 12) and Anne Enright (2005: 13) describe, getting pregnant is often seen by the mothers of Irish women as the worst thing that can happen to their daughters. Melissa Benn in her book, *Madonna and Child: Towards a New Politics of Motherhood*, states it this way: 'The values of our time tell us that each of us can 'make it', woman or man, mother or childfree' (Benn 1998: 8). It is from this paradigm that the dilemma emerges as to whether being a mother accords with such values or whether, like the Bad Sisters in

Cinderella, we must cut off a bit of ourselves so that the magic slipper of motherhood completes an acceptable social identity. Often, women reach their decision having reflected on social constraints on the one hand and biological constraints and concerns about aging on the other. Anne Enright (2005: 13) said she spent most of her thirties 'facing a glass wall': 'On the other side of this wall, were women with babies – mothers, you might call them' (ibid.). She struggled with the notion of what it might be like on the other side of that glass wall, with that contested mothering identity. Women are affected as much by a 'sense of dividedness' about what constitutes individual achievement (de Marneffe 2006: 55) as by the 'low cultural value' attached to their desire to mother, evidenced by putdowns such as 'getting broody' (Sevlón 2005: 472).

The contradictions of motherhood have long been contested terrain. Writing of her experience of motherhood in 1950s America, Adrienne Rich said that it 'seemed to me the most painful, incomprehensible, and ambiguous that I had ever travelled, a ground hedged by taboos, mined with false namings' (1979: 15). Rich identified the ways in which 'institutionalized motherhood' as a construction of patriarchy was cast as demanding 'selflessness rather than self-realization, relation to others rather than the creation of self' (ibid.: 42). Rich's identification of 'sacred motherhood' with this sharp dichotomy between selflessness and selfishness became a fundamental issue within second-wave feminism of the 1970s and 1980s and is one with which feminist writers from many different perspectives continue to struggle (Brush 1996; Kawash 2011). Feminist scholars and activists have worked to isolate the social, cultural and economic conditions which sustain an ideology of mothering as selflessness at the expense of the everyday lives of women in unequal and stratified societies. They have also tried to honour the specificity of each woman's decisions about motherhood and how women care as mothers, however limited each woman may find herself in responding to conditions not necessarily of her own making (see Hays 2004; Ladd-Taylor and Umansky 1998; Oaks 2015; Lowe 2016). The arguments needed to explore the value of motherhood – its gains and losses – and to deal with its contradictions head on, what kind of undertaking it is. This is important work particularly amidst the current contest with resurgent conservative values that assign motherhood to women as the most 'natural' and 'best' status they can obtain.[2] Women need to ask can being a mother 'support women's personhood and claims to integrity, autonomy, dignity, security, and political voice'? (Brush 2006: 430; Hays 1996).

For Irish women, this sharp dichotomy has lessened but remains a constant preoccupation. It is arguable that the widespread experience for Irish women of the conventional nuclear family was concentrated within three short decades in the middle of the twentieth century before women once more sought other options (F. Kennedy 2001: 4–5; 1989: 9). Yet the public regime of gender relations, which had been contested by women at the outset of the state (O'Dowd 1987; Connolly 2003) has continued largely uninterrupted up to the Citizens Assembly on Gender Equality in 2021 which at least recommended changes to the 1937 Constitution, including the removal of Article 41.2, the so-called woman in the home clause.[3]

Pat O'Connor draws on work by R.W. Connell, Denise Richardson and Heidi Hartmann on heterosexuality to show how 'hegemonic masculinity' is maintained through 'social and cultural privileging' (P. O'Connor 1998: 69), often in subtle ways so that it becomes 'difficult to see how our sense of ourselves could be other than incomplete' (ibid.: 83). For Anne Enright, the problem of motherhood and how it cuts across what is deemed valuable work is acutely evident to a woman as soon as her baby is born:

---

2   The resurgence of conservative values and the extent to which they risk hard won gains for women are seen in the struggle to hold the line over reproductive rights in the United States, most especially that of legal abortion, and are also apparent in the punitive impacts of the 1996 welfare reform act on single parents (Hays 2004; Edin and Kefalas 2005; Solinger 2013; Briggs 2017). In Ireland, the Merrion Square Dublin-based Iona Institute for Religion and Society (2021) is a hub for promoting conservative views on heterosexual families, abortion, school choice, and 'the freedom of conscience and religion'.

3   The Citizens Assembly which met remotely through the Covid-19 pandemic, released its recommendations in April, 2021, including the deletion and replacement of Article 41.2, the so-called woman in the home clause and replace it with a non-gender specific clause obliging the state to take 'reasonable measures to support care within the home and the community' (Citizens Assembly 2021).

> It comes to you in a rush with the first baby – the unfairness of it. You become blind
> with a fury that is not quite your own – thousands of years of rage have been waiting
> until just this moment to say Hello. Why should your time, as a woman, be so little
> valued? Why should you be the one to give, and to bend? (Enright 2005: 155)

Pat O'Connor argues that while in theory childbearing women should
be recognised for the caring work they do, in practice, this does not
happen: 'There is little evidence to suggest that it is accorded high social
value' in Irish society (2000: 90). One of the 'forty-something' aged
women interviewed by Victoria White in her book, *Mother Ireland*, put
it this way:

> For women to reclaim motherhood it has to be safe. The woman, the mother, has
> to be respected and not rendered vulnerable to being abused, demeaned, devalued
> for the role she assumes. I am very aware that in this country we are not there yet.
> Motherhood is not valued. It is actively devalued. ('Maria', quoted in White 2010: 161)

Irish social and political institutions are hardly alone in extolling
motherhood and selfless domesticity as the centre of family life, while
also failing to support women as mothers (Kennedy 2004; Hilliard 2004).
The ideology of the selfless mother was widespread in nineteenth and
early twentieth-century Britain, United States, Canada and elsewhere,
having an enormous impact on social thinking about an ideal family life
(Cott 1997; Laslett and Brenner 1989; Williams 1991 2001; Lowe 2016).
Although the material work women did as mothers and wives was part of
their 'calm, devoted, and self-abnegating' presence (Cott 1997: xiii), then
as now, it was also simultaneously disavowed (Boydston 1994). This had
troubling consequences, perhaps most of all for those from working class;
marginalised ethnic, racial and indigenous backgrounds; and those women
with any form of disability (Ross 1993; Pooley 2013; Kline 1993; Kallianes
and Rubenfeld 1997; Horgan 2004). Excluded from the better-resourced
domain of White middle-class life, these were women who were frequently
judged not to measure up to the ideals that formed 'compulsory motherhood' and as a result, risked running afoul at the very least of public health
strictures and child welfare laws (Kline 1993).
  In one form or another, the ideological power of the selfless mother
carried through to the late twentieth century even as women worked in

increasing numbers outside the home, trapping them remorselessly between selfless mother and good worker (Hays 1996). This ideology was accompanied by strong regulatory frameworks of women's actions as mothers in western welfare states, often with punitive effects (Ross 1993, 1995) and these trends have continued into the twenty-first century directed especially against impoverished women, often of marginalised ethnic or racial status (Edin and Kefalas 2005). The force of this ideology was and remains sufficient to permit it to be redeployed purely in the terms of reference most useful to the state and its allied agencies which then impose these on the individual woman in the worst and most vulnerable of circumstances (Bridges 2011; Oaks 2015).

Feminist legal scholar Joan Williams (2001: 1442) argues that the notion of domesticity, at the core of which is the selfless mother, needs to be understood as an organising principle of the sex-gender system we have come to know so well. The essentialising role of motherhood is what second-wave feminist scholars and advocates strenuously rejected and often along with it, the very notion of being a mother. They rejected the heavy loading for women of caring work, citing its long-term damage to women's psychological well-being. Sheila Rowbotham describes the latter simply: 'We wanted new relationships and conditions in which we could have children and lead fuller lives' (1989: 86), but how were women to get those conditions? In Ireland, Jenny Beale (1986) argued that there must be a rejection of the exclusive role of woman in the home, be it in urban or rural, fast-urbanising, locations, precisely because of the impact of isolation and subordination for women as they endeavoured to fulfil their domestic roles. As Beale put it, the demands on women at home were increasing within a growing consumerist society, placing yet more pressure on women: 'People today expect more elaborate meals than boiled potatoes and brown bread' (ibid.: 46). Leaving the home behind and going into paid employment seemed a solution to some of the immediate psychological pressures.

However, this move itself made possible by the changing requirements of neoliberal capitalism and the shift to a service sector in so-called developed economies (Hardt and Negri 2000: 286–7), was built into a discriminatory, sex-segregated economy with the majority of working women in either full-time or part-time service jobs (Drew 1992; Ruane and Sutherland 2001: 36–7). Here and elsewhere, this shift corresponds to the second stage of Williams' two-phase model. If the first stage entailed the 'sacralization of childcare' in the Breadwinner/Housewife model, running from roughly 1780 to 1970, the second phase is the Ideal Worker/ Marginalised Caregiver 1970 to the present (2001: 1447–8). The ways we have approached this second phase have not solved the problem of the tensions women feel, the conflict now being between their roles as 'moral mothers' and 'ideal workers' (Williams 1991: 82) because the selfless mother must endure at all costs.

These 'recycled patterns' about gender and domesticity continue to frame women's daily material experiences of work and family. They also 'pit women against other women' in ways which are 'corrosive' about how they mother, given their responsibilities external to the family (Williams 2001: 1450, 1457). This conflict spills into and saturates the seemingly endless debates which have been termed the 'mammy/mummy/mommy' wars (the designation changes depending on geographical location) where women struggle with the implications of trying to fulfil both commitments, formal work and motherhood, or reject the former in favour of the latter.[4] Some women can do so from a position of relative privilege, examining minutely the voluminous research for and against nursery and childcare facilities for very young children (White 2010). Many must think through this struggle from positions where they are already on the social and economic margins, where to work for a minimum entry-level wage in an unskilled job, with only poor quality childcare available that is itself poorly regulated, jeopardises still further what they can do for their children (Benn 1998; Hays 2004; C. O'Brien 2013; Murphy-Lawless and Edwards 2014). All of these concerns are played out against a background of public debate by professional experts about every single aspect of mothering and parenting in what seems an ever more tightly drawn scrutiny of maternal actions from pregnancy onward.

In a compelling opinion piece, Irish novelist Emma Donoghue (2011) begs women to end their 'mutual surveillance' of one another in the mammy

---

4   Kawash (2011: 970) notes that in 2003–4 alone, there were over thirty academic books published on motherhood in the United States.

wars, pointing out that as mothers, we need to bring to a close the 'strange tendency to slide from the descriptive to the prescriptive to the proscriptive'. She can see the energy and investment in our identities as mothers but wonders at the origins of the 'tense scrutiny' which leads to the formation of myriad 'hostile tribes'. Daphne de Marneffe too objects to the 'noisy extremism' (2006: 145) of the mammy wars, arguing that it obfuscates crucial discussions about 'the hard, undramatic choices involved in providing enough care for our children' (ibid.). While the concept of 'choice' is itself problematic for poorer women in a 'society of consumers' (Bauman 1998: 39–40; Solinger 2002; Edin and Kefalas 2005), de Marneffe's argument is ruthless in its clarity. She wants us to consider the distinctly unglamorous work of having and rearing children and how it raises a problem of imagination for every woman who thinks about motherhood. Each one of us must try to make sense of 'what kind of a person … would be willing or interested in putting together that kind of devotion and attention' (2006: 272). Each one does so in social and political contexts inimical to the notion of support for mothering, so that a 'crisis of self' reflects 'a crisis of society' (ibid.). Arlie Hochschild (1997: 249) has described the ambivalence and conflict aroused by this crisis as 'the most difficult and frightening aspect' of contemporary parenthood, 'the need for "emotional investment" in family life in an era of familial divestiture and deregulation' (ibid.).

Yet the satisfactions are undeniable as read through the work of poets like Nuala Ní Dhomhnaill, whom Patricia Kennedy (2004) includes in her exploration of Irish motherhood. These are a few of the lines from Ní Dhomhnaill's poem, 'Feeding a Child':

> the sun rises up the back
> of bare hills,
> a guinea gold to put in your hand
> my own

Kennedy writes of the poem, 'We can sense the soft skin of both the baby's hand small hand and the mother's breast from which the child drinks its fill' (2004: 17). However, as much as we may be able to feel the force of this poetic image of nurturing and responding, it is becoming a curiously unmentionable experience. De Marneffe warns that maternal desire 'has become increasingly problematic' whereas sexual desire is taken for granted: 'It is almost as if women's desire for sex and their desire to mother have switched places in terms of taboo' (2006: 4).

Economic and demographic changes through the Celtic Tiger years

There have been multiple challenges for Irish women for whom child-bearing continues to be an important experience amidst the entwined impacts of a patriarchal overhang, a neoliberal economy, and the problem of domesticity. Some women have vastly greater agency to make a decision to become pregnant or not, or to keep a pregnancy, compared with others, but for all women these decisions are threaded through a range of personal complexities of each woman's life and hopes set within class, sexuality, ethnicity, and so on but also within a changed Ireland.[5]

The Malthusian alarms over too high a population in Ireland is a long-vanished discourse, and while the large family as a typical cultural phenomenon survived into the twentieth century, it had come to an end by the beginning of the 1980s.[6] There are always anxieties on the part of the state about the size and composition of the population and these are never ethically neutral (Douglass 2005). We have already seen how women's emigration and the decline in marriages were viewed as evoking a crisis for

5   In Ireland, because of the continuing tensions around access to abortion, we have seen in Chapter 4, the conflicts thrown up for women up to the referendum on the Eighth Amendment in 2018, though difficulties remain; see Chapter 6.

6   The total fertility rate (TFR) fell steadily from a peak rate in the mid-twentieth century of 4.07 in 1964 to 3.26 by the end of the 1970s to 2.08 by the end of the 1980s. It remained below replacement level throughout the 1990s. At its lowest, it was 1.85 in 1994 and 1995. The downward trend was then slightly reversed so that through the latter end of the Celtic Tiger years, with the TFR reaching 2.07 in 2008, just as the economy began to collapse (McGrath et al. 2006; CSO 2012a) before it began to drop again reaching below replacement level by 2011 (CSO 2017).

Irish society in the mid-twentieth century and the fear that the Irish would simply disappear (O'Brien 1954). This fear about population decline has a problematic history on par with that of discourses on over-population, and is used to frame powerful images of national decline (Douglass 2005: 6), just as it did in 1950s Ireland. Since the state's foundation, the dependency ratio – the number of people between the working ages of roughly 15–65 who can be classified as 'economically productive', in comparison with the numbers dependent on family and, crucially, the state's resources – has been a continuing preoccupation for Irish politicians and policymakers, albeit always within a masculinist frame of reference. Since the programmes for economic expansion from 1958 onwards successive Irish governments have courted economic growth in the hopes of stemming emigration (Lee 1989). Since the 1980s this preoccupation has been bound up with gaining the un-trammelled economic expansion associated with globalised neoliberal markets (Harvey 2005). These moves have impacted on women's working lives with the number of women in the paid workforce expanding steadily since 1986. By 2004, it was just over 55 per cent of all women between the ages of 15–64 were in paid employment. With the demise of the Celtic Tiger, this figure dropped to a low of 46.7 per cent in 2011, but then recovered to 64.2 per cent by 2019 (CSO 2005, 2012d, 2020a). However, Irish women continue to work fewer hours than men and earn less than men (ibid.) and this is centred on what Ursula Barry and Pauline Conroy-Jackson term 'the classic form of a deregulated labour market in that prevailing gender norms are reflected on the labour market – flexibility means different experiences for women and men workers' (Barry and Conroy 2012).

It is a labour market profile which also very directly concerns the motherhood dilemma and the consequent need to work part-time. 'Ireland's welfare regime is a mixed hybrid model combining strong elements of market-organised and delivered services with women in the family expected to deliver care and support across a range of social needs … caring for children and persons who are long-term frail or with disabilities' (Barry and Conroy 2012: 2).

During the Celtic Tiger era, in 2004, the fall in the dependency ratio was cited as a 'demographic dividend' because more people were available for employment and thus for paying taxes, while at the same time, the state could reduce its provision of essential services to the populace (P. Sweeney 2004), in line with the demands of globalised state economics. However, the need for the 'right' demographic profile was cut across by a sudden increase in inward migration, with people coming both from other EU countries and as asylum seekers (Kennedy and Murphy-Lawless 2003; Fanning 2007).[7] Women's personal decisions about motherhood inevitably carry the burden of state macroeconomic thinking. According to the OECD, Ireland now has the third highest rate of childlessness in OECD countries (K. Byrne 2019) and if we do give birth, we do so later: more than two years later from the beginning of the Celtic Tiger to its denouement, and now three years later (CSO 2019a). Women have felt able to shape their own circumstances about motherhood, at least in part, but the difficulty about popular media discussions on mothering and 'lifestyle' is that they can cover up so much, including substantive inequalities amongst women (Barry 2008) while the stark realities of an economy that has become entirely dependent on the vagaries of global consumer capitalism (O'Toole 2003a; Allen 2007) have created still more strains and disaffections for individual women. Our interviews were conducted in the final few years of the Celtic Tiger when the economy was already contracting, and before its calamitous implosion in 2008. However, almost none of the problems women discussed in relation to motherhood have gone away. If anything, they have redoubled in force.

7   In a very real sense the patriarchal state is never satisfied. At the same time that nation states across Europe are preoccupied about the dearth of babies and the impact on dependency ratios, arguing about the way to get what they see as the 'right' kind of population growth (Douglass 2005; Kligman 1998), there is concern about the 'wrong' sort of growth which is entangled with perceived threats to the national coffers and ever-present latent racism. Thus EU states, despite an overall rhetoric about human rights, have periodically tightened coercive strategies, including legislation, so as to limit inward migration from non-EU societies, as happened during the 2015 'migration crisis' (Hintjens 2019). Ireland did so with its 2004 Citizenship Referendum (Fanning 2016: 11–2; see also Chapter 6) though even this did not prevent Ireland from becoming a truly multi-ethnic society (ibid.).

Thinking about motherhood and counting the cost

Within this context, central to women's thoughts about motherhood are the timing of it and the subsequent costs. The irony of effective contraception is that most women will need to decide when they wish to become pregnant, or whether they wish to take on motherhood at all. It is not a straightforward decision within contemporary relationships. As Sarah, 30 years of age, puts it, when her female friends tell her that they are pregnant by choice,

> I'm like 'You actually *what*? You actually *planned* to do this!' like 'Wow!' With planned pregnancy having become the norm for many women, the issue of choice is inescapable and becomes almost a kind of burden. How prepared must one be to decide to become a mother, how mature, how sure of oneself and one's partnership? (Sarah, 30, teacher, metropolitan area)

Other women shared their perspectives, elaborating on the complexities of their decision-making:

> I think it's really more pressured, the choice. I mean it's better having the choice, obviously, but there's lots of pressures – 'Am I not being a full woman if I don't work and have interests, am I not being a proper mother if I don't stay at home and mind children and all.' You know, even delaying when you start having the family or the choices around that. Playing God almost, I suppose, 'I'll take contraception until this time and then I'll stop, and then I'll want a baby'. That's what we're deciding. Whereas before that decision wasn't really there. (Marcella, 28, civil servant, small town)

> For me, it's kind of like, I just don't feel ready. (Emily, 29, community worker, small town)

> I'm nowhere even near dealing with it. Because you see I still think of myself as being like, about twenty, really. (Sarah, 30, teacher, metropolitan area)

> I mean, you have a child, you can't put it on hold for a couple of years and do something else, it's such a huge commitment. I would find a lot of people in their thirties are … they still consider themselves to be sorting themselves out, you know?! They're still getting there, you know? (Cliona, 32, systems analyst, metropolitan area)

The construction of selfhood and of women's perceptions of their sense of self and their current way of life, and how children disrupt those meanings are reflected back to them by their wider family and friends with queries about starting a family:

> The five year plan thing kind of worries me, I try not to have one, but there's nearly a pressure to have one. And when will you have your children is the question that's being asked of us since we got married. Christmas cards we get saying 'We're waiting for the patter of tiny feet!' and you're kind of going 'Help! I don't think so!' So it's kind of funny. And it's a joke and all that, but I'm kind of going 'Hmm, I dunno about all of this.' I'd be very alarmed about women trying to be Wonder Women, trying to do everything. And just conscious of the influence of advertising, and all these women's magazines, and programmes from the US even, this whole Delia Smith [British celebrity chef] type 'This is a perfect dinner to make, and this is the way your Christmas table should look' and I just get really frightened by that. I can see friends of mine being absolutely frazzled and stressed out and feeling that they're not a good mother, and really beating themselves up. (Siobhan, 30, trainee solicitor, rural area)

> The pressure is off a little bit from my parents, because my sister had a baby two weeks ago! So the first grandchild is born, phew! So I'm off the hook. But yeah there are definitely pressures, and more so, I have this aunt who sits me down every time she sees me and tells me the statistics of getting pregnant at my age. (Jane, 28, scientist, small city)

> Well I'm not really getting that pressure from my parents, now my mother would be very good and she says enjoy my life, well enough settling down at thirty. And my dad doesn't ever say anything like so I'm grand that way. But I find there's a big pressure around friends and just general chatting like, just about settling down. (Niamh, 26, nurse, small city)

The work of seeing 'self' and accurately assessing selfhood runs parallel to and often merges with major practical considerations, especially perceived financial needs and anxieties:

> I mean, I like the idea of an unexpected joyful pregnancy, but unexpected and joyful if all the pre-conditions are already in place! Then it can be as unexpected and as joyful as it likes! But not if I happen to be unexpectedly and joyfully on the dole in a bedsit. (Mona, 26, health worker, small town)

> If you can't financially afford it, you can't buy a new car, you know, if you can't pay for childcare, if you don't have a house, or can you have an extra child … you know, I think there are very real problems. If you can't afford to give up your job, and if

you don't have a partner to support you, they're all very kind of practical things as well. (Sinead, 30, nurse, small city)

The felt need to establish career prospects while sustaining a relationship and then to add in the realities of having children contribute to an intricate and difficult, if not impossible balancing act:

It's impossible. At the moment, I'm working full time, I've had to do overtime at my work, and then college two nights a week and every second Saturday, and then trying to fit in study. And even trying to meet up with friends or wash clothes during that week is very, very difficult. And I just think if I had the added responsibility of a child I'd have a nervous breakdown by now, I really would! (Abby, 27, media officer, suburban area)

One woman queried how comfortable she and her partner were without children:

Possibly to us, I mean, we've reached our current advanced day, and we have a comfortable lifestyle, and don't want to compromise it too greatly, in a 'Aah, live in a shoe box on the side of the road, raise our children on lentils and so forth' way … I don't know. That was actually something I was talking about with my sister over the holidays, was have we, because we haven't had … I mean, she's twenty eight and I'm thirty one, and neither of us have even sort of begun to think of planning a family so far. Are our expectations of our potential level of material comfort, have they become inflated by our years of childlessness? And there are non-financial reasons why I don't have any children yet. My musical work often takes up an enormous amount of time. So I don't think either of us are really ready to make that jump either. But it would be nice if and when we do, that we were in a position to do so. Does that make sense? (Sadhbh, 31, computer operative, metropolitan area)

The cost of housing and the quality and cost of childcare are ever-present concerns and most women voiced their uneasiness about these factors:

I have seen it absolutely grind people's lives to a halt. And it doesn't matter how much you earn, well, it does, if you're earning a hundred thousand, then that's grand. But you know, your friends might be earning on average thirty five thousand each a year, so that adds up to what, seventy grand a year, and they're renting. And the conditions of renting, I mean the conditions, No pets, No children, No this, No that, No permanency, one year lease, no security, not at all. And I have seen people just stuck. And I'm thinking in particular of a friend of mine who is heading for forty. And just missed the boat and just no security at all. So how can you possibly have children? And it's not just about having children, how can you build a life? How can you make plans? You know? Basic things. (Sarah, 30, teacher, metropolitan area)

We've been together for a few years now and I think we're definitely planning a life together … but I don't think financially we're in a place where we can talk about it in comfort. So it's definitely because of the lack of assistance in terms of childcare, and the fact that I couldn't really be at home, we'd need the income coming in. Because of the difficulties of finding adequate childcare as well, a place that you're comfortable as a mother to leave your child, I don't think we're ready for it at all, there's a lot more thinking needed. (Joan, 34, civil servant, small town)

How do people do it, I mean, I struggle from week to week to pay my bills, and then a crèche on top of that, and then a small amount left over then to go out and have a few drinks, where would you bring the money in? It's a hundred and fifty euro a week in a subsidised crèche at work. (Nora, 27, local authority worker, small city)

Seeing the impact of these pressures on other couples, that sense of grinding to a halt induces still more anxiety as couples struggle with the decision to have children. For one woman and her partner, these pressures led to a decision to move away altogether from Dublin, where house costs remain highest:

In Dublin I think that house prices for young couples is a major issue. I think that when you're starting out, you're getting married, obviously your house is the priority. And then you eventually move on to children. And that's when it's a big crisis of life. Particularly for women … So that's more pressure. Like for me, that's one of the reasons we left Dublin. (Ann, 33, rural tourist guide, rural area)

Without an ongoing partnership as an anchor for motherhood, there is still that sense of the importance of financial security and support before making a decision to have a child, as with this woman below who is single:

For me it's not essential to have a partner in my life … But definitely, to be secure would be the main thing, financially, emotionally, because it's a huge thing to go through. And definitely with good support systems in place, be it friends, family. (Aoife, 22, shop manager, city)

Some women have begun to think differently about maintaining a job and a home life with children and to consider if it would be possible to withdraw from the workplace without losing the status of an independent woman, and not be judged harshly for doing that:

> I mean, we have been very open from the start. We knew very quickly that we were going to get married to each other. And have been very open about things like children, and how long we'll wait, and even how many we'd like to have! So I think I wouldn't like to work. I'd like to have a few years to rear my children. Even just to see them into their twos or threes. Just to have time to spend with them as babies, and just kind of be around. Just to see them and be with them and bond with them. Something I'd like, so I'd like to not work outside the home for a few years. (Nuala, 24, voluntary organisation worker, suburban area)

> But my sense is that it's nearly turning again, especially where I come from at home, it's nearly OK to take five years off and bring up your children. It's now seen as a luxury if you can afford to do that, you're giving your kids the best start in life. If you can survive economically, it's kind of the ideal option. I'd certainly love to not work for five years. And I wouldn't perceive myself as lazy. (Ciara, 27, midwife, small city)

> For a long time, it was just, my career was it. I just wanted to start a business, run a business and be successful at that. And make money and then that was the way that I could prove my whatever. So for many years I had decided that's it, motherhood is just not for me. And I was clear that I was not going to be a mother because I don't have any maternal instincts. Seeing women with babies was just like 'keep them away from me. I don't know those things.' But now I definitely feel some kind of a biological clock ticking. (Maureen, 33, self-employed, small town)

Making the choice not to have children

Given the pressures of negotiating between self, partnership, work and motherhood, some women are deciding not to prioritise motherhood at all. The growth from the late 1990s in much better paid careers, combined with sexual freedom, means that some Irish women are now in a position to state openly that motherhood is not their preferred option. Although there is talk about the feeling of 'baby hunger' (Hewlett 2002; *The Irish Times* 2003b) for women as they grow older in countries like the United States and Britain, perhaps for the first time in Irish society,

women have been able to state their positions openly, resisting certain
censure about this decision.

> When I was twenty-five, twenty-six, I'd see little children and go 'Oh God, aren't
> they gorgeous, I want to have one' ... and then suddenly that wore thin very fast
> when I started babysitting my friends' kids, and my nephews ... And now I'm kind
> of thinking 'Do I really want to have children? Like really?' So it's very interesting
> how I've changed in the space of a few years. And I don't know is it that whole selfish
> reason. Is it because they're very expensive? Is it because I want to go on and further
> my career? Is it because I want to have like ten holidays a year? I don't know why.
> (Siobhan, 30, trainee solicitor, rural area)

> I'd have to do a couple of years' experience here, and then I'd like to go and work
> various places abroad. And I'd be like 'when do I fit it in!' And would I really want to
> do it? You know? I think I'd ... Because I really want, I really like travelling, I could
> happily spend my days travelling round the world, and it would be a lot easier too,
> without a baby in tow. And my boyfriend has said, he's like 'if you want to have a
> baby then I'm happy enough to have one with you, but if you don't that's fine by me.'
> So he's kind of leaving it totally up to me. So, I dunno. Maybe like if it happened
> accidentally, grand, get on with it. But at the moment I can't see myself planning to
> have any. (Shauna, 26, student nurse, small city)

> I'm twenty-nine now and I don't feel a bit maternal to be honest. Maybe in my mid-
> thirties I will think about it. (Molly, 29, restaurant worker, small city)

> I'm not interested in children at all. I want to continue with my career and it's just
> not my thing. (Hazel, 29, sales manager, city)

Decision-making about having children and thinking about their
care can and does shift for women in their late thirties and early forties, as
Maureen summed up so well:

> I think the pressures on women are huge. It's really difficult to invest fifteen or twenty
> years into a career and then have a child, and hand that child over to someone else to
> raise. Or try to step out of that career for a number of years to be with that child, and
> also probably the financial burden in today's day and age. Or finding a man that can
> actually, who has a good enough job that can pay for a woman not to work. I know
> that I picked men that I didn't want to have children with. So it was really easy for
> me to concentrate on a career, concentrate on relationship, and handle contracep-
> tion. Now, because I've begun to think about having a child, I've actually had to
> have conversations with this new guy about what it would take for me to continue
> my business, maybe at a much lower level, what it would cost, what I would expect
> of him. (Maureen, 33, self-employed, small town)

These negotiations with oneself, with one's partner, about introducing a child into one's life have become ever more pressing.

Unplanned pregnancies

The core assumption that the responsible management of self means managing one's fertility decisions, and whether and when to have a baby, does not preclude unplanned pregnancies where the woman opts to keep the pregnancy. One large-scale study during the Celtic Tiger period, the 'Growing Up in Ireland' project, reported 41 per cent of women having an unplanned pregnancy (Williams et al. 2010). As we set forth in Chapter 4, the official definition of a crisis pregnancy is one which is not planned and not desired by the woman involved. It is usefully broad so as to encompass the range of circumstances women may have. However, it can be argued that such a definition inadvertently places a premium on the rational, if not fail-proof, management of fertility, so that any unplanned pregnancy is an event deemed to be a crisis. The Irish Contraception and Crisis Pregnancy study found that 29 per cent of women said they were either 'happy' or 'calm and peaceful' during their pregnancy, but negative emotions in varying degrees were reported by a substantial number of women who defined their pregnancy as a crisis pregnancy (Rundle et al. 2010: 144).

The 'best time' to have a baby weighs heavily on women, as we have already seen. Timing was an issue for this young woman who had sought an abortion when she became pregnant in her first year in college. Yet she did feel able to accommodate a second unplanned pregnancy with her long-term boyfriend on the equally rational ground that there was no 'good reason' not to carry through an unplanned pregnancy:

> I was finished college, and things were different and I just kind of thought like, well once I spoke to him, and he was completely okay about it, and he was really good about it. And I thought there wasn't really any good reason not to do this. I mean, I was going to either go straight into work after finishing college, and then in a few years take a year out and have a baby, you know. Or else take a year out and have a

baby and then go to work next year. So it was decided it didn't make any difference. (Marie-Therese, 24, retraining scheme, village near a small town)

Some younger women and women on their own remembered strongly negative emotions, their own feelings and family reactions:

It's hard for anybody I think, if it's not planned, it's hard for a woman who is married, with a house, a car and a job. Even under them circumstances it's hard when it's unplanned, but in my circumstances, I had just started in the job. Me and the baby's father hadn't been together long. He wasn't in a great job. I was 18. So it was hard. It was very, very hard. I would say for about six months I was in denial I'd say. Just 'Don't talk to me about it, I don't want to know'. (Liz, 20, bank clerk, small city)

Yeah, and it would have been the Catholic background, rural area, huge shock, to the family, and to the … it happens to someone else, it doesn't happen, it never happens to us, only happens to other people. (Evelyn, 34, rural tourism manager, rural area)

One woman in our group of interviewees became pregnant when she had just turned fifteen. An early school-leaver in a very small town, she was already in an established sexual relationship with her boyfriend, albeit with no contraception, and had begun to work in a local hotel when she discovered she was pregnant. She 'put off' telling anyone for three months:

At the start, I didn't want to tell anyone more because of the rejection. My mam was upset and that. She said that she had reared her children and she would not rear my child for me. It was a very hard time. (Karen, 23, back to work trainee, village)

It was only after her baby was born that the young woman had the confidence to seek out contraception, asking a local GP for the pill. She had to leave her parental home soon after the baby was born and find rented accommodation and then her boyfriend left her. The experience of one crisis pregnancy and then being on her own at such a very young age, she was then 16, with her young baby made her constantly worried that the pill would fail or that she would forget to take it, and she not want to face another crisis pregnancy:

I did some research for myself, got hold of information on different types of contraception. I went on to Depo-Provera for a few years. That worked for me. It was a great relief. It fit in and I trusted it. (Karen, 23, back to work trainee, village)

Good education and work opportunities were seriously limited for this young woman and for others in our group who were from a working-class background where early school-leaving was a reality. An unplanned pregnancy in these circumstances held different meanings, including a sense of self-blame for not asserting a wish not to have sex or the necessity of asking a male partner to use contraception. In practical terms, there was also the likely reliance on social welfare as a single parent with no training or qualifications.

> Totally unplanned! I had to tell my family straight away, because I was in a relationship at the time and he had told his mum. And I thought I'd better tell mine before they found out from somebody else, which would more than likely happen. My family didn't react to it well at all. I was left on my own for months on end. My mum, it was anger. Like how could I be so stupid and … but at the end of the day I didn't hear anything from them about sex education or anything. I learned all I knew from friends or magazines or TV. To be honest I'm not blaming it on this or anything, but to me, I was never taught to say 'No', or you could say No like. And that's a couple of years, like she's three now. And whenever I started becoming sexually active or whatever, that I didn't realise, it was probably stupid of me, but I didn't think 'Jesus you know, I can say No here'. (Pauline, 23, unemployed, village near small town)

> When I got pregnant with my daughter, it was, I will be honest, it was kind of a shock. I slept with this bloke twice, and I fell pregnant by him. I was young. Looking back I don't regret my child, but I wish I had waited and did something with my life, because now I can't do anything. Can't work. It's quite hard. And that's a situation I do kind of regret. And obviously I was young and I should have used protection and I didn't. (Marie-Therese, 24, retraining scheme, village near a small town)

It seems likely that younger women giving birth under the age of 20 may have represented a lower socio-economic background with still quite limited access to reproductive health resources like contraception. The inter-related complexity of social inequalities and social exclusion (Mayock and Byrne 2004: 34) needed serious attention for younger women who in practical terms lacked access to age-appropriate contraception support clinics (Kavanagh 2005; Higgins and Murphy-Lawless 2009). The number of women giving birth in this age range have fallen steadily since Celtic Tiger times: in 2004, 2,560 women under the age of 20 gave birth while these numbers were down by two-thirds in 2019 (CSO 2004: 27; CSO 2019a).

Women from Dublin's inner city pointed how the vulnerabilities of very young women were impossible to disentangle from the realities of an area abandoned for two decades to widespread unemployment and an illegal drugs culture:

> It hasn't changed that much since me Ma's day. Not greatly. You probably have more choices, but you still don't have the option of accessing the services that's needed … I know there's girls working, and they're in to their ninth month pregnant. And they're into street prostitution in Dublin, some people in the hospital, the workers in the hospital, they know that in the hospital. But yet it's allowed continue. The only thing that happens is the social worker comes in, and yeah, for the child's benefit, but where does the mother, and where does the support come for the mother? And I see the problem now is worse, because they're younger. I see them, fifteen and sixteen years olds living on the streets, and they're more vulnerable. (Deirdre, 30, community worker, metropolitan inner-city)

It was also noted that far from having 'choice', young woman drug users could face pressure to accept injectable contraception alongside methadone treatment:

> She has no choice, she isn't given the methadone unless she takes this contraceptive. I mean, that choice is taken away from them. (Sharon, 28, voluntary drugs worker, metropolitan inner-city)

The vicious outcomes of social exclusion and economic marginalisation in a deeply unequal society (Coulter and Nagle 2015; see Murphy and Rosenbaum 1999) distort women's decisions and experiences of pregnancy and motherhood.

The chronic problem of Irish maternity services[8]

Alongside the power exerted over women's lives by church and state in twentieth-century Ireland, a third entrenched group, the medical

8   Chapter 6 provides a more detailed analysis of the cumulative damage done by this professional monopoly.

profession, exercised control over pregnant women's bodies and the issue of where and how to give birth. Dogmatic ideologies, principally the 'active management of labour' (O'Driscoll and Meagher 1980) aided a professional monopoly over the care of pregnant women and operated as an unquestioned national health policy for seven decades (O'Connor 1995; Kennedy and Murphy-Lawless 1998; Dunlea 2021). Women became trapped in the outdated 1954 Maternity and Infant Care Scheme which marginalised midwives working in the community while putting in place conditions for an expanded obstetric–led centralised hospital system of maternity care which further compromised the professional autonomy of midwives (Dunlea 2021). Women have learned to put up with a medicalised production line with fragmented care, steadily worsening ratios of midwifery staff to women creating unsafe conditions, a bare minimum of postnatal support once discharged, and one of the lowest rates of breastfeeding in Europe (M. O'Connor 1995; Kennedy and Murphy-Lawless 1998; P. Kennedy 2002; Dunlea 2021). It has created yet another conflicted arena which women must learn to negotiate:

> I just get a real sense from watching people who I know who have children, they're like these little isolated cells without any sense of there being anything there for them that they don't have to work really, really hard for, and beg for and kick for. And it's hard enough work having a child without having to scream for anything you need. And I'm not even talking about entitlements, just in terms of having to find, you know, if you want to go any alternative route, you have to go and find it and you have to face all the ill feeling and the people clicking their tongues and going 'Oh my God! You're having it at home! I wouldn't do that!' If you don't want an epidural everyone around you goes 'Aha! Wait till the third hour and you'll want it then!' So just the lack of any alternatives. (Mona, 26, health worker, small town)

Unusually, in a country where there has been virtually no support from the extant health structures for home birth up to very recently, one of the women was born at home. However, it did not seem a realistic prospect for her to do as her mother had done, as she reflected on what she sees as the risks in birth:

> I was a home birth myself, I suppose I like that idea. Then again it scares me greatly if anything went wrong. After going through nine months and something going wrong, it's very scary. A pregnancy here is a gamble one way or another. You can do things

to the letter of what every book tells you and it can still work out wrong. (Denise, 25, office worker, suburban area)

A health worker in a smaller rural setting understood how maternity care is constrained by the production line approach bringing with it wide-scale interventions; she linked it to cutbacks and closures of local hospital-based maternity services:

I know there are issues around the caesarean sections, and the numbers of them that are happening, and around home births not being actually, that's not an option for a women, and the cutbacks mean that some hospitals are losing their maternity services, and what that means for women living three hours from a hospital, from a maternity service. People living in rural areas where the closest hospital is one that's, you know, hours away. And all about that kind of timing your birth, and making sure it happens on a Monday at four o'clock, and that's it, because you live so far away. (Kate, 30, health services administrator, rural area)

For several women we interviewed who had already given birth, the lack of support in hospital tainted their entry into new motherhood. The woman who had been 15 when she gave birth did not attend antenatal classes. But she did try to read about the pregnancy and her boyfriend was with her when her son was born:

The labour was hard and a nurse said to me, 'What do you expect when you didn't go to antenatal classes?' My boyfriend replied, 'What the fuck are you on about?' (Karen, 23, back to work trainee, village)

The fragmented care told heavily for Liz who was young and at the beginning of a career path when an unplanned pregnancy changed her circumstances. She felt entirely unsupported going through the hospital system with complications including a breech position which she could feel but which staff neither picked up on nor did they listen to her:

It would have been the second appointment I had, they did a urine sample and there was blood in the urine. And obviously being a first time mother I said 'God, like, what's that?' 'Oh you don't need to know about that.' So I said 'Well, you know I'd like to know about it.' 'No, you don't need to know about it.' And I'd say on my third last appointment I said to them 'Do you think that everything's okay' because you could feel it. You know. The head like [of the baby]. And they said 'Yeah, yeah, you're grand.' So the day I went into labour I went in and the nurse said 'Let's have a look at you.' And literally, I just pulled up my top to show the bump and she said 'How long have you been breach?' So it shows that I was nothing but a number. Every doctor I went to – a different doctor every time because I went public – and every doctor I went to must have said to himself 'Ah sure she'll be here next month and it will be somebody else's – it will be another doctor's problem.' (Liz, 20, bank clerk, small town)

After focusing on how her own experience of pregnancy was dismissed, compromising her and her baby's health, Liz reveals that hospital policy prohibited her from having support during labour and delivery:

They wouldn't let my partner in because it was an emergency. But if they had of listened to me it wouldn't have been an emergency. In my opinion they really, really, really have an awful lot to learn … for them to tell you there's nothing wrong, and then to go in and find that there is something wrong. It's very strange.

Nuala, a voluntary organisation worker in a suburban area, understood how this system of care is not sufficient for women's needs:

I wouldn't like to have a caesarean section. Definitely not, no. I definitely want to have a relationship with the person who is going to be with me, to deliver the baby and everything. And I think I'd like to have a midwife. I don't know if there's midwives at all births. I don't know a lot about maternity services. But, just to have gone through the pregnancy and birth with the same person. And maybe even aftercare. Like, to have a relationship … I'd hate to be pregnant, and all of a sudden go into labour and be rushed off to somebody that I didn't know. It just seems panicky. I just want to be assured that everything will be well, and that I'd know the person and they'd know me. They'd know what type of a person I was even or I'd know what type of a person they are. Just to be comfortable and used to them, and used to the baby. (Nuala, 24, voluntary worker, suburban area)

In talking with young women about their desires and experiences of maternity care, we were aware that women were little able to spare the time to focus on the issue of giving birth and saw no immediate route to having different more supported birthing.[9]

9　What is striking is that these were women with relatively straightforward support needs. For women experiencing domestic violence in pregnancy, so much more

What are state supports for pregnant and new mothers?

The Maternity Protection Acts 1994–2004, with statutory amendments in 2001 and 2006, appears to give reasonable statutory protection to working women in respect of twenty-six weeks of paid maternity leave, plus, if a woman chooses, sixteen weeks of unpaid maternity leave. She is meant to have protection of all her employment rights. She has protected paid time off for antenatal and postnatal appointments, for breastfeeding (if workplace facilities for breastfeeding are not provided by the employer, a reduction in working hours with payment in lieu must be provided), and time off if the baby requires hospitalisation.[10] No woman can be dismissed for being pregnant and women are entitled to return to their same position with the same contract they held before becoming pregnant. The length of paid maternity leave has been extended twice since it was first instituted in 1981, when it was fourteen weeks long. Some employers, generally larger organisations, will top up statutory maternity leave payments to an employee's full wage for the twenty-six weeks. This package could be far better, but the legislation seeks to protect a woman from discrimination simply because she has become pregnant with the Maternity Protection Acts operate alongside the Employment Equality Acts 1998–2008. The Equality Authority has the task of ensuring that all statutory entitlements for women are observed (Equality Authority 2012). Nonetheless, taking maternity leave has proven to be a minefield

needs to be done. Although Ireland did pass the Domestic Violence Act 2018 in line with its obligations to ratify the 2015 Council of Europe Convention on Preventing and Combating Violence against Women and Domestic Violence, known as the Istanbul Convention, the threadbare nature of our maternity services, the lack of autonomy for midwives, the lack of community midwifery all put pregnant women experiencing domestic violence at still greater risk at one of the most vulnerable points in their lives (Webster 2019; O'Brien-Green 2020).

10 The Acts have since been supplemented by the Paternity Leave and Benefit Act 2016 which allows a fortnight's paid leave for the father, partner, whether spouse, civil partner or cohabitant, and for the parent of a donor-conceived child.

(C. Taylor 2015), especially for women in the services or retail sectors (Banks and Russell 2011).[11]

In the early 2000s, women were still required to begin their maternity leave a fortnight before their due date.[12] This simply did not match their realities. Even now most women who are in employment try to position their maternity leave as carefully as possible to take into account all of the competing pressures of caring for a very young baby, paying the cost of housing, be it rent or mortgage repayments, and having to anticipate and pay for childcare. Whether women have managed successfully has been dependent on differing employment sectors, with those employed in smaller, private sector companies and retail/wholesale sectors often harder hit. At the time of our interviews, outright lying about due dates was a common coping tactic. Here, a woman speaks about her sister's experience:

> My sister's just had a baby. She took two weeks beforehand. She did the usual Irish thing and she diddled her dates so she could work as long as possible so she could use the time after the birth, rather than before. She had a very healthy pregnancy so she was in a position where she could do that. Now that she's on maternity leave, she's no top up pay, just the state maternity pay which certainly doesn't cover the cost of the mortgage, which they took on the assumption that they would have two wages coming in. So that is a huge issue, and obviously means a lot of compromise

11 A detailed review of fifty-four cases of pregnancy-related discrimination between 1999 and 2008, the timeframe between the two Equality Acts, revealed that women face a number of negative consequences in their workplaces, including dismissal from their jobs, merely for becoming mothers (Banks and Russell 2011). Organising adequate representation for cases which are heard by the Equality Tribunal or the Labour Court is important for outcomes (ibid.: 28) with compensation in these cases ranging from €2,000 to €85,000 (ibid.). Many thousands of queries flow each year to the Equality Authority about entitlements and rights under the legislation (Kirwan 2011). However legislation itself does not prevent poor treatment. In a 2011 national survey of 2,300 women, a substantial minority of women, 30 per cent, reported poor treatment, ranging from being given unfair workloads to loss of salary to loss of promotion to outright dismissal (Russell, Watson and Banks 2011: xi–xii).

12 This has since changed. Women are asked to give four weeks' notice that they will be taking maternity leave and although employers would still prefer women to begin that leave a fortnight before the expected date of birth, there is now more room for women to adjust that pre-birth interval to their own needs.

and a lot of sacrifices on the altar of motherhood, or of parenthood. (Joan, 34, civil servant, small town)

Women watch one another in the workplace and can see for themselves that working up to the fortnight beforehand brings its own stresses:

No space to centre yourself about 'Oh my God, my baby's going to be born next week,' getting your head around it. (Bernadette, 30, catering manager, small city)

I know a couple of women that actually did do it, but then, once it came they actually had to leave the few weeks early because they just weren't physically able to stand on their two feet, so they had to leave. But you'd see them, and I be there saying 'When are you due?' and they'd be eyeing you saying whatever date fitted like, because the manager would be around, like, you know. The managers would know that they're lying about it, but they can't prove it, you know what I mean. (Jacqueline, 30, financial services, suburban area)

Despite the seeming extent of statutory protection, many women feel the pressure of having to plan pregnancies to satisfy workplace commitments:

The whole planning around important aspects of your job. I mean, you hear some women talking about that, 'Oh September's a very important time in work, so I couldn't be off on maternity leave.' You know? Not being allowed to have your baby and enjoy the baby. So you very much have to fish around, and get a sense of what your future bosses' views are on that. I always ask that as a question now. And it raises a lot of eyebrows. I was in a job interview there this time last year, and I asked what was their policy on, I suppose family friendly policies, and if I was to decide that I was to have three children in the next five years, what procedures would be there, you know, crèche facilities, all this. And they were just completely going 'Em, well, we've never been asked that at interview before.' And they were like 'Do you want to tell us something? Are you pregnant? You need to tell us this.' (Agnes, 29, financial advisor, metropolitan area)

The sense of having to satisfy employers about availability is a barrier for some women when seeking new employment:

It's like, people shouldn't be regarded as an impediment to business success for being pregnant. If that's something that's unconsciously going through a prospective employer's mind, when I, as a woman of childbearing age, go to interview for a job there, I don't want them to think 'Hmm, it could be her, but it could be this man, or this post-menopausal lady, or somebody else who is equally unlikely to give birth in the next ten years.' (Eve, 29, marketing assistant, metropolitan area)

I've had a relatively heated discussion with some friends on the subject, because one of them manages a small business. And he was 'You don't know how terrible this is, these women running off and having babies and taking maternity leave.' It was interesting to see his perspective on it, much as I felt it was unreasonable. (Cliona, 32, systems analyst, metropolitan area)

These pressures are cumulative and support for difficult decisions women must make about their jobs, about even telling their employers they are pregnant, is not necessarily forthcoming from friends, employers, or partners:

I've a couple of friends who've had children within the last year. One of whom I see fairly regularly. It's kind of an odd issue for me with the girl I see fairly regularly, because, I think we're very good friends, but she made a very definite 'I am going to stay at home with my baby' decision. Which she made before her maternity leave, and she didn't tell her employer she wasn't coming back. And obviously she had her reasons for doing so. But I've been trying to keep disapproval out of my voice lest I sound like some sort of spokesperson for IBEC [Irish Employers and Business Federation]. And obviously I don't know what decisions I'm going to end up making, if and when I have children. (Sarah, 30, teacher, metropolitan area)

But it's worrying as well that people are afraid to tell employers that they are pregnant, and are putting themselves and their unborn child at risk, health and safety aspects of the job. I did a lot of agency work as a nurses' aide, to get money, and it's a dreadful job, and ugh, I wouldn't go back to it if I can, ever. But a lot of women, they have no skills, they left school early, and that's a job that's easiest to get into, and they're not trained properly, so they're putting themselves at risk, and then a lot of them are pregnant. There are no hoists in place, which there should be by law, and they're lifting heavy men and women with strokes say. And you really wonder about miscarriages and things like that just happening from pure physical stress and strain of these poor people who have to keep working to try and pay the rent. (Fiona, 24, health worker, metropolitan area)

A friend of mine, her husband was just made redundant, and she's on maternity leave, they just had their second child there, and same age as me, twenty nine. And she had to leave her maternity leave early to go back to work, to try and get some money coming up to Christmas. Because Santy and all, the whole trimmings of Christmas have to be paid for. And it's awful, because she's really struggling now. She was struggling as it was, but with the second child now, who wasn't planned either, I really

worry about them, and how they're going to cope. And the relationship is coming
under strain, and they're fighting a lot more, and the husband's drinking a lot more.
It's that whole horrible situation that you read about, and I can see it developing
before my eyes. (Emily, 29, community worker, small town)

Several women cited a clearer framework for maternity rights as lacking
and state support for pregnant and new mothers as a clear policy failure.

Most of the jobs I've done are temporary. So therefore, if I did get pregnant, my
maternity benefit would be minimal. I'd have no job security. I think for part time
workers and women working in these, I hate these categories, but in the whole non-
professional jobs, where they would be able to speak up for themselves. I know
there's all these regulations and directives coming in, but are these really enforced,
you know? (Nuala, 24, voluntary organisation worker, suburban area)

I think I do see it, maternity cover, as something where I feel, the same as with house
prices, that it's somewhere the state has let us down. There's just no feeling of accepted responsibility for you or any children you produce. It's almost like anything
is begrudged to you. And it makes me really fucked off, because I have the opportunity to get up and leave, but what about the people who don't? (Mona, 26, health
worker, small town)

Mona articulates the exact problem for many women, especially in lower-
waged work. They have no reasonable work alternatives and have to carry
on regardless.

Working mothers: Shouldering the pressures of work, home and childcare

The overwhelming majority of women take the current paid maternity
leave package and a large majority then return to work, but that is not
an easy decision or transition. It is women without the treasured middle
class career path, lower paid women, women with two or more children and women who are single parents who find it especially difficult
to return to work and who are most vulnerable to the combined impact
of workplace practices and economic and organisational pressures, chief

amongst which is the cost of childcare. State spending on and state subsidies for childcare remain amongst the lowest in the EU while childcare costs remain amongst the highest with the burden falling on the shoulders of the individual (Russell et al. 2018).

Despite the fact that the rapidly expanding workforce relied on women's vastly greater levels of employment to help create the so-called Celtic Tiger economy, where GDP grew by 9.3 per cent on average each year between 1994 and 2000 (O'Toole 2003a: 10), supporting women workers with children was a non-priority by the Irish state. An issue that should have been the focus for collective political action for all women was, and remains, a divisive one between women with the argument being raised whether it is responsible to have children at all:

> It's awful, I just see so many people nowadays having all these kids, but because of the fact that they have to go out to work, they end up spending no time with them at all. And I kind of, I really think it defeats the purpose of having a child at all. That you send them off to their creche at seven o'clock in the morning and don't see them until six, and by that stage they're asleep so. It's terrible because you have to work to support having the children, but then because of that you don't see them. It's a real Catch-22 situation. (Abby, 27, media officer, suburban area)

> Even last night I was thinking about it on the DART, when you see these girls that are so young, and they have all their babies with them, and they're obviously not doing everything all day long. And it makes me kind of think, well, I'm not having a child because I can't afford one, that's not fair. They're obviously on the dole, and they're so much younger than me, not that I want one now, but I actually considered the fact that I can't afford a child. That's one, the main factor why I wouldn't. I mean there's people working horrendous hours and not seeing their kids, and then there's the people not bothering, who don't have the money, bringing up all these kids. (Jacqueline, 30, financial services, suburban area)

These realities which are there for all women but with differing burdens in relation to class and resources exist entirely outwith the current minimalist statutory framework and split women amongst themselves as to who or what is responsible when the glittering life of partner, work and a young family proves to be fool's gold. One single parent, who became a mother when she was fifteen, carried significant pressures as a very young single mother and early school-leaver. Dependent on a low-waged job in the local hotel, she was told by the hotel manager that she needed to return to work three months after the baby was born and she knew too little to raise any objection. In that same interval, she struggled with accommodation for herself and her baby, first trying to live with her parents and then with her boyfriend's family. Tensions were great on all sides and without concrete support for her with the baby's care, she had to give up work and rely on the single parent's allowance, beginning to retrain only when her son turned eight:

> I went back to work shortly afterwards, part-time. I only had 12 or 13 weeks maternity leave. I only managed to stay a few shifts. The baby was so young. (Karen, 23, back to work trainee, village)

A somewhat older single mother with somewhat better prospects as a trainee bank clerk was also struggling over the sheer cost of childcare and resented other single mothers for accepting the state allowance and not working:

> I think some people get everything and other people don't get anything at all. I mean there's loads of people that I know who have babies and are receiving an awful lot of benefit from the government, where as I would receive nothing. And to be honest with you in my opinion it's because I'm out working, and I am willing to give it a go, and give it a try and I mean it is hard. It's finding childcare that I can afford. I pay 700 euro a month, childcare, I mean that's half my wages. When there's people sitting at home and they're getting everything handed to them, oh it is very, very frustrating. (Liz, 20, bank clerk, small city)

It is indeed frustrating and the issues of cost and availability and the juggling with time pressures that accompany a return to work rightly preoccupy women:

> It is very hard to combine everything. Work and relationship you can do. Work and one child, you can just about do, but when it comes to certainly work and two children? The price of childcare is so, so expensive, so that almost even rules out working for a lot of women. Certainly for me it does, thinking about it. And because working hours having got so long, it's very difficult. Who's going to pick up the child from the crèche? Your husband or partner may be working till maybe ten o'clock at night. And then it falls on you. So it's very difficult, for me it would be very difficult to have any kind of career. (Agnes, 29, financial adviser, metropolitan area)

Well yeah, because they're just stuck with the childcare issue, aren't they? I mean, with lower paid couples, it's not an option for both of them to work. And then grandparents are stepping in and like, the whole structure or strength of this family unit is being stretched and twisted. It's not necessarily that people aren't trying, they are. But they definitely need more help. And not handouts as such, but positive support. Like, be it childcare within the workforce or whatever, that they can actually work, and they can effectively raise their own children, and feel powerful enough to be a family unit. (Bernadette, 30, catering manager, small city)

Stress. Big stress. Yeah, and you see it in them when you meet them like. Because it's not all about you any more, you lose the, like, everything about yourself, it's all about what the baby needs, and you know, it's a struggle like, it's just such a struggle. And especially like, even people who are renting, they just have no chance of getting a house, it's just not going to happen. And because they have a baby, and all their extra cash that they would have saved if they didn't have the child, goes towards the child, and you never manage to build up savings, because there's always something. (Shauna, 26, student nurse, small city)

What is telling about these pressures is the lack of any sense of collective response to them in order to gain any substantive support at policymaking levels.

The realities of rural contexts

Women living in more rural settings had more limited career options, but also felt they could manage work more readily because there remains enough of a more traditional extended family network to help take some of the strain out of the decision to have children:

I left today, dropped two boys up to my parents, they're both in their eighties. And then tonight we'll go out, and the mother-in-law will take over. So they're very lucky children that they have all their family, their aunts, their uncles, me, their father. We're very lucky, we live with my mother-in-law, and she's great. Most of the time! And then my parents are the other side of me, moved down from ___ to live down this side of the country. (Brenda, 28, farmer, rural area)

But I think the family network is so important. And if people don't have it, if their grandparents are nowhere near them ... I think that's very sad. Maybe because we're from large families that help, everybody helps everybody. And I think that we're very privileged to have it. (Patricia, 32, small business owner, rural area)

Greater involvement of men

Women also cited the cultural shift which has made possible far greater involvement by partners and husbands in the care of children:

> Guys are playing a much bigger part in rearing their kids at a younger age. Because like if the mother's going out to work, then a lot of people are doing shift work at different times of the week so that the father can be there during the day and then Mum's gone at night. I think economically it kind of dictates it as well. Either you cannot pay for childcare or you cannot afford to have your kid or you don't want to have your kid in a crèche, five hours five days a week, so definitely, looking at my friends who are my age who have become daddies, planned or not planned, they have been really involved with the rearing of their children. (Ciara, 27, nurse, small city)

> It's great to see now, fellas pushing prams, and they no longer get the jokes like years ago. I think it's now seen as part of society. That's though from the outside, I don't know, I have no personal view of how they are behind closed doors or anything. Just from outside it looks better. (Elizabeth, 27, occupational therapist, small city)

> It's about equality, in terms of bringing men into that, of welcoming men into that scene as well, and it's not just a female domain. A lot of men want to be more involved like, and it's not really fair to say 'Oh well, men don't really care about childcare.' I think that they do, but it's very difficult for them to express those kinds of feelings. (Kate, 30, health services administrator, rural area)

One woman from a rural setting demurred:

> I was at a childcare conference about two weeks ago, the county childcare committee. And there was two men in the audience, and four at the top table. And they were talking about how things have changed in Ireland around childcare, and I know they have. But you just looked at that audience, and it was just full of women. There's more and more happening around parents, parenting programmes and more support for fathers, and that's all very good. But just that day I thought, 'This is just the same as it's always been.' (Caoimhe, 25, rural project manager, rural area)

A tiny number of men are full-time fathers in a two-parent household and that number has seen modest growth. At the time when we did our interviews, there were 4,900 men engaged in full-time home duties; a decade later there were 9,200 men (CSO 2016). The number of men who are single parents had grown somewhat: 10,100 in 2006, 12,900 in 2016 (ibid.). However women as mothers are overwhelmingly carrying on with what Arlie Hochschild and Anne Machung (2012) have named 'the second shift'. The price of their entering the labour force in massive numbers has been the related pressures to do the double workday: paid employment and the everyday work of parenting and organisation of the household.

Where are we going as women and mothers?

The women we talked with had much to say about the challenges of motherhood and the struggles for working mothers. Women see and know these challenges in advance at least in part. They see the realities of the 'second shift', making the prospect of taking on motherhood daunting:

> Two people that work with me have two children each, with one, there is a three year old and one's just been born this year. And they have to work full time, Monday to Friday, they have to travel up from the country 'cos it's too expensive to live in Dublin. They're leaving their house at six in the morning, they're not getting back until maybe half six at night. Their children are babies, in crèches, the crèches are costing them a thousand Euro a month. So even with our pay, which isn't huge, I mean, they're not actually walking away with a lot of money, by the time you take off petrol, travelling costs, babysitting. But the little bit that they are getting, they have to have that because the mortgage is so high. So if they stopped working for four or five years, they wouldn't be able to even afford to pay the mortgage. So it's a very kind of, trapped nearly. I think they are very, very stressed out, because they can't do their job as well, because they're exhausted. Absolutely exhausted. By the time they get into work. And then they'll be leaving early if the child's sick ... Financially they're all very stressed as well. So it's something that I would have no interest in that at all. (Fiona, 24, health worker, metropolitan area)

Yet the larger social expectations about mothering remain and women still respond to this:

> But yeah, Ireland, is, that's what you're supposed to be doing. There is that thing when you're in a long term relationship, OK they might accept now that you're not going to get married, but will you hurry up and have the babies please? (Bernadette, 30, catering manager, small city)

Despite many decades of feminists writing and campaigning and despite efforts to build more equal relationships in the home and in the workplace, all the messy contradictions and the sheer graft for women are still there. Women face an uncertain relationship to the labour market, along with the economic devaluing of their caring work. They work fewer hours in the formal labour market and earn less than men (CSO 2019b) and they do so to enable them to do that second shift, they do it to be able to mother. Given the embedded social inequalities in Irish society, the stratified nature of mothering remains unchanged. For women in well-developed careers with good pay, it is hard. For women lower down the qualifications and employment ladder, for women surviving at the very margins, they simply cannot see their daily lives reflected in the consumer-oriented glossy weekend supplements available in every corner shop. At the height of the Celtic Tiger, the evidence pointed to single parent female-headed households as those most likely to be poor (P. O'Connor 2000: 91) and if anything, this has worsened since the austerity cuts imposed following the collapse of the Celtic Tiger. As Victoria White (2010: 45) has argued, Irish women have to make 'stark choices'. Women are detrimentally affected by economic currents over which we as a society have chosen to exercise no control whatsoever. For example, we have seen that the price of housing, bought or rented, the profit-taking on this core need for all families, fuelled the Celtic Tiger and has been a recurrent preoccupation for women thinking about becoming mothers. It clouds their individual ambitions and their dreams and leaves them querying how they can afford to be mothers. Celtic Tiger Ireland, with all that excess of economic growth, had no political agenda to radically improve the conditions in which women take on motherhood.

It could have radically reshaped our families and our communities. That time is gone and with a decided lack of commitment on the part of the state to even consider economic support for new mothers and new parents, women have been left to search out for themselves individual and often deeply unsatisfactory solutions to their dilemmas about core needs for them and their children. In this late modern capitalist society of ours, women continue to become mothers and try to 'eke out the satisfactions of mothering' (de Marneffe 2006: 136) as best they can but as Rachel Thomson and her co-researchers have argued, 'working and mothering are entangled and entwined, creating insights that are both exciting and intolerable' (Thomson et al. 2011: 193). This sums up the perceptions we have presented in this chapter, and that combination of the exciting and the intolerable throws light on the undone work that lies before us.

Loss, Athwartness, Resistance[1]

The story of the men who loved Ireland has often been told, but of Irishwomen the hero tale has not been told.
— Susan Mitchell 1919

So many things get covered up these days, I am just so thankful that this has come out.
— Catherine Corless 2017

Women have died, women will die … these are the daughters of Ireland.
— Emma Mhic Mhathuna, message to the Taoiseach, 8 May 2018

Thinking again about Ireland's peculiar history

In the first chapter, we referred to Yeats' poem, 'Down by the Salley Gardens', the source for this book's title. The story it presents is of the man who regrets a love lost to him, who has failed to act on his desire for a life with the woman who is confident in hers. Through the lines of the poem, we glimpse a woman who is unafraid to take command of her relationship with that man. Untroubled, she places her hand on his shoulder and urges him to be as free in himself as she is in herself, standing in the field by that river alongside the salley trees. The grace and fluency conveyed to us in the second verse of the poem embodies all we might want for

---

1   We use the term 'athwartness' from David Lloyd's (2008) work to emphasize how Irish women's lives are shaped in opposition to an expected or socially accepted course of action, particularly in an oblique direction and in response to the need for resistance.

women who seek to live their lives with genuine agency. An old woman's memory of a country song, refashioned by Yeats into those well-known verses after he encounters her on a walk, gives us a hopeful image of what all women in contemporary Ireland have the potential to be, strong, able, confident about desire, about sex and about motherhood should we wish it. It is a hope yet unrealised in its totality. Inadvertently, Yeats and the old woman, who herself will have been born before the Famine, bring us to consider the steep gradient of loss and dislocation for women that has made up much of our history in post-Famine Ireland.

Through all the phases of modernisation that Irish society has traversed, through its singular demographic regime of depopulation along with staggeringly high rates of fertility persisting well into the twentieth century, to the pressing realities women face currently: this is what the quotations above, from women spanning the last 100 years, also bring us to as with a clarion call. All three of those women, Susan Mitchell, the republican essayist from the privileged social background shared with the Yeats family, who argued for the importance of not excluding women's experiences from Irish public life; the local historian Catherine Corliss to whom the country is indebted for revealing the numbers and location of babies and young children who died in the Tuam Mother and Baby home in the twentieth century; and Emma Mhic Mhathuna who lost her life in 2018 to the CervicalCheck scandal[2] draw attention to the specific consequences for women of that long historical epoch. The post-independence Irish state, endeavouring to 'put all that behind us', that is, the backward, impoverished, largely agrarian society with its problems of acute poverty, over-population and its presumed fecklessness, sexual and social, which had been endlessly critiqued in classical nineteenth-century commentaries (McLean 2004), was as integral as the Catholic church in fashioning a climate where women's voices were silenced.

Ironically, the wave of economic and political adjustments in the late twentieth century which ushered in the Celtic Tiger era led to the perfect

---

2   Emma Mhic Mathuna was one of several hundred women affected by the initial CervicalCheck scandal. Mother of five children, she died aged 37, five months after a High Court settlement in her favour against the state for non-disclosure of her original smear test results from 2010 to 2013. See also note 11.

Irish subject. This was the one longed for by those political economists, often British, writing before the Famine and put forward as a solution to the 'Irish problem', where abandoning subsistence agriculture, 'the vigorous, sexually active body' (McLean 2004: 53) would be disciplined into a well-ordered hierarchy of work and production within conventional relations of capital (ibid.: 53–7). We certainly got there in the end: the consumer capitalism of late modernity has created 'the radically individualized subject' (ibid.: 44) schooled into being the 'smart woman ... with good make-up and carrying some fashionable shopping bags', that 'better class of women' whom Ann Marie Hourihane (2000: 5) notes in her tour of Celtic Tiger Ireland, the women flying to New York City to shop, spending approximately €2,400 on each trip (Milne 2019: 193). However, our participation in the globalised consumer economy has been at the price of our also accepting a deeply unequal society, with many women left behind, many struggling, and all of us still having to deal with deeply unequal gender relations with concrete consequences in a state which remains a consummately patriarchal undertaking.[3]

In this concluding chapter, we return to aspects that the women we interviewed spoke about in light of what has changed in the last fifteen years. We then set out what still urgently needs to happen at ordinary everyday levels for women. The heterosexual women whose stories and analyses appear in Chapters 2 through 5 were taking on their adult lives exploring sexual desire, making decisions about their relationships and about motherhood in the expansive Celtic Tiger years, a time of far greater affluence than Irish society has ever before known. Women have been freer

---

3   Murphy (2018) argues that the 'lingering effects' of Ireland's traditional male bread-winner model is still evident in the Irish taxation and social welfare regimes. In the latter, when women with caring duties register as unemployed, the state's assumption is that they are available for work full-time, an assumption which ignores their caring obligations. Unless they fulfil that full-time requirement, women are ineligible for important ancillary training and support services. Barry and Feeley describe how such structural aspects cumulatively end in great economic disadvantage for women because of how the unacknowledged 'gendered nature' of caring relationships continues to reinforce 'damaging patriarchal notions of male hegemony' (2016: 45).

than any generation before them to shape their sexual lives and to access in
ever greater numbers social and sexual freedoms. Yet their efforts to get to
grips with what they wanted or needed, the problems they have encountered along the way, have been far from straightforward. Many critical
matters remain unresolved.

Despite the profound relief over the success of the 2018 referendum repealing the anti-abortion Eighth Amendment, we face a social landscape of
undone work, much of which is connected to the nature of a still avowedly
patriarchal Irish society. At first glance, patriarchy appears to be an archaic
notion out of step with the free-flowing sophistication we display in our new-
found consumer ways of life, but it is there daily reflected in the actions and
non-actions of the state and in our principal institutions. Many do benefit
from current social arrangements in the short-term, including many men. In
the long term we must do the political work of seeing far, of connecting and
of imagining anew what is needed for a much different society for the better-
ment of circumstances for everyone.

If we construct a timeline between the X case in 1992 and the Repeal referendum, we can name what ebbed away, most notably the rapid decline of
the Catholic church in the wake of the avalanche of sexual abuse cases. There
was also growing openness about sex but it was not matched by comprehensive education and health services from institutions like schools and health
centres which are all basic undertakings of the state and which could have made
a concrete contribution to individual well-being amidst the cultural change
about sex. An exception to this was the work of the Crisis Pregnancy Agency
set up by government initiative as a statutory agency in 2001. The Agency developed a floodtide of creative initiatives and research to begin to equip young
women (and young men) with that greater understanding of being sexually
active safely. Nonetheless, openness about sex continued to be jeopardised by
the feeling that sex, especially the conditions of safe sex, was something to be
embarrassed about and worse. This emerged in our interviews, for example,
in the lengths women had to go to and the questions they were asked if they
required emergency contraception.

Although every society creates its own dysfunctional myths about
sex, the particular Irish elements at work here bear recalling because of
the critical overhang of older mores that constrained and even imprisoned

women for so long.[4] The influence of the twentieth-century Irish Catholic church as a signal dimension imposed on women is only one part of that *longue durée* which formed the mores of post-Famine society such as we find recounted in John Throne's *The Donegal Woman* (2006). We need to see how and why the post-independence Irish state has retained its conservative, patriarchal rootedness affecting women's status even as it has attempted successfully to 'align itself with an emergent global order' (McLean 2004: 160). As Walter Benjamin writes on the uses of memory, we must 'not be afraid to return again and again to the same matter … to turn it over as one turns over soil' (2005: 576) if we are to make sense of what has still to be accomplished. For women, this actually takes in post-Famine times with the memory of Famine death and ongoing social dread: of poverty, of the loss of land and status, and above all for women, the loss of social respectability because of their out-of-place bodies in a history which has had especially long-lasting impacts.

'Liquid modernity' (Bauman 2005) itself has brought its own constraints and downsides, like the pressure to have sex because contraception is taken as a given, often before very young teenaged women feel ready to do so. We must deal with these pressures which are part of our contemporary culture in parallel with the often-unspoken aspects of our punitive history which remain strewn across our current scene 'not simply as past but as an abiding, if unacknowledged, contemporary presence' (McLean 2004: 157). These present dilemmas for both women and men. Younger teenaged women continue to deal with 'the reductive prism of the male gaze' and feel it necessary to protect themselves from that gaze (Orenstein

4   Leane (2014), in her analysis of interviews with older Irish women born between 1914 and 1955, quotes an Irish social worker in London employed during the late 1960s and 1970s in an agency supporting unmarried mothers. She stated that even when dealing with women from traditional 'Catholic' countries like Italy and Spain, Irish women appeared to carry a far greater burden of shame about being pregnant outside marriage: 'They were the most difficult to deal with, you know, because … they had all the baggage. A huge amount of it. And the *contortions* that a number of Irish girls went through … the sense of being … of having misbehaved, was a very strong reflection of Irish attitudes' (quoted in Leane 2014: 47–8).

2016), while teenaged boys continue to be socialised into masculinist attitudes towards women which border on the abusive, abetted by the rapidly expanding commodification of sex including the widespread consumption of pornography (MacNeela et al. 2018; Dawson et al. 2019; Orenstein 2020; J. O'Connell 2021).

We argue that matters are far better for women in knowledge and material terms now but hardly fully better especially when we take in the reality that contemporary Irish society is brutally unequal.[5] With a more complex picture, we can understand how much work lies ahead and the nature and forms of activism we require. That unrealised fragment from a distant past, the woman standing confidently by the salley trees, can help us 'through the ruins of progress' (Lloyd 2008: 71). It can inspire us through all our damaged pasts and presents to imagine the alternatives we wish to reach. If we summon our resistance, if we stand to one side of the Irish state, athwart as David Lloyd (2008) puts it, and outwith the official Irish establishment of our managed 'increasingly administered society' (Brown 2001: 12), we can seize our 'politics out of history' (ibid.) to help us get to that project of a 'still-to-be-realized alternative' future (Lloyd 2008: 72).

---

5   Unemployment rates which stood at 4.8 per cent just prior to the collapse of the Celtic Tiger in 2008 rose to 15.5 per cent by 2012 but by 2017 had dropped to 8.4 per cent. However, the austerity measures, tax increases and social welfare cuts imposed on Ireland in the wake of the 2008 crash by the European Central Bank, the European Commission and the International Monetary Fund have had short and long-term consequences, with average incomes of the poorest 10 per cent much lower still by 2010 (OECD 2013), and even with a partial economic recovery by 2019, single parent households with one or more children under the age of 18 had the highest at risk rate of poverty, 29.7 per cent compared with 6.1 per cent in two person households with one or more children under the age of 18 (CSO 2020c). The overall percentage of women in Ireland at risk of living in poverty stands at 14.9 per cent. Women are over-represented in the numbers of people on minimum waged work, 55 per cent females to 45 per cent males (Burke-Kennedy 2019). Ireland is rated 'as one of the most market unequal countries in the EU' (P. Sweeney 2020: 20). See also note 9.

'Uneven modernity'

In Chapter 2, we encountered a thoughtful reflection from Christine, age 31, unemployed and living in a small town, who said of women and sex: 'Sex has become an almost subliminal programming by people in suits to sell products and the "humanity" has been stripped away.' This reworking of sex, where it has become entangled in an uncomfortable dynamic with the reinvention of self, shaped in the marketplace of late capitalism, has also changed how we view the meaning and force of sexual desire. Anna Clark (2008: 11) argues that the older radical tradition of sexual desire 'as a way of transcending self – whether in a greater love for the divine, for nature, or revolution – to celebrating sexual desire as a way of knowing and expressing the innermost self' leaves us with a conundrum: 'Sex [as] the truth about the self can be just as rigid and imprisoning as earlier restrictions, because it prescribes boundaries for the self in terms of identity' (2008: 11).

This current problematic about sex is one we did not anticipate as women activists in the 1970s, 1980s and 1990s, as we endeavoured to roll back both Irish public attitudes about sex freely chosen and official state restrictions preventing those individual decisions by women. Ireland's peculiar history has left us well behind in shedding those earlier constraints on the pursuit of sexual desire compared with other western societies which had begun to change by the 1960s. Hera Cook (2004: 281) points out that in Britain as early as 1964, half a million women were prescribed the contraceptive pill on their own request and this rose by 1989 to include over 75 per cent of all women born between 1945 and 1959, regardless of marital status. Our near neighbour's shifting social attitudes to what was then called premarital sex, underpinned by unconditional access to safe oral contraception by 1975, preceded by the iconic 1967 legislation on abortion, created spaces within that high period of modernity where women's sexual desire might now interact openly with the values and weight of liberal individualism and autonomy, albeit in a predominantly heterosexual culture (ibid.).

Our struggles in Ireland were darker and more prolonged within a timeframe that carried late into the twentieth century and has touched the first two decades of the twenty-first century. The restrictions on sexual expression imposed by the rigidly conservative male-dominant social order of post-Famine Ireland in their cruelty oppressed women, creating 'fallen women' but never 'fallen men' (Ferriter 2009: 17), and that order carried over forcibly into the first seven decades of Ireland as an independent state, its hold loosening only slowly in the 1990s. Not only did sex and sexual desire remain hidden (ibid.: 15), women were forced into a myriad of painful contradictions as they sought to deal with the impact of this social order imposed on their private everyday lives.

As always in this struggle, the poorer a woman was, the harder it bore upon her. At the same time Michael Solomons was working with a group of socially conscientious doctors to set up the first family planning clinic in the late 1960s and early 1970s (Solomons 1992), the trend towards early marriage since the 1940s had culminated in 64 per cent of all women being married by 24 years of age (Murphy-Lawless 1987). The subsequent family size was largest amongst poorer women who had far poorer health and who were living in deeply inadequate conditions. The raft of state-sponsored housing programmes between 1932 and 1942 dramatically reduced the numbers of families living in slums in urban areas, especially Dublin (Lee 1989: 193), was important also in retaining cheap labour on site in the centre of the city. These housing schemes, like the complex of over 400 flats built in Sheriff Street in the Dublin docklands continued to cheat the lives of poor working-class women throughout the 1960s and 1970s. Without access to any form of contraception, they endeavoured to rear large families, twelve children not untypical, in tiny two-bedroomed flats which had only a toilet, a small sitting space with a table for meals and a scullery in which children were washed and food was prepared.[6] These were the social conditions that drove Solomons and his group to found the Irish Family Planning Association against public opposition. Completed family

6   The Sheriff Street flats were demolished by 1998 and the site sold to developers as part of the expansion of private luxury housing and upmarket retail outlets to sit alongside the International Financial Services Centre. Rita Fagan, one of the leaders of the women's group fighting for regeneration and community control of St Michael's estate in south inner-city Dublin, has argued, 'poor people live on very rich land in this city' (2016: 383).

sizes of 7–9 children in 1971 (Murphy-Lawless 1987) impinged above all on the lives and health of poorer women from urban and rural backgrounds alike. The Coombe Hospital, one of the three public maternity hospitals in Dublin, continued to celebrate its status as 'the home of grand multiparty' (Feeney, quoted in Murphy-Lawless 2002: 913), that is, seven or more children, at the same time refusing to offer anything other than a clinic with the 'rhythm method' of contraception. Working-class women attending the Coombe in the 1970s were seeking the contraceptive pill and their lack of interest in the 'rhythm method' led to the undersubscribed clinic being closed down for lack of clients (Solomons 1992: 27). Middle-class women were already using the contraceptive pill from the 1960s onward, but they had recourse to private medicine. Like their mothers before them who had been able to seek out contraceptive devices discreetly from the time of the 1929 ban on contraceptives (Ferriter 2009: 193–4), thousands now availed of prescriptions for the pill as a 'cycle regulator' obtained from their own GPs (Solomons 1992: 23).

These class differences and the consequent stark outcomes in many women's lives did not feature in the Irish state's account of itself, its 'mythic patriarchal narratives' (Gibbons 1996: 4) effectively denying women's quotidian realities. The shifts in government policy from the late 1950s onward, opening the country's lacklustre economy to foreign direct investment and then to the expanding liberalised markets that accompanied EEC entry in 1973, played an unexpectedly vital role in changing the contexts about sex and motherhood and gradually breaking up the conservative hegemony about women's roles being primarily in the home which had held sway for so long. Terence Brown notes that the changes brought in by the EEC were viewed by a few prescient voices for their potential to 'alter the face and mind of the nation' heretofore bound by its mythology of a 'traditional Ireland' (Brown 1981: 231) in which women's rights, for example, were at best those that stemmed 'from their relationship with an individual man' (P. O'Connor 1998: 4). In 1961, in what was characterised as a low-skill, low pay economy (P. Sweeney 2004: 14), there were 379,000 people employed in agriculture. This sector shrank rapidly over the next twenty years, so that by the 1980s, farming was already half the size it had been. By 2004, under markedly different conditions of a globalised economy, agriculture represented only 6 per cent of the work force while the service sector represented 66 per cent (ibid.), a proportion of which was also low-waged. Those same decades saw a complete inversion of the once universal norms about women's work, and a society which had been socialised with images of women's contented domesticity and promoting her principal role as wife and mother with her extensive unpaid labour had vanished. By the 2000s, a raft of legislation and incentives reflecting the demands of a rapidly expanding consumer economy had brought about the recognition in law of women's rights in their own names, for example, employment and social welfare entitlements, though the 'consistently grudging' state response to childcare (Russell, McGinnity and O'Connell 2017: 394) revealed the continuing 'ambiguous status of women in the public arena' (P. O'Connor 1998: 4). This was despite the fact that, by then, 65 per cent of women were employed by then in the formal labour market, dominated by the services industry.

Lee (1989: 651) argues that 'the post-famine image makers' had set about 'chiselling a face and a form for Caitlín Ní hUallachain' drawing on a 'highly selective construction of reality' which pointed to a 'capacity for self-deception on a heroic scale' about 'traditional Ireland' (ibid.: 652–3), one which was carefully curated by the Irish establishment.[7] However, this understanding was threadbare by the 1950s, the point at which the population fell to its lowest ebb since censuses commenced in the early nineteenth century. There was 'no alternative self-portrait ... to command similar conviction' (ibid.: 653). An account of economic progress and a national identity facing outwards took its place and 'in the collective memory' the 1960s were 'seen as a period when a new Ireland began to come to life' (Brown 1981: 229–30). This 'collective memory', again a highly selective one, was

---

7   MacCurtain (1995: 55) cites Irish governments up to the mid-twentieth century which saw no great issue with young women emigrating to work as domestic servants, deeming it a 'freedom of movement', but failing always to ask why women, especially those facing certain drudgery here and to where they were going, wanted to leave. Lee (1989: 377) notes that of every 100 girls in Connaught between 15–19 in 1946, 45 had emigrated by 1951, and quotes the great AE who wrote that younger women seeing the 'wrinkled face and bent back and rheumatic limbs' of their mothers chose to try their chances away from Ireland (ibid.: 376).

now in the hands of still more image-makers, the authors of the modernising Ireland project like the Industrial Development Authority (Peillon 2002: 40) who sought to market abroad Ireland's economic potential along with the attractions of its 'traditional' culture. The latter were never closely defined, but somehow implied 'values' rooted in familial and community structures which also remained conveniently vague (ibid. 2002: 40–1).

A patriarchal state to its core, the Irish political and administrative wings were well able to maintain a distance from some of the most savage aspects of this traditional culture which it wished to sell abroad. The state contracted out the work of overseeing women who were denied personal agency for having sex in unauthorised social spaces or having sex forced upon them, leaving it to the Magdalene laundries or the county homes to penalise, if not criminalise them while the state deliberately stepped aside from all regulatory responsibilities (O'Rourke and Smith 2016). The international profile of a new Ireland as a place to relocate industry or to come on holiday certainly did not draw attention to the state's alliance with Catholic female religions orders to carry out this work on its behalf.[8] Although such carceral homes were not an Irish creation, as Caelainn Hogan has written, 'independent Catholic Ireland brought them to a sort of dark perfection' (2019b: 29).

In the midst of this 'uneven modernity' (Peillon 2002: 40), it was no surprise that a new push for a return to an imagined cohesive national identity emerged. By the 1970s, the country had net emigration for the first time in the twentieth century as rising economic prospects enabled numbers of Irish people to return home, many from Britain bringing their

---

8   Female religious orders carried out much of the country's day-to-day health, social and educational care, but also undertook the 'dirty' work of containing women in the mother and baby homes network as both dangerous objects and stark warning about unacceptable sexual behaviours. In 1900 there were approximately 8,000 nuns in Ireland, dispersed among 35 religious orders and 368 convents (MacCurtain 1995: 54). By 1980, numbers had swollen to 11,415 living in 128 religious congregations (ibid.), but this era was effectively coming to an end. The state had finally professionalised the care and teaching duties which had once given a form of continuing employment to younger women from inordinately large Irish families who neither emigrated nor married, but had found openings in convent life.

experiences with them. These were not necessarily the stereotypical Irish Catholic immigrants either, for as Ann Rossiter (2009) documents, immigrant or second-generation Irish women were part of feminist groups in Britain exploring more radical political and social concerns from the 1960s onward. Similarly, Connolly and O'Toole (2005: 3) describe the 1970s women's movement here as a 'fundamental challenge to the cultural conservatism that characterised Irish society' nowhere more so than in relation to long-established attitudes about women's roles which 'permeated public institutions and private life' (ibid.). In its diversity, this 'second wave of feminisms' enabled women to begin to say in public that they were 'unmarried mothers', as happened at a meeting in the Mansion House in 1971, to speak out about the assaults on women's sexuality and well-being in many forms: domestic violence, rape, the lack of access to abortion and contraception (ibid.).

Joe Lee (1989: 653–4) argues that the Pro-Life Amendment Campaign established in 1981 was bound up with the call to withstand the 'liberal' values that were beginning to emerge, with PLAC becoming 'a rallying point for a variety of mentalities resentful at recent social changes' (ibid.: 653; see also Rynne 1982). Lee writes that with many still eager to deceive themselves about official Ireland's 'authorised self-portrait' about traditional sexual mores, conservative Catholics mounted a 'bitter resistance' (ibid.) which pushed the country into the 1983 abortion referendum and thereafter as we know, into the thirty-five-year struggle to abolish the Eighth Amendment. That PLAC came into being in the sombre decade of the 1980s when Irish society once more faced recession and emigration and was finally openly confronted with the stark realities of women's sexual oppression is itself distressing. PLAC's success indicates how far powerful groupings were prepared to go to use state machinery to deny the lived realities of women whose names still resonate in our memories. Nonetheless, the success of the 1983 referendum and the numbers of pro-life groups in the 1990s and 2000s could not prevent women from seizing, wherever possible, every chance they could to redefine sex in their own terms. Women discovered networks of support enabling them to act for themselves, however challenging it proved, as with the Irish Women's Abortion Support Group that enabled women to travel safely to London (Rossiter 2009). Artists like

Alanna O'Kelly and Pauline Cummins challenged the weight of official representations of Irish women tied to the allegory of a maternal self-sacrificing 'Mother Ireland', and instead exerted women's sexual and social autonomy through their performance art (Antosik-Parsons 2014). Activism across multiple fronts involved sharpened political and legal contests with an obdurate state dragging its heels and battle by battle, women secured greater support for and openness about our sexual and reproductive needs and desires (Connolly and O'Toole 2005).

By 2010, when *The Irish Times* carried out a wide-ranging survey on sex and relationships, Ian McShane (2010) commented that the results indicated a 'generally relaxed attitude of Irish people towards sex' and women laid claim to expressing their individual desires as they wished. Maria Luddy was able to write that 'sexual desire and sexual practices are integral to how we create our identities, and shape our interactions with the world' (2015: xvii), a project of self-formation with far less jeopardy now attached to it. Although our book has dealt with heterosexual women and their relationships during the Celtic Tiger era, that same sense of freedom around sexual desire, accompanied by razor sharp activism, opened up explorations of LGBTQ sexualities which were reflected in radically changed public discourses and laws. Personal and family responses in favour of a necessary freedom in people's lives were exemplified by the overwhelmingly successful 2015 Marriage Equality Referendum which secured the twenty-fourth amendment to the Constitution (S. Healy et al. 2016).

Complexities of self and sexual relationships

And yet Christine's observation at the outset of this concluding chapter raises queries about this project of self and sexuality and about the contemporary context which has shaped it. In 2008, Tom Inglis, a fierce critic of Catholic control of sexual mores in the long post-Famine century and a half, began to articulate concerns similar to Christine's about the ways in which Irish people in a globalised economy have acquired self-determination about sexual pleasure. Sex has virtually ceased to be an issue of public concern and, lifting a huge burden from people's shoulders, the agency to have sexual partners for one encounter or short-term or long-term relationships is a taken-for-granted personal good. This and similar social attitudes about the 'plurality of choices' late modern selfhood affords us (A. Giddens 1991: 82) locate us very close to our peers in economically advanced economies. Inglis, however, is cautious, pointing out that the ending of silence about sex in Ireland and the public acceptance that our private sexual pleasures are part of our rightful pursuits, whatever we choose, is simultaneously shot through with our contemporary Irish behaviours as globalised 'over-stimulated consumer capitalists' (2008: 186).

From another direction, the Israeli sociologist, Eva Illouz (2007) describes how within this era of consumer capitalism, the 'cold intimacies' of sexual selves, how we relate to one another, take place within an expanding 'commodification of selfhood'. An evolving conditionality shapes emotions as a form of rationalised capital in which the balance between selfhood and relationship is weighed in quantitative terms (ibid.: 109). Amongst other effects, Inglis sees how this has become translated into 'everyday life [with] the sense of self hav[ing] been colonized by an obsession with the body and being sexually attractive' (2008: 187). The unexpected downside then of our freedoms about sex and sexuality is the freight of contradictions that envelops each of us as we juggle reflexively in a process of 'chronic revision' (A. Giddens 1991: 20) about self, need and choice.

Placing this nexus in the context of what he terms 'liquid modernity', Zygmunt Bauman argues that sex must now be '"self-sufficient" … to be judged solely by the satisfaction it may bring on its own' (2003: 45). The raison d'être of liquid modernity is 'the promise to satisfy human desire in a way no other society in the past could … dream of doing' (2005: 81). It brings with it the weight of permanent 'non-satisfaction' of our desires which themselves become 'the fly-wheels of the consumer-targeted economy' (ibid.). The promise of no-strings attached sexual pleasure, an encounter where the only purpose is 'pleasure and joy' (2003: 46) does not work out quite as we might have hoped: Bauman cautions that 'sex is not liberated from supernumerary, superfluous, useless, cumbersome, and cramping loads. It is on the contrary, *overloaded*. Overflowing with expectations beyond its capacity to deliver' (2003: 47, original emphasis).

Little wonder then that the desired goal of the perfect sexual body undertaking perfect sexual relationships becomes a target of the multiple strategies to keep those 'fly-wheels' of consumer capitalism spinning while the numbers of people seeking help because of the associated mental unwellness with this struggle increases. For example, both young women and men 'constantly bombarded with notions of the perfect image' (Larkin, quoted in McCormack 2015) and higher numbers are seeking treatment for eating disorders. A psychiatrist who has practiced for over four decades explains that those in the 25–35 age group are particularly affected due to stress around maintaining relationships and employment and that 'today's culture values visual stimulation rather than older moral or political or social values' (Larkin, quoted in McCormack 2015).

This is one picture of how the exploitative capacity of liquid modernity spills over into constant anxiety about the broader choices we make in respect of sex and relationships, and the nagging sense that one has to hedge one's bets as the potential of 'durable engagements' mutates and is recast as 'incapacitating dependency' (Bauman 2003: 47). The decision to become a couple, as distinct from having sex, becomes ever more fraught around the question of how to define commitment to self as much as commitment to the other: 'There is always a suspicion … that one is living a lie or a mistake; that something crucially important has been overlooked, missed, neglected, untried and unexplored; that a vital obligation to one's authentic self has not been met' (2003: 55). Illouz argues that the self each of us must manage within the boundaries of late modern capitalism does so in conformity with the 'logic of economic relations and exchange' (2007: 5). Bauman identifies how we reconstruct the continuing work of self-development 'as the right way to the proper/desirable sexual identity' (2003: 55) as both right and obligation. He describes this cultural vocabulary, encouraged on all sides and normalised in everyday discourses, as a rational calculation to commit to 'more self-appreciation, self-concern, and self-care' while seeking 'less "dependence" on others, and less attention to others' demands for attention and care, more distance and sobriety' (ibid.).

Along the way, marriage, or the long-term partnership, has become 'a relationship initiated for, and kept going for as long as it delivers emotional satisfaction' with the decision to have children becoming 'a source of "inertial drag" on possible separation, rather than [an] anchoring feature of the relationship' (Giddens 1991: 89). Effective contraception has delivered into our own hands the decision about having children but conception and pregnancy become caught up in 'the new frailty of family structures' (Bauman 2003: 41). Parallel to the growing instabilities of work, unstable jobs, too often insecure housing and unstable life prospects, this decision to have children, which will entail sacrifice of self, possibly putting limits on hoped for careers and so on, is akin to 'signing a mortgage contract with undisclosed and indefinitely long repayments' (ibid.: 42). Bauman argues that 'the most nerve-straining and tension-generating decision' (ibid.), dislodges the habits and training of 'prudent' consumerism, of reading the specified terms and conditions: 'Having children means weighing the welfare of another, weaker and dependent being against one's own comfort', an 'obligation that goes against the grain of liquid modern life' (ibid.).

These are unexpected, unanticipated outcomes: the 'agonies of *homo sexualis* are those of *homo consumens*. They have been born together' (Bauman 2003: 49). What emerges is a calculation of 'the balance of reasonable hopes of gains and realistic prospects of losses' (ibid.: 58). Tom Inglis sees each one of us acting as our own 'moral arbiters' (Inglis 2014a: 12), managing our selfhood as best we can. The position is a demanding one from which to deal with the ceaseless discourses about romantic love which are 'deeply embedded in consumer capitalism' (ibid.: 157) itself seeking to reduce us to consuming as our principal undertaking.

Inglis examines how Irish people are managing to create changing senses of self within this globalised commodified worldview, suggesting that we can reach personal accommodations in ways which are 'voluntary and strategic' (2014b: 226), despite Ireland being one of the most globalised countries internationally, 'a prime example of reflexive accumulation' (Cronin 2002: 56–7). Inglis argues that we are undertaking a more nuanced interplay where we are constructing our 'personal identities and sense of self' (2008: 254) by actively creating 'strong webs of meaning' that may well include family and caring duties, but which give us space to reflect critically on how we are living as individuals outside what was once an 'all-embracing ideology' (2014a: 12). That ideology as we know entailed a massive sacrifice for women. The issue then is how we use the spaces within this current dynamic and whether the contemporary work of self can be flexible enough to keep us from being totally reducible to the commodification and cold individualism of late modernity. There is some overlap between what Inglis presents in his arguments about strong webs of meaning and what Todd May argues, that 'although neoliberalism pervades our culture, it has not overtaken us' and if we can recognise how our relationships 'lend our lives the meaning they do', we have a chance to not become subject to neoliberal self-conceptions' (2012: 141) which carry a high ethical price in 'the hurried, emergency culture of consumerist society' (Bauman 2008: 159). Here is a case for seeing how Irish sociality with 'overlapping complex webs … woven by individuals in their everyday lives' can draw on or create sufficiently fruitful modalities while recognising that what appears to be shared perceptions are 'contradictory and sometimes irreconcilable' (Inglis 2014a: 34). And this is precisely why in making use of this relativised space for self and social reflection, we nonetheless have an absolute obligation to keep those contradictions to the fore. Personal agency exercised in this manner might help to place us at a usefully oblique angle with our complex past while simultaneously going against the grain of late modernity and its glittering consumer capitalism, the progressive Europe that it evokes, towards which official Ireland has moved with such alacrity.

Contradictions and remnants

However, our problems abound still. The complex webs Inglis deciphers may themselves run too close to the ongoing depiction of Irish women as 'strong, coping and courageous' (P. O'Connor 1998: 244) while not challenging the tenacious presence of a state facing in two directions, late modern in its economics and globalised culture, and back to its still standing patriarchal core. Pat O'Connor notes that there has been a steady erosion of 'taken-for-granted' male authority across all 'the major institutional structures' of state, church and the very economic system (ibid.: 245). At the same time, the continuing salience of the concept of women's caring centred on a history of familialism, sits uneasily alongside 'a heightened need for an awareness of gendered self-interest' both measured against a continuing problem of 'the perceived legitimacy' of women's voices, especially as they 'articulate women's needs and perspectives' (ibid.). We need to think through the logic and extent of these many contradictions in order to act with political effect, acknowledging that our commodified present thrives on widespread inequalities, many women prospering, many struggling daily, while none of the remnants of our past have really subsided.[9] O'Connor reminds us of this when she quotes J. P. O'Carroll's analysis of the 1983 pro-life referendum: 'The alternative vision offered by female knowledge and insight is suspect and a source of fear' (J. P. O'Carroll in P. O'Connor 1998: 245).

Suspicion of the female body continues to hold sway and is at the heart of the controversy with such strong historical roots. All of this leapt into public consciousness yet again in early 2021 with the publication of the report by the Commission of Investigation on Mother and Baby Homes. The Commission was established by the government in 2015, in the wake of extensive documentary evidence collated and first published in 2012 by local historian Catherine Corliss on the burial of 796 babies in an unmarked mass grave at the rear of the Tuam Bon Secours Mother and Baby Home. The Commission's report, covering eighteen homes only of the extensive network 'involved in separating mothers and children in twentieth century Ireland' has proven damaging to the survivors, with multiple inaccuracies and omissions: of the experiences of the women directly involved who gave their testimony, of family members who endured forced separation, of the extent of illegal adoptions (O'Rourke and McGettrick 2021) and of specific information on the babies who died from institutional

---

9   Lone parent households, which comprise one in six of all household units in
      Ireland, are 86 per cent female-headed (OneFamily 2020) and are at greatest risk
      of poverty (Byrne and Treanor 2020). They also suffer the realities of homelessness
      disproportionately to other household formations (Loftus 2019).

neglect. The narrowness of the terms of reference set by the government, the omission of a human rights framework to guide the Commission, its lack of transparency, the lack of written transcripts, the destruction of the original tape recordings of witnesses, for the survivors compounded the wrongs of the historic abuse so that the report as a whole 'denied the people affected access to the language, personal records and administrative archives required to record and articulate their history' (ibid.). There was a storm of public protest, detailed critiques throughout the media about the Commission and its report, objections from human rights groups like Clann representing the survivors,[10] and Oireachtas motions demanding an extension to the Commission's work to right some of these wrongs, all to no avail. In a lengthy review article, Clair Wills (2021) commented that the Commission's data which showed an increased intake of women into the homes throughout the 1960s and 1970s points to the repeated (and one must presume deliberate) failure of the Irish state to develop any concrete financial measures to support single mothers outwith the homes until the early 1970s. Wills also comments how her eyes were glazed with absorbing the extensive financial details as to how the homes actually ran; in this at least there was no lack of information about the maze of bureaucratic structures required in the operations of the homes (ibid.).

The state's insistence that the Commission's final report must stand unchanged as the official record has done grievous damage to people's experiences within living memory, let alone to the women who have long since died. However, in trying to close off the inquiry, and close down their voices, the state will be unable to hold and shape that history of women as it might intend because memory itself is too potent. Already matters have shifted under a groundswell of activism. After an Oxford University, UK event in June 2021 when one of the Commission's members finally broke the silence about how they had carried out their work, the government was urged to repudiate the report under the weight of detail the Commission member revealed (Horgan-Jones et al. 2021; J. McCarthy 2021). At least

10   Clann is a joint initiative set up by the Justice for Magdalenes group, the Adoption Rights Alliance and the legal firm Hogan Lovells to discover exactly what happened to incarcerated unmarried mothers and their children in twentieth-century Ireland and to support all survivors in seeking justice from the Irish state.

eight survivors of the Mother and Baby Home regime, including Philomena Lee, whose long search for her son was chronicled in the 2009 book, *The Lost Child of Philomena Lee*, have brought judicial reviews before the High Court on the grounds that the Commission's actions, inaccuracies, redactions, omissions and conclusions violate their rights both constitutionally and under the European Convention on Human Rights (Carolan 2021; Bray 2021). Without question, the final report violates their voices. Without question, their voices will not be silenced again.

As Walter Benjamin argued, memory is 'the dark loam', 'the medium in which the past is experienced': 'Genuine memory must … yield an image of the person who remembers, in the same way a good archaeological report not only informs us about the strata from which its findings originate, but also gives an account of the strata which first had to be broken through' (2005: 576). The collective work of retrieving women's stories and accounts that the state would have never wanted to excavate gives us 'an account of the resistances and problems experienced on the way to finding them' and 'does not so much reveal the past as jolt us into a mode of critical inquiry' (Arnold-de Sinime 2013: 71). The urgency of this political work of critical inquiry across the cultural landscape brings us into the territory explored by writers and artists like Anne Enright in her novel *The Gathering* and Alanna O'Kelly in her Famine work. O'Kelly uses the 'richness of memory' of women's fecundity and the harshness of the Famine to 'subvert dominant cultural narratives' (Levin 1999: 32; Antosik-Parsons 2014: 211) and in this sense, women are 'guardians of the past' (McLean 2004: 140).

We return once more to considering what we can still usefully glean from our 'cultural remnants' (Lloyd 2008: 70), the effects of the unutterably cruel post-Famine epoch which women endured generation after weary generation. The range of women's voices we have encountered in previous chapters, their individual struggles for selfhood as sexual beings and, if they have so chosen, as mothers and carers, have come at the endgame of a claustrophobic society which appeared to effortlessly support a state prepared to drive women into the tightest of constrained definitions of how they might live their lives. Lloyd's 'cultural remnants' were dragged and drawn into that contorted twentieth-century society. If that claustrophobia itself has ebbed, its effects have spilled over into twenty-first-century Ireland and are revealed through contemporary women's stories. These stories may help us to identify political spaces which have the potential for vital collectivity against the darker consequences of late modernity which women must now also confront.

Loss and connection

In his essay, 'The Concept of History', Benjamin writes of the urgent need to seize 'memory as it flashes up in a moment of danger' (2003: 391). Such a moment arrives when the dominant story of the 'present' in its conformism with the account of the 'victors' deliberately seeks not to recognise the pain it imposed on those who were made lose in the past and yet the loss must be confronted (ibid.). David Lloyd has argued that there is an acute problem in how we view the project of Irish modernity which valorises 'progress', as defined by the victors, and which in producing its account of contemporary Irish society seeks to bury 'recalcitrant' social spaces (Lloyd 1999: 77). The intent, as Lloyd describes it, is to fold beneath the dominant story, the 'alternative histories' that state-legitimated forgetting wishes to discard as events in a past which are of no consequence in its narrative about its own ongoing success. The exposure of these stubborn 'recalcitrant spaces', hidden within the history of what is sanctioned as acceptable, is nowhere more acute than in relation to women and their bodies. Each time these events re-emerge, and they do, they pose a danger to the current social order in the form 'of newly antagonistic practices … this rhythm of return is that of the alternative social imaginations amid the ruins of shattered cultures and the traces of state violence' (ibid.: 78).

Each time we use the commonplace statement 'in this day and age' to help us make sense of the accounts we are hearing of women's lives from decades ago, we stumble uncomfortably not only over the past that has been buried, but the means by which this has been accomplished. Thus, in response to the extent of the damage done to women in the Magdalene laundries finally and definitively being exposed by the survivors, we want to say it would not happen now. And then almost at once we are forced to recognise that the scandals which are currently engulfing women's lives, 'in this day and age', such as the non-disclosure by the state health services of adverse test results about cervical cancer,[11] have not alone affinity, but actual continuity, with the way past histories about women have been buried, not least by being cloaked in the silence that mainstream institutions of the state are so adroit at constructing. Inevitably, it shakes our confidence in this thing called 'progress' which is useful if we can take on, as Lloyd suggests we should, the political work of constructing alternative antagonistic practices.

These spaces in relation to women's lives periodically 'disrupt the timeline' of the conservative post-1922 Irish state (Lloyd 1999: 78). Without warning, they break into our lives and are the reasons why Irish feminist historians were impelled to undertake such a wide body of work from the 1990s onward (ibid.). For Lloyd the problem is what the official Irish account dare not say of itself without running the risk of interrogating too closely the underpinnings of that conservative petty bourgeois state in all its particular cruelties.[12] The 'strong farmers' with their consolidated landholdings

11   The CervicalCheck scandal involved many women who attended the state's cervical screening service but who were not subsequently informed that the results of their tests were incorrect and that in fact there were abnormalities; 221 women at least went on to develop cancer of the cervix. Vicky Phelan (2019) documents how she came to discover the scandal and then mounted an effective public campaign to expose the state's cover-up along with other affected women and their husbands, including Stephen Teap, whose wife Irene died from cervical cancer in 2019. By the time Phelan discovered her records, leading her to the records of the others, seventeen women had already died. Ruth Morrissey, who also went to the High Court in 2018, had to take her case to the Supreme Court; the High Court finding in her favour was contested by the HSE and the labs involved, fourteen of which were located outside Ireland. In the Supreme Court hearing in 2019, the issue of the 'internationally unprecedented' decision by the HSE to outsource 90 per cent of the lab work that came from CervicalCheck was raised in detail. In March 2020, the Supreme Court upheld the High Court ruling that the HSE and the outsourced labs had been negligent and that both had failed to apply an adequate procedural standard to the work of screening. Morrissey died four months later in July 2020 without the state ever issuing her an apology for the 'magnitude of harm' (Bowers 2020b).

12   Many thousands of babies from both Catholic and Protestant mother and baby homes were caught up in unregulated and illegal adoptions from the 1940s through

who emerged as the dominant class in post-Famine Ireland, aided and abetted by an expanding church machinery hungry for power, sought also to consolidate that conservatism. The price, Lloyd argues, was to implant an 'anxiety' not alone about the 'spectres of the dead' (2008: 64) whereby those landholdings were increased, but dread about 'the loss of forms of agency and of social relations that cannot be fully named' (2008: 65). These come back as threats to haunt the structures of conformism that remain the single strongest trait of twentieth-century Ireland. This surely is the story of the Tuam Mother and Baby home, itself built on the site of a former workhouse whose history stretches back to Famine times. The bodies of dead babies and children were denied a burial in accordance with Catholic rites and instead discarded by Catholic nuns in a mass grave, much of which appeared to be made up of disused sewage chambers (Wills 2021). This is so discordant because their actions open our eyes to those unremitting social fears of post-Famine Ireland, the fear of poverty, the fear of how pregnancy might connect to poverty and loss of status if it occurred in proscribed social spaces made wrong by the memory and legacy of famine.

The image drags us back to that time of Famine when, as Stuart McLean (2004) relates, women were seen as the carriers of extremes: the accounts of bereaved mothers holding the bodies of their dead children in their arms as they walked for hours and days, searching desperately for a way to give them a Christian burial, their actions underscoring the 'dehumanizing effects of famine' (ibid.: 135). If through these and similar desperate actions for themselves and their children, women were viewed as 'symptoms of social pathology … a disruptive force' at a time of hunger and social collapse (ibid.: 136), the nuns at a later point also become carriers of extremes. Their actions are dehumanising in relation to what should have been a strong adherence to a core religious obligation, properly observed, burial in consecrated ground, not bodies discarded; the nuns too become

the 1960s. This included an extensive foreign adoption trade with the United States. It required the ongoing involvement in Ireland of a number of senior figures including obstetricians like Professor Eamon deValera, son of the country's President, who privately arranged the adoptions for childless couples of babies born to vulnerable women, a practice that continued well after legislation to regulate adoption had been passed in 1952 (Hegarty 2021).

'symptoms of social pathology' of a century later. Tuam underscores the extremes of fear that mainstream Irish society has consistently reinforced about women and sex in post-Famine Irish society if they are not constrained by those patriarchal terms of reference.

The loss that is at the heart of Famine and post-Famine Ireland, these profoundly troubling 'cultural remnants', tear through the timelines of our own lives and bring us face to face with glimpses of how these losses have borne so heavily on women. They jolt us when we connect them to the loss of agency, the loss of the social relations we want and welcome and for which we are still struggling, albeit within the changed circumstances of well-off contemporary Ireland.

At the margins of the past, say, how workhouses record the disciplining of their inmates, or how the upper classes endeavour to secure the marital futures of their daughters amidst threats that their houses will be burnt to the ground, we find innumerable stories of seduction and pregnancy; for example, the glimpse of Mary Tobin and the brief story of May Gould. Mary Tobin, the widow and inmate of the Lismore workhouse during the Famine we discuss in Chapter 1, fares badly when she becomes pregnant in 1849. May Gould is the fictional upper-class young woman from Galway in George Moore's 1886 *A Drama in Muslin*, when the country is awash with local insurrections about land. Unlike Mary Tobin, whose already meagre food rations are cut in half to punish her when her pregnancy begins to show, May Gould is fortunate enough to be secreted away in Dublin for the duration of her pregnancy, supported financially by her stalwart older friend Alice Barton who writes to escape the emptiness of the gentry's marriage market. Through her friend, May Gould gratefully avoids any social opprobrium, not least because her baby dies days after birth.

We do not know Mary Tobin's fate, only that she suffers shaming by the workhouse governor and near starvation while pregnant in the midst of the Famine. We can hope that her agency extended beyond meeting a man along the road to Tallow, but her precarious social position would most likely have dictated otherwise. Moore gives more agency to the upper-class May Gould who 'determined to be a good woman yet' (Moore, Chapter VIII) sells her best hunter to pay for a wedding present for her good friend Alice, who has defied parental anger marrying the local doctor who is beneath her social status and leaves all these constraints behind her, emigrating to

London. As David Lloyd writes, the 'recovery of silhouettes that rise up on the horizon of official discourse' (1999: 77) becomes the source for complex projects of retrieval and connection with those who were defeated, who grieved and died, and who were often wordlessly grieved in turn.

In the late decades of the twentieth century, we gradually learned to turn wordless grief about all that women had endured into action: Ann Lovett's death was the touchstone and no anniversary of that bitter January day in 1984 goes unheeded. Yet in order to fully understand the actions we need to pursue, we also need to see the continuity we still face in the clash with the conforming institutions, discourses and practices of contemporary Ireland. As Nell McCafferty observed, the state's investigations did everything necessary not to ask any relevant questions in the wake of this tragedy, most especially of her family, with whom the Gardaí had 'not been able to secure an interview' ten days after she died (McCafferty 1997: 49). The unspoken acquiescence of the Gardaí held the line with a patriarchal family model.

We have learned to identify how alternative forms of agency and voice have come about in spite of monumental efforts to suppress and delimit them, and thus we understand more about the contemporary forms of agency we need, always remembering how women as sexual beings, very often as mothers, can be pushed into shame and silence. The difference between these fragments from the distant past, Mary Tobin, and the traces of women's stories from the recent past in Ireland, is not so great when looked at through the continuing challenges women face. Agency comes hard fought for, women seeking out others to help when they can, but recognising that if no help is forthcoming, their stories may worsen appreciably as was Ann Lovett's unspeakable fate, a young adolescent woman who paid with her life because of a sexual encounter about which we can know virtually nothing except that she had no option but to continue the pregnancy.[13] Matters did change insofar as fifteen years later, Karen, whom we met in Chapter 2, also

---

13 In 2018, *The Irish Times* published a lengthy interview with Richard 'Ricky' McDonnell, Ann Lovett's boyfriend, breaking his silence of over three decades about his relationship with Ann and how her death has affected his life ever since (Boland 2018). His description of Ann as a loving person who was 'very sharp, very witty' girl who was 'brilliant at drawing' gave us resonant images to think again about the truly awful dimensions of her tragic death.

living in a small town, experienced a markedly different outcome. Karen wanted to have sex when she was 13, and when she gave birth to her son at 15, although the atmosphere was heavy with social disapproval – her family, her school which she left, the hospital staff where she gave birth – she became a single parent, kept her son and reared him, and managed to return to a training scheme and paid work by the time she was 20.

The more distant silhouettes and fragments continue to throw out for consideration the patriarchal power copper-fastened by that conservative post-1922 state, but they also help us question whether we are now at the right end of history with the kinds of agency we require currently. As Christa Craven and Dána-Ain Davis argue, we need a sharp lens to document how women's lived experiences under neoliberalism are testament to different forms of increasing inequalities and the deliberate undermining of social justice, hampering how we live our lives, erasing 'the particularity of women's experience', bidding us instead to accept the atrophied forms of marketplace engagement (Craven and Davis 2011: 192). If the official wish is to forget, to deny, we must work to create greater agency in order to make the state uneasy, to make use of the institutional and political anxiety that underpins the state's need to forget. Our stories, our lives contest the forgetting, and this is why we must challenge at every turn if we are to shape a society with a more just future. Eng and Kazanjian argue that working with the past 'in a continued and open relationship', engaging with the loss, generates sites for memory and history, for the rewriting of the past as well as the reimagining of the future' (2003: 4).

Individually, women have endeavoured to rewrite their present and deal with their past as sexual beings. Any woman in Ireland now over the age of 50 carries these traces of our past in the scenes and stories which have shaped urgent political activism over the last several decades about women's needs, about what we have come to define as reproductive justice. The stories come unexpectedly. One of us remembers back to the mid-1970s, when there was no chance whatsoever of an outpost of the Irish Family Planning Association for women living in the Connemara Gaeltacht, no motorways, negligible public transport. On holiday from Dublin with a young child who played happily with the family of children living in the cottage across the road, imagine what it felt like to be invited in for cup of tea, a shop-bought cake on the table which itself would have taken effort to obtain, and to listen to an anguished request for oral contraception from the young mother with four children and a new baby who took her chance with a stranger. She was suffering acute postnatal depression and said she simply could not have another baby, begging for help, which on return to Dublin was organised as best as could be done in those times.

On a summertime flight to the UK for a holiday, three years before the abortion referendum of 2018, one of the authors settled into a seat, and politely greeted the much older woman in the next seat. And, when that flight was delayed disembarking at its destination for over an hour because of a security scare, the much older woman in conversation suddenly began to relate her past. From an impoverished small farm in the midlands and finding herself pregnant at 16 by a local lad, she went to the local GP who then went to her parents with the story that his mother in Galway was ill and needed a live-in helper and surely the 16-year-old could be given up for such work. Class relations kicked in and the young woman's parents at once gave way to the request from the respectable and powerful local doctor in collusion with the local priest. It was 1958 and the young woman was sent to a mother and baby home in a distant county. Days after she gave birth, the nuns put her back to work in the laundry, perishingly cold and with no care for her post-pregnant well-being. Sitting on an aeroplane on a sunny bright morning, a completely incongruous setting given all she was saying, she related the detail that her nipples were so badly cracked, her milk was laced with blood as her baby nursed. She fought signing the adoption papers and lost. She returned home briefly and was turned out. She built a life elsewhere outside Ireland, never forgetting her baby while she had other children, but never disclosing to her English husband what had occurred, the family who had disowned her, the baby she had been forced to surrender. After her husband died, she went searching and found her adult son and was reunited with him.

There is rightly a huge range of literature over recent decades which explores these and similar circumstances. We understand far better how many knew, how many helped in the silencing and why they did so (see Garrett 2016),[14] and thus we understand the need not to be silenced now.

---

14   Garrett suggests that in the changing climate of the late 1960s when the phrase 'single parenthood' was beginning to emerge, it became important to reassess the strategies of containment for pregnant women, not least because the 1967 Abortion

In 2017, the journalist Justine McCarthy wrote of the agonising loss of her beautiful older sister, similarly exiled, but in her case, forced by their mother to have her child put up for adoption, forced as McCarthy conveys, because in the Ireland of the 1970s, her mother who was a widow with four children, simply could not sustain the local pressures if the truth came out. Instead by her action, taking her pregnant daughter to England, 'our family was splintered for ever' and a 'shroud of secrecy hung over us all' (McCarthy 2017). McCarthy's mother kept a tiny photograph of the baby in her purse and 'never stopped pining for her first born grandchild' (ibid.). McCarthy's sister never came home, dying at 51. Her adopted son found his aunts after her death and they discovered that their sister, his mother, had written a letter to him when she signed the papers, a letter that survived the years and was given to him on his eighteenth birthday to tell him that she loved him. Both women, mother and grandmother, forced to be prudent in accordance with the strictures of an utterly unjust society, tempered such loss as best they could.

These potent memories of pain and loss may help us extend our knowledge of the current regimes in Ireland within which women are living their lives. Far from a progressive account, we see instead the machinations of what we might name a technocratic governance built on neoliberal doctrines replete with different inventions of inequity which trap and continue to dispossess many of us, neutralising and diluting our experiences and understandings (Craven and Davis 2011), and thus silencing us once more.

Our 'progress' in a patriarchal state

Pat O'Connor (2000) has written about the extent to which Ireland remains a 'man's world', one where the 'patriarchal nature of Irish public life' continues to deliver the 'dividend' of 'male privileging'. This appears to

Act in England opened a new possibility for them, seeking not just to go to England to have a baby but to have an abortion, so that limiting the ' "temptation of a very serious nature before the distraught unmarried mother" ', became a key rationale for the introduction of the Unmarried Mothers Allowance in 1973 (2016: 721).

be gifted to men as individuals rendering men 'unwitting beneficiaries' if not outright 'oppressors' (ibid: 83) as such. However, O'Connor urges us to see how beyond the level of each individual the impacts of male privileging are sustained throughout our public institutions, within and by the state itself. This state, as Lloyd (1999) reminds us, from 1922 onward employed the paradoxical instrument of the conservative traditionalisms of post-Famine society alongside the safety valve of emigration, a crucial escape route for women, not least when they became pregnant (Rossiter 2009). This same instrument of state governmentality enabled our successful 'entry into global capitalism and modernity … a rapid transition through the 1960s and 1970s from an isolated economy to a classic instance of "dependence" … advantageously located within the European Community' (Lloyd 1999: 86). This instrument, this presentation of conservative catholic nationalism, exactly leant itself to the dependency status we assumed internationally even as we appeared to shed its most objectionable and highly visible aspects. What Pat O'Connor terms 'invisible patriarchy' (1995) remains deeply embedded in the structures of this state and despite the changes which have flowed from EEC/EU membership, the structural shifts in Ireland to conform with EU law have never entirely dislodged the underpinnings of 'the patriarchal Irish cultural tradition' (P. O'Connor 1995: 182). The 'dominant structural realities' which remain in place are centred on women's caring and service (ibid.: 178). This is why O'Connor (2000) argues that we require gender as a crucial body of theory to analyse how women, and men, continue to live within this patriarchal state. The same female-attributed qualities of caring and service, the mainstay of Irish domestic life in the twentieth century, are still perceived as invaluable within the public domain, if never adequately paid for and resourced, as with the predominantly female professions of midwifery and nursing (INMO 2019).

The Irish state in its unvarnished realities as distinct from its sleek modernising guise on the global scene, remains a 'reluctant assentor' (P. O'Connor 1995: 177) to an EU legal framework on rights that directly affect women, a framework which privileges women's conditions in relation to employment and social security within the EU economy as a primary policy. With nothing beyond threadbare rhetoric from the state to seriously carry through on women's human rights, Irish women like A, B and C between

2005 and 2010, and Amanda Mellett between 2011 and 2016, have learned to trudge down the legal route to either the European Court of Human Rights as the body which oversees the 1950 European Convention on Human Rights as part of the Council of Europe or to the United Nations Human Rights Committee to seek a lawful ruling against that same patriarchal state (IFPA 2018). These four women all sought a legal medical abortion on the grounds of risk to life for A, B and C and for Amanda Mellett, on the grounds that her baby had a fatal foetal anomaly which forced her to leave Ireland to access a medical termination of pregnancy at twenty-two weeks for which she and her husband had to pay in full.

Women, now, in contemporary globalised Ireland, must continue to deal with 'invisible patriarchy' which flows through the realities of state, church, family and community often in perverse alignment against them (P. O'Connor 1995: 178). 'Invisible patriarchy' cuts across the everyday worlds of women's lived experiences and reframes them in discourses which we must assume fit the ill-defined needs of a range of public and publicly funded institutions and policies, not women. In the introduction to their useful collection of essays on women's bodies, motherhood and space, Sarah Hardy and Caroline Wiedmer note that the expanding number of roles which women took on following widespread entry into paid employment in the latter third of the twentieth century entailed seeing themselves as 'multiply constructed subjects and embodied beings' (2005: 4) in order to carry out their prescribed roles as mothers and workers and, we should add, as consumers in the globalised economy.

While women have attempted some resistance individually and collectively to the force of these public discourses, they have also often already accepted that they form 'part of their own restrictions' (Marotta 2005). The spaces between the material and discursive which women must negotiate 'constitute a powerful force that helps shape their subjectivities and their possibilities (Marotta 2005: 15). Childcare provision in Ireland provides a continuing example of how these spaces translate into multiple contradictions for women, in this instance stemming from poor policymaking on the part of a state which assumes limited responsibility for supporting women as mothers and as workers. This throws up extensive conflicts for women in respect of material time and space, leaving them often with a burden of guilt as they try to negotiate the incommensurable spaces of the workforce and the lives of young children. These conflicts are the more acute in a society as unequal as Ireland where access to childcare is stratified; economically more secure women are able to purchase the best resourced and more expensive forms of childcare while lower down the scale of paid employment, women make and mend in radically different social spaces, often as paid carers for other women's children (Hardy and Wiedmer 2005: 6–7). This might be in their own homes or inadequately funded and scarce public nurseries, or private for-profit nurseries where rates of pay for mostly female staff are at the lower end, or as women immigrants whose own children are in far different geographical locations being reared by older family members relying on wages being sent back to them as emigrants' remittances in Brazil or the Philippines and so on. With this last, how can we not see what has been part of our own history as women emigrants?

The overriding issue of invisible patriarchy is there in the absolute drift of state policies on childcare. In 1998, the Chair of the National Women's Council of Ireland, Katherine Zappone, commissioned research on the best direction for childcare in Ireland to contribute recommendations to a government Expert Working Group (Coveney et al. 1998). Zappone wrote in her Forward that 'the National Women's Council Childcare Campaign has been driven by the conviction that childcare should be shifted as a matter of private responsibility on the part of the individual woman to a matter of public responsibility on the part of the state' (ibid.: 4). These were Celtic Tiger times and should have been a period of extensive state investment in line with the European models which enabled women to enter the paid workforce in huge numbers. It did not happen, leaving women we interviewed in Chapter 5 with the burden of 'choosing' between home and paid work:

> I think it is very hard to combine everything. Work and relationship you can do. Work and one child, you can just about do, but when it comes to work and two children, the price of childcare is so, so expensive. So that almost even rules out working for a lot of women. (Agnes, 29, Financial adviser, Metro area)

Over twenty years on from that NWCI campaign, the childcare sector remains fragmented, largely privately run, with a poorly paid workforce, and is exorbitantly expensive for the individual household. Fees for full-time childcare cost as much as €184 per week in the rest of the country, rising to over €200 per week in the greater Dublin area (Taft 2020). Ireland has been ranked last in state childcare support and maternity leave of the original 15 EU countries while the cost of childcare must be shouldered by women in the 'maximum private responsibility' market approach of the Irish state (O'Hagan 2015: 211). All the state has managed to assemble during the period of the Celtic Tiger years of funding largesse is a regulatory agency to review childcare provision, and a subsidised means-tested Early Childhood Care and Education Scheme, providing two years of free pre-school care for three hours a day, five days a week, thirty-eight weeks of the year only. Once more, the material labour of seeking out an available place, of leaving off and collecting children, despite the daily stress of traffic jams and poor public transport, for example, falls to women in a make and mend undertaking that leaves them struggling between their perceived role as a 'good' mother and what Williams (1991) refers to as an 'ideal' worker. Women find themselves accepting limited childcare options, often regardless of cost in order to at least partially fulfil both those roles, carrying the weight of what appears to be their individual failure, while the state effectively absents itself. It should be noted that even if this policy lacuna were viewed solely in relation to the narrowest of conventional economic targets, this 'grudging reluctance' to deal effectively with childcare (Russell et al. 2017: 394), with its sheer waste of women's time and labour makes no sense whatsoever except as part of the unquestioned paradoxical 'man's world' of the Irish state.[15]

Women also continue to make and mend, at best, in the critical spheres of their reproductive health. We met younger women in Chapter 3 who encountered significant problems of both access to and cost of contraception. These problems remain. There is currently a government pledge

15   In February 2020, Helen McEntee, a member of government and a senior Cabinet Minister, announced that she was going to take her full six months maternity leave for her first baby, not least to 'pave the way' for other women TDs for whom there is no automatic maternity leave entitlement. It will require new legal and constitutional provision to make this possible (Finn 2021; McConnell 2021).

to introduce free contraception for all (see H. O'Connell 2020), and in advance of that measure being undertaken, a review report for the then Minister for Health drew attention to continuing problems of lack of access locally, cost and lack of knowledge about the best methods of contraception especially for women who are in any way socially vulnerable or from marginalised groups such as women who are homeless or who are from minority ethnic groups (Pollak 2019). A 2020 survey carried out on behalf of the Dublin Well Woman Clinic also drew attention to these same exclusion issues while commenting that there is a lack of knowledge of what is best suited for women as individuals. For example, there is a reliance on emergency contraception rather than women being able to determine from the outset the most efficacious contraception that suits their circumstances (Dublin Well Woman 2020). Both reports urged that resources be put in place to help women with the initial consultation and with the cost of long-acting reversible contraceptives. These necessary actions should form part of a national sexual health strategy, but here too the absence of relevant policymaking is striking. Between 2002 and 2009 the Crisis Pregnancy Agency advocated for a reworked national relationships and sex education programme along with a comprehensive sexual health strategy. The Agency consistently reflected the complexity of women's voices and groups across Ireland endeavouring to support young women; its calls for action were based on the Agency's well-articulated collaborative outreach and extensive research, carried out until it met a fate similar to the Women's Health Council. It was dissolved as a statutory agency and its changed remit absorbed into the rigid machinery of the HSE by 2010. The HSE finally published a National Sexual Health Strategy in 2015 with a series of public health targets which were clinically based and which lacked the strength of grassroots collaboration. Its Mid-Term Review in 2018 noted the slowness of change in expanding even clinical services across the country, the absence of adequate funding to secure expansion and the consequent frustration of health care workers (HSE 2018). Non-action by the state has been calamitous for the sexual well-being of many young people.

Even getting to a place where younger women can more readily attain a confident understanding of sex and sexuality remains difficult. Our interviewees, adults by the time of the Celtic Tiger, had endured minimal if not dishonest approaches to sex education in their schools, with that sense of shame always lurking in the background. In formal discussions, they rarely fared better than the description given by Bernadette in Chapter 3:

> I mean, ours was drawings, cross sections, and a sample of a tampon, that was it like. That's what we had. But certainly nothing about relationships and emotions. (Bernadette, 30, catering manager, small city)

Ellen Coyne writes, hilariously and pointedly, about the failures of school-based sex education for her generation of young women coming of age in a small town at the height of the Celtic Tiger: 'If you'd like to create a total frenzy around sex, might I recommend a Catholic education for your young and impressionable adolescent?' (Coyne 2020: 38). Her experiences have told her that if anything 'the way I felt – the way loads of us felt about sex and shame and women was much more complicated than simply claiming that the Church tried to turn misogyny into a Catholic virtue' (ibid.: 35).

The ongoing entanglement of church control of state-funded education, with parents often having no choice as to which schools their children attend, has cut off the wide-ranging knowledge base of sex, sexuality and relationships that young people need.[16] The falling away of nominally Catholic parents from active weekly religious practice, now down to 35 per cent (O'Toole 2018) and the 2016 Census figures with a drop, albeit small, from 84 per cent to 78 per cent of Census respondents listing themselves as Catholic, suggests that Coyne is correct in that the problem of inadequate sex and relationships education is now a multi-layered one, with parents themselves failing to respond to their growing children. A recent ESRI survey which has recommended an overhaul of the school syllabus on sex education indicates that although at 17 years of age, 33 per cent of young people have had sexual intercourse, at 13 years of age, only 45 per cent of respondents had discussed sex with their parents (Nolan and Smyth

---

16   In April 2021, the Irish Catholic Bishops Conference published its new programme on relationships and sexuality as a resource for primary schools which reinforced its traditional Catholic teaching about marriage and single sex relationships amongst other aspects (C. O'Brien 2021).

2020). We still have irrelevant, unsatisfactory school-based sex education and a percentage of parents who do not connect effectively with their children. Coyne recounts in vivid detail how her friends scraped the money for emergency contraception together for one of them, not neglecting any coins which might have fallen under the furniture (Coyne 2020: 35–7). Similarly, our interviewees relied on a peer network to survive as recounted in Chapter 3, making use of what they had to help young people navigate increasingly ambiguous terrain. The further dimension here is that the far greater focus in our consumer society on sex and its availability makes participation important for the individual as was expressed by women like Ciara, quoted in Chapter 2:

> One of your friends slept with a boy, and they tell you, and how great it was, and you're going to sit there and think 'Oh, that sounds good, I might have a go.' (Ciara, 27, nurse, small city)

If younger teenaged women want to explore more nuanced understandings of their self-identity as sexual beings and how emotions and relational aspects figure strongly in what they come to know, and they do want this (Higgins and Murphy-Lawless 2009), we still lack the dedicated skills and spaces for them. How can this be?

Turning to the state's changed position on abortion, despite the relatively rapid setting up of abortion services in the wake of formal legislation being signed into law in December 2018, many problems remain. Amongst the total 6,666 abortions carried out in 2019, the vast majority of women were able to deal with their decisions through clinic and outpatient treatment. However, only ten of the country's nineteen public hospitals offer abortion care and community provision of early abortion care is sketchy, while the cut-off mark of twelve weeks is creating difficulties forcing some women to still travel abroad for the care they need (Bowers 2020a; Cullen 2020). The Department of Health is currently carrying out a review the Health (Regulation of Termination of Pregnancy) Act 2018. There are a number of inter-related issues which will need to be challenged: the three-day waiting period, far too few GPs who offer abortion care, only one in ten, uneven geographical access to abortion services, limitations on the clinical interpretations of fatal foetal anomalies, and finally, the twelve-week limit on when abortions can be performed (Ní Aodha 2021). All of these issues mean that some women must still leave the country for abortions.[17]

Ireland's maternity services present a further arena of struggle, past and present. A past struggle relates to justice about the extent of the practice of symphysiotomy in Irish maternity hospitals. This controversial surgery entailed cutting through a woman's pregnant pelvis and damaging her permanently and continued until at least the early 1990s and affecting approximately 1,500 women, leaving them with pain, incontinence and a range of other severe consequences. The rationale, to 'help' anticipated 'obstructed labour', was itself a contentious if familiar frame of reference from the male-dominant obstetric establishment. Symphysiotomy is another unvarnished reality about which the women immediately involved have had to struggle to find scope to access the extremely limited redress scheme which the state finally offered to them after a concerted campaign over some years (M. O'Connor 2011: 2016). The avoidance of where responsibility rests for this decades-long scandal reaches from the maternity hospitals to medical professional bodies to the state's legal machinery and comprises a special example of patriarchy in action. Whatever about the obstetricians, the state blocked any 'avenues that might offer survivors a determination of truth or a mechanism for justice' (M. O'Connor 2016: 171). Linda Connolly, writing about the failure of the official review which women had long sought, carried out by the government-appointed Maureen Harding-Clarke, concluded that the total fund set aside to compensate the women, €34 million, was itself 'a clear admittance of wrongdoing on the part of the State, despite what the report intimates about "victims", bloggers, misguided applications and advocacy groups … it remains yet another example of Irish women's bodies on trial' (Connolly 2016). Of course, women who acted and organised would be dismissed as 'misguided'.

In Chapter 5, we encountered women going through our maternity services very often unsupported. For an aspect so central to our reproductive selves as the moment when we give birth, the site of power affecting

---

17   In 2020, despite travel restrictions as a result of the Covid-19 pandemic, 194 women travelled from Ireland to the UK for abortions and giving Irish addresses: sixty-two women travelled because of fatal foetal anomalies and 132 because the pregnancy was judged a risk to their physical or mental health (Holland 2021b).

us is 'hidden in plain sight' (Hynan 2018: 124). The maternity services are anchored in an enduring patriarchal structure which has at its roots the favoured 'Mastership' system dating from the eighteenth century (Hynan 2018; Devane et al. 2020). Irish maternity care is largely midwife-delivered but obstetric-governed and operates through a clearly delineated obstetric hierarchy in the nineteen maternity units around the country, including five standalone hospitals. These units account for place of birth for virtually all 59,796 women who gave birth in Ireland in 2019, excepting a tiny group of women, less than 200, who managed to have a home birth. The three Dublin standalone hospitals which are amongst the largest and busiest in Europe all have named 'Masters' at their apex elected for a seven-year term by their respective governing boards. These are powerful positions which have had a decisive impact on the increasingly medicalised direction of maternity provision countrywide (Murphy-Lawless 2021). Over 120 obstetric consultants at the top of this hierarchy with lucrative careers in our public-private system (M. O'Connor 2006), retain what Bridget McAdam-O'Connell (1998: 23) terms a 'free pass' in how they exercise their extensive power. She draws attention to how a photograph of a newly born baby published in 1992 in *The Irish Times* is used to celebrate the anniversary of the foundation the National Maternity Hospital. The photograph is of the then Master standing to the forefront with the newborn in his arms, while the woman who gave birth is in the background sitting up in bed. Commenting that 'even though the photograph shows an ostensibly happy trio, doctor, baby, mother, the placing of the obstetrician centre stage' sends the message as to where the power lies and McAdam-O'Connell concludes 'the woman has given birth in the hospital and will have done so according to the hospital rationales, set by doctors. So she has lost, not least because she does not command resources in that setting to win' (McAdam-O'Connell 1998: 24).

The unparalleled power of obstetrics, exercised through a maze of state-sanctioned legal and regulatory practices has favoured obstetric dominance (M. O'Connor 2006) and in turn, given the absence of effective oversight of how obstetrics functions, has led to abuses such as the Neary scandal. Neary was a consultant obstetrician in Our Lady of Lourdes Hospital Drogheda who conducted at least 188 hysterectomies, some on very young women, without due medical cause between 1974 and 1998 (records were subsequently discovered to be missing so the full number of women affected is unknown), until an anonymous midwife whistleblower reported Neary to authorities (Matthews and Scott 2008). It was women's activism which kept the issue in the public eye and eventually in 2003, Neary was struck off by the Irish Medical Council. The subsequent Lourdes Hospital Inquiry resulted in a compensation bill estimated between €45 and €50 million which was paid out by the state. Neary kept his full state pension.

The tragic death of Savita Halappanavar in 2012 occasioned a highly critical report by a state agency (HIQA 2013) which drew attention, amongst other factors, to the need for a specific up to date maternity policy. This policy arena of women's care has remained unchanged by the state in its organisational tenets since the early 1950s while obstetric power has flourished to the detriment of women (Dunlea 2021; Stach 2020).[18] We come off badly to the point of embarrassment in comparison to our near neighbours, Northern Ireland and Scotland, where the configuration of maternity services is significantly different and in line with current international evidence. There are well-established midwifery-led units and flexible home

18 The pressure to hold a referendum to effectively renege on the clause in the 1998 Good Friday Agreement guaranteeing that all people born on the island of Ireland are entitled to citizenship was a sustained campaign mounted by the Masters of Dublin's three maternity hospitals acting in concert. An internal memo released in 2004 from the Department of Justice revealed that the Masters had sought meetings and exchanged correspondence over an 18-month period in 2002–3 with then Minister for Justice Michael McDowell, expressing their 'disquiet' that non-national women, principally from Africa and Eastern Europe, were coming to Ireland in the late stages of pregnancy for the sole purpose, the Masters argued, of gaining citizenship for their babies. They 'pleaded for constitutional change' because the hospitals were being stretched to the limit of their capacities and that 'something needs to be done to tighten up controls in the immigration area' (Brennock 2004). What they refused to address, in addition to the need for urgent reform of the maternity services to address the overcrowding, was the legal standing of asylum seekers under international human rights conventions (Kennedy and Murphy-Lawless 2003). In the event, the referendum was held and carried in June, 2004 with a majority of 79 per cent. The racist undertones (Mancini and Finlay 2008), the absolute non-status of what Agamben (1998) terms 'bare life' was there for all to see.

birth policies as measures of national policies in these jurisdictions which have been responsive to women's needs and women's activism. Here, we have only two midwifery-led units which have remained on a 'pilot' basis since the early 2000s. Moreover, the National Maternity Strategy (2016–26) which arose from the 2013 HIQA report, actually reinforced obstetric decision-making for women, despite decades of activism in the Republic to bring midwives and midwifery-led care to the centre (Murphy-Lawless 2021). This is the strength of hidden-in-plain-sight patriarchal power.

The recent death of the well-known and respected independent midwife Philomena Canning brought this home with particular savagery (Clifford 2019; Murphy-Lawless 2019). Philomena was suspended from her home birth practice in 2014 by the HSE with no clear evidence or reason. At the time, she had twenty-nine women on her books, some weeks from giving birth. Eventually she was declared free to return to her practice in 2016 but with no concrete recompense for her ensuing legal fees, the reputational damage she sustained, and the loss of her employment. A settlement was finally secured under severe public pressure soon after an interview with her was published by the campaigning journalist, Mick Clifford in February 2019, by which time Philomena was weeks from her death due to ovarian cancer. There is no woman who attended her funeral a month later, the service itself sensitively chosen by Philomena before she died, who was not acutely aware of how wrong it was for the state to pursue Philomena without any cause whatsoever, merely because she pursued what she had always believed in and practised as an independent midwife, the best possible care of a pregnant woman. The paper trail leading to Philomena's suspension has never been recoverable in the public domain.

Perhaps most unsettling in the ongoing patriarchal marking of our public institutions is the continuing reliance on the 'cultural depiction of men as the appropriate authority figures' (P. O'Connor 1995: 86). This extends to the acceptability of what we may term official discourse tainted with a kind of legalistic masculinity. As activists and feminist scholars, we also need to acknowledge how this use of a template of male authority has been advantageously taken up by women in senior positions in Irish institutional life who use those same discourses and tactics of male privileging, including a reliance on hierarchical structures and relations, to reinforce

their own scope of power, thus colluding with the patriarchal dividend
(P. O'Connor 2000: 98). These remain 'dominant structural realities' of
a patriarchal underpinning (P. O'Connor 1995: 178) the complexity and
density of which come tumbling into public consciousness as bizarre coincidence. In April 2017, on the same day that the Citizens Assembly on the
anti-abortion Eighth Amendment reported its recommendation to hold a
referendum on whether or not the Eighth should be repealed, there were
widespread protests across Dublin about the behind-the-scenes agreement
between the National Maternity Hospital and St Vincent's Hospital placing
the new maternity hospital under the ownership of the Sisters of Charity.
    The protests resulted in the government returning to formal medi-
ation with the religious order which has owned St Vincent's Hospital to
resolve the issue of immediate governance and ownership (Mudiwa 2017),
but the ensuing agreement is still the subject of political controversy three
years on, with concerns that it will tie the new maternity hospital, for
which overall costs the state is paying, to restrictive Catholic rulings on
abortion and a range of other vital interventions for women's reproductive
health (Horgan-Jones and Wall 2021). The government is renewing its efforts to buy the site set aside on the St Vincent's Hospital campus for the
new hospital so that ownership and governance are clearly in the hands of
the state (ibid.). But the holding company which has taken over from the
Sisters of Charity and which is claiming charitable status, the St Vincent's
Hospital Group, has declared it must retain ownership of the site (Bray
and O'Halloran 2021).[19] Originally, the hospital was due to open in 2021.

19   The concerns about ownership and control of clinical decision-making about
     women's reproductive care are well understood. In 2017, Dublin's Mater Hospital, a
     major site of acute clinical care, teaching and research in Ireland originally founded
     and run by a religious order, the Sisters of Mercy, does not provide from its in-house
     pharmacy any access to oral contraception although doctors are free to prescribe it.
     Women who may be bedridden must access their own prescriptions outside the hos-
     pital (O'Malley/Newstalk 2017). Although circumstances are changed now in that
     women can obtain their contraception externally, this issue invokes the dreadful
     case of Sheila Hodgers who died in 1983 days after giving birth to her third baby,
     and as it happened, just before the referendum to insert the Eighth Amendment
     into the Constitution. She had terminal breast cancer held in check by her drug
     treatment which was stopped in Our Lady of Lourdes Hospital in Drogheda when

Our past continues to bleed into our present and for much the same reasons: as Ferriter (2017) writes in his analysis of the National Maternity Hospital debacle 'for all the focus on religion and ethos, money and power are also central to the controversy'. The St. Vincent's Hospital campus itself relied on state monies to be built but state oversight and concern were too often lacking as in so many other critical areas related to women's health.

Connecting then with now

The journalist Catherine Shanahan (2018), calling for an end to paternalism in health care, has recounted the fate of the Women's Health Council originally set up in 1997. This was just after Bridget McCole's death from advanced liver disease in 1996, the outcome of her having been infected with contaminated anti-D immunoglobin during late pregnancy in 1977 to deal with her Rhesus-negative status. The ensuing Hepatitis C scandal, the full details of which only began to be revealed by the state in 1994, impacted on the lives of some 1,600 women. The Women's Health Council about which there had been extensive consultations the length of the country to give a strong direction to its remit appeared to be a genuine token of earnest on the part of the state to begin to take seriously women's health needs. It was set up by law as a permanent statutory agency to give it sufficient force. Shanahan reminds us how it was revealed in 1997 that the state had decided to treat Bridget McCole as an adversary in a court process which put maximum pressure on her as a plaintiff.[20] Shanahan also reminds us that the Women's Health Council itself was abolished eleven

she became pregnant lest the drugs harm the foetus. She is said to have died in agony (O'Reilly 1992; O'Toole 2003b).

20 *The Irish Times* commented in 1997 on Bridget McCole's circumstances: 'In a functioning democracy, the word "versus" in the title of the legal case "Bridget Ellen McCole versus the Minister for Health", setting the interests of a citizen against the interests of her political protector, would have no conceivable meaning. But to a dying and grossly-wronged woman, to her husband and children, its meaning was made all too clear … The simple answer to the question put by the McCole family

years later in 2008 by a female Minister for Health whose argument in so doing was that health sector agencies required rationalisation. In whose interests are such actions taken is what we needed to ask then and now.

Shanahan wrote her piece shortly after the Northern Ireland professor of public health, Gabriel Scally, had published his 200-page review for the government on the CervicalCheck scandal (Scally 2018; and see notes 2 and 11). It is a rarity in Ireland for a medical person to speak with comprehensive honesty about what has been done to women through professional and state negligence. On the basis of intensive interviews, Scally described how these traumatic events had left the 221 women who had developed cervical cancer and their families with 'deep hurt, anguish and resentment' (ibid.: 141). Not alone had the women been let down by consecutive catastrophic failures of the state's health, administrative and legal systems alongside medical consultants who were consistently autocratic and paternalistic, women also experienced the complete failure on the part of these individuals and systems to accept their wrongdoing: 'At the heart of this issue lies the willingness and strength to speak the truth, as well as the willingness and ability to listen when others speak it' (ibid.: 142). At the press conference launching the report, Scally drew attention to several quotations from the interviews presented in bold on page 20 of the report:

'Why does it always happen to women?'

'I think there is a history of looking at women's health services as being secondary.'

'Women and women's rights are not taken seriously.'

'Paternalism is alive and well.' (Scally 2018: 20)

And he concluded that the male-dominant Irish medical system had led women to inexorable tragedy: 'Many of the major controversies

---

is that their State saw Bridget Ellen McCole as an enemy' (*The Irish Times* 1997). This same logic has carried into the lives, and deaths, of the women who have been forced to fight the HSE in court over CervicalCheck negligence.

about maltreatment of patients or denial of reproductive rights in the Irish healthcare system have involved women being damaged' (ibid.).

The woman to speak out first about the appalling failure of CervicalCheck was Vicky Phelan on the steps of the High Court in 2018 after successfully suing the state for what had occurred (Phelan 2019). We need to celebrate Vicky Phelan and Bridget McCole two decades before her, both of whom had to stand up against the state's malfeasance, as citizens whose lives the state and its institutions ruined. The lines of power along which a host of these and similar institutional actions have run, such as the government decision to seal the archives of the survivors of the mother and baby homes (McConnell 2020), or the denials of birth certificates to those born in Magdalene homes, are a kind of casual abuse of power and positionality. They are inaccessible to us as ordinary women, but like live electricity wires, we sense where they are. We know they damage and even kill, and we know that too many women, past and present, have had no free pass in Irish society to build their lives safely.

Past to present, our gains however critical as with the removal of the Eighth Amendment have been far fewer than we required and there is far less recognition, often by women themselves, of all that is needed. In June 2018 as part of a special commemorative event and gathering, over 220 survivors of the Magdalene regime were first honoured at Áras an Uachtaráin by President Higgins with a heartfelt apology to them for how the state, the church and society had incarcerated them and cast them aside. The women were then brought to the Mansion House for a gala dinner (Hogan 2019a: 162–3). A call went out over social media from the event organisers asking people to gather in Dawson Street to welcome the women as they got off the buses which had brought them from the Áras. Despite a perfect early summer's evening, just at closing time for the streets of offices and shops nearby, younger women were not present in any significant number in the crowd of approximately 200 people who made their way to the Mansion House to greet the women. It should have been possible to be part of that welcoming crowd for a brief half hour or so, as requested over social media, and then go on one's way to an evening drink or meal or entertainment.

Again, in the early hours of a bitterly cold night on 27 January 2020, a vulnerable young woman gave birth on a street corner in the centre of Dublin amidst a tangle of cardboard boxes for shelter (Feehan 2020). The incident, covered in the national press a few hours later, took place during a general election campaign. It was luck alone that there were still a few passers-by at 1 a.m. who rang for an ambulance to take the young woman and her baby to hospital. Otherwise the country would have awakened to a tragedy that would have invoked images of Ann Lovett's death. Yet there was no massive outcry on social media in the days following. No women's group, no women's spokesperson of any national political party made any statement about the occurrence. How do instances like these, critical to how we see ourselves, because as McLean writes, these are the 'interimplications of pasts, presents and futures' (2004: 160), how do they connect to Irish women in the post-Repeal the Eighth climate? What are women not recognising, what are they choosing to ignore in their lives and the lives of their daughters, in the lives of all women into the future? What are they risking by not seeing the implications of non-action? Bauman writes of how the late modern order of 'liquid modernity' flourishes on the 'universal contingency of the consumer life' (2005: 58). How are we to move beyond that unstable, unsustainable consumer life which promotes a detachment of cold calculation of self, and instead create and pursue a politics of engagement that encompasses the ongoing needs of all women in Ireland? Unless we have the courage to see.

In their discussion of reproductive justice, Zakiya Luna and Kristen Luker (2013) employ this definition from Asian Communities for Reproductive Justice (an organisation now called Forward Together):

> the complete physical, mental, spiritual, political, economic, and social well-being of women and girls [that] will be achieved when women and girls have the economic, social and political power and resources to make healthy decisions about our bodies, sexuality and reproduction for ourselves, our families and our communities in all areas of our lives. (ACRJ, 2005: 1, quoted in Luna and Luker, 2013: 328; see also Luna 2020; Zavella 2020)

We have nothing even remotely close to this in late modern Ireland.

Being Athwart: Resistance and exuberance

Pat O'Connor has concluded that while many women have changed 'the parameters of their own private lives' over these last few decades, it is ironic that they have failed to understand 'the implicit male bias' in Irish institutions and thus have completely under-estimated 'the strength and flexibility of the processes and practices involved in the maintenance of patriarchy' (1998: 250). And which will continue to be maintained unless we can begin to take account of the loss and pain which stretches back through our history and build it into vital political thinking.

In the same week that the current government announced its decision to seal the Mother and Baby Home archives, the Department of Health reneged on its promise to the 221 CervicalCheck survivors to establish a non-adversarial tribunal. Following a Supreme Court decision that the HSE held the principal responsibility for the entire screening programme and thus there was no necessity to sue both the HSE and the laboratories to whom the histology work had been outsourced, the group had argued that the way was clear for a non-adversarial setting (Bray 2020). Instead, the state announced, without further consultation with the 221Plus group, that there will be a tribunal process which will be adversarial in nature to deal with the remaining cases on the grounds that the laboratories must be represented and the women questioned by their lawyers (ibid.). Daniel McConnell wrote of both these events in detail observing that this was 'A truly terrible week for this state ... the State itself has moved again to fail the people it has hurt the most' (McConnell 2020). Vicky Phelan's response was 'Why is it so hard to do what is right for women who have already been failed by the State?' (quoted in Loughlin 2020). Why indeed?

That was Emma Mhic Mhathuna's question in the weeks before she died of her cervical cancer undisclosed until it was too late. Mother of five children, she said of her situation: 'I shouldn't be dying, that's what makes this a tragedy ... I feel like I've essentially been murdered. I should be here another 50 years' (Mhic Mhathúna 2018). Why must it happen? Why must the Irish state perpetrate such violence against women with such incontro-vertible intent? Lloyd (1999: 82) points to the 'assiduous preservation of the apparatuses, ideological and repressive' gained from British imperialism, ideas about tradition and masculinity, for example, which were reshaped and re-deployed to suit the purposes of the post-1922 state as it slid into its version of modernity, with the consequence of marginalising 'unassimilable and recalcitrant social groups, cultural forms and political projects', all having a massive effect on gender relations, Lloyd concludes, in modern Ireland (ibid.). Women's lives, our lives, our bodies, formed and reformed by an obstructive masculinist culture have been 'both object of forgetting and repository of memory' (McLean 2004: 148). To make sense of this was the work of im-agination and connection set out by Doireann Ní Ghríofa in her exploration of the life of Eibhlín Dubh Ní Chonaill, *A Ghost in the Throat*, women's lives then and now, the absolute 'force of female desire' (2020: 182). Given our times, there is no little political urgency in positioning that desire in all the many forms and shapes against this masculinist state and asking why? Why continue to deny us? Why grudgingly accept us on your terms only?

We need that fundamental understanding about how overarching structures of forgetting have been used against our lives, we need that connection of remembering to get to the social change that can realise the futures of the young women from the Celtic Tiger years whom we have interviewed (some of whom will now have their own daughters to mentor), the futures of the already adult children who were illegally adopted out of the mother and baby homes, the futures of the children of the women whose lives have been lost to the scandals of the state's reproductive ser-vices, the futures of the emigrant women who have come to live here since the early 2000s, opening Ireland at last to many multi-ethnic identities, the futures of the socially and economically marginalised women straight across contemporary Ireland. We need to confront this masculinist Irish state differently, a state peerless in its capacity to deny many truths, denying also that its version of equality is profoundly undemocratic to everyone, women and men, citizens, migrants, asylum seekers, all. This is why we need truth-telling in all its dimensions as never before. And we need to deploy the long arc of our recalcitrance as a potent disrupter of how our pasts have been told against us and equally how our futures are even now being constrained by the state within its stunted parameters of what is of-ficially deemed an appropriate late modern society.

We honour the recalcitrance of Emma Mhic Mhathuna wearing a dramatic full-length red ball gown into the High Court on the day of her settlement against the HSE, declaring afterwards 'I wasn't going to come into court the victim … I came in a victor and so red is a symbol of standing for women' (quoted in Murtagh 2018). In the face of her impending death, Emma's was an action of 'subversive reimagining' (McLean 2004: 161) of our past and our future that we require many times over. We have begun already through our truth-telling about this patriarchal state.

In his essays on 'fearless speech' in the classical Greek texts, Foucault (2001) asks us to consider the fundamental role that *parrhesia*, truth-telling, plays in a free society and what happens when you are prevented from speaking because of your lack of social status: 'If you are not a regular citizen in the city, if you are exiled, then you cannot speak … If you do not have the right of free speech, you are unable to exercise any kind of power … and without the right of criticism, the power exercised by a sovereign is without limitation' (ibid.: 29). Those who seize the ground to speak then will always do so from 'below' (ibid.: 18) and they become the *parrhesiastes*, the truth-tellers. Foucault adds 'if there is a kind of "proof" of the sincerity of the *parrhesiastes* it is his courage' (ibid.: 14).

Her courage, hers: our truth-tellers have been the women who have spoken out against this obdurate state. Much of the power of the Irish state up to the last third of the twentieth century, deploying its strong partnership with the educational and social care institutions of the Irish Catholic church and all the church's cultural machinery aimed towards suppression, stemmed from how women were prevented from speaking by obliterating even their names. One reason why the sealing up of names from the Mother and Baby Commission is so raw for us as bystanders and supporters of the survivors is that the sum of all our history cries out how immeasurably wrong this is.

Individual women have thrown aside the myriad efforts to silence them, cumulative scandal upon scandal. This is the importance of Vicky Phelan standing on the steps of the High Court after she had refused to sign the confidentiality agreement without which the state's legal team would not even discuss a settlement:

I thought about that dotted line that I would have to sign. Like an ellipsis ... the ellipsis of the story of my life ... But that's just the thing, I thought. My life won't be continued. This might be the full stop. Where the story ends, because of what happened to me. The irony of that ellipsis makes me angry. And what about the other women, or the families of those who have died. The lives that already had come to an end. If I signed, they would never know the truth. 'I can't sign that, I said to Cian' [her solicitor]. (Phelan 2019: 239)

It is the importance of Roisin Molloy's actions she undertook with her husband, Mark, after their baby, Mark, had died in Portlaoise Hospital in January 2012. In her testimony to the Oireachtas Committee on Health and Children in May 2015, Roisin described how, traumatised and grief-stricken by her baby's death and by the utter lack of care meted out to her and Mark afterwards and with four young children to care for, she 'became the crazy mother telling everybody that my child had died when he should not have died' (Oireachtas Joint Committee on Health and Children 2015). Roisin knew she had been lied to and she and Mark relentlessly pursued every possible official channel over several years until an RTE *Primetime* programme in January 2014 took up their case, revealing other families who had experienced the same disastrous outcome and had also been lied to, leading ultimately to an HSE investigation and a HIQA report which confirmed the parents' accounts (Flaherty 2015; Murphy-Lawless 2015). Imagine having the courage to describe yourself as 'the crazy mother' to get your voice heard; courage in truth-telling, courage indeed.

It is the absolute importance of Joanne Hayes who endured unspeakable crimes committed against her in the course of the so-named Kerry Babies scandal, crimes violating her very person, physically and mentally, committed by the state's Garda Síochána, medical and legal 'authorities' in accusing her of a baby's murder, who along with her siblings has finally achieved a settlement in the High Court of the damages owing to her for the ordeal of thirty-six years ago and restitution of her and her siblings' good names. A series of declarations said about her and her family in police and medical reports and the tribunal itself constituted absolute lies will now be appended to every single official record of the case (O'Faolain 2020). It is reported that Ms Justice Leonie Reynolds who handed down this ruling along with the state's apology on 18 December 2020 was emotional, feelings echoed by women across the country who felt the weight of truth and a good name restored after the most intense suffering.

We can see the project which has emerged here: in what Lloyd (2003) sees as a counterhegemonic struggle, women who have spoken out have acted on their individual and collective loss, have transmuted it into a clarity of intent so that not accepting their great loss, they reject the state which has imposed it, anxious always to keep its power. In their resistance, they have decided not to 'lose [their] loss in order to become [the] good subjects of modernity' (ibid. 2003: 220), the good subjects of that state which would now prefer a modernised subjectivity compliant with a globalised way of life, one which has set its own traps for women. Instead, it is women of Ireland who can place themselves athwart this version of modernity and demand something human, far more whole in their lives, in the lives of their partners, families and children, who will take up the case of a young woman giving birth amidst some cardboard boxes on a street corner in the middle of a freezing January night, and demand far-reaching social change for all.

The pregnant Nigerian asylum seeker who died in the Rotunda Hospital in 2010, Bimbo Onanuga, would have remained nameless but for the actions of a courageous group of midwifery students who in refusing to be silenced made it possible to begin the fight for her public inquest (Murphy-Lawless 2014, 2018). That work moved on to the formation of the Elephant Collective, activists who worked with the Independent4Change politician Clare Daly and a group of widowers for six years to gain the Coroners (Amendment) Act 2019, ensuring mandatory public inquests for all women who die in our maternity services. The law places Ireland in accordance with Article 2 of the European Convention on Human Rights, the right to life, and is the first such legislation in Europe. This lengthy campaign took the absolute loss of women's lives and built a work of social solidarity and no little exuberance, with countless acts of friendship at its base, cutting across the structural violence of Irish society and facing down a government which in harming women would rather pay out hundreds of millions in damages than to act with honesty and humility.

These are feisty women, the truth-tellers, who have created 'new modes of non-modern recalcitrance' (Lloyd 1999: 78) or what the film-maker

Emma O'Grady has named as *Mad, Bad and Dangerous Women* in her recent series of the same title, women who are unafraid to take on that vital 'subversive reimagining' of which McLean writes. One of the women interviewed in the *MBD* film was the distinguished artist Pauline Cummins who recounts being asked to do a mural for the National Maternity Hospital in 1984, a year of otherwise grim events including Ann Lovett's death and the beginning of Joanne Hayes' horrific ordeal at the hands of a punitive state. Moving counter-intuitively, all too aware of the trauma people were experiencing in the wake of these shocking events and herself pregnant at the time, Pauline balanced on scaffolding to paint across the expanse of one of the old hospital's external walls a larger-than-life mural of two naked women carrying aloft a third woman naked and pregnant, dancing for the sheer joy of being alive.

The fact that the hospital scrubbed away the mural in weeks, of course without asking Pauline's permission, was an indication of exactly how dangerous we are when we dare to tell the truth and remain athwart. The mural also calls attention to why in early Irish culture the goddess figures of Bridget and Macha in all their strength were prized. Pauline's mural and its story were a glorious light in that bleak year of 1984. More recently, the portrayal of Brigid by Sophie Merry, in a Bridget story for our times, the short film produced for the Repeal the Eighth campaign, left us grinning in recognition of all we are when we stand confidently to set aside a male establishment.

We have the knowledge and the tools to build tough, relentless political spaces of dissent to which we bring 'a proliferation of present-pasts and present-futures' (McLean 2004: 160) in order to yield forms of genuine equality, wrenched free from the current social and economic conformities of Irish society. Drawing on our particular history of loss and silencing, we can create these dissenting political spaces alongside the abundant energies of women who have come to Ireland in their many thousands in the last two decades with their particular histories of loss and silencing so that we can justly anchor all our lives. The political creativity, the exuberance, the truth-telling can and will command a different future.

As the poet Rita Ann Higgins (2011) writes, 'Ireland is changing Mother, tell your sons.'

Note on the Cover Artist

Credit for cover art of a *sailleach*, salley, willow tree and a woman with her children by Martina Hynan. Martina is a maternal artist, curator and birth activist based in Ennis, Co. Clare, Ireland. She is a PhD researcher with the Centre for Irish Studies, NUI Galway and member of The Elephant Collective, a birth activist group. Her feminist practice-with-research project explores the entanglements of birth with place, exploring how the transition from home to hospital birth affects both the relationship with the experience of childbirth and the place of birth, particularly in rural Ireland.

To view her work, please visit: <www.martinahynan.com>

Cover image: The book cover has been designed by Martina Hynan and is in memory of Mary Martin and Margaret Martin.

Bibliography

Abortion Rights Campaign. (nd). *Abortion Law in Ireland*. Available from: <https://www.abortionrightscampaign.ie/abortion-law-in-ireland/>, accessed 8 July 2018.

Agamben, G. (1998). *Homo Sacer: Sovereign Power and Bare Life*. Palo Alto, CA: Stanford University Press.

Almeling, R. (2020). *GUYnecology: The Missing Science of Men's Reproductive Health*. University of California Press.

Allen, K. (2000). *The Celtic Tiger: The Myth of Social Partnership in Ireland*. Manchester: Manchester University Press.

—— (2007). *Ireland's Economic Crash: A Radical Agenda for Change*. Dublin: The Liffey Press.

Allison, J. (2013). *Motherhood and Infertility in Ireland: Understanding the Presence of Absence*. Cork: Cork University Press.

Andersen, K. (2010). 'Irish Secularization and Religious Identities: Evidence of an Emerging New Catholic Habitus', *Social Compass*, 57 (1), 15–39.

Antosik-Parsons, K. (2014). ' "Caoineadh na mairbh": Vocalising Memory and Otherness in the Early Performances of Alanna O'Kelly', *Nordic Irish Studies*, 13 (1), 205–21.

Arnold-de Sinime, S. (2013). *Mediating Memory in the Museum: Trauma, Empathy, Nostalgia*. London: Palgrave Macmillan.

Bacik, I. (2013). 'Abortion and the Law in Ireland', In A. Quilty, S. Kennedy., and C. Conlon (eds), *The Abortion Papers Ireland: Volume II*, pp. 104–117. Dublin: Attic Press.

Baker, J., Lynch K., Cantillon S., and Walsh J. (2004). *Equality: From Theory to Action*. Houndmills, Basingstoke, Hampshire, England: Palgrave Macmillan.

Bakhru, T. S. (2014). 'Movement, Consumption and Choice in Neoliberal Reproductive Health Discourses: An Irish Case Study'. In D. Nititham and R. Boyd (eds), *Heritage, Diaspora and the Consumption of Culture: Movements in Irish Landscapes*, pp. 219–34. Abingdon: Routledge.

Banks, J. and Russell, H. (2011). *Pregnancy Discrimination in the Workplace: Legal Framework and Review of Legal Decisions 1999 to 2008*. Dublin: HSE Crisis Pregnancy Programme and the Equality Authority.

Bardon, S. (2018). 'Ireland Votes to Remove Constitutional Ban on Abortion by Resounding Two-Thirds Majority', *The Irish Times*, 26 May, <www.irishtimes.com/news/politics/ireland-votes-to-remove-constitutional-ban-on-abortion-by-resounding-two-thirds-majority-1.3510068>, accessed 27 May 2018.

Barmpouti, A. (2019). *Post-War Eugenics, Reproductive Choices and Population Policies in Greece, 1950s–1980s*. London: Palgrave Macmillan.

Barry, U. (2008). *Where Are We Now? New Feminist Perspectives on Women in Contemporary Ireland*. Dublin: TASC at New Ireland.

—— (2018). 'What do We Mean by Bodily Autonomy? And What does Bodily Autonomy Mean for Women in Particular?' In K. D'Arcy (ed.), *Autonomy*, pp. 180–92. Cork City: New Binary Press. <https://researchrepository.ucd.ie/handle/10197/9738>

Barry, U., and Conroy, P. (2012). 'Ireland 2008–2012 Untold Story of the Crisis – Gender, Equality and Inequalities', *Tasc Thinkpieces*, May, 1–26. Dublin: TASC.

Barry, U., and Feeley, M. (2016). 'Gender and Economic Inequality in Ireland'. In R. Hearne and C. McMahon (eds), *Cherishing All Equally 2016: Economic Inequality in Ireland*, pp. 45–55. Dublin: TASC.

Bauman, Z. (1993). *Postmodern Ethics*. Oxford: Blackwell Press.

—— (1998). *Work, Consumerism and the New Poor*. Maidenhead, Berkshire, England: Open University Press.

——(2003). *Liquid Love*. London: Polity Press.

——(2004). *Identity*. London: Polity Press.

——(2005). *Liquid Life*. London: Polity Press.

—— (2008). *Does Ethics Have a Chance in a World of Consumers?* Cambridge, MA: Harvard University Press.

Beale, J. (1986). *Women in Ireland: Voices of Change*. Dublin: Gill and Macmillan.

Beesley, A. (2005). 'Shopping Centre Boom Shows Little Sign of Abating Next Year', *Irish Times*, 30 December, <https://www.irishtimes.com/business/shopping-centre-boom-shows-little-sign-of-abating-next-year-1.1288710>, accessed 31 December 2005.

Benjamin, W. (2003). 'On the Concept of History'. In H. Eiland and M. W. Jennings (eds), Walter Benjamin: *Selected Writings, 4, 1938–1940*, pp. 389–400. London: Belknap Press of Harvard University Press.

—— (2005). 'Excavation and Memory'. In M. Jennings, H. Eiland and G. Smith (eds), *Selected Writings, Volume 2, Part 2, 1931–1934*, p. 576. London: Belknap Press of Harvard University Press.

Benn, M. (1998). *Madonna and Child: Towards a New Politics of Motherhood*. London: Jonathan Cape.

Best, A. (2005). 'Abortion Rights along the Irish-English Border and the Liminality of Women's Experiences', *Dialectical Anthropology*, 29 (3/4), 423–37.

Bicheno, J. E. (1830). *Ireland, and its Economy: Being the Result of Observations Made in a Tour Through the Country in the Autumn of 1829*. London: John Murray.

Blofield, M. (2008). 'Women's Choices in Comparative Perspective Abortion Policies in Late-Developing Catholic Countries', *Comparative Politics*, 40 (4), 399–419.

Bogle, K. A. (2008). *Hooking Up: Sex, Dating, and Relationships on Campus*. New York: NYU Press.

Boland, R. (2009). 'A Town Torn', *The Irish Times*, 19 December, <https://www.irishti mes.com/culture/books/a-town-torn-1.793083>, accessed 21 December 2009.

—— (2018). 'Ann Lovett: Death of a "strong, kick-ass girl"', *The Irish Times*, 24 March, <https://www.irishtimes.com/life-and-style/people/ann-lovett-death-of-a-strong-kick-ass-girl-1.3429792>, accessed 24 March 2018.

—— (2020). 'Ireland's Abandoned Babies: "Stories of Unimaginable Fear"', *The Irish Times*, 11 January, <https://www.irishtimes.com/life-and-style/health-fam ily/ireland-s-abandoned-babies-stories-of-unimaginable-fear-1.4134033>, ac- cessed 11 January 2020.

Bourke, A. (1993). 'More in Anger than in Sorrow: Irish Women's Lament Poetry'. In J. N. Radner (ed.) *Feminist Messages: Coding in Women's Folk Culture*, pp. 160– 81. Urbana: University of Illinois Press.

Bourke, J. (1993). *Husbandry to Housewifery: Women, Housework and Economic Change 1890–1914*. Oxford: Oxford University Press.

Bourke, A., et al. (2015). 'Factors Associated with Crisis Pregnancies in Ireland: Findings from Three Nationally Representative Sexual Health Surveys', *Reproductive Health*, 12 (1), 14–25.

Bowers, S. (2020a). 'Over 90% of Women who Accessed Early Abortion Service did not Require Hospital Visit', *The Irish Times* 17 November, <https://www.irishti mes.com/news/health/over-90-of-women-who-accessed-early-abortion-serv ice-did-not-require-hospital-visit-1.4410894>, accessed 18 December 2020.

—— (2020b). 'State did not Apologise to Ruth Morrissey "now it is too late", says Husband after her Death', 19 July, *The Irish Times* <https://www.irishtimes. com/news/health/state-did-not-apologise-to-ruth-morrissey-now-it-is-too- late-says-husband-after-her-death-1.4308145>, accessed 20 December 2020.

Boydston, J. (1994). *Home and Work: Housework, Wages and the Ideology of Labor in the Early Republic*. New York: Oxford University Press.

Boylan, P. (2019). *In the Shadow of the Eighth: My Forty Years Working for Women's Health in Ireland*. Dublin: Penguin Ireland.

Boyle, P. P., and Ó Gráda, C. (1986). 'Fertility Trends and Excess Mortality in the Great Irish Famine', *Demography*, 23 (4), 543–62.

Bray, J. (2019a). 'Abortion in Ireland: Four Weeks in, How's it Working?', *The Irish Times*, 26 January, <www.irishtimes.com/life-and-style/health-family/ abortion-in-ireland-four-weeks-in-how-s-it-working-1.3770442>, accessed 26 January 2019.

—— (2019b). 'A Tale of Two Abortions in Ireland: One Legal, One Criminal', *The Irish Times*, 13 April, <www.irishtimes.com/life-and-style/health-family/a-tale-of-two-abortions-in-ireland-one-legal-one-criminal-1.3857189>, accessed 13 April 2019.

—— (2020). 'Q and A CervicalCheck Tribunal', *The Irish Times*, 28 October, <https://www.irishtimes.com/news/health/q-a-cervicalcheck-tribunal-1.4393633>, accessed 29 October 2020.

—— (2021). 'Murphy Hits Back Hard at Critics over Mother and Baby Home Report', *The Irish Times*, 11 June, <https://www.irishtimes.com/news/ireland/irish-news/murphy-hits-back-hard-at-critics-over-mother-and-baby-home-report-1.4591058>, accessed 11 June 2021.

Bray, J., and O'Halloran, M. (2021). 'St Vincent's Says it must Retain Ownership of National Maternity Hospital Site', *The Irish Times*, 22 June, <https://www.irishtimes.com/news/health/st-vincent-s-says-it-must-retain-ownership-of-national-maternity-hospital-site-1.4600564>, accessed 22 June 2021.

Brennan, J., et al. (1938). 'The Population Problem: A Radio Discussion', *Journal of Statistical and Social Inquiry Society of Ireland*, 16 (1), 112–21.

Brennock, M. (2003). 'One in Four 15 to 17 year-olds have had Sex – Poll', *The Irish Times*, 19 September, <https://www.irishtimes.com/news/one-in-four-15-to-17-year-olds-have-had-sex-poll-1.376914>, accessed 8 August 2005.

——. (2004). 'McDowell Changes Argument on Referendum', *The Irish Times*, 9 April, <https://www.irishtimes.com/news/mcdowell-changes-argument-on-referendum-1.1307408>, accessed 28 May 2006.

Bresnihan, V. (2004). 'Mind-Maps: Motherhood and the Political Symbolism in the Irish Pro-Life Movement'. In P. Kennedy (ed.), *Motherhood in Ireland: Creation and Context*, pp. 117–26. Cork: Mercier Press.

Bridges, K. (2011). *Reproducing Race: An Ethnography of Pregnancy as a Site of Racialization*. Berkeley, CA: University of California Press.

Briggs, L. (2018). *How All Politics Became Reproductive Politics: From Welfare Reform to Foreclosure to Trump*. Berkeley, CA: University of California Press.

Brush, L. (1996). 'Love, Toil, and Trouble: Motherhood and Feminist Politics', *Signs: Journal of Women in Culture and Society*, 21 (2), 429–54.

Burke, S. (2009). *Irish Apartheid: Healthcare Inequality in Ireland*. Dublin: New Island.

Burke-Kennedy, E. (2019). 'Women More Likely to be Earning Minimum Wage than Men', *The Irish Times*, 26 April, <https://www.irishtimes.com/business/economy/women-more-likely-to-be-earning-minimum-wage-than-men-1.3872576>, accessed 8 March 2020.

Burley, J., and Regan, F. (2002). 'Divorce in Ireland: The Fear, the Floodgates and the Reality', *International Journal of Law, Policy and the Family*, 16, 202–22.

Butler, J. (1990). *Gender Trouble: Feminism and the Subversion of Identity*. New York: Routledge.

Brown, T. (2004). *Ireland: a Social and Cultural History, 1922–2002*. London: Fontana.

Browne, K., and Calkin, S. (eds) (2020). *After Repeal: Rethinking Abortion Politics*. London: Zed Books.

Browne, K., and Nash, C. (2017). 'Heteroactivism: Beyond Anti-Gay', *ACME: An International Journal for Critical Geographies*, 16 (4), 643–52.

Browne, K., and Nash, C. (2019). 'Losing Ireland: Heteroactivist Responses to the Result of the 8th Amendment in Canada and the UK'. In S. Calkin, and K. Browne (eds) *After Repeal: Rethinking Abortion Politics*, pp. 205–23. London: Zed Books.

Browne, K., Nash, C., and Gorman-Murray, A. (2018). 'Geographies of Heteroactivism: Resisting Sexual Rights in the Constitution of Irish Nationhood', *Transactions of the Institute of British Geographers*, 43 (4), 526–39.

Byrne, A. (2003). 'Developing a Sociological Model for Researching Women's Self and Social Identities', *European Journal of Women's Studies*, 4, 443–64.

Byrne, E. A. (2012). *Political Corruption in Ireland 1922–2010: A Crooked Harp?* Manchester: Manchester University Press.

Byrne, K. (2019). 'More Women in Ireland are Choosing to be 'Voluntarily Childless'. Are You One of Them?' *Irish Independent*, 17 July. <https://www.independent. ie/life/more-women-in-ireland-are-choosing-to-be-voluntarily-childless-are-you-one-of-them-38321146.html>, accessed 2 June 2021.

Byrne, D., and Treanor, M. (2020). *Income, Poverty and Deprivation among Children: A Statistical Baseline Analysis*. Dublin: Department of Children, Equality, Disability, Integration and Youth.

Campbell, B. (2013). *End of Equality: The Only Way is Women's Liberation*. London: Seagull Books.

Canvin, K. et al. (2007). 'Can I Risk Using Public Services? Perceived Consequences of Seeking Help and Health Care among Households Living in Poverty: Qualitative Study', *Journal of Epidemiology and Community Health*, 61, 984–89.

Carberry, G. (2008). 'Eileen Flynn, Teacher Sacked in 1982, Dies', *The Irish Times*, 11 September, <https://www.irishtimes.com/news/eileen-flynn-teacher-sacked-in-1982-dies-1.937690>, accessed 13 September 2008.

Carey, S. (2015). 'Why Has Ireland So Many Childless Women?', *Irish Independent*, 19 April, <http://www.independent.ie/opinion/columnists/sarah-carey/arti cle31153766.ece>, accessed 25 April 2015.

Carolan, M. (2019). 'HSE Apologises to Family of Pregnant Woman Kept on Life Support', *The Irish Times*, 20 November, <https://www.irishtimes.com/news/crime-and-law/courts/high-court/hse-apologises-to-family-of-pregnant-woman-kept-on-life-support-1.4089397>, accessed 20 November 2019.

——(2021). 'Philomena Lee among Five Given Leave to Challenge Mother and Baby Homes Report', *The Irish Times*, 12 April, <https://www.irishtimes.com/news/crime-and-law/courts/high-court/philomena-lee-among-five-given-leave-to-challenge-mother-and-baby-homes-report-1.4535356>, accessed 12 April 2021.

Carpenter, L. (2005). *Virginity Lost: An Intimate Portrait of First Sexual Experiences.* New York: NYU Press.

Chan, S. (2018). 'Speaking of Silence, Speaking of Art, Abortion and Ireland'. *Irish Studies Review*, 27 (1), 73–93.

Chodorow, N. (1999). *The Reproduction of Mothering: Psychoanalysis and the Sociology of Gender* (2nd ed.). Berkeley, CA: University of California Press.

Citizens Assembly (2021). 'Recommendations of the Citizens' Assembly on Gender Equality', Press Release, 24 April 24. <https://www.citizensassembly.ie/en/news-publications/press-releases/recommendations-of-the-citizens-assembly-on-gender-equality.html>, accessed 2 June 2021.

Clancy, P. (1986). 'Socialisation, Selection and Reproduction in Education'. In P. Clancy et al. (eds), *Ireland: A Sociological Profile*, pp. 116–36. Dublin: IPA.

Clark, A. (2005). 'Wild Workhouse Girls and the Liberal Imperial State in the Mid-Nineteenth Century Ireland', *Journal of Social History*, 2, 389–409.

——(2008). *Desire: A History of European Sexuality.* London: Routledge.

Clark, S. (1979). *Social Origins of the Irish Land War.* Princeton, NJ: Princeton University Press.

Clarke, R. (2021). *Breathtaking: Inside the NHS in a Time of Pandemic.* Boston, MA: Little, Brown Book Group.

Clear, C. (2000). *Women of the House: Women's Household Work in Ireland 1922–1961.* Dublin: Irish Academic Press.

——(2007). *Social Change and Everyday Life in Ireland, 1850–1922.* Manchester: Manchester University Press.

Coakley, A. (2004). 'Mothers and Poverty'. In P. Kennedy (ed.), *Motherhood in Ireland: Creation and Context*, pp. 207–17. Cork: Mercier Press.

Cohen, D. (1993). 'Private Lives in Public Spaces: Marie Stopes, the Mothers' Clinics and the Practice of Contraception', *History Workshop Journal*, 35 (Spring), 95–116.

Cohen, D. S., and Joffe, C. (2020). *Obstacle Course: The Everyday Struggle to Get an Abortion in America.* Berkeley, CA: University of California Press.

Colen, S. (1995). ' "Like a Mother to Them": Stratified Reproduction and West Indian Childcare Workers and Employers in New York'. In F. D. Ginsburg and R. Rapp (ed.), *Conceiving the New World Order: The Global Politics of Reproduction*, pp. 78–102. Berkeley, CA: University of California Press.

Collier, J. F. (1997). *From Duty to Desire: Remaking Families in a Spanish Village*. Princeton, NJ: Princeton University Press.

Combat Poverty Agency. (2005). *Mapping Poverty: National Regional and County Patterns*. Dublin: Stationery Office.

Commiskey, G. (2015). 'Winning is the Lifeblood of Ireland's Women Rugby Champions: The Strength of our Women Rugby Players should be Cherished', *The Irish Times*, 23 March <http://www.irishtimes.com/sport/rugby/intern ational/winning-is-the-lifeblood-of-ireland-s-women-rugby-champions-1.2149070>, accessed 23 March 2015.

Conlon, C. (2006). 'Concealed Pregnancy: A Case-study Approach from an Irish setting'. *Crisis Pregnancy Agency Report*. Dublin: CPA. <https://www.lenus.ie/handle/10147/43751>

Conlon, C., O'Connor, J., and Chathain, S. N. (2012). *Attitudes to Fertility, Sexual Health and Motherhood amongst a Sample of Non-Irish National Minority Ethnic Women*. Dublin: Health Service Executive. <https://www.lenus.ie/handle/10147/304950>

Connell, K. H. (1956). 'Marriage in Ireland after the Famine: The Diffusion of the Match'. *Journal of the Statistical and Social Inquiry Society of Ireland*, 159, 82–103.

—— (1958). 'The Land Legislation and Irish Social Life'. *The Economic History Review*, Second Series, 1 (August), 1–7.

——(1965). 'The Potato in Ireland', *Clogher Record*, 5 (3), 281–95.

Connolly, E. (2003). 'Durability and Change in State Gender Systems: Ireland in the 1950s', *European Journal of Women's Studies*, 10 (1), 65–86.

Connolly, L. (2003). *The Irish Women's Movement: from Revolution to Devolution*. Dublin: Lilliput Press.

—— (2016). 'Symphysiotomy Report Begets More Questions', *Irish Examiner*, 29 November, <https://www.irishexaminer.com/opinion/commentanalysis/arid-20432728.html>, accessed 30 November 2016.

Connolly, S. J. (1985). 'Marriage in Pre-Famine Ireland'. In A. Cosgrove (ed.), *Marriage in Ireland*, pp. 78–98. Dublin: College Press.

——(2011). 'Society and Economy'. In D. Ó Corráin and T. O'Riordan (eds), *Ireland 1815–1870: Emancipation, Famine and Religion*, pp. 33–42. Dublin: Four Courts Press.

Connolly, L., and O'Toole, T. (2005). *Documenting Irish Feminisms: The Second Wave*. Dublin: Woodfield Press.

Conroy, P. (2004). 'Maternity Confined – The Struggle for Fertility Control'. In P. Kennedy (ed.), *Motherhood in Ireland: Creation and Context*, pp. 127–38. *Cork: Mercier Press.*

Constitution Review Group. (1996). *Report of the Constitution Review Group.* Dublin: Stationery Office.

Cook, H. (2004). *The Long Sexual Revolution: English Women, Sex and Contraception 1800–1975.* Oxford: Oxford University Press.

Cosgrove, A. (1985). 'Introduction'. In A. Cosgrove (ed.), *Marriage in Ireland*, pp. 1–4. Dublin: College Press.

Cott, N. F. (1997). *The Bonds of Womanhood: "Woman's Sphere" in New England, 1780–1835.* New Haven, CT: Yale University Press.

Coulter, C., and Nagle, A. (2015). *Ireland Under Austerity: Neoliberal Crisis, Neoliberal Solutions.* Manchester: Manchester University Press.

Coveney, E. et al. (1998). *Caring for All Our Futures. Models of Childcare Based on the NOW Projects.* Dublin: National Women's Council of Ireland.

Cowley, M. (1984). 'Parents Did Not Know Ann Lovett was Pregnant', *The Irish Times*, 22 February, n.p.

Coyne, E. (2020). *Are You There, God? It's Me, Ellen.* Dublin: Gill Books.

Craig, P. (2007). *Asking for Trouble: The Story of an Escapade with Disproportionate Consequences.* Belfast: Blackstaff Press.

Craven, C., and Davis, D. A. (2011). 'Revisiting Feminist Ethnography: Methods and Activism at the Intersection of Neoliberal Policy', *Feminist Formations*, 23 (2), 190–208.

Crawford, E. M. (1995). 'Food and Famine'. In C. Pórtéir (ed.), *The Great Irish Famine: The Thomas Davis Lecture Series*, pp. 60–73. Cork: Mercier Press.

Crisis Pregnancy Agency. (2002). *Towards a Strategy to Address the Issue of Crisis Pregnancy.* Dublin: Crisis Pregnancy Agency. <https://www.lenus.ie/bitstream/handle/10147/43756/3961.pdf?isAllowed=y&sequence=1>

—— (2003). *Strategy Summary: To Address the Issue of Crisis Pregnancy.* Dublin: Crisis Pregnancy Agency. <www.lenus.ie/bitstream/handle/10147/305324/StrategySummary200420061.pdf?sequence=1&isAllowed=y>

—— (2014). *Summary Report of the Consultation for the Strategy to Address the Issue of Crisis Pregnancy*, no. 3. Dublin: Crisis Pregnancy Agency.

Crittenden, A. (2010). *The Price of Motherhood: Why the Most Important Job in the World is Still the Least Valued*, 10th Anniversary Edition. New York: Picador.

Cronin, M. (2002). 'Speed Limits: Ireland, Globalisation and the War against Time'. In K. Peadar, L. Gibbons, and M. Cronin (eds), *Reinventing Ireland: Culture, Society and the Global Economy*, pp. 54–66. London: Pluto Press.

Crossman, V. (2006). 'Viewing Women, Family and Sexuality through the Prism of the Irish Poor Laws', *Women's History Review*, 15 (4), 541–50.

Crowe, C. (2021). 'The Commission and the Survivors', *The Dublin Review*, Summer. <https://thedublinreview.com/article/the-commission-and-the-survivors/>

CSO (Central Statistics Office). (2003). *Vital Statistics, 4th Quarter and Yearly Summary 2002.* Dublin: Government Publications Office.

—— (2004). *Vital Statistics, 4th Quarter and Yearly Summary 2003.* Dublin: Government Publications Office.

—— (2005). Women and Men in Ireland, 2004, <https://www.cso.ie/en/csolatestnews/pressreleases/2004pressreleases/womenandmeninireland2004/>

—— (2010). *Vital Statistics, 4th Quarter and Yearly Summary 2009.* Dublin: Government Publications Office.

—— (2012a). *Measuring Ireland's Progress, 2011.* Dublin: Government Publications Office.

—— (2012b). *Statistical Yearbook of Ireland.* Dublin: Government Publications Office.

—— (2012c). *Profile 5, Households and Families.* Dublin: Government Publications Office.

—— (2012d). Women and Men in Ireland 2011, Central Statistics Office, press release. <https://www.cso.ie/en/csolatestnews/pressreleases/2012pressreleases/pressreleasewomenandmeninireland2011/>

—— (2012e). *Vital Statistics, Marriages Report 2009.* Dublin: Government Publications Office.

—— (2014). *Vital Statistics, Fourth Quarter and Yearly Summary 2013.* Dublin: Stationery Office.

—— (2016). *Women and Men in Ireland 2016.* Cork: Central Statistics Office. <https://www.cso.ie/en/releasesandpublications/ep/p-wamii/womenandmeninireland2016/>

—— (2017). 'Population and Labour Force Projections 2017–2051', Fertility Assumptions, <https://www.cso.ie/en/releasesandpublications/ep/p-plfp/populationandlabourforceprojections2017-2051/fertilityassumptions/>

—— (2018). *Ireland's Economic Crisis – 10 Years On.* Cork: Central Statistics Office. <https://www.cso.ie/en/releasesandpublications/ep/p-macip/macip17/irelandseconomiccrisis-10yearson/>

—— (2019a). *Vital Statistics Yearly Summary 2019.* Cork: Central Statistics Office. <https://www.cso.ie/en/releasesandpublications/ep/p-vsys/vitalstatisticsyearlysummary2019/>

—— (2019b). *Women and Men in Ireland 2019.* Cork: Central Statistics Office. <https://www.cso.ie/en/releasesandpublications/ep/p-wamii/womenandmeninireland2019/>

—— (2020a). *Survey on Income and Living Conditions (SILC) 2019*. Cork: Central
    Statistics Office. <https://www.cso.ie/en/releasesandpublications/ep/p-silc/
    surveyonincomeandlivingconditionssilc2019/>

—— (2020b). *Women and Men in Ireland 2019*, <https://www.cso.ie/en/releases
    andpublications/ep/p-wamii/womenandmeninireland2019/>

—— (2020c). *Survey on Income and Living Conditions (SILC) 2019*. Cork: Central
    Statistics Office. <https://www.cso.ie/en/releasesandpublications/ep/p-silc/
    surveyonincomeandlivingconditionssilc2019/>

Cullen, L. M. (1968). *Life in Ireland*. London: Batsford.

Cullen, M. (1990). 'Breadwinners and Providers: Women in the Household
    Economies of Labouring Families 1835–6'. In M. Luddy and C. Murphy (ed.),
    Women Surviving, pp. 85–116. Dublin: Poolbeg Press.

Cullen, P. (2020). 'Total of 6,666 abortions carried out under new legislation last
    year', *The Irish Times*, 30 June, <www.irishtimes.com/news/health/total-of-
    6-666-abortions-carried-out-under-new-legislation-last-year-1.4292507>,
    accessed 30 June 2020.

Cullen, P., and Korolczuk, E. (2019). 'Challenging Abortion Stigma: Framing
    Abortion in Ireland and Poland', *Sexual and Reproductive Health Matters*,
    27 (3), 6–19.

Culliton, G. (1996). 'Last Days of a Laundry', *The Irish Times*, 25 September,
    <https://www.irishtimes.com/culture/last-days-of-a-laundry-1.89388>,
    accessed 25 September 1996.

Daly, C. (2015). 'Ireland's First Abortion Legislation', In A. Quilty, S. Kennedy.,
    and C. Conlon (eds), *The Abortion Papers Ireland: Volume II*, pp. 263–69.
    Dublin: Attic Press.

Daly, M. E. (1981). *A Social and Economic History of Ireland Since 1800*. Dublin:
    Educational Company of Ireland.

—— (2006). *The Slow Failure: Population Decline and Independent Ireland, 1920–
    1973*. Madison, Wisconsin: University of Wisconsin Press.

Davies, S. E. (2013). 'Respectful, Evidence-Based Care for Women with a High BMI
    Increases Satisfaction and Reduces Physical and Psychological Morbidity'.
    Dignity in Childbirth Forum, 16 October, Royal Society of Medicine.

Dawson, K. et al. (2019). *PornReport*. Galway: School of Psychology, National
    University of Ireland Galway. De Beaumont, G. (2006). *Ireland: Social,
    Political and Religious*. Cambridge, MA: Belknap Press/Harvard University
    Press.

De Certeau, M. (1988). *The Practice of Everyday Life*. Berkeley, CA: University of
    California Press.

De Londras, F. (2020). '"A hope raised and then defeated?" The Continuing Harms
    of Irish Abortion Law', *Feminist Review*, 124 (1), 33–50.

De Londras, F., and Enright, M. (2018). *Repealing The 8th: Reforming Irish Abortion Law*. Bristol: Policy Press.

De Londras, F., and Markicevic, M. (2018). 'Reforming Abortion Law in Ireland: Reflections on the Public Submissions to the Citizens' Assembly', *Women's Studies International Forum*, (70), 89–98.

de Marneffe, D. (2006). *Maternal Desire: On Children, Love and the Inner Life*. London: Virago.

de Tocqueville, A. (1990). *Alexis de Tocqueville's Journey in Ireland, July-August, 1835*. [Translated by Larkin, E.]. Dublin: Wolfhound Press.

Dean, M. (2002). 'Powers of Life and Death beyond Governmentality', *Cultural Values*, 6 (1–2), 119–38.

Delay, C. (2018). 'Kitchens and Kettles: Domestic Spaces, Ordinary Things, and Female Networks in Irish Abortion History, 1922–1949', *Journal of Women's History*, 30 (4), 11–34.

—— (2019a). 'From the Backstreet to Britain: Women and Abortion Travel in Modern Ireland'. In C. Beyer et. al. (eds), *Travellin' Mama: Mothers, Mothering, and Travel*, pp. 217–34. Ontario, Canada: Demeter Press.

—— (2019b). 'Pills, Potions, and Purgatives: Women and Abortion Methods in Ireland, 1900–1950', *Women's History Review*, 28 (3), 479–99.

—— (2019c). 'Wrong for Womankind and the Nation: Anti-abortion Discourses in 20th-century Ireland', *Journal of Modern European History*, 17 (3), 312–25.

Delay, C., and Liger, A. (2019). 'Bad Mothers and Dirty Lousers: Representing Abortionists in Post-Independence Ireland', *Journal of Social History*, 54 (1), 286–305.

Deegan, G. (2019). 'More Babies Taken into Care than Any Other Age Group', *The Irish Times*, 12 March, <https://www.irishtimes.com/news/social-affairs/more-emergency-care-orders-sought-for-babies-than-any-other-age-group-1.3822125>, accessed 12 March 2019.

Devane, D., Webster, J., Murphy-Lawless, J., and Hughes, P. (2020) 'COVID-19: Challenging Ireland to Move from Mastership to Midwifeship'. *Medical Anthropology Quarterly* Rapid Response Blog Series. <http://medanthroquarterly.org/?p=526>

Devine, D., Grummell, B., and Lynch, K. (2011). 'Crafting the Elastic Self? Gender and Identities in Senior Appointments in Irish Education'. *Gender, Work and Organization*, 18 (6), 631–49.

Dillon, M. (1993). *Debating Divorce: Moral Conflict in Ireland*. Lexington: University Press of Kentucky.

Doherty, G. M., and O'Riordan, T. (2011). 'The Synod of Thurles, 1850: Discipline and Education'. In D. Ó Corráin and T. O'Riordan (ed.), *Ireland 1815–1870: Emancipation*, pp. 183–94. Dublin: Four Courts Press.

Donoghue, E. (2011). 'I'm Sick of All this Mutual Surveillance – Let's Put a Stop to the Mummy Wars'. *The Guardian*, 23 April, <http://www.theguardian.com/commentisfree/2011/apr/23/emma-donoghue-mummy-wars-parenting>, accessed 23 April 2011.

Donovan, D., and Murphy, A. E. (2004). *The Fall of the Celtic Tiger: Ireland & the Euro Debt Crisis*. Oxford: Oxford University Press.

Douglass, C. B. (2005). 'Introduction'. In C. Douglass (ed.), *Barren States: The Population Implosion in Europe*, pp. 1–28. Oxford: Berg.

Drew, E. (1992). 'Part-time Working in Ireland: Meeting the Flexibility Needs of Women Workers or Employers?' *Canadian Journal of Irish Studies*, 18 (1), 95–109.

Drew, E. et al. (1998). *Women, Work and the Family in Europe*. London: Routledge.

Dublin Well Woman Centre. (2020). *The Contraception Conversation*. Available from <https://wellwomancentre.ie/new-research-shows-majority-of-women-in-ireland-are-using-ineffective-contraception-to-prevent-pregnancy/>, accessed 19 December 2020.

Duggan, C. (1987). 'Farming Women or Farmer's Wives? Women in the Farming Press'. In Curtin, C. et al. (eds), *Gender in Irish Society*, pp. 54–69. Galway: Galway University Press.

Duncombe, J., and Marsden, D. (1996). 'Whose Orgasm is this Anyway? "Sex Work" in Long-term Heterosexual Couple Relationships'. In J. Weeks and J. Holland (eds), *Sexual Cultures: Communities, Values and Intimacy*, pp. 220–38. London: Palgrave Macmillan.

Dunlea, M. (2021). 'An Institutional Ethnography of Antenatal Care: The Nature and Meaning of the Antenatal Encounters'. Open access Ph.D., University of Dublin, Trinity College.

Durham, M. G. (2009). *The Lolita Effect: The Media Sexualisation of Young Girls and What We Can Do About It*. London: Duckworth Overlook.

Earner-Byrne, L. (2006). 'Managing Motherhood: Negotiating a Maternity Service for Catholic Mothers in Dublin, 1930–1954', *Social History of Medicine*, 19 (2), 261–77.

—— (2009). *Mother and Child: Maternity and Child Welfare in Dublin, 1922–60*. Manchester: Manchester University Press.

Earner-Byrne, L., and Urquhart, D. (2019). *The Irish Abortion Journey, 1920–2018*. London: Palgrave Pivot.

Eastern Health Board. (1995). *Review of Family Planning Services and Proposals for Further Development.* Dublin: Eastern Health Board. <https://www.lenus.ie/handle/10147/46260>

—— (2009). *The Perinatal Statistics Report, 2007.* Dublin: ESRI.

—— (2012). *The Perinatal Statistics Report, 2010.* Dublin: ESRI.

Edin, K., and Kefalas, M. (2005). *Promises I Can Keep: Why Poor Women Put Motherhood before Marriage.* Berkeley, CA: University of California Press.

Edkins, J. (2000). *Whose Hunger? Concepts of Famine, Practices of Aid.* Minneapolis: University of Minnesota Press.

Eng, D. L., and Kazanjian, D. (2003). 'Introduction: Mourning Remains'. In D. L. Eng and D. Kazanjian (eds), *Loss: The Politics of Mourning*, pp. 1–28. Berkeley, CA: University of California Press.

Enloe, C., Graff, A., Kapur, R., and Walters, S. D. (2019). 'Ask a Feminist: Gender and the Rise of the Global Right', *Signs: Journal of Women in Culture and Society*, 44 (3), 823–44.

Enright, A. (2005). *Making Babies: Stumbling into Motherhood.* London: Vintage Books.

Equality Authority. (2012). *Your Maternity Leave Rights Explained. Plain English Guide to the Maternity Protection Acts 1994–2004.* Roscrea, Co. Tipperary: Equality Authority

Eurostat Press Office. (2016). 'Part-time Employment of Women in the EU Increases Drastically with the Number of Children: Women Earned on Average 16% Less than Men in the EU'. *Eurostat News Release*, 8 March, <http://ec.europa.eu/eurostat/documents/2995521/7202372/3-07032016-AP-EN.pdf>

Fallon, B. (2019). 'I'm Not a Mother. Please Don't Judge Me', *The Irish Times*, 15 December, <https://www.irishtimes.com/life-and-style/health-family/i-m-not-a-mother-please-don-t-judge-me-1.4104446>, accessed 15 December 2019.

Fanning, B. (2016). 'Immigration, the Celtic Tiger and the Economic Crisis', *Irish Studies Review*, 24 (1), 9–20.

—— (2007). *Immigration and Social Change in the Republic of Ireland.* Manchester: Manchester University Press.

Farrell, E. (ed.) (2012). *'She Said She Was in the Family Way:' Pregnancy and Infancy in Modern Ireland.* London: University of London Press, Institute of Historical Research.

Feeney, J. K. (1955) 'The Grand Multipara: Trauma of Labour', *Journal of the Irish Medical Association*, 36 (214), 112–4.

Fegan, E., and Rebouche, R. (2003). 'Northern Ireland's Abortion Law: The Morality of Silence and the Censure of Agency', *Feminist Legal Studies*, 11 (3), 221–54.

Ferguson, H., and Hogan, F. (2007). *Men, Sexuality and Crisis Pregnancy: A Study of Men's Experiences*. Dublin: Crisis Pregnancy Agency, <www.lenus.ie/handle/ 10147/305195>

Ferriter, D. (2004). *The Transformation of Ireland, 1900–2000*. London: Profile Books.

—— (2009). *Occasions of Sin: Sex and Society in Modern Ireland*. London: Profile Books.

—— (2014). 'The Irish Abortion Question Has Always Been Linked to Class, Secrecy and Moral Judgment', *The Irish Times*, 23 August, <https://www.irishtimes. com/news/social-affairs/the-irish-abortion-question-has-always-been-linked-to-class-secrecy-and-moral-judgment-1.1905362>, accessed 21 April 2021.

—— (2018). 'Irish Catholicism is Rooted in Class Prejudice', *The Irish Times*, 25 August, <https://www.irishtimes.com/opinion/diarmaid-ferriter-irish-cath olicism-is-rooted-in-class-prejudice-1.3606614>, accessed 25 August 2018.

Field, L. (2018). 'The Abortion Referendum of 2018 and a Timeline of Abortion Politics in Ireland to Date', *Irish Political Studies*, 33 (4), 608–28.

Fields, J. (2008). *Risky Lessons: Sex Education and Social Inequality*. New Brunswick, NJ: Rutgers University Press.

Fields, J., and Tolman, D. (2006). 'Risky Business: Sexuality Education and Research in U.S. Schools', *Sexuality Research and Social Policy*, 3 (4), 63–76.

Fine, M. (1988). 'Sexuality, Schooling, and Adolescent Females: The Missing Discourse of Desire', *Harvard Educational Review*, 58 (1), 29–53.

Finn, C. (2019). 'Harris Wants VAT Removed on Condoms and Menstrual Cups', *The Journal.ie* 12 August <https://www.thejournal.ie/simon-harris-vat-cond oms-menstrual-cups-4759193-Aug2019/>, accessed 12 March 2021.

—— (2021). 'Justice Minister to Take 6 Months Paid Maternity Leave from 30 April', *thejournal.ie*, 11 March, <https://www.thejournal.ie/helen-mcentee-matern ity-leave-2-5378276-Mar2021/>, accessed 11 March 2021.

Fischer, C. (2011). 'Re-visioning Ireland: Lessons from Feminist Care Ethics'. *Studies: An Irish Quarterly Review*, 100 (39), 63–72.

—— (2020). 'Feminists Redraw Public and Private Spheres: Abortion, Vulnerability, and the Affective Campaign to Repeal the Eighth Amendment', *Signs: Journal of Women in Culture and Society*, 45 (4), 985–1010.

Fisher, K. (2006). *Birth Control, Sex, and Marriage in Britain 1918–1960*. Oxford: Oxford University Press.

Fitzpatrick, D. (1985). 'Marriage in Post-Famine Ireland'. In A. Cosgrove (ed.), *Marriage in Ireland*, pp. 116–31. Dublin: College Press.

—— (1987). 'The Modernisation of the Irish Female'. In P. O'Flanagan, P. Ferguson, and K. Whelan (eds), *Rural Ireland 1600–1900: Modernisation and Change*, pp. 162–80. Cork: Cork University Press.

—— (1990). '"A Share of the Honeycomb": Education, Emigration and Irishwomen'. In M. Daly and D. Dickson (eds), *The Origins of Popular Literacy in*

Ireland: Language Change and Educational Development 1700–1920, pp. 167–87. Dublin: Tony Moreau.

—— (1997). 'Women and the Great Famine'. In M. Kelleher and J. Murphy (eds), *Gender Perspectives in Nineteenth Century Ireland*, pp. 50–69. Dublin: Irish Academic Press.

Flaherty, R. (2015). 'Varadkar: Parents of Babies Who Died at Portlaoise Hospital "were lied to"', *The Irish Times*, 17 May, <https://www.irishtimes.com/news/politics/varadkar-parents-of-babies-who-died-at-portlaoise-hospital-were-lied-to-1.2215623>

Fletcher, R. (2005). 'Abortion Needs or Abortion Rights? Claiming State Accountability for Women's Reproductive Welfare', *Feminist Legal Studies*, 13, 123–34.

Foster, R. (1988). *Modern Ireland 1600–1972*. London: Allen Lane.

Foucault, M. (1981a). 'The Politics of Health in the Eighteenth Century'. In C. Cordon (ed.), *Power/Knowledge: Selected Writing and Interviews and Other Writings 1972–1977*, pp. 166–82. Brighton: Harvester Wheatsheaf.

—— (1981b). *The History of Sexuality, Volume One: An Introduction*. Harmondsworth: Penguin.

—— (1984). 'What is Enlightenment?' In P. Rabinow (ed.), *The Foucault Reader: An Introduction to Foucault's Thought*, pp. 32–50. Harmondsworth: Penguin.

—— (1997). 'Security, Territory and Population'. In P. Rabinow (ed.), *Ethics: Essential Works of Foucault 1954–84, Volume 1*, pp. 67–72. London: Penguin.

—— (2001). *Fearless Speech*. Joseph Pearson (ed.). Los Angeles: Semiotext(e).

—— (2002). 'Truth and Juridical Forms'. James Faubion (ed.). In *Power: Essential Works of Foucault 1954–1984*, pp. 1–89. London: Penguin.

—— (2004). 'The Risks of Security'. In J. Faubion (ed.), *Power: Essential Works of Foucault 1954–1984, Volume 3*, pp. 365–81. London: Penguin.

—— (2008). *The Birth of Biopolitics: Lectures at the Collège de France 1978–1979*. G. Burchall (ed.). New York: Picador.

Francis, G. (2021). *Intensive Care: A GP, a Community and Covid-19*. London: Profile Books Lt.

Fuller, L. (2002). *Irish Catholicism Since 1950: The Undoing of a Culture*. Dublin: Gill and Macmillan.

Fuszara, M. (1991). 'Legal Regulation of Abortion in Poland'. *Signs: Journal of Women in Culture and Society*, 17 (1), 117–28.

Galvez, A. (2011). *Patient Citizens, Immigration Mothers: Mexican Women, Public Prenatal Care, and the Birth-Weight Paradox*. New Brunswick, NJ: Rutgers University Press.

Garcia, L. (2012). *Respect Yourself, Protect Yourself: Latina Girls and Sexual Identity*. New York: NYU Press.

Garrett, P. M. (2016). ' "Unmarried Mothers" in the Republic of Ireland', *Journal of Social Work*, 16 (6), 708–25. doi:10.1177/1468017316628447.

Geary, P. (1992). 'Ireland's Economy in the 1980s: Stagnation and Recovery a Preliminary Review of the Evidence', *Economic and Social Review*, 23 (3), 253–81.

Geary, R. C. (1954/5). 'The Family in Irish Census of Population Statistics', *Journal of Statistical and Social Inquiry Society of Ireland*, XXIX, Part III, 1–30.

Georges, E. (2008). *Bodies of Knowledge: The Medicalization of Reproduction in Greece*. Nashville: Vanderbilt University Press.

Gibbons, L. (1996). *Transformations in Irish Culture*. Cork: Cork University Press.

Giddens, A. (1991). *Modernity and Self-Identity: Self and Society in the Late Modern Age*. Palo Alto, CA: Stanford University Press.

Gilmartin, M., and White, A. (2011). 'Interrogating Medical Tourism: Ireland, Abortion, and Mobility Rights', *Signs: Journal of Women in Culture and Society*, 36 (2), 275–80.

Ginsburg, F. D. (1998 [1984]). *Contested Lives: The Abortion Debate in an American Community* (2nd ed.). Berkeley, CA: University of California Press.

Ginsburg, F. D., and Rapp, R. (1995a). 'Introduction: Conceiving the New World Order'. In F. D. Ginsburg and R. Rapp (eds), *Conceiving the New World Order: The Global Politics of Reproduction*, pp. 1–17. Berkeley, CA: University of California Press.

—— (eds) (1995b). *Conceiving the New World Order: The Global Politics of Reproduction*. Berkeley, CA: University of California Press.

Glaser, E. (2021). 'Parent Trap: Why the Cult of the Perfect Mother has to End', *The Guardian*, 18 May. <https://www.theguardian.com/lifeandstyle/2021/may/18/parent-trap-why-the-cult-of-the-perfect-mother-has-to-end>, accessed 18 May 2021.

Glass, L. et al. (2013). 'Mothering, Poverty and Consumption'. In S. O'Donohue et al. (eds), *Motherhood, Markets and Consumption: The Making of Mothers in Contemporary Western Cultures*, pp. 199–209. Abingdon, Oxford: Routledge.

Goldberg, M. (2010.) *The Means of Reproduction: Sex, Power and the Future of the World*. New York: Penguin Press.

Gomperts, R. (2002). 'Women on Waves: Where Next for the Abortion Boat?' *Reproductive Health Matters*, 10 (19), 180–83.

Gramsci, A. (1971). *Selections from Prison Notebooks*. Q. Hoare and G. Nowell Smith (eds). London: Lawrence and Wishart.

Grant, E. (2004). *The Highland Lady in Ireland: Elizabeth Grant of Rothiemurchus, Journals 1840–1850*. Edinburgh: Canongate.

Grant, L. (1994). *Sexing the Millenium: Women and the Sexual Revolution*. New York: Grove.

Gray, B. (2004). *Women and the Irish Diaspora*. London: Psychology Press.

Gray, J., Geraghty, R., and Ralph, D. (2013). 'Young Grandchildren and their Grandparents: A Secondary Analysis of Continuity and Change across Four Birth Cohorts', *Families, Relationships, and Societies*, 2, 289–98.

Griffin, G., O'Connor, O., Smyth, A., and O'Connor, A. (eds) (2019). *It's a Yes! How Together for Yes Repealed the Eighth and Transformed Irish Society*. Dublin: Orpen Press.

Grosz, E. (1994). *Volatile Bodies: Towards a Corporeal Feminism*. Bloomington, IN: Indiana University Press.

Guinnane, T. (1998). *The Vanishing Irish: Households, Migration, and the Rural Economy*. Princeton, NJ: Princeton University Press.

Gutiérrrez, E. R. (2008). *Fertile Matters: The Politics of Mexican-Origin Women's Reproduction*. Austin: University of Texas Press.

Halkias, A. (2004). *Empty Cradle of Democracy: Sex, Abortion, and Nationalism in Modern Greece*. Durham: Duke University Press.

Hannan, D., and Katsiaouni, L. (1977). *Traditional Families? From Culturally Prescribed to Negotiated Roles in Farm Families*, ESRI Paper. No. 87. Dublin: ESRI.

Hardiman, A. (1999). 'Green Paper on Abortion Clarifies a Complex Issue', *The Irish Times*, 15 September, <www.irishtimes.com/culture/green-paper-on-abortion-clarifies-a-complex-issue-1.22755>, accessed 22 August 2005.

Hardt, M., and Negri, A. (2000). *Empire*. Cambridge, MA: Harvard University Press.

Hardy, S., and Wiedmer, C. (eds) (2005). *Motherhood and Space: Configurations of the Maternal in Politics, Art and the Every-day*. London: Palgrave Macmillan.

Harvey, D. (2005). *A Brief History of Neoliberalism*. Oxford: Oxford University Press.

Haugeberg, K. (2017). *Women Against Abortion: Inside the Largest Moral Reform Movement of the Twentieth Century*. Urbana: University of Illinois Press.

Hays, S. (1996). *The Cultural Contradictions of Motherhood*. London: Yale University Press.

—— (2004). *Flat Broke with Children: Women in the Age of Welfare Reform*. London: Oxford University Press.

Health Education Bureau. (1984). *Public Attitudes Towards Family Planning*. Survey Carried Out with Irish Marketing Surveys, March. Dublin: Health Education Bureau.

Healy, A. (2005). 'Mother of Baby Found Dead in Bin Unlikely to Face Charges', *The Irish Times*, 14 May, <https://www.irishtimes.com/news/mother-of-baby-found-dead-in-bin-unlikely-to-face-charges-1.441982>, accessed 14 May 2005.

Healy, K. (2007). 'Abandoned Babies'. ABC News, 19 June. <www.abc.net.au/news/stories/2007/06/20/1956243.htm>, accessed 25 June 2007.

Healy, S. et al. (2013). *What Would Real Recovery Look Like? Securing Economic Development, Social Equity and Sustainability*. Dublin: Social Justice Ireland.

Hearn, M. (1990). 'Women Surviving'. In M. Luddy and C. Murphy (eds), *Life for Domestic Servants in Dublin, 1880–1920*, pp. 148–79. Dublin: Poolbeg Press.

Hearne, R. (2020). *Housing Shock: The Irish Housing Crisis and How to Solve It*. Bristol: Policy Press.

Hegarty, A. (2021). 'Eamonn De Valera Jr Repeatedly Arranged Illegal Adoptions', RTÉ, 4 March, <https://www.rte.ie/news/investigations-unit/2021/0303/1200525-de-valera-jr-repeatedly-facilitated-illegal-adoptions/>, accessed 4 March 2021.

Hesketh, T. (1990). *The Second Partitioning of Ireland: The Abortion Referendum of 1983*. Dublin: Brandsma Books.

Higgens, R. A. (2011). *Ireland is Changing Mother*. Northumberland, UK: Bloodaxe Books.

Higgins, A., and Murphy-Lawless, J. (2009.) *Helping Young Women to Understand Sex and Sexuality: An Evaluation of the Pilot Holistic Sexual Education Programme, Letterkenny Women's Centre, 2008–2009*. Unpublished report, Crisis Pregnancy Agency.

Hilliard, B. (2004). 'Motherhood, Sexuality and the Catholic Church'. In P. Kennedy (ed.), *Motherhood in Ireland*, pp. 139–59. Cork: Mercier Press.

—— (2006). 'Changing Gender Roles in Intimate Relationships'. In J. Garry, N. Hardiman and D. Payne (eds), *Irish Social and Political Attitudes*, pp. 33–42. Liverpool: Liverpool University Press.

Hinsliff, G. (2012). *Half a Wife: The Working Family's Guide to Getting a Life Back*. London: Chatto and Windus.

Hintjens, H. (2019). 'Failed Securitisation Moves during the 2015 "Migration Crisis"', *International Migration*, 57(4), 181–96.

Hochschild, A. R. (1997). *The Time Bind: When Work Becomes Home and Home Becomes Work*. New York: Metropolitan Books.

Hochschild, A., and Machung, A. (2012). *The Second Shift: Working Families and the Revolution at Home*. New York: Penguin.

Hogan, C. (2019a). 'Why Ireland's Battle over Abortion is Far from Over', *The Guardian*, 3 October, <https://www.theguardian.com/lifeandstyle/2019/oct/03/why-irelands-battle-over-abortion-is-far-from-over-anti-abortionists>, accessed 3 October 2019.

—— (2019b). *Republic of Shame: Stories from Ireland's Institutions for Fallen Women*. Sandycove: Penguin Random House Ireland.

Holland, K. (2012). *Savita: The Tragedy that Shook a Nation*. Dublin: Transworld Ireland.

—— (2017a). 'Protection of Life During Pregnancy Act is "Unworkable"', *The Irish Times*, 13 June, <https://www.irishtimes.com/news/social-affairs/protection-of-life-during-pregnancy-act-is-unworkable-1.3117350>, accessed 6 June 2020.

—— (2017b). 'Abortion Movement has been Hijacked by the Middle Class', *The Irish Times*, 1 May, <https://www.irishtimes.com/opinion/abortion-movement-has-been-hijacked-by-the-middle-class-1.3066835>, accessed 6 June 2020.

—— (2018a). 'Savita Halappanavar's Father urges Yes Vote in Abortion Referendum', *Irish Times*, 11 April, <www.irishtimes.com/news/social-affairs/savita-halappanavar-s-father-urges-yes-vote-in-abortion-referendum-1.3457368>, accessed 11 April 2018.

—— (2018b). 'Abortion, Regret and Choice'. In U. Mullally (ed.), *Repeal the 8th*, pp. 43–53. London: Unbound.

—— (2018c) 'Suicide on the Rise among Mothers in Poorer Dublin Areas', *Irish Times*, 21 May, <https://www.irishtimes.com/news/social-affairs/suicide-on-the-rise-among-mothers-in-poorer-dublin-areas-1.3502336>, accessed 2 June 2021.

—— (2020). 'Covid Restrictions Make it Difficult for Irish Women Seeking Abortions to Travel', *The Irish Times*, 28 October, <https://www.irishtimes.com/news/social-affairs/covid-restrictions-make-it-difficult-for-irish-women-seeking-abortions-to-travel-1.4391601>, accessed 28 October 2020.

—— (2021a). 'Part-time Work "of little benefit" to Families Seeking to get out of Poverty', *The Irish Times*, 31 May, <https://www.irishtimes.com/news/social-affairs/part-time-work-of-little-benefit-to-families-seeking-to-get-out-of-poverty-1.4579490>

—— (2021b). 'Almost 200 Women and Girls Travelled to Britain for Abortions in 2020', *The Irish Times*, 10 June, <https://www.irishtimes.com/news/social-affairs/almost-200-women-and-girls-travelled-to-britain-for-abortions-in-2020-1.4589703>, accessed 10 June 2021.

Holland, M. (2000). 'Report on Abortion Reeks of Hypocrisy', *The Irish Times*, 23 November, <https://www.irishtimes.com/opinion/report-on-abortion-reeks-of-hypocrisy-1.1117310>, accessed 31 October 2020.

Holland, K., and Mac Cormaic, R. (2014). 'Woman in Abortion Case Tells of Suicide Attempt', *The Irish Times*, 19 August, <https://www.irishtimes.com/news/health/woman-in-abortion-case-tells-of-suicide-attempt-1.1901256>, accessed 10 June 2021.

Hooks, B. (2000). *Feminism is for Everybody: Passionate Politics*. Cambridge, MA: South End Press.

Horgan, G. (2004). 'Mothering in a Disabling Society'. In P. Kennedy (ed.), *Motherhood in Ireland: Creation and Context*, pp. 194–206. Cork: Mercier Press.

Horgan-Jones, J. et al. (2021). 'Mother and Baby Homes Commission Urged to Address Oireachtas Committee', *The Irish Times*, 3 June, <https://www.iri shtimes.com/news/ireland/irish-news/mother-and-baby-home-commiss ion-should-do-the-right-thing-and-address-oireachtas-1.4583046>, accessed 3 June 2021.

Horgan-Jones, J., and Wall, M. (2021). 'Government to Renew Effort to Purchase National Maternity Site', *The Irish Times*, 21 June, <https://www.irishtimes. com/news/ireland/irish-news/government-to-renew-effort-to-purchase-natio nal-maternity-hospital-site-1.4598760>, accessed 21 June 2021.

Horton, R. (2021). *The COVID-19 Catastrophe: What's Gone Wrong and How to Stop It Happening Again* (2nd ed.). Cambridge: Polity Press.

Hourihane, A. M. (2000). *She Moves Through the Boom*. Dublin: Sitric Books.

HSE Crisis Pregnancy Program. (2010). 'Number of Women Giving Irish Addresses at UK Abortion Clinics Decreases for Eighth Year in a Row According to Department of Health UK', Press release, 25 May, <http://www.crisispregna ncy.ie/news/number-of-women-giving-irish-addresses-at-uk-abortion-clinics- decreases-for-eighth-year-in-a-row-according-to-department-of-health-uk/>, accessed 25 May 2010.

Hug, C. (1999). *The Politics of Sexual Morality*. Basingstoke: Macmillan Press.

Hyde, A., and Howlette, E. (2004). *Understanding Teenage Sexuality in Ireland*. Dublin : Crisis Pregnancy Agency, <https://www.lenus.ie/bitstream/handle/ 10147/305327/understandingteensexualityinIreland.pdf?sequence=1&isAllo wed=y>

Hynan, M. (2018). 'Hidden in Plain Sight: Mapping the Erasure of the Maternal Body from Visual Culture', In N. Edwards, R. Mander and J. Murphy-Lawless (eds), *Untangling the Maternity Crisis*, pp. 124–32. London: Routledge.

Illouz, E. (2007). *Cold Intimacies: The Making of Emotional Capitalism*. Cambridge, Oxford: Polity.

Inglis, T. (1987). *Moral Monopoly: The Rise and Fall of the Catholic Church in Modern Ireland*. Dublin: Gill and Macmillan.

—— (1997). 'Foucault, Bourdieu and the Field of Irish Sexuality', *Irish Journal of Sociology*, 7, 5–28.

—— (2003). *Truth, Power and Lies: Irish Society and the Case of the Kerry Babies*. Dublin: UCD Press.

—— (2008). *Global Ireland: Same Difference*. New York: Routledge.

—— (2014a). *Meanings of Life in Contemporary Ireland: Webs of Significance*. London: Palgrave Macmillan.

Inglis, T. (ed.) (2014b). *Are The Irish Different?* Manchester: Manchester University Press.

IOL. (2005). 'Body of Newborn Baby Discovered in Ballina', 20 February, <https://www.rte.ie/news/2005/0220/60130-baby/>, accessed 20 February 2005.

Iona Institute for Religion and Society. (2021). 'About the Iona Institute', <https://ionainstitute.ie/about-the-iona-institute/>

Ireland, Constitution Review Group. (1996). *Report of the Constitution Review Group*. Dublin: Stationery Office.

Ireland, Department of the Taoiseach. (1999). *Green Paper on Abortion*. <http://www.taoiseach.gov.ie/eng/Publications/Publications_Archive/Publications_2006/Publications_for_1999/GreenPaperOnAbortion.pdf>

Ireland, Government. (2009). *Commission to Inquire into Child Abuse Report, Volumes. I–V*. Dublin: Stationery Office.

Irish Examiner. (2018). 'Women are Happier but Lonelier Since Becoming Mothers, Survey Shows', 22 October, <https://www.irishexaminer.com/news/arid-30877331.html>, accessed 6 June 2021.

Irish Family Planning Association. (2000). *The Irish Journey: Women's Stories of Abortion*. Dublin: IFPA.

—— (2010). *Sexual Health and Asylum: Handbook for People Working with Women Seeking Asylum in Ireland*. Dublin: IFPA. <https://www.lenus.ie/handle/10147/622871>

—— (nd). 'History of Abortion in Ireland'. IFPA. <https://www.ifpa.ie/advocacy/abortion-in-ireland-legal-timeline/>

Irvine, J. M. (2002). *Talk About Sex: The Battles Over Sex Education in the United States*. Berkeley, CA: University of California Press.

Isis Research Group. (1998). *Caring for All Our Futures: Policy Recommendations for Establishing a National Childcare Strategy*. Dublin: NWCI.

Jackson, P. (1992). 'Abortion Trials and Tribulations', *The Canadian Journal of Irish Studies*, 18 (1), 112–20.

Johnson, R. (1992). 'The X Case and Rights: An Analysis of Letters to the Press on the Abortion Debate in Ireland'. Unpublished M.Phil. Dissertation. Dublin: Centre for Gender and Women's Studies, Trinity College Dublin.

Jackson, S., and Cram, F. (2003). 'Disrupting the Sexual Double Standard: Young Women's Talk about Heterosexuality', *British Journal of Social Psychology*, 42, 113–27.

Joffe, C. (2010). *Dispatches from the Abortion Wars: The Costs of Fanaticism to Doctors, Patients, and the Rest of Us*. Boston, MA: Beacon Press.

Kallianes, V., and Rubenfeld, P. (1997). 'Disabled Women and Reproductive Rights', *Disability & Society*, 12 (2), 203–22.

Kamen, P. (2000). *Her Way: Young Women Remake the Sexual Revolution*. New York: NYU Press.

Kaplan, L. (2017). *The Story of Jane: The Legendary Underground Feminist Abortion Service* (2nd ed.). Chicago: University of Chicago Press.

Kavanagh, R. (2005). *A Survey of Young Women's Understanding of their Sexual Health Needs and their Perceptions of the Letterkenny Women's Health and Planning Clinic* (unpublished). Dublin: Crisis Pregnancy Agency.

Kawash, S. (2011). 'New Directions in Motherhood Studies', *Signs: Journal of Women in Culture and Society*, 36 (4), 969–1003.

Kelleher, M. (1995). 'Irish Famine in Literature'. In C. Pórtéir (ed.), *The Great Irish Famine: The Thomas Davis Lecture Series*, pp. 232–47. Cork: Mercier Press.

—— (1997). *The Feminization of Famine: Expressions of the Inexpressible?* Durham: Duke University Press.

Kelly, M. P. F. (1992). 'A Chill Wind Blows: Class, Ideology, and the Reproductive Dilemma'. In C. Backhouse (ed.), *Challenging Times: The Women's Movement in Canada and the United States*, pp. 252–67. Montreal: McGill-Queen's University Press.

Kennedy, F. (1989). *Family, Economy, and Government in Ireland*. Dublin: Economic and Social Research Institute.

—— (2001). *Cottage to Crèche: Family Change in Ireland*. Dublin: Institute of Public Administration.

—— (2004a). 'Introduction'. In P. Kennedy (ed.), *Motherhood in Ireland: Creation and Context*, pp. 7–8. Cork: Mercier Press.

—— (2004b). 'Creation and Context'. In P. Kennedy (ed.), *Motherhood in Ireland: Creation and Context*, pp. 11–36. Cork: Mercier Press.

Kennedy, M. (2015). 'After Scandals, Ireland is no Longer the "Most Catholic Country in the World,"' *NPR*, 26 August, <https://www.npr.org/2015/08/26/434821443/after-scandals-ireland-is-no-longer-the-most-catholic-country-in-the-world>, accessed 29 March 2021.

Kennedy, P. (2002). *Maternity in Ireland: A Woman-Centred Perspective*. Dublin: Liffey Press.

Kennedy, P., and Murphy-Lawless, J. (1998). *Returning Birth to Women: Challenging Policies and Practices'*. Dublin: Centre for Women's Studies, Trinity College Dublin and Women's Education, Research, and Resource Centre, University College Dublin.

—— (2003). 'The Maternity Care Needs of Refugee and Asylum-seeking Women in Ireland', *Feminist Review*, 73, 39–53.

Kennedy, R. E. (1973). *The Irish: Emigration, Marriage and Fertility*. Berkeley, CA: University of California Press.

Keohane, K., and Kuhling, C. (2004). *Collision Culture: Transformations in Everyday Life in Ireland*. Dublin: Liffey Press.

Kiely, E. (2005). 'Where is the Discourse of Desire? Deconstructing the Irish Relationships and Sexuality Education (RSE) Resource Materials', *Irish Educational Studies*, 24 (2–3), 253–66.

——(2015). 'School-Based Sex Education in Ireland, 1996–2002: The Public Debate'. In J. Redmond, S. Tiernan, S. McAvoy and M. McAuliffe (eds), *Sexual Politics in Modern Ireland*, pp. 109–26. Sallins, Kildare: Irish Academic Press.

Kiely, E., and Máire, L. (2014). 'Lessons in Sexual Citizenship: The Politics of Irish School-Based Sexuality Education'. In L. Máire (ed.), *Sexualities and Irish Society: A Reader*, 297–320. Dublin: Orpen Press.

Kilfeather, S. (2002). 'Sexual Expression and Genre, 1801–1917'. In A. Bourke (ed.), *The Field Day Anthology of Irish Writing: Irish Women's Writing and Traditions, Volume 4*, pp. 825–33. Cork: Cork University Press.

Kilfeather, S. (2005). 'Irish Feminism'. In J. Cleary and C. Connolly (eds), *The Cambridge Companion to Modern Irish Culture*. Cambridge: Cambridge University Press.

Kinealy, C. (1997). *A Death-Dealing Famine: The Great Hunger in Ireland*. London: Pluto Press.

Kirwan, M. (2011). 'Legal Matters: Pregnancy Discrimination', *Irish Independent*, August 1, <https://www.independent.ie/life/family/mothers-babies/legal-matters-pregnancy-discrimination-26757139.html>, accessed 8 March 2021.

Kligman, G. (1998). *The Politics of Duplicity: Controlling Reproduction in Ceaucescu's Romania*. Berkeley, CA: University of California Press.

—— (2005). 'A Reflection on Barren States: The Demographic Paradoxes of Consumer Capitalism'. In C. Douglass (ed.), *Barren States: The Population Implosion in Europe*, pp. 249–60. Oxford: Berg.

Kline, M. (1993). 'Complicating the Ideology of Motherhood: Child Welfare Law and First Nation Women', *Queen's Law Journal*, 18 (2), 306–34.

Ladd-Taylor, M., and Umansky, L. (eds) (1998). *Bad Mothers: The Politics of Blame in Twentieth-Century America*. New York: NYU Press.

Lane, S. (2008). *Why Are Our Babies Dying? Pregnancy, Birth and Death in America*. Boulder, CO: Paradigm Publishers.

Lanzieri, G. (2013). 'Towards a "Baby Recession" in Europe? Differential Fertility Trends during the Economic Crisis', *Eurostat*, Statistics in Focus, M/D. <http://epp.eurostat.ec.europa.eu/portal/page/portal/product_details/publication?p_product_code=KS-SF-13-013>

Layte, R., and McGee, H. (2007). 'Regret about the Timing of First Sexual Intercourse: The Role of Age and Consent', ESRI Working Paper No. 217, November. Dublin: ESRI.

Leahy, P. (2018). 'Cancer Scandal: After Vicky Phelan's Anger came Emma Mhic Mathúna's Raw Reality', *The Irish Times*, 11 May, <https://www.irishtimes.com/news/politics/cancer-scandal-after-vicky-phelan-s-anger-came-emma-mhic-math%C3%BAna-s-raw-reality-1.3490959>, accessed 11 May 2018.

Lee, E. (2003). *Abortion, Motherhood, and Mental Health: Medicalizing Reproduction in the United States and Great Britain* (2nd ed.). Piscataway: Aldine Transaction.

Lee, J. (1973). *The Modernisation of Irish Society 1848–1918*. Dublin: Gill and Macmillan.

—— (1977). 'Women and the Church since the Famine'. In M. MacCurtain and D. Ó'Corráin (eds), *Women in Irish Society: The Historical Dimension*, pp. 37–45. Dublin: Arlen House.

—— (1989). *Ireland 1912–1985: Politics and Society*. Cambridge: Cambridge University Press.

Lee, E., and Jenkins, T. (2002). 'Introduction'. In E. Lee and T. Jenkins (eds), *Debating Matters: Teenage Sex: What Should Schools Teach Children*, pp. xiii–xxi. London: Institute of Ideas and Hodder and Stoughton.

Lees, S. (1986). *Losing Out: Sexuality and Adolescent Girls*. London: Hutchinson.

Legg, S. (2005). 'Foucault's Population Geographies: Classifications, Biopolitics and Governmental Spaces', *Population, Space and Place*, 11 (3), 137–56.

Lerner, G. (1979). *The Majority Finds Its Past: Placing Women in History*. Oxford: Oxford University Press.

Levitas, R. (2012). 'The Just's Umbrella: Austerity and the Big Society in Coalition Policy and Beyond', *Critical Social Policy*, 32 (3), 320–42.

Littlejohn, K. E. (2021). *Just Get on the Pill: The Uneven Burden of Reproductive Politics*. Berkeley, CA: University of California Press.

Lloyd, D. (1999). *Ireland After History*. Cork: Cork University Press.

—— (2003). 'The Memory of Hunger'. In D. Eng and D. Kazanjian (eds), *Loss: The Politics of Mourning*, pp. 205–28. Berkeley, CA: University of California.

—— (2008). *Irish Times: Temporalities of Modernity*. Dublin: Field Day.

Lodge, A., and Lynch, K. (2004). *Diversity at School*. Dublin: IPA/Equality Authority.

Loftus, C. (2019). 'With over a Thousand Lone Parent Families Homeless, are we Repeating the Mistakes of our Past?' 27 September, available at: <https://www.focusireland.ie/with-over-a-thousand-lone-parent-families-homeless-are-we-repeating-the-mistakes-of-our-past/>, accessed 19 February 2021.

Lopez, I. (2008). *Matters of Choice: Puerto Rican Women's Struggle for Reproductive Freedom*. New Brunswick: Rutgers University Press.

Lowe, P. (2016). *Reproductive Health and Maternal Sacrifice: Women, Choice, and Responsibility*. London: Palgrave Macmillan.

Lowe, P., and Page, S-J. (2019). 'Rights-based Claims Made by UK Anti-abortion Activists', *Health and Human Rights Journal*, 21 (2), 133–44.

—— (2020). 'Sophie's Choice: Narratives of "Saving" in British Public Debates on Abortion', *Women's Studies International Forum*, 79, 1–7.

Lubhéid, E. (2004). 'Childbearing against the State? Asylum Seeker Women in the Irish Republic', *Women's Studies International Forum*, 27, 335–49.

—— (2006). 'Sexual Regimes and Migration Controls: Reproducing the Irish Nation-State in Transnational Contexts', *Feminist Review*, 83, 60–78.

Lucey, B. et al. (eds) (2019). *Recalling the Celtic Tiger*. Oxford: Peter Lang Publishers.

Luddy, M. (2011). 'Unmarried Mothers in Ireland, 1880–1973', *Women's History Review*, 20 (1), 109–26.

—— (2015). 'Foreword'. In J. Redmond et al. (eds), *Sexual Politics in Modern Ireland*, pp. xiv–xvii. Sallins: Irish Academic Press.

Ludlow, J. (2008a). 'Sometimes, It's a Child and a Choice: Toward an Embodied Abortion Praxis', *NWSA Journal*, 20 (1), 26–50.

—— (2008b). 'The Things We Cannot Say: Witnessing the Trauma-tization of Abortion in the United States', *WSQ: Women's Studies Quarterly*, 36 (1/2), 28–41.

Luker, K. (1991 [1978]). *Taking Chances: Abortion and the Decision Not to Contracept* (2nd ed.). Berkeley, CA: University of California Press.

—— (1984). *Abortion and the Politics of Motherhood*. Berkeley, CA: University of California Press.

—— (2006). *When Sex Goes to School: Warring Views on Sex Since the Sixties*. Boston, MA: W. W. Norton & Company.

Luna, Z. (2020). *Reproductive Rights as Human Rights: Women of Color and the Fight for Reproductive Justice*. New York: NYU Press.

Luna, Z., and Luker, K. (2013). 'Reproductive Justice', *Annual Review of Law and Social Science*, 9, 327–52.

Lunn, P., and Fahey, T. (2011). *Households and Family Structures in Ireland: A Detailed Statistical Analysis of Census 2006*. Dublin: ESRI.

Lynch, K. (2001). 'Equality in Education', *Studies: An Irish Quarterly Review*, 90 (360), 395–411.

—— (2006). 'Neo-liberalism and Education'. In S. Healy, B. Reynolds and M. L. Collins (eds), *Social Policy in Ireland: Principles, Practice and Problems*, pp. 297–328. Dublin: The Liffey Press.

Lynch, K., Baker J., and Lyons, M. (2009). *Affective Equality: Love, Care and Injustice*. Houndmills, Basingstoke, Hampshire, England: Palgrave Macmillan.

Lynch, K., and Lodge, A. (2002). *Equality and Power in Schools: Redistribution, Recognition, and Representation*. London: Routledge Falmer.

Lynd, R. (1909). *Home Life in Ireland*. London: Mills and Boon.

Mac Laughlin, J. (2001). *Reimagining the Nation-State: The Contested Terrains of Nation-Building*. London: Pluto Press.

MacCurtain, M. (1987). 'Moving Statues and Irishwomen', *Studies: An Irish Quarterly Review* 76 (302): 139–47.

—— (1993). 'The Real Molly Macree'. In A. Dalsimer (ed.), *Visualizing Ireland: National Identity and the Pictorial Tradition*, pp. 9–21. Boston, MA: Faber and Faber.

——(1995) 'Late in the Field: Catholic Sisters in Twentieth-Century Ireland and the New Religious History', *Journal of Women's History*, 6 (4)/7 (1), 49–63.

MacDonagh, O. (2003). *The Union and Its Aftermath*. Dublin: UCD Press.

MacKeogh, C. (2004). *Teenagers and the Media: A Media Analysis of Sexual Content on Television*. Dublin: Crisis Pregnancy Agency. <https://www.lenus.ie/handle/10147/305163>

MacNeela, P., O'Higgins, S., McIvor, C., Seery, C., Dawson, K., and Delaney, N. (2018). *Are Consent Workshops Sustainable and Feasible in Third Level Institutions? Evidence from Implementing and Extending the SMART Consent Workshop*. National University of Ireland Galway.

Mahon, E. (1994). 'Ireland: A Private Patriarchy?' *Environment and Planning A: Economy and Space*, 26 (8), 1277–296.

Mahon, E., Conlon C., and Dillon, L. (1998). *Women and Crisis Pregnancy: A Report Presented to the Department of Health and Children*. Dublin: Stationery Office.

Malthus, T. R. (2004). *An Essay on the Principle of Population* (2nd ed.), P. Appleman (ed.). New York: W.W. Norton and Co.

Mancini, J. M., and Finlay, G. (2008). 'Citizenship Matters': Lessons from the Irish Citizenship Referendum', *American Quarterly*, 60 (3), 575–99.

Marmot, M. G. (2010). *Fair Society, Healthy Lives: The Marmot Review; Strategic Review of Health Inequalities in England post-2010*. London: Marmot Review.

Marotta, M. (2005). 'MotherSpace: Disciplining through the Material and Discursive'. In S. Hardy and C. Wiedmer (eds). *Motherhood and Space: Configurations of the Maternal through Politics, Home, and the Body*, pp. 15–33. New York: Palgrave Macmillan.

Mason, C. (2019). 'Opposing Abortion to Protect Women: Transnational Strategy since the 1990s', *Signs: Journal of Women in Culture and Society*, 44 (3), 665–92.

Matthews, A., and Scott, P. A. (2008). 'Perspectives on Midwifery Power: An Exploration of the Findings of the Inquiry into Peripartum Hysterectomy at Our Lady of Lourdes Hospital, Drogheda, Ireland', *Nursing Enquiry*, 15 (2), 127–34.

Mayock, P., and Byrn, T. (2004). *A Study of Sexual Health Issues, Attitudes and Behaviours: The Views of Early School-Leavers*. Dublin: Crisis Pregnancy Agency.

Mayock, P. et al. (2007). *Relationships and Sexuality Education (RSE) in the Context of Social, Personal and Health Education (SPHE): An Assessment of the Challenges to Full Implementation of the Programme in Post-Primary Schools*. Dublin: Crisis Pregnancy Agency.

McAuliffe, M., and Kennedy, S. (2017). 'Defending Catholic Ireland'. In R. Kuhar and D. Parnotte (eds), *Anti-Gender Campaigns in Europe: Mobilizing against Equality*, pp. 133–50. London: Rowman and Littlefield International.

McBride, O., Morgan, K., and McGee, H. (2010). *Irish Contraception and Crisis Pregnancy Study 2010*. Dublin: Crisis Pregnancy Programme.

McCafferty, N. (1997). 'The Death of Ann Lovett'. In *The Best of Nell: A Selection of Writings over Fourteen Years*, pp. 48–54. Dublin: Attic Press.

—— (2010). *A Woman to Blame: The Kerry Babies Case*. Cork: Cork University Press.

—— (2018). 'Strange Fruit'. In U. Mullally (ed.), *Repeal the 8th*, pp. 191–6. London: Unbound.

McCaffrey, L. (2005). 'Sean O'Faolain and Irish Identity', *New Hibernia Review*, 9 (4), 144–56.

McCarthy, J. (2017). 'I idolised my big sister, but society cast her out when she got pregnant', *The Times*, 19 March, <https://www.thetimes.co.uk/article/i-idolised-my-big-sister-but-society-cast-her-out-when-she-got-pregnant-sx3hqx ghp>, accessed 3 May 2021.

—— (2021). 'State Should Disown Baby Home Report', *The Sunday Times*, Irish edition, 13 June, <https://www.thetimes.co.uk/article/justine-mccarthy-state-dis own-baby-home-report-ireland-8sj7qlw2g>, accessed 13 June 2021.

McConnell, D. (2020). 'Mother and Baby Homes Records to be Sealed for 30 Years as Controversial Bill Passes'. *Irish Examiner*, 23 October. <https://www.irishe xaminer.com/news/arid-40069511.html>, accessed 2 June 2021.

—— (2021). 'Heather Humphreys to Replace Helen McEntee as Justice Minister while on Maternity Leave', *Irish Examiner*, 11 March, <https://www.irishexami ner.com/news/arid-40242338.html>, accessed 11 March 2021.

McCormack, C. (2015). 'Boys' Quest for "Perfect Body" Fuels Rise in Eating Disorders', *Irish Independent*, 22 February, <https://www.independent.ie/ irish-news/health/boys-quest-for-perfect-body-fuels-rise-in-eating-disorders-31011395.html>, accessed 22 February 2015.

McCormick, L. (2009). *Regulating Sexuality: Women in Twentieth Century Northern Ireland*. Manchester: Manchester University Press.

McGarry, P. (2018). 'Cura, The Catholic Church Crisis Pregnancy Agency, to Close on Friday', *The Irish Times*, 13 June, <https://www.irishtimes.com/news/soc ial-affairs/religion-and-beliefs/cura-the-catholic-church-crisis-pregnancy-age ncy-to-close-on-friday-1.3529428>, accessed 17 May 2020.

McGrath, D., O'Keeffe S., and Smith, M. (2006). *Crisis Pregnancy Agency Statistical Report 2005: Fertility and Crisis Pregnancy Indices*. Dublin: CPA. <https://www.lenus.ie/handle/10147/305230>

McHugh, R. (1956). 'The Famine in Irish Oral Tradition'. In R. Dudley Edwards and D. Williams (eds), *The Great Irish Famine*, pp. 391–435. Dublin: Browne and Nolan.

McLean, S. (2004). *The Event and Its Terrors: Ireland, Famine, Modernity*. Stanford: Stanford University Press.

McLoughlin, D. (1990.) 'Workhouses and Irish Female Paupers, 1840–70'. In M. Luddy and C. Murphy (eds), *Women Surviving*, pp. 117–47. Dublin: Poolbeg Press.

—— (2001). 'Women and Sexuality in Nineteenth Century Ireland'. In A. Hayes and D. Urquhart (eds), *The Irish Women's History Reader*, pp. 81–6. London: Routledge.

—— (2002). 'Workhouses'. In Angela Bourke et al. (eds), *Field Day of Anthology of Irish Writing Volume V*, pp. 722–26. Cork: Cork University Press.

McNay, L. (2000). *Gender and Agency: Reconfiguring the Subject in Feminist and Social Theory*. London: Polity Press.

McRobbie, A. (2008). 'Young Women and Consumer Culture: An Intervention', *Cultural Studies*, 22 (5), 531–50.

McShane, I. (2010). 'Survey Reveals more Relaxed Attitude to Sex', *The Irish Times*, 15 September. <www.irishtimes.com/news/survey-reveals-more-relaxed-attitude-to-sex-1.650855>, accessed 31 October 2020.

Meredith, F. (2018). 'The UK Supreme Court says Northern Ireland Legislation Contravenes the European Convention on Human Rights, and the Public Backs a Change in the Law', *The Irish Times*, 9 June, Weekend, p. 3.

Meyer, C. L., and Oberman, M. (2001). *Mothers Who Kill Their Children: Understanding the Acts of Moms from Susan Smith to the 'Prom Mom'*. New York: NYU Press.

Mhic Mhathúna, E. (2018). 'I'm Dying Because of Human Error and That's Disgusting', *The Irish Times*, 10 May, <https://www.irishtimes.com/news/social-affairs/emma-mhic-mhath%C3%BAna-i-m-dying-because-of-human-error-and-that-s-disgusting-1.3490935>, accessed 10 May 2018.

Miller, A. (1987). *Timebends*. New York City: Grove Press.

Miller, K., Doyle, D., and Kelleher, P. (1997). '"For Love and Liberty": Irish Women, Migration and Domesticity in Ireland and America, 1815–1920'.

In P. O'Sullivan (ed.), *Irish Women and Irish Migration, Volume Four, The Irish World Wide: History, Heritage, Identity*, pp. 41–65. London: Leicester University Press.

Milne, I. (2019). 'Shopping Trips to New York'. In B. Lucey et al. (eds), *Recalling the Celtic Tiger*, pp. 293–95. Oxford: Peter Lang Publishers.

Mishtal, J. (2015). *The Politics of Morality: The Church, the State, and Reproductive Rights in Postsocialist Poland*. Ohio: Ohio University Press.

—— (2017). 'Quiet Contestations of Irish Abortion Law: Abortion Politics in Flux'. In S. Stettner, K. Ackerman, K. Burnett, and T. Hay (eds), *Transcending Borders: Abortion in the Past and Present*, pp. 187–202. London: Palgrave Macmillan.

Mitchell, C. (2005). 'Catholicism and the Construction of Communal Identity', *Irish Journal of Sociology*, 14 (1), 110–30.

Moane, G. (1999). *Gender and Colonialism: A Psychological Analysis of Oppression and Liberation*. London: Macmillan Press.

Mockery, J., and Gráda, C. Ó. (1988). 'Poor and Getting Poorer? Living Standards in Ireland Before the Famine', *Economic History Review*, 41 (2), 209–35.

Mokyr, J., and Ó Gráda, C. (1988). 'Poor and Getting Poorer? Living Standards in Ireland before the Famine', *The Economic History Review*, 41 (2), 209–35.

Moore, G. (1886). *A Drama in Muslin, A Realistic Novel*. London: Vizetelly & Co.

Moral, P. G., and Korteweg, A. C. (2012). 'The Sexual Politics of Citizenship and Reproductive Rights in Ireland: From National, International, Supranational and Transnational to Postnational Claims to Membership?', *European Journal of Women's Studies*, 19 (4), 413–27.

Moriarty, A. (2018). 'Why Contraception isn't Just about Condoms and the Pill', *The Irish Times*, 20 September, <https://www.irishtimes.com/life-and-style/hea lth-family/why-contraception-isn-t-just-about-condoms-and-the-pill-1.3626 966>, accessed 18 May 2021.

Mudiwa, L. (2017). 'New National Maternity Hospital Governance Crisis Resolved', *Irish Medical Times*, 29 May, <https://www.imt.ie/news/new-national-matern ity-hospital-governance-crisis-resolved-29-05-2017/>, accessed 15 June 2021.

Muldowney, M. (2015). 'Breaking the Silence: Pro-choice Activism in Ireland since 1983.' In J. Redmond, S. Tiernan, S. McAvoy, and M. McAuliffe (eds), *Sexual Politics in Modern Ireland*, pp. 127–50. Co. Kildare: Irish Academic Press.

Mullally, S. (2005). 'Debating Reproductive Rights in Ireland', *Human Rights Quarterly*, 27 (1), 78–104.

Mullally, U. (ed.) (2018). *Repeal the 8th*. London: Unbound.

Mullaney, J. L. (2006). *Abstinence and Personal Identity: Everyone is NOT Doing It*. Chicago: University of Chicago Press.

Muncy, R. (1991). *Creating a Female Dominion in American Reform, 1880–1935*. New York: Oxford University Press.

Munson, Z. W. (2009). *The Making of Pro-life Activists: How Social Movement Mobilization Works*. Chicago: University of Chicago Press.

Murphy, M. (2018). *Male Breadwinner Activation, Wifely Labour and the Irish Patriarchy: The Lingering Effects of Traditional Gender Assumptions*, 23 May, Progressive Economy@TASC, Dublin. <https://www.tasc.ie/blog/2018/05/23/male-breadwinner-activation-wifely-labour-and-the/>, accessed 12 March 2021.

Murphy-Lawless, J. (1987). *Fact Sheets on Fertility*. Dublin: Health Education Bureau.

—— (1993). 'Fertility, Bodies and Politics: The Irish Case', *Reproductive Health Matters*, 1 (2), 53–64.

—— (1998). *Reading Birth and Death: A History of Obstetric Thinking*. Cork: Cork University Press.

—— (2005). 'Bodies Coming and Going: Women and Fertility in Postmodern Ireland'. In C. B. Douglass (ed.), *Barren States: The Population 'Implosion' in Europe*, pp. 229–48. New York: Routledge.

—— (2006). *A Follow-up Project on Perceptions of Women about Fertility, Sex, and Motherhood: Probing the Data Further*. Report No. 17. Dublin: Crisis Pregnancy Agency.

—— (2015). 'Sally Rowlette's Inquest', *AIMS Journal*, 27 (2), 6–9.

—— (2021). 'Strange Times in Ireland: Death and the Meaning of Loss Under COVID-19'. In D. Lupton and K. Willis (eds), *The COVID-19 Crisis: Social Perspectives*, pp. 131–43. London: Routledge.

Murphy-Lawless, J., and Edwards, N. (2014). 'Marginality and Social Exclusion: Jeopardising Health and Life Chances'. In R. Deery et al. (eds), *Sociology for Midwives*, pp. 175–93. London: Polity Press.

Murphy-Lawless, J., Higgens, A., and Pembroke, S. (2008). *The Impact of the WISE UP Programme for Women Living and Working with Social Exclusion: An Evaluation for the Irish Family Planning Association*. Dublin: IFPA.

Murphy-Lawless, J., and McCarthy, J. (1999). 'Social Policy and Fertility Change in Ireland: The Push to Legislate in Favour of Women's Personal Agency', *European Journal of Women's Studies*, 6 (1), 69–96.

Murphy-Lawless, J., Oaks, L., and Brady, C. (2004). *Understanding how Sexually Active Women Think about Fertility, Sex, and Motherhood*. Report No. 6. Dublin: Crisis Pregnancy Agency.

Murphy-Tighe, S. (2017). 'Regaining Agency and Autonomy: A Grounded Typology of Concealed Pregnancy in 21st Century Ireland'. Open access Ph.D., University of Dublin, Trinity College.

Murtagh, P. (2018). 'Emma Mhic Mhathúna: "I wasn't going to come into court the victim", *The Irish Times*, 30 June <https://www.irishtimes.com/news/crime-and-law/courts/high-court/emma-mhic-mhath%C3%BAna-i-wasn-t-going-to-come-into-court-the-victim-1.3548627>, accessed 23 April 2021.

Nack, A. (2008). *Damaged Goods? Women Living with Incurable Sexually Transmitted Diseases*. Philadelphia: Temple University Press.

Nally, D. (2008). 'That Coming Storm: The Irish Poor Law, Colonial Biopolitics, and the Great Famine', *Annals of the Association of American Geographers*, 98 (3), 714–41.

Nelson, J. (2003). *Women of Color and the Reproductive Rights Movement*. New York: NYU Press.

—— (2015). *More than Medicine: A History of the Feminist Women's Health Movement*. New York: NYU Press.

Ní Aodha, G. (2018). 'Here's the Number of Abortion Pills Seized in Ireland in the Past 10 Years', *The Journal.ie*, 3 April, <www.thejournal.ie/abortion-pill-use-in-ireland-3892752-Apr2018/>, accessed 10 October 2020.

—— (2021). 'Three Years After the Referendum Vote, Just One in 10 GPs are Offering Abortion Services', *The Journal.ie*, 25 May. <https://www.thejournal.ie/one-in-10-gps-in-ireland-offering-medical-abortions-5447262-May2021/>, accessed 28 May, 2021.

Ní Chonchuir, S. (2014). 'Two is Really Company for Childless Couples', *Irish Examiner*, 20 April, <www.irishexaminer.com/lifestyle/healthandlife/relationships/two-is-really-company-for-childless-couples-265701.html>, accessed 15 July 2021.

Ní Ghríofa, D. (2020). *A Ghost in the Throat*. Dublin: Tramp Press.

Nicholson, A. (1998). *Annals of the Famine*. M. Murphy (ed.). Dublin: Lilliput Press.

Nolan, T. (1995). 'The Lismore Poor Union and the Famine'. In D. Cowman and D. Brady (eds), *The Famine in Waterford 1845–1850: Teacht na bprátaídubha*, pp. 101–18. Dublin: Geography Publications.

Nolan, A., and Smyth, E. (2020). *Talking about Sex and Sexual Behaviour of Young People in Ireland*. Dublin: ESRI.

NWCI (National Women's Council of Ireland). (2015). 'How Poverty and Inequality are Affecting Women', press release, 29 January, <https://www.nwci.ie/learn/article/how_poverty_and_inequality_are_affecting_women_in_ireland_in_europe_and_acr>

—— (2006). *An Accessible Childcare Model*. Dublin: National Women's Council of Ireland.

Oaks, L. (1998). 'Irishness, Eurocitizens, and Reproductive Rights'. In S. Franklin and H. Ragoné (eds), *Reproducing Reproduction: Kinship, Power, and Technological Innovation*, pp. 132–55. Philadelphia: University of Pennsylvania Press.

—— (1999). 'Irish trans/national Politics and Locating Fetuses'. In L. M. Morgan and M. W. Michaels (eds), *Fetal Subjects, Feminist Positions*, pp. 175–198. Philadelphia: University of Pennsylvania Press.

—— (2002). ' "Abortion is part of the Irish experience, it is part of what we are": The Transformation of Public Discourses on Irish Abortion Policy', *Women's Studies International Forum*, 25 (3), 315–33.

—— (2003). 'Antiabortion Positions and Young Women's Life-Plans in Contemporary Ireland', *Social Science and Medicine*, 56, 1973–86.

—— (2015). *Giving Up Baby: Safe Haven Law, Motherhood and Reproductive Justice*. New York: NYU Press.

O'Brien, C. (2013). 'Creche Crisis: The Staff Speak', *The Irish Times*, 31 May, <www.irishtimes.com/life-and-style/creche-crisis-the-staff-speak-1.141334>, accessed 5 July 2020.

—— (2018). ' "Baptism Barrier" to Catholic Schools to Go Next Year', *The Irish Times*, 9 May, <https://www.irishtimes.com/news/education/baptism-barrier-to-catholic-schools-to-go-next-year-1.3488198>, accessed 17 June 2021.

—— (2021). 'New Catholic Primary School Sex Education Programme Published', *The Irish Times*, 26 April, <https://www.irishtimes.com/news/education/new-catholic-primary-school-sex-education-programme-published-1.4547221>, accessed 26 April 2021.

O'Brien, E. (2007 [1960]). *The Country Girls*. London: Orion Books.

O'Brien, J. (1954). 'The Irish Enigma'. In J. O'Brien (ed.), *The Vanishing Irish: The Enigma of the Modern World*, pp. 3–10. London: W. H. Allen.

O'Brien, T. (1998). 'Abortion Law in the Republic of Ireland'. In E. Lee (ed.), *Abortion Law and Politics Today*, pp. 110–5. London: Palgrave Macmillan.

O'Brien-Green, S. (2020). 'Domestic Violence and Pregnancy in Ireland: Women's Routes to Seeking Help and Safety'. Open access Ph.D., University of Dublin, Trinity College. <http://hdl.handle.net/2262/91289>

O'Connell, H. (2020). 'Free Contraception for All Women Aged 17 to 25 Under New Plan', *Independent.ie*, 16 December, <https://www.independent.ie/irish-news/free-contraception-for-all-women-aged-17-to-25-under-new-plan-39868598.html>, accessed 15 January 2021.

O'Connell, J. (2021). 'How to Build a Modern Man: Helping Boys to Grow up Happy', *Irish Times*, 10 April. <https://www.irishtimes.com/life-and-style/health-family/parenting/how-to-build-a-modern-man-helping-boys-to-grow-up-happy-1.4527180>, accessed 10 April 2021.

O'Connor, A. (1991). 'Women in Irish Folklore: The Testimony Regarding Illegitimacy, Abortion and Infanticide'. In M. MacCurtain and M. O'Dowd (eds), *Women in Early Modern Ireland*, pp. 304–317. Edinburgh: Edinburgh University Press.

——(2005). *The Blessed and the Damned: Sinful Women and Unbaptised Children in Irish Folklore*. Oxford: Peter Lang Publishers.

O'Connor, L. (2002). 'The "War of the Womb": Folklore and Nuala Ní Dhomhnaill'. In Angela Bourke et al. (eds), *The Field Day Anthology of Irish Writing. Volume V: Irish Women's Writing and Traditions*, pp. 1639–45. Cork: Cork University Press in association with Field Day.

O'Connor, M. (1995). *Birth Tides: Turning Towards Home Birth*. London: Harper Collins.

——(2007). *Emergency: Irish Hospitals in Chaos*. Dublin: Gill and Macmillan.

—— (2010). *Bodily Harm: Symphysiotomy and Pubiotomy in Ireland, 1944–92*. Cathair na Mart: Evertype.

O'Connor, P. (1998). *Emerging Voices: Women in Contemporary Irish Society*. Dublin: IPA.

——(2000). 'Ireland: A Man's World?' *The Economic and Social Review*, 31 (1), 81–102.

——(2006). 'Young People's Constructions of the Self: Late Modern Elements and Gender Differences', *Sociology*, 40 (1), 107–24.

——(ed.) (2008). *Irish Children and Teenagers in a Changing World*. Manchester: Manchester University Press.

O'Connor, P. (2003). 'Feminism and Politics of Gender'. In M. Adshead and M. Millar (eds), *Public Administration and Public Policy in Ireland: Theory and Methods*, pp. 50–63. London: Routledge.

——(2008). 'The Irish Patriarchal State: Continuity and Change'. In M. Ahdshead, P. Kirby, and M. Millar (eds), Contesting the State: Lessons from the Irish Case, pp. 143–164. Manchester: Manchester University Press.

Ó Danachair, C. (1985). 'Irish Folk Tradition'. In A. Cosgrove (ed.), *Marriage in Ireland*, pp. 99–115. Dublin: College Press.

O'Dowd, L. (1987). 'Church, State and Women: The Aftermath of Partition'. In C. Curtin et al. (eds), *Gender in Irish Society*, pp. 3–36. Galway: Galway University Press.

O'Dowd, M. (2002). 'Property, Work and the Home: Women and the Economy, c. 1170–1850'. In A. Bourke et al. (eds), *The Field Day Anthology of Irish Writing Volume V*, pp. 464–71. Cork: Cork University Press.

O'Driscoll, K., and Meagher, D. (1980). *Active Management of Labour: The Dublin Experience*. London: W.B. Saunders.

OECD. (2013). *Crisis Squeezes Income and Puts Pressure on Inequality and Poverty*. Results from the OECD Income Distribution Database, May, <https://www.oecd.org/els/soc/OECD2013-inequality-and-poverty-8p.pdf>

—— (2014). *Childlessness*. OECD Family database, Social Policy Division SF2.5. <http://www.oecd.org/els/family/SF_2_5_Childlessness_June2014.pdf>

O'Faolain, A. (2020). '"Suffering and Stress of this Ordeal is Finally Behind Us" – Joanne Hayes Issues Statement Following State Apology over Kerry Babies Case', *The Irish Times*, 18 December, <https://www.irishtimes.com/news/crime-and-law/courts/high-court/kerry-babies-suffering-and-stress-of-ordeal-finally-behind-us-joanne-hayes-1.4440521>, accessed 18 December 2020.

—— (2021). 'HSE Secures Order Allowing Doctors to Carry Out C-section on Prisoner with Mental Illness', *Irish Examiner*, 24 May. <https://www.irishexaminer.com/news/courtandcrime/arid-40297352.html>, accessed 24 May.

O'Faolain, S. (1954). 'Love Among the Irish'. In J. O'Brien (ed.), *The Vanishing Irish: The Enigma of the Modern World*, pp. 105–116. London: W.H. Allen.

Ó Gráda, C. (1999). *Black '47 and Beyond: The Great Irish Famine in History, Economy and Memory*. Princeton, NJ: Princeton University Press.

Ó hAllmhuráin, G. (2005). 'Dancing on the Hobs of Hell: Rural Communities in Clare and the Dance Halls Act of 1935', *New Hibernia Review*, 9 (4), 9–18.

O'Hagan, C. (2015). *Complex Inequality and 'Working Mothers'*. Cork: Cork University Press.

O'Hara, P. (1998). *Partners in Production?: Women, Farm and Family in Ireland*. Oxford: Berghahn Books.

O'Higgins-Norman, J. (2009). 'Still Catching up: Schools, Sexual Orientation and Homophobia in Ireland', *Sexuality and Culture*, 13 (1), 1–16.

Ohlmeyer, J. (2003). 'A Laboratory for Empire? Early Modern Ireland'. In K. Kenny (ed.), *Ireland and the British Empire*, pp. 26–60. Oxford: Oxford University Press.

Oireachtas Joint Committee on Health and Children. (2015). 'Joint Committee on Health and Children Debate', 14 May, <https://www.oireachtas.ie/en/debates/debate/joint_committee_on_health_and_children/2015-05-14/2/?highlight%5B0%5D=roisin&highlight%5B1%5D=roisin>, accessed 17 May 2021.

O'Malley, L./Newstalk. (2017). 'Mater Hospital Patients Refused the Contraceptive Pill'. *Newstalk*, 21 April, <https://www.newstalk.com/news/mater-hospital-patients-refused-contraceptive-pill-539604>, accessed 24 February 2018.

O'Morain, P. (2019). 'Love Island's Maura Higgins Dances on Grave of Official Ireland', *The Irish Times*, 1 August, <https://www.irishtimes.com/life-and-style/health-family/love-island-s-maura-higgins-dances-on-grave-of-official-ireland-1.3965783>, accessed 14 June 2021.

OneFamily. (2020). 'Facts and Figures'. Available at <https://onefamily.ie/media-policy/facts-figures/>, accessed 27 May, 2021.

O'Reilly, A. (2010a). *21st Century Motherhood: Experience, Identity, Policy and Agency*. New York: Columbia University Press.

O'Reilly, A. (ed.) (2010b). *Encyclopedia of Motherhood*. Thousand Oaks, CA: Sage Publications.

O'Reilly, E. (1992). *Masterminds of the Right*. Dublin: Attic Press.

Orenstein, P. (2001). *Flux: Women on Sex, Work, Love, Kids and Life in a Half-Changed World*. New York: Anchor Books.

—— (2016). *Girls & Sex: Navigating the Complicated New Landscape*. New York: Harper.

—— (2020). *Boys & Sex: Young Men on Hookups, Love, Porn, Consent, and Navigating the New Masculinity*. New York: Harper.

O'Riordan, C. (2018). *Debating the Eighth: Retain or Repeal?* Dublin: Orpen Press.

O'Rourke, M., and McGettrick, C. (2021) 'Mother and Baby Homes Inquiry's Lack of Transparency was Damaging', *The Irish Times*, 25 January, <https://www.irishtimes.com/opinion/mother-and-baby-homes-inquiry-s-lack-of-transparency-was-damaging-1.4466658>, accessed 25 January 2021.

O'Rourke, M., and Smith, J. M. (2016). 'Ireland's Magdalene Laundries: Confronting a History not yet in the Past'. In A. Hayes and M. Meagher (eds), *A Century of Progress? Irish Women Reflect*, pp. 1–15. Dublin: Arlen House.

Orr, J. (2017). *Abortion Wars: The Fight for Reproductive Rights*. Bristol: Policy Press.

Ostrach, B. (2018). *Health Policy in a Time of Crisis: Abortion, Austerity, and Access*. New York: Routledge.

O'Sullivan, K. (2019). 'Decision-making: From "Participatory Citizenship" to Active Citizenship. A Feminist Activist Ethnography of Parent-School Relations in a DEIS School Context'. Open access Ph.D., University of Dublin, Trinity College.

O'Toole, B. (2015). '1831–2014: An Opportunity to Get it Right this Time? Some Thoughts on the Current Debate on Patronage and Religious Education in Irish Primary Schools', *Irish Educational Studies*, 34 (1), 89–102.

O'Toole, F. (1994). *Black Hole, Green Card: The Disappearance of Ireland*. Dublin: New Island Books.

—— (1998). *The Lie of the Land: Irish Identities*. Dublin: New Island Books.

—— (1999). *The Irish Times Book of the Century*. Gill and Macmillan: Dublin.

—— (2002). 'Still Failing to Protect Our Children', *The Irish Times*, 23 July <https://www.irishtimes.com/opinion/still-failing-to-protect-our-children-1.1089498>, accessed 10 February 2005.

—— (2003a). *After the Ball*. Tasc/New Island: Dublin.

—— (2003b). 'The Ugly Politics of the Womb', *The Irish Times*, 5 August, <https://www.irishtimes.com/opinion/the-ugly-politics-of-the-womb-1.368580>, accessed 17 May 2021.

—— (2010). *Enough is Enough: How to Build a New Republic*. London: Faber and Faber.

Ó Tuathaigh, G. (1972). *Ireland before the Famine 1798–1848*. Dublin: Gill and Macmillan.

Peillon, M. (2002). 'Culture and State in Ireland's New Economy'. In P. Kirby, L. Gibbons, and M. Cronin (eds), *Reinventing Ireland: Culture, Society, and the Global Economy*, pp. 38–53. London: Pluto Press.

Petchesky, R. P. (1990 [1984]). *Abortion and Woman's Choice: The State, Sexuality, and Reproductive Freedom* (Rev. ed.). Boston, MA: Northeastern University Press.

Pimenta, D. (2020). *Duty of Care: One NHS Doctor's Story of the Covid-19 Crisis*. London: Wellbeck Publishing Group.

Pollak, S. (2019). 'Free Contraception Should Start with Young Women, Report Recommends', *The Irish Times*, 29 October, <https://www.irishtimes.com/news/health/free-contraception-should-start-with-young-women-report-rec ommends-1.4065020>, accessed 29 October 2019.

Porter, E. (1996). 'Culture, Community and Responsibilities: Abortion in Ireland', *Sociology*, 30 (2), 279–98.

Quinn, G. (1969). 'The Changing Pattern of Irish Society, 1938–1951'. In K. Nowlan and T. D. Williams, *Ireland in the War Years and After, 1939–51*, pp. 120–133. Dublin: Gill and Macmillan.

Ramaswami. R. (2012). *Why Migrant Mothers Die in Childbirth in the UK* [Online]. Open Democracy. Available from <http://www.opendemocracy.net/5050/ramya-ramaswami/why-migrant-mothers-die-in-childbirth-in-uk>, accessed 14 November 2018.

Rattigan, C. (2008). '"I thought from her appearance that she was in the family way": Detecting Infanticide Cases in Ireland, 1900–1921', *Family and Community History*, 11 (2), 134–51.

——(2012). *'What else could I do?' Single Mothers and Infanticide, Ireland 1900–1950*. Dublin: Irish Academic Press.

Reagan, L. J. (1997). *When Abortion Was a Crime: Women, Medicine, and the Law in the United States, 1867–1973*. Berkeley, CA: University of California Press.

Redfern, C., and Aune, K. (2010). *Reclaiming the F Word: The New Feminist Movement*. London: Zed Books.

Redmond, J., Tiernan, S. McAvoy, S., and McAuliffe, M. (eds) (2015). *Sexual Politics in Modern Ireland*. Co. Kildare: Irish Academic Press.

Reid, L. (2004). 'Appeal Made to Mother of Baby Found at Church', *The Irish Times*, 19 April, <https://www.irishtimes.com/news/appeal-made-to-mother-of-baby-found-at-church-1.1308609>, accessed 19 April 2004.

Reilly, G. (2012). 'How Much does the Average Irish Girl Spend on her Debs?', *The Daily Edge*, <https://www.dailyedge.ie/cost-of-average-debs-586552-Sep2012/>, accessed 28 April 2021.

Rich, A. (1979). *Of Woman Born: Motherhood as Experience and Institution*. London: Virago.

Riegel, R. (2018). 'Coveney Reveals What Convinced Him to Back Abortion', *Irish Independent*, 30 April. <www.independent.ie/irish-news/abortion-referendum/coveney-reveals-what-convinced-him-to-back-abortion-36857139.html>, accessed 30 April 2018.

Roberts, D. (1998). *Killing the Black Body: Race, Reproduction, and the Meaning of Liberty*. New York: Vintage.

Robinson, J. (2004). 'Health Visitors or Health Police?' *AIMS Journal*, 16(3), <http://www.aims.org.uk/Journal/Vol16No3/HealthVisitors.htm>, accessed December 20, 2004

Roche, B. (2004). 'Body of Baby Found in West Cork', *The Irish Times*, 8 September, <https://www.irishtimes.com/news/body-of-baby-found-in-west-cork-1.1156578>, accessed 12 December 2014.

Rosen, M. (2021). *Many Different Kinds of Love*. London: Ebury Press.

Ross, E. (1993). *Love and Toil: Motherhood in Outcast London, 1870–1918*. New York: Oxford University Press.

——(1995). 'New Thoughts on "The Oldest Vocation": Mothers and Motherhood in Recent Feminist Scholarship', *Signs: Journal of Women in Culture and Society*, 21 (2), 397–413.

Rossiter, A. (2009). *Ireland's Hidden Diaspora: The Abortion Trail and the Making of a London Irish Underground, 1980–2000*. London: IASC Publishing.

Rothman, B. K. (2003). 'Caught in the Current'. In J. S. Taylor, L. L. Layne, and D. F. Wozniak (eds), *Consuming Motherhood*, pp. 279–88. New Brunswick: Rutgers University Press.

—— (2009). 'Mothering Alone: Rethinking Single Motherhood in America', *Women's Studies Quarterly*, 37 (3/4), 323–8.

Rotunda Hospital. (2014). *Clinical Report, 1st January- 31st December 2013*. Dublin: The Rotunda Hospital.

Rowbotham, S. (1989). 'To Be or Not to Be: The Dilemmas of Mothering', *Feminist Review*, 31 (1), 82–93.

Ruane, M. (2000). 'Introduction'. In *The Irish Journey: Women's Stories of Abortion*, pp. 6–10. Dublin: IFPA.

——(2010). 'When Irish Women Took Control of Their Destiny – and Their Bodies', *Irish Independent*, 1 May. <https://www.independent.ie/opinion/comment/medb-ruane-when-irish-women-took-control-of-their-destiny-and-their-bodies-26654330.html>, accessed 4 November 2020.

Ruane, F., and Sutherland, J. (2001). *Women in the Labour Force*. Dublin: Employment Equality Agency.

Rundle, K., Leigh C., McGee H., and Layte R. (2004). *Irish Contraception and Crisis Pregnancy [ICCP] Study: A Survey of the General Population*. Dublin: Crisis Pregnancy Agency.

Rupp, L. J., Taylor, V., Regev-Messalem, S., Fogarty, A. C. K., and England, P. (2014). 'Queer Women in the Hookup Scene: Beyond the Closet?' *Gender & Society*, 28 (2), 212–35.

Russell, H. et al. (2011). 'Pregnancy at Work: A National Survey'. Dublin: Dublin and Roscrea, Co. Tipperary: HSE Crisis Pregnancy Programme and the Equality Authority.

—— (2018). 'Maternal Employment and the Cost of Childcare in Ireland'. ESRI Research Series Number 73. Dublin: ESRI/POBAL.

Russell, H., McGinnity, F., Fahey, E., and Kenny, O. (2018). *Maternal Employment and the Cost of Childcare in Ireland*. Research Series No. 73. Dublin: ESRI.

Russell, H., McGinnity, F., and O'Connell, P. (2017). 'Gender Equality in the Irish Labour Market, 1966–2016: Unfinished Business?', *The Economic and Social Review*, 48 (4), 393–418.

Russell, H., Watson, D., and Banks, J. (2011). *Pregnancy at Work: A National Survey*. Dublin: Crisis Pregnancy Programme/Employment Equality Authority.

Ryan, P. (2011). *Asking Angela MacNamara: An Intimate History of Irish Lives*. Dublin: Irish Academic Press.

Rynne, A. (1982). *Abortion: The Irish Question*. Dublin: Ward River Press.

Sawicki, J. (1991). *Disciplining Foucault: Feminism, Power and the Body*. New York: Routledge.

Scally, G. (2018). *Scoping Inquiry into the CervicalCheck Screening Programme*. [Online] Available from <http://scallyreview.ie/> [14 March 2021].

Scally, D. (2021). *The Best Catholics in the World*. London: Penguin.

Segal, L. (2015). *Straight Sex: Rethinking the Politics of Pleasure*. London: Verso.

Sevlón, E. (2005). 'Timing Motherhood: Experiencing and Narrating the Choice to Become a Mother', *Feminism and Psychology*, 15 (4), 461–82.

Shanahan, C. (2018). 'Put Paternalism to Bed in our Health Service', *Irish Examiner*, 14 September, <https://www.irishexaminer.com/opinion/commentanalysis/arid-30868885.html>, accessed 14 September, 2018.

Shannon, J. (2017). 'Learning Lessons from Savita', *Irish Medical Times*, 28 April, <https://www.imt.ie/features-opinion/interview-features-opinion/learning-lessons-from-savita-28-04-2017/>, accessed 6 June 2021.

Sheehan, S. et al. (2014). *Annual Clinical Report 2013*. Dublin: Coombe Women and Infants University Hospital.

Side, K. (2006). 'Contract, Charity and Honourable Entitlement: Social Citizenship and the 1967 Abortion Act in Northern Ireland after the Good Friday Agreement', *Social Politics: International Studies in Gender, State and Society*, 13 (1), 89–116.

—— (2011). 'A.B.C. v. Ireland: A New Beginning to Access Legal Abortion in the Republic of Ireland?', *International Feminist Journal of Politics*, 13 (3), 391–413.

—— (2016). 'A Geopolitics of Migrant Women, Mobility and Abortion Access in the Republic of Ireland', *Gender, Place & Culture*, 23 (12), 1788–99.

—— (2020). 'Visual Realignment? The Shifting Visual Terrains of Anti-abortion Strategies in the Republic of Ireland'. In R. A. J. Hurst (ed.), *Representing Abortion*, pp. 104–118. London: Routledge.

Silliman, J., and Bhattaharjee, A. (eds) (2002). *Policing the National Body: Race, Gender and Criminalization in the United States.* Boston, MA: South End Press.

Singer, E. O. (2017). 'Lawful Sinners: Reproductive Governance and Moral Agency Around Abortion in Mexico', *Culture, Medicine, and Psychiatry*, 42 (1), 11–31.

—— (2019). 'Realizing Abortion Rights at the Margins of Legality in Mexico', *Medical Anthropology: Cross-Cultural Studies in Health and Illness*, 38 (2), 167–81.

Slattery, L. (2010). 'Fruits of Boom Largely Wasted, says Davy Report', *The Irish Times*, 20 February <https://www.irishtimes.com/business/fruits-of-boom-largely-wasted-says-davy-report-1.624267>, accessed 21 March 2021.

Smith, J. (2007). *Ireland's Magdalen Laundries and the Nation's Architecture of Containment.* Manchester: Manchester University Press.

Smyth, A. (1992a). 'A Sadistic Farce: Women and Abortion in the Republic of Ireland, 1992'. In A. Smyth (ed.), *The Abortion Papers Ireland*, pp. 7–24. Dublin: Attic Press.

—— (2018). 'The Obvious Explanations of how Power is Held and Exercised over Women are Very Basic'. In U. Mullally (ed.), *Repeal the 8th*, pp. 129–42. London: Unbound.

Smyth, A. (ed.) (1992b). *The Abortion Papers Ireland.* Dublin: Attic Press.

Smyth, L. (1998). 'Narratives of Irishness and the Problem of Abortion: The X Case 1992', *Feminist Review*, 60, 61–83.

—— (2002). 'Feminism and Abortion Politics: Choice, Rights, and Reproductive Freedom', *Women's Studies International Forum*, 25 (3), 335–45.

—— (2005). *Abortion and Nation: The Politics of Reproduction in Contemporary Ireland.* Hants, England: Ashgate.

—— (2006). 'The Cultural Politics of Sexuality and Reproduction in Northern Ireland', *Sociology*, 40 (4), 663–80.

Snitow, A. (1992). 'Feminism and Motherhood: An American Reading', *Feminist Review*, 40 (1), 32–51.

Solinger, R. (2002). *Beggars and Choosers: How the Politics of Choice Shapes Adoption, Abortion, and Welfare in the United States.* New York: Hill and Wang.

—— (2013). *Reproductive Politics: What Everyone Needs to Know.* New York: Oxford University Press.

Solomons, M. (1992). *Pro Life? The Irish Question.* Dublin: Lilliput Press.

Speed, A. (1992). 'The Struggle for Reproductive Rights: A Brief History in its Political Context'. In A. Smyth (ed.), *The Abortion Papers Ireland*, pp. 85–98. Dublin: Attic Press.

Stach, M. (2020) 'Deceptive Promises: Women's Understandings of Technology in Maternity Care'. Open access Ph.D., University of Dublin, Trinity College. <http://hdl.handle.net/2262/92447>

Stepp, L. S. (2007). *Unhooked: How Young Women Pursue Sex, Delay Love and Lose at Both*. New York: Riverhead Books.

Stettner, S., Ackerman, K., Burnett K., and Hay, T. (eds) (2017). *Transcending Borders: Abortion in the Past and Present*. London: Palgrave Macmillan.

Sweeney, P. (2004). 'The Irish Experience of Economic Lift Off: With a Focus on the Contribution of Social Partnership and the Potential Contribution of Life-long Learning'. The Workplace of the Future Colloquium, 27 May. Bishops University, Canada.

Sweeney, T. (2019). 'Love Island: Maura Higgins from Longford gives Two Fingers to Toxic Masculinity', *The Irish Times*, 26 June, <https://www.irishtimes.com/culture/tv-radio-web/love-island-maura-higgins-from-longford-gives-two-fingers-to-toxic-masculinity-1.3938068>

Sweetman, R. (1979). *On Our Backs: Sexual Attitudes in a Changing Ireland*. London: Pan Books.

——(2020). *Feminism Backwards*. Cork: Mercier Press.

Szreter, S., and Fisher, K. (2010). *Sex Before the Sexual Revolution: Intimate Life in England, 1918–1963*. Cambridge: Cambridge University Press.

Taft, M. (2020). 'The Irish Childcare Model is Broken', *The Irish Times*, 3 January, <https://www.irishtimes.com/opinion/the-irish-childcare-model-is-broken-1.4128802>, accessed 3 January 2020.

Tanenbaum, L. (2000). *Slut! Growing Up Female with a Bad Reputation*. New York: Perennial/HarperCollins.

Tanturri, M. et al. (2015). 'Childlessness in Europe. Families and Societies, Working Paper Series, 32', Changing Families and Societies, <http://www.familiesandsocieties.eu/wp-content/uploads/2015/03/WP32TanturriEtAl2015.pdf>

Taylor, C. (2015). 'Pregnant and Working? You May Still Face Discrimination', *The Irish Times*, 14 August, <https://www.irishtimes.com/business/work/pregnant-and-working-you-may-still-face-discrimination-1.2314872>, accessed 10 June 2021.

Taylor, J. (1999). 'Case X: Irish Reproductive Policy and European Influence', *Social Politics: International Studies in Gender, State & Society*, 6 (2), 203–29.

The Irish Times. (1966). 'Women Give Views of Family Planning', *The Irish Times*, 14 October, p. 1.

—— (1997). 'Letter Shows State Saw Bridget McCole Not as the Victim but as the Enemy', *The Irish Times*, 2 August, <https://www.irishtimes.com/news/letter-shows-state-saw-bridget-mccole-not-as-the-victim-but-as-the-enemy-1.93343>, accessed 15 June 2021.

—— (2003a). 'Remembered as Judge who Refused Teacher's Appeal', *The Irish Times*, Obituaries, Justice Noel Ryan, 19 April, <https://www.irishtimes.com/news/remembered-as-judge-who-refused-teacher-s-appeal-1.356300>, accessed 23 May 2021.

—— (2003b). 'Ravaged by "Baby Hunger"', *The Irish Times*, 26 July, <https://www.irishtimes.com/news/ravaged-by-baby-hunger-1.367593>, accessed 3 May 2021.

—— (2003c). 'Crisis Pregnancy Website Available', *The Irish Times*, 5 September, <www.irishtimes.com/news/crisis-pregnancy-website-available-1.373378>, accessed 8 February 2004.

—— (2004a). 'For the First Time, the Situation was Fully Explained', *The Irish Times*, 9 June, <www.irishtimes.com/news/for-the-first-time-the-situation-was-fully-explained-1.114400>, accessed 8 February 2004.

—— (2004b). 'Insight, Empathy and Judgment', *The Irish Times*, 12 June, <https://www.irishtimes.com/news/insight-empathy-and-judgment-1.1144628>, accessed 8 February 2004.

—— (2004c). 'Plea for Mother of Foetus to Seek Help', *The Irish Times*, 4 August, p. 7.

—— (2007). 'High Court grants "Miss D" right to travel', *The Irish Times*, 5 September, <https://www.irishtimes.com/news/high-court-grants-miss-d-right-to-travel-1.806706>, accessed November 1, 2007.

—— (2017). 'Obituary: Sherie de Burgh', *The Irish Times*, 15 April, <https://www.irishtimes.com/life-and-style/people/obituary-sherie-de-burgh-1.3049102>, accessed 10 October 2020.

Thompson, S. (1996). *Going All the Way*. New York: Hill and Wang Publishers.

Thomson, J. (2018). *Abortion Law and Political Institutions: Explaining Policy Resistance*. London: Palgrave MacMillan.

Thomson, R., Kehily, M. J., Hadfield, L., and Sharpe, S. (2011). *Making Modern Mothers*. Bristol: Policy Press.

Throne, J. (2006). *The Donegal Woman*. Derry: Drumkeen Press.

Tobin, C., Murphy-Lawless, J., and Tatano Beck, C. (2014). 'Childbirth in Exile: Asylum Seeking Women's Experience of Childbirth in Ireland', *Midwifery*, 30 (7), 831–8.

Tolman, D. (2002). *Dilemmas of Desire: Teenage Girls Talk about Sexuality*. Cambridge, Mass: Harvard University Press.

Tsing, A. L. (1990). 'Monster Stories: Women Charged with Perinatal Endangerment', In F. Ginsburg, and A. L. Tsing (eds), *Uncertain Terms: Negotiating Gender in American Culture*, pp. 282–99. Boston, MA: Beacon Press.

Valenti, J. (2009). *The Purity Myth: How America's Obsession with Virginity is Hurting Young Women*. New York: Seal Press.

Wade, L. (2017). *American Hookup: The New Culture of Sex on Campus*. New York: W. W. Norton Company.

Walby, S. (1990). *Theorizing Patriarchy*. Oxford: Blackwell.

—— (1997). *Gender Transformations*. London: Routledge.

Walkerdine, V., Lucey, H., and Melody, J. (2001). *Growing Up Girl: Psychosocial Explorations of Gender and Class*. Basingstoke, Hampshire: Palgrave.

Webster, J. (2019). 'An Exploration of the Views and Experiences of Midwives who Routinely Screen for Domestic Violence in an Irish Antenatal Setting', *MIDIRS Midwifery Digest*, 29 (4), 451–7.

Weeks, J. (1997). *The World We Have Won: The Remaking of Erotic and Intimate Life*. London: Routledge.

Whelan, K. (1995). 'Pre and Post-Famine Landscape Change'. In C. Pórtéir (ed.), *The Great Irish Famine: The Thomas Davis Lecture Series*, pp. 19–33. Cork: Mercier Press.

—— (2005). 'The Cultural Effects of the Famine'. In J. Cleary and C. Connolly (eds), *The Cambridge Companion to Modern Irish Culture*, pp. 137–54. Cambridge: Cambridge University Press.

White, V. (2010). *Mother Ireland: Why Ireland Hates Motherhood*. Dublin: Londubh Books.

Wilde, W. (1850). *Ireland: Her Wit, Peculiarities and Popular Superstitions*. Gloucester: Dodo Press.

Williams, R. (1983). *Keywords: A Vocabulary of Culture and Society* (2nd ed.). Oxford: Oxford University Press.

Williams, J. C. (1991). 'Domesticity as the Dangerous Supplement to Liberalism', *Journal of Women's History*, 2, 69–88.

—— (2001). 'From Difference to Dominance to Domesticity: Care as Work, Gender as Tradition', *Chicago-Kent Law Review*, 76, 1441–93.

Williams, J., Greene, S., McNally, S., Murray, A., and Quail, A. (2010). *The Infants and their Families: Growing Up in Ireland. National Longitudinal Study of Children*. Dublin: ESRI/Trinity College Dublin. Office of the Minister for Children and Youth Affairs.

Wills, C. (2021). 'Architectures of Containment', *London Review of Books*, 43(10), <https://www.lrb.co.uk/the-paper/v43/n10/clair-wills/architectures-of-cont ainment>, accessed 22 May 2021.

Yeates, N. (1999). 'Gender, Familism, and Housing: Matrimonial Property Rights in Ireland', *International Women's Studies Forum*, 22 (6), 607–18.

Yeats, W. B., and Albright, D. (eds) (1992). *The Poems*. London: David Campbell Publishers.

Yogalingam, K., Kelleher, C., Bourke, A., Boduszek, D., McGee, H., and K Morgan, K. (2013). 'Experiences of Crisis Pregnancy Among Irish and non-Irish Adults Living in Ireland: Findings From the Irish Contraception and Crisis Pregnancy Survey 2010 (ICCP-2010)', *Irish Journal of Medical Science*, 182 (4), 633–8.

Young, A. (1897). *A Tour in Ireland, 1776–1779*. London: Cassell and Company.

Zavella, P. (2020). *The Movement for Reproductive Justice: Empowering Women of Color through Social Activism*. New York: NYU Press.

Index

Reimagining Ireland

Series Editor: Dr Eamon Maher, Technological
University Dublin

The concepts of Ireland and 'Irishness' are in constant flux in the wake of an ever-increasing reappraisal of the notion of cultural and national specificity in a world assailed from all angles by the forces of globalisation and uniformity. Reimagining Ireland interrogates Ireland's past and present and suggests possibilities for the future by looking at Ireland's literature, culture and history and subjecting them to the most up-to-date critical appraisals associated with sociology, literary theory, historiography, political science and theology.

Some of the pertinent issues include, but are not confined to, Irish writing in English and Irish, Nationalism, Unionism, the Northern 'Troubles', the Peace Process, economic development in Ireland, the impact and decline of the Celtic Tiger, Irish spirituality, the rise and fall of organised religion, the visual arts, popular cultures, sport, Irish music and dance, emigration and the Irish diaspora, immigration and multiculturalism, marginalisation, globalisation, modernity/postmodernity and postcolonialism. The series publishes monographs, comparative studies, interdisciplinary projects, conference proceedings and edited books. Proposals should be sent either to Dr Eamon Maher at eamon.maher@ittdublin.ie or to ireland@peterlang.com.

www.ingramcontent.com/pod-product-compliance
Lightning Source LLC
Chambersburg PA
CBHW071835270326
41929CB00013B/2003